SPECIAL FUNCTIONS

(for Physicists and Engineers)

BY THE SAME AUTHOR

Mechanics
Mathematical Physics—Part I
Mathematical Physics—Part II
Mathematical Physics—Part III
A Textbook of Differential Equations
A Textbook of Integral Calculus
A Textbook of Mechanics
A Textbook of Statics
A Textbook of Trigonometry
Analytical Geometry
Fundamentals of Mechanics and General Properties of Matter
Fourier Series, Transforms and Their Applications
Integral Transforms for Engineers and Physicists
Introduction to Matrices (For Engineering and Physics Students)
Partial Differential Equations in Physics
Tensor Analysis for Scientists
Theory of Functions of a Real Variable
Vectors for Scientists
A Textbook of Group Theory
A Textbook of Sound
Special Functions
Waves and Oscillations
Computer Oriented Numerical Methods in Technology
Modern Algebra
A Textbook of Differential Geometry

SPECIAL FUNCTIONS

(for Physicists and Engineers)

(Revised Edition)

Dr. P. K. Mittal

Head, Department of Mathematics,
P.L.M.S. Govt. P.G. College,
Rishikesh

Prof. Jai Dev Anand (Retd.)

Department of Physics and Astrophysics,
Delhi University

HAR-ANAND
PUBLICATIONS PVT LTD

HAR-ANAND PUBLICATIONS PVT LTD
E-49/3, Okhla Industrial Area, Phase-II, New Delhi-110020
Tel.: 41603490 Fax: 011-41708607
E-mail: info@haranandpublications.com
Website: www.haranandpublications.com

Revised Edition, 2011

Published by Ashok Gosain and Ashish Gosain for
Har-Anand Publications Pvt Ltd

Printed in India at Saujanya Printing Press

Preface

It gives us great pleasure in bringing out new edition of the book 'Special Functions' (For Physicists and Engineers) which meets the requirement of the students of physics and engineering. The book has been revised by taking into account the suggestions of students and teachers.

It is hoped that the book will be found quite useful for students and teachers. Suggestions for still improvements from all well wishers will be greately acknowledged.

We appreciate the efforts of our publisher Ashok Gosain and Ashish Gosain of Har-Anand Publications in bringing out the new edition of the book in a very short time.

Dr. P. K. Mittal
Jai Dev Anand

CONTENTS

1 Introduction

1.1 Special Functions

We are familiar with the exponential function e^x, as the infinite series

$$1 + x + \frac{x^2}{2!} + \frac{x^3}{3!} + \ldots$$

But it can also be defined as the solution of the differential equation

$$\frac{d^2y}{dx^2} - y = 0 \qquad \text{...(i)}$$

Similarly, the trigonometric ratios define sine and cosine functions. Also, we have

$$\cos x = 1 - \frac{x^2}{2!} + \frac{x^4}{4!} - \ldots$$

and
$$\sin x = x - \frac{x^3}{3!} + \frac{x^5}{5!} - \ldots$$

But they are also the solutions of the differential equation

$$\frac{d^2y}{dx^2} + y = 0 \qquad \text{...(ii)}$$

Under the condition $y = 0$ when $x = 0$, the solution of (ii) is $y = \sin x$, while with the condition $y = 1$ when $x = 0$, its solution is $y = \cos x$.

We can, therefore, define the fuction e^x as the solution of differential equation (i) and also, functions $\sin x$ and $\cos x$ as the solutions of equation (ii) with the conditions as stipulated above. We do not, however, proceed to define them as such because they are well-known from earlier context.

More generally, the solutions of the differential equation

$$\frac{d^2y}{dx^2} + m^2 y = 0 \qquad \text{...(iii)}$$

with the above conditions are $\sin mx$ and $\cos mx$; and one solution of the differential equation

$$\frac{d^2y}{dx^2} - k^2 y = 0 \qquad \text{...(iv)}$$

is the function e^{kx}.

The differential equations (i), (ii), (iii) and (iv) have solutions which can be expressed in terms of known functions; but the differential equation

$$(1 - x^2)\frac{d^2y}{dx^2} - 2x\frac{dy}{dx} + n(n+1)y = 0 \qquad ...(v)$$

can not be solved in terms of known elementary functions. Hence in this case we define new functions in terms of the solution of (v). We call equation (v) as the *Legendre's equation,* and the solutions of this equation are known as *Legendre's functions.*

The problems of mathematical physics lead us to determine the solutions of differential equations which satisfy certain prescribed conditions. These solutions turn out to be new functions which possess interesting properties; and there are many differential equations of this type. Thus the theory of differential equations has originated a large number of new functions. We call them **special functions**, special in the sense that they arise as the solutions of special problems.

1.2 Spherical Harmonics

In dealing with the theory of potential, we commonly use the Laplace's equation

$$\frac{\partial^2 V}{\partial x^2} + \frac{\partial^2 V}{\partial y^2} + \frac{\partial^2 V}{\partial z^2} = 0$$

Any solution V_n of this equation, which is a homogeneous polynomial of degree n, in x, y, z is called the **Solid Spherical Harmonics.**

Laplace's equation in polar or spherical polar coordinates is written as

$$\frac{\partial^2 V}{\partial r^2} + \frac{2}{r}\frac{\partial V}{\partial r} + \frac{1}{r^2}\frac{\partial^2 V}{\partial \theta^2} + \frac{\cot\theta}{r^2}\frac{\partial V}{\partial \theta} + \frac{1}{r^2\sin^2\theta}\frac{\partial^2 V}{\partial \varphi^2} = 0$$

Let V_n; when expressed in polar coordinates take the form $V_n = r^n \cdot U_n(\theta, \phi)$, where $U_n(\theta, \phi)$ is a function of θ and ϕ only.

Then $U_n(\theta, \phi)$ is called the **Surface Spherical Harmonics** of degree n.

Obviously, when $r = 1$, $V_n = U_n$.

Hence surface spherical harmonics is the value of the corresponding solid spherical harmonics on the surface of a unit sphere whose centre is the origin.

1.3 Legendre's equation from Laplace's equation

Laplace's equation in spherical coordinates is

$$\frac{\partial}{\partial r}\left(r^2\frac{\partial V}{\partial r}\right) + \frac{1}{\sin\theta}\frac{\partial}{\partial\theta}\left(\sin\theta\frac{\partial V}{\partial\theta}\right) + \frac{1}{\sin^2\theta}\frac{\partial^2 V}{\partial\phi^2} = 0 \qquad ...(i)$$

Let us put $V = r^n U_n$, where U_n is a function of θ and ϕ only, so that

$$\frac{\partial V}{\partial r} = nr^{n-1}U_n, \quad \frac{\partial V}{\partial \theta} = r^n\frac{\partial U_n}{\partial \theta}.$$

$$\frac{\partial^2 V}{\partial \phi^2} = r^n \frac{\partial^2 U_n}{\partial \phi^2}.$$

Substituting in (i), we get

$$\frac{\partial}{\partial r}(nr^{n+1} U_n) + \frac{1}{\sin\theta}\frac{\partial}{\partial\theta}\left(r^n \sin\theta \frac{\partial U_n}{\partial\theta}\right)$$

$$+ \frac{1}{\sin^2\theta} . r^n \frac{\partial^2 U_n}{\partial \phi_2} = 0$$

or $$n(n+1)r^n U_n + \frac{r^n}{\sin\theta}\frac{\partial}{\partial\theta}\left\{\sin\theta \frac{\partial U_n}{\partial\theta}\right\}$$

$$+ \frac{r^n}{\sin^2\theta} \cdot \frac{\partial^2 U_n}{\partial\phi^2} = 0$$

Let us suppose, that U_n is independent of ϕ.

Then $$n(n+1)U_n + \frac{1}{\sin\theta}\frac{\partial}{\partial\theta}\left(\sin\theta \frac{\partial U_n}{\partial\theta}\right) = 0 \qquad \text{...(ii)}$$

Putting $\mu = \cos\theta$ and $U_n = y$

so that $$\frac{\partial U_n}{\partial\theta} = \frac{\partial y}{\partial\theta} = \frac{\partial y}{\partial\mu} \cdot \frac{\partial\mu}{\partial\theta}$$

$$= -\sin\theta \frac{\partial y}{\partial\mu}.$$

Substituting in (ii), we get

or $$n(n+1)y + \frac{1}{\sin\theta}\frac{\partial}{\partial\theta}\left(-\sin^2\theta \frac{\partial y}{\partial\mu}\right) = 0$$

or $$n(n+1)y + \frac{1}{\sin\theta}\frac{\partial}{\partial\mu}\left(-(1-\mu^2)\frac{\partial y}{\partial\mu}\right) \cdot \frac{\partial\mu}{\partial\theta} = 0$$

$$\frac{\partial}{\partial\mu}\left\{(1-\mu^2)\frac{\partial y}{\partial\mu}\right\} + n(n+1)y = 0 \qquad \text{...(iii)}$$

which is **Legendre's equation.**

Solution $P_n(\mu)$ of Legendre's equation is the surface spherical harmonic of degree n, which is free from ϕ.

1.4 Bessel's Equation from Laplace's Equation

We have Laplace's equation in cylindrical coordinates as

$$\frac{\partial^2 V}{\partial r^2} + \frac{1}{r}\frac{\partial V}{\partial r} + \frac{1}{r^2}\frac{\partial^2 V}{\partial\theta^2} + \frac{\partial^2 V}{\partial z^2} = 0 \qquad \text{...(i)}$$

Now, let $V = R\,\Theta' Z'$ where R, Θ', Z' are the functions of r, θ and z alone respectively.

Substituting in (i), we have

$$\Theta' Z' \frac{d^2 R}{dr^2} + \frac{1}{r} \Theta' Z' \frac{dR}{dr}$$

$$+ \frac{1}{r^2} RZ' \frac{d^2\Theta'}{d\Theta^2} + R\Theta' \frac{d^2 Z'}{dz^2} = 0$$

or
$$\frac{1}{R}\left(\frac{d_2 R}{dr^2} + \frac{1}{r}\frac{dR}{dr}\right) + \frac{1}{r^2} \cdot \frac{1}{\Theta'} \cdot \frac{d^2\Theta'}{d\Theta^2}$$

$$+ \frac{1}{Z'} \cdot \frac{d^2 Z'}{dz^2} = 0 \qquad \text{...(ii)}$$

Since the first three terms are independent of z, therefore the fourth term must also be independent of z. Thus the fourth term must be equal to a constant,

i.e.,
$$\frac{1}{Z'}\frac{d^2 Z'}{dz^2} = C \text{ (constant)}$$

or
$$\frac{d^2 Z'}{dz^2} = CZ' \qquad \text{...(iii)}$$

Similarly third term must be free from θ and hence, it must also be equal to a constant, i.e.,

$$\frac{1}{\theta} \cdot \frac{d^2\Theta'}{d\theta^2} = D \text{ (constant)}$$

or
$$\frac{d^2\Theta'}{d\theta^2} = D\Theta' \qquad \text{...(iv)}$$

With the help of (iii) and (iv) equation (ii) becomes.

$$\frac{1}{R}\left(\frac{d^2 R}{dr^2} + \frac{1}{r}\frac{dR}{dr}\right) + \frac{1}{r^2} D + C = 0$$

or
$$r^2 \frac{d^2 R}{dr^2} + r\frac{dR}{dr} + (D + Cr^2) R = 0 \qquad \text{...(v)}$$

Let $kr = v$, so that $\frac{dR}{dr} = \frac{dR}{dv} \cdot \frac{dv}{dr} = k\frac{dR}{dv}$

and
$$\frac{d^2 R}{dr^2} = k\frac{d^2 R}{dv^2} \cdot \frac{dv}{dr} = k^2 \frac{d^2 R}{dv^2}.$$

By putting these values in (v), we get

$$k^2 r^2 \frac{d^2 R}{dv^2} + kr\frac{dR}{dv} + \left(D + C\frac{v^2}{k^2}\right) R = 0.$$

Putting $C = k^2$ and $D = -n^2$, we get

$$v^2 \frac{d^2 R}{dv^2} + v\frac{dR}{dv} + (v^2 - n^2) R = 0.$$

Again, putting $R = y$ and $v = x$, we have

$$x^2 \frac{d^2 y}{dx^2} + x\frac{dy}{dx} + (x^2 - n^2) y = 0 \qquad \text{...(vi)}$$

This is Bessel's equation.

The solution of this equation is called the cylindrical function or Bessel's function of order n.

2 Legendre's Polynomials and Functions

2.1 Legendre's Equation (Definition)

The differential equation of the form

$$(1 - x^2)\frac{d^2y}{dx^2} - 2x\frac{dy}{dx} + n(n+1)y = 0 \qquad \text{...(i)}$$

is called **Legendre' differential equation** or simply **Legendre's equation,** where n is a constant.

This equation can also be written as

$$\frac{d}{dx}\left\{(1 - x^2)\frac{dy}{dx}\right\} + n(n+1)y = 0.$$

2.2 Solution of Legendre's Equation

The Legendre's equation (i) can be solved in series of ascending or descending powers of x. The solution in descending powers of x is more important than the one in ascending powers.

Let us assume, $$y = \sum_{r=0}^{\infty} a_r x^{k-r} \qquad \text{...(ii)}$$

$$\therefore \quad \frac{dy}{dx} = \sum_{r=0}^{\infty} a_r (k-r) x^{k-r-1}$$

and $$\frac{d^2y}{dx^2} = \sum_{r=0}^{\infty} a_r (k-r)(k-r-1) x^{k-r-2}$$

Substituting these values in (i), we get

$$(1 - x^2)\sum_{r=0}^{\infty} a_r (k-r)(k-r-1) x^{k-r-2}$$

$$- 2x = \sum_{r=0}^{\infty} a_r (k-r) x^{k-r-1} + n(n+1)\sum_{r=0}^{\infty} a_r x^{k-r} = 0$$

or $$\sum_{r=0}^{\infty} a_r [(k-r)(k-r-1)x^{k-r-2} + \{n(n+1) - (k-r)(k-r-1) - 2(k-1)\}x^{k-r}] = 0$$

or $$\sum_{r=0}^{\infty} a_r [(k-r)(k-r-1)x^{k-r-2} + \{n(n+1) - (k-r)(k-r+1)\}x^{k-r}] = 0$$

or $$\sum_{r=0}^{\infty} a_r [(k-r)(k-r-1)x^{k-r-2} + \{n^2 - (k-r)^2 + \{n-(k-r)\}x^{k-r}] = 0$$

or $$\sum_{r=0}^{\infty} a_r [(k-r)(k-r-1)x^{k-r-2} + (n-k+r)(n+k-r+1)x^{k-r}] = 0 \quad \text{...(iii)}$$

Now (iii) being an identity, we can equate to zero the coefficients of various powers of x.

∴ Equating to zero the coefficient of highest powers of x, i.e., of x^k, we have

$$a_0 (n-k)(n+k+1) = 0.$$

Now, $a_0 \neq 0$, as it is the coefficient of first term with which the series starts.

$$\therefore \quad \left.\begin{aligned} k &= n \\ k &= -(n+1) \end{aligned}\right\} \quad \text{..(iv)}$$

Equating to zero the coefficient of the next lower power of x, *i.e.*, of x^{k-1}, we have

$$a_1 (n-k+1)(n+k) = 0$$

∴ $a_1 = 0$, since neither $(n-k+1)$ nor $(n+k)$ is zero by virtue of (iv).

Again equating to zero the coefficient of the general term, *i.e.*, of x^{k-r}, we have

$$a_{r-2}(k-r+2)(k-r+1) + (n-k+r)(n+k-r+1)a_r = 0$$

$$\therefore \quad a_r = -\frac{(k-r+2)(k-r+1)}{(n-k+r)(n+k-r+1)} a_{r-2} \quad \text{...(v)}$$

putting $r = 3$

$$a_3 = -\frac{(k-1)(k-2)}{(n-k+3)(n+k-2)} a_1 = 0, \text{ since } a_1 = 0.$$

∴ We have, $a_1 = a_3 = a_5 = \ldots = 0$ (each)

Now two cases arise:

Case I. When $k = n$,

From (iv), we have

$$a_r = -\frac{(n-r+2)(n-r+1)}{r \cdot (2n-r+1)} a_{r-2}$$

Putting $r = 2, 4 \ldots$ etc.

$$a_2 = -\frac{n(n-1)}{2 \cdot (2n-1)} a_0$$

$$a_4 = -\frac{(n-2)(n-3)}{4\cdot(2n-3)}\cdot a_2$$

$$= \frac{n(n-1)(n-2)(n-3)}{2.4.(2n-1)(2n-3)}\cdot a_0 \text{ etc.}$$

$$\therefore \quad y = a_0 x^n + a_2 x^{n-2} + a_4 x^{n-4} + \ldots.$$

$$\text{or } y = a_0\left[x^n - \frac{n(n+1)}{2.(2n-1)}\cdot x^{n-2} + \frac{n(n-1)(n-2)(n-3)}{2.4(2n-1)\cdot(2n-3)}x^{n-4}\right] \quad \ldots\text{(vi)}$$

which is one solution of Legendre's equation.

Case II. When $k = -(n+1)$ then from (iv), we have

$$a_r = -\frac{(n+r-1)(n+r)}{r\cdot(2n+r+1)}a_{r-2}$$

Putting $r = 2, 4, \ldots$ etc.

$$a_2 = \frac{(n+1)(n+2)}{2.(2n+3)}a_0$$

$$a_4 = \frac{(n+3)(n+4)}{4.(2n+5)}a_2$$

$$= \frac{(n+1)(n+2)(n+3)(n+4)}{2.4.(2n+3)(2n+5)}a_0 \text{ etc.}$$

$$\therefore \quad y = \sum_{r=0}^{\infty} a_r x^{-n-1-r}$$

$$= a_0 x^{-n-1} + a_2 x^{-n-3}\ a_4 x^{-n-5} + \ldots$$

$$= a_0\left[x^{-n-1} + \frac{(n+1)(n+2)}{2.(2n+3)}x^{-n-2}\right.$$

$$\left. + \frac{(n+1)(n+2)(n+3)(n+4)}{2.4.(2n+3)(2n+5)}x^{-n-4} + \ldots\right] \quad \ldots\text{(vii)}$$

which is the other solution of Legendre's equation.

2.3 Legendre's function of the first kind or Legendre's polynomial of degree n. Definition

The solution of Legendre's equation is called Legendre's function.

When n is a positive integer and

$a_0 = \dfrac{1.3.5.(2n-1)}{n!}$, the solution (vi) of §2.2 is denoted by $P_n(x)$ and is called **Legendre's function of the first kind.**

$$\therefore \quad P_n(x) = \frac{1.3.5\ldots(2n-1)}{n!}\left[x^n - \frac{n(n-1)}{2.(2n-1)}x^{n-2}\right.$$

$$\left. + \frac{n(n-1)(n-2)(n-3)}{2.4.(2n-1)(2n-3)}x^{n-4}\ldots\right] \quad \ldots\text{(viii)}$$

$P_n(x)$ is a terminating series and gives what are called **Legendre's Polynomials** for different values of n.

We can write

$$P_n(x) = \sum_{r=0}^{n/2}(-1)^r\frac{(2n-2r)!}{2^n r!(n-2r)!(n-r)!}x^{n-2r} \quad \ldots\text{(ix)}$$

where $\left(\frac{n}{2}\right) = \begin{cases} n/2 & \text{if } n \text{ is even} \\ (n-1)/2 & \text{if } n \text{ is odd.} \end{cases}$

Legendre's Function of the second kind. Definition.

When n is a positive integer and

$$a_0 = \frac{n!}{1.3.5....(2n+1)}$$

the solution (vi) of § 2.2 is denoted by $Q_n(x)$ and is called the **Legendre's function of the second kind.**

$$\therefore \quad Q_n(x) = \frac{n!}{1.3....(2n+1)}\left[x^{-n-1} + \frac{(n+1)(n+2)}{2(2n+3)}x^{-n-2}\right.$$

$$\left. + \frac{(n+1)(n+2)(n+3)(n+4)}{2.4.(2n+3)(2n+5)}x^{-n-3} + ...\right] \qquad ...(x)$$

$Q_n(x)$ is an infinite or non-terminating series, as n is positive.

2.4 General solution of Legendre's equation

The most general solution of Legendre's equation is

$$y = A\,P_n(x) + B\,Q_n(x) \qquad ...(xi)$$

where A and B are arbitrary constants.

2.5 Generating function for Legendre polynomials

To show that $P_n(x)$ is the coefficient of h^n in the expansion of $(1-2xh+h^2)^{-1/2}$ in ascending powers of h.

Or

Show that $(1-2xh+h^2)^{-1/2} = \sum_{n=0}^{\infty} h^n P_n(x), |x| \le 1, |h| < 1$

We have $(1-2xh+h^2)^{-1/2} = \{1-h(2x-h)\}^{-1/2}$

$$= 1 + \frac{1}{2}h(2x-h) + \frac{1.3}{2.4}h^2(2x-h)^2$$

$$+ ... + \frac{1.3...(2n-3)}{2.4...(2n-3)}h^{n-1}(2x-h)^{n-1}$$

$$+ \frac{1.3...(2n-1)}{2.4...(2n)}h^n(2x-h)^n + ...$$

$\therefore$ Coefficient of h^n

$$= \frac{1.3...(2n-1)}{2.4...2n}\cdot(2x)^n + \frac{1.3...(2n-3)}{2.4...(2n-2)}$$

$$^{n-1}C_1(2x)^{n-2} + \frac{1.3...(2n-5)}{2.4...(2n-4)}\,^{n-2}C_2(2x)^{n-4} + ...$$

$$= \frac{1.3...(2n-1)}{n!}\left[x^n - \frac{2n}{2n-1}(n-1)\frac{x^{n-2}}{2^2} + \right.$$

$$\left. + \frac{2n(2n-2)}{(2n-1)(2n-3)}\cdot\frac{(n-2)(n-3)}{2!}\cdot\frac{x^{n-4}}{2^4}...\right]$$

$$= \frac{1.3\ldots(2n-1)}{n!}\left[x^n - \frac{n(n-1)}{2(2n-1)}x^{n-2}\right.$$

$$\left. + \frac{n(n-1)(n-2)(n-3)}{2.4(2n-1)(2n-2)} \cdot x^{n-4} \ldots\right]$$

$$= P_n(x).$$

Thus we can say that

$$\sum_{n=0}^{\infty} h^n P_n(x) = (1-2xh+h^2)^{-1/2}.$$

$(1-2xh + h^2)^{-1/2}$ is called the generating function of the Legendre Polynomials.

ILLUSTRATIVE EXAMPLES

Ex. 1. *Show that* $P_0(x) = 1$, $P_1(x) = x$, $P_2(x) = \frac{(3x^2-1)}{2}$,

$P_3(x) = \frac{1}{2}(5x^3-3x)$, $P_4(x) = (35x^4 - 30x^2 + 3)/8$.

Solution. We know that

$$\sum_{n=0}^{\infty} h^n P_n(x) = (1-2\,hx+h^2)^{-1/2}$$

$$= \{1 - h(2x-h)\}^{-1/2}$$

$$= 1 + \frac{h}{2}(2x-h) + \frac{1.3}{2.4}h^2(2x-h)^2$$

$$+ \frac{1.3.5}{2.4.6}h^3(2x-h)^3 + \frac{1.3.5.7}{2.4.6.8}h^4(2x-h)^4 + \ldots$$

or
$$P_0(x) + h\,P_1(x) + h^2 P_2(x) + h^3 P_3(x) + h^4 P_4(x)$$

$$+ \ldots = 1 + x.\,h + \frac{1}{2}(3x^2-1)\,h^2 + \frac{1}{3}(5x^3-3x)h^3$$

$$+ \frac{1}{3}(35x^4 - 30x^2 + 3)\,h^4 + \ldots$$

Equating the coefficients of like powers of h, we get

$$P_0(x) = 1,\ P_1(x) = x,\ P_2(x) = \frac{(3x^2-1)}{2},$$

$$P_3(x) = \frac{(5x^3-3x)}{2},\quad P_4(x) = \frac{35x^4-30x^2+3}{8}$$

Ex. 2. *Express* $P(x) = x^4+2x^3+2x^2-x-3$ *in terms of Legendre's polynomials.*

Solution. From Ex. 1, we have

$$P_0(x) = 1,\ P_1(x) = x,\ P_2(x) = \frac{(3x^2-1)}{2},$$

$$P_3(x) = \frac{(5x^3-3x)}{2},\quad P_4(x) = \frac{35x^4-30x^2+3}{8}$$

Now,

from
$$P_4(x) = \frac{1}{8}(35x^4 - 30x^2 + 3),$$

$$x^4 = \frac{8}{35} P_4(x) + \frac{6}{7} x2 - \frac{3}{35},$$

from $\quad P_3(x) = \frac{1}{2}(5x^3 - 3x), x_3 = \frac{2}{5} P_3(x) + \frac{3}{5} x,$

from $\quad P_2(x) = \frac{1}{2} 3x^2 - 1), x^2 = \frac{2}{3} P_2(x) + \frac{1}{3}$

and $\quad x = P_1(x); \; 1 = P_0(x)$

Substituting these values, we have

$$P(x) = \frac{8}{35} P_4(x) + \frac{6}{7} x^2 - \frac{3}{35} + 2x^3 + 2x^2 - x - 3.$$

$$= \frac{8}{35} P_4(x) + 2x^3 + \frac{20}{7} x^2 - x - \frac{108}{35}$$

$$= \frac{8}{35} P_4(x) + 2\left[\frac{2}{5} P_3(x) + \frac{3}{5} x\right] + \frac{20}{7} x^2 - x - \frac{108}{35}$$

$$= \frac{8}{35} P_4(x) + \frac{4}{5} P_3(x) + \frac{20}{7} x^2 + \frac{1}{5} x - \frac{108}{35}$$

$$= \frac{8}{35} P_4(x) + \frac{4}{5} P_3(x) + \frac{20}{7}\left[\frac{2}{3} P_2(x) + \frac{1}{3}\right] + \frac{1}{5} x - \frac{108}{35}$$

$$= \frac{8}{35} P_4(x) + \frac{4}{5} P_3(x) + \frac{40}{21} P_2(x) + \frac{1}{5} x - \frac{224}{105}$$

$$= \frac{8}{35} P_4(x) + \frac{4}{5} P_3(x) + \frac{40}{21} P_2(x) + \frac{1}{5} P_1(x) - \frac{224}{105} P_0(x)$$

Ex. 3. *Prove:* $1 + \frac{1}{2} P_1(\cos\theta) + \frac{1}{3} P_2(\cos\theta) + \ldots$

$$+ \ldots + \ldots = \log\left[\left(1 + \sin\frac{\theta}{2}\right) \Big/ \left(\sin\frac{\theta}{2}\right)\right]$$

Solution. From the generating function, we have

$$\sum_{n=0}^{\infty} h^n P_n(x) = (1 - 2hx + h^2)^{-1/2} \qquad \ldots\text{(i)}$$

Integrating w.r.t. h from 0 to 1, we get

$$\sum_{n=0}^{\infty} \int_0^1 h^n P_n(x)\, dh = \int_0^1 \frac{dh}{\sqrt{(1 - 2hx + h^2)}} \qquad \ldots\text{(ii)}$$

Replacing x by $\cos\theta$ on both sides, (ii) gives

$$\sum_{n=0}^{\infty} P_n(\cos\theta) \int_0^1 h^n\, dh = \int_0^1 \frac{dh}{\sqrt{(1 - 2h\cos\theta + h^2)}}$$

or
$$\sum_{n=0}^{\infty} P_n(\cos\theta) \left[\frac{h^{n+1}}{n+1}\right]_0^1 = \int_0^1 \frac{dh}{\sqrt{(h - \cos\theta)^2 + \sin^2\theta)}}$$

or
$$\sum_{n=0}^{\infty} \frac{P_n(\cos\theta)}{n+1} = \log(h - \cos\theta) + \sqrt{[(h - \cos\theta)^2 + \sin^2\theta]}_0^1$$

$$= \log\{1 - \cos\theta) + \sqrt{[(1 - \cos\theta)^2 + \sin^2\theta]}\} - \log(1 - \cos\theta)$$

$$= \log\{(1 - \cos\theta) + \sqrt{[2(1 - \cos\theta)\}]} - \log(1 - \cos\theta)$$

$$= \log \frac{(1 - \cos\theta) + \sqrt{2}\sqrt{(1 - \cos\theta)}}{(1 - \cos\theta)}$$

$$= \log \frac{\sqrt{\{(1 - \cos\theta)\}}\sqrt{\{(1 - \cos\theta)\}} + \sqrt{2}\sqrt{\{(1 - \cos\theta)\}}}{\sqrt{\{(1 - \cos\theta)\}}\sqrt{\{(1 - \cos\theta)\}}}$$

$$= \log \frac{\sqrt{[(1 - \cos\theta)]} + \sqrt{2}}{\sqrt{[(1 - \cos\theta)]}}$$

$$= \log \frac{\sqrt{\left\{\left(2\sin^2\frac{\theta}{2}\right)\right\}} + \sqrt{2}}{\sqrt{\left\{\left(2\sin^2\frac{\theta}{2}\right)\right\}}}$$

$$= \log \frac{1 + \sin\frac{\theta}{2}}{\sin\frac{\theta}{2}}$$

$$\therefore \quad \frac{P_0(\cos\theta)}{1} + \frac{1}{2}P_1(\cos\theta) + \frac{1}{3}P_2(\cos\theta) + \ldots = \log \frac{1 + \sin\frac{\theta}{2}}{\sin\frac{\theta}{2}}$$

or

$$1 + \frac{1}{2}P_1(\cos\theta) + \frac{1}{3}P_2(\cos\theta) + \ldots$$

$$= \log \frac{1 + \sin\frac{1}{2}\theta}{\sin\frac{1}{2}\theta} \quad [\because P_0(\cos\theta) = 1]$$

Ex. 4. *Show that (a)* $P_n(1) = 1$

(b) $P_n(-x) = (-1)^n P_n(x)$

Hence deduce that $P_n(-1) = (-1)^n$.

Solution. We know that

$$\sum_{n=0}^{\infty} h^n P_n(x) = (1 - 2xh + h^2)^{-1/2}$$

Putting $x = 1$

$$\sum_{n=0}^{\infty} h^n P_n(1) = (1 - 2h + h^2)^{-1/2}$$

$$= (1 - h)^{-1}$$

$$= 1 + h + h^2 + \ldots + h^n + \ldots$$

$$= \sum_{n=0}^{\infty} h^n$$

Equating the coefficients of h^n, we get $P_n(1) = 1$.

(b) we have,

$$(1 - 2xh + h^2)^{-1/2} = \sum_{n=0}^{\infty} h^n P_n(x)$$

Now, $(1+2xh+h^2)^{-1/2} = \{1-2x(-h)+(-h)^2\}^{-1/2}$

$$= \sum_{n=0}^{\infty} (-h)^n P_n(x)$$

$$= \sum_{n=0}^{\infty} (-1)^n h^n P_n(x) \qquad \text{...(i)}$$

Again, $(1+2xh+h^2)^{-1/2} = \{1-2(-x)h+h^2\}^{-1/2}$

$$= \sum_{n=0}^{\infty} h^n P_n(-x) \qquad \text{...(ii)}$$

From (i) and (ii) we have

$$= \sum_{n=0}^{\infty} h^n P_n(-x) = \sum_{n=0}^{\infty} (-1)^n h^n P_n(x)$$

Equating the coefficients of h^n from both sides, we get

$$P_n(-x) = (-1)^n P_n(x).$$

Deduction. Putting $x = 1$, we have

$$P_n(-1) = (-1)^n P_n(1) = (-1)^n \{\because P_n(1) = 1\}.$$

Ex. 5. *Prove that* (*a*) $P_n'(1) = \frac{1}{2} n(n+1)$

(*b*) $P_n'(-1) = (-1)^{n-1} \frac{1}{2} n(n+1)$

Solution. $P_n(x)$ satisfies Legendre's equation

$$(1-x^2)\frac{d^2y}{dx^2} - 2x\frac{dy}{dx} + n(n+1)y = 0$$

$$(1-x^2)P_n''(x) - 2xP_n'(x) + n(n+1)P_n(y) = 0 \qquad \text{...(i)}$$

(a) Putting $x = 1$, in (i), we have

$$-2P_n'(1) + n(n+1)P_n(1) = 0$$

$$\therefore \quad P_n'(1) = \frac{1}{2} n(n+1) P_n(1)$$

$$= \frac{1}{2} n(n+1) \qquad [\because P_n(1) = 1].$$

(b) Putting $x = -1$ in (i), we get

$$2P_n'(-1) + n(n+1)P_n(-1) = 0$$

$$\text{or} \quad P_n'(-1) = -\frac{1}{2} n(n+1) P_n(-1)$$

$$= (-1)^{n-1} \cdot \frac{1}{2} n(n+1) \qquad [\because P_n(-1) = (-1)^n].$$

Ex. 6. *Prove that* $P_n(0) = 0$, *for n odd and*

$$P_n(0) = \frac{(-1)^{n/2} n!}{2^n \{(n/2)!\}^2}, \text{ for } n \text{ even.}$$

Solution

(i) We know that

$$P_n(x) = \frac{1.3.5 \ldots (2n-1)}{n!}$$
$$\left[x^n - \frac{n(n-1)}{2(2n-1)} x^{n-2} + \frac{n(n-1)(n-2)(n-3)}{2.4.(2n-1)(2n-3)} x^{n-4} - \ldots\right]$$

when n is odd, say $n = (2m+1)$, then

$$P_{2m+1}(x) = \frac{1.3.5 \ldots \{2(2m+1)-1\}}{(2m+1)!}$$
$$\times \left[x^{2m+1} - \frac{(2m+1)(2m+1-1)}{2.\{2(2m+1)-1\}} x^{2m+1-2} + \ldots\right]$$

Putting $x = 0$, we get $P_{2m+1}(0) = 0$,

i.e., $P_n(0) = 0$ when n is odd.

Also, we have

$$\sum_{n=0}^{\infty} h^n P_n(x) = (1 - 2xh + h^2)^{-1/2}$$

or
$$\sum_{n=0}^{\infty} h^n P_n(0) = (1 + h^2)^{-1/2} = \{1 - (-h^2\}^{-1/2}$$

$$= 1 + \frac{1}{2} \cdot (-h^2) + \frac{1.3}{2.4} (-h^2)^2$$
$$+ \frac{1.3.5}{2.4.6} (-h^2)^3 + \ldots$$
$$+ \frac{1.3.5 \ldots (2r-1)}{2.4 \ldots 2r} (-h^2) r + \ldots$$

Hence all powers of h on the R.H.S. are even.

Equating the coefficient of h^{2m} on both sides, we have

$$P_{2m}(0) = \frac{1.3.5 \ldots (2m-1)}{2.4.6 \ldots 2m} (-1)^m$$
$$= (-1)^m \frac{(2m)!}{2^{2m} (m!)^2}$$

i.e., When $n = 2m$, then

$$P_n(0) = \frac{(-1)^{n/2} n!}{2^n \left\{\left(\frac{n}{2}\right)!\right\}^2}.$$

Ex. 7. *Prove that* $(1 - 2xz + z^2)^{-1/2}$ is a solution of the equation

$$z \frac{\partial^2 (zv)}{\partial z^2} + \frac{\partial}{\partial x}\left\{(1 - x^2) \frac{\partial v}{\partial x}\right\} = 0$$

Solution. Let

$$v = (1 - 2xz + z^2)^{-1/2} = \sum_{n=0}^{\infty} z^n P_n$$

or
$$zv = \sum_{n=0}^{\infty} z^{n+1} P_n$$

$$\therefore \qquad z\frac{\partial^2}{\partial z^2}(zv) = \sum_{n=0}^{\infty} (n+1)nz^n P_n.$$

Also
$$\frac{\partial v}{\partial x} = \sum_{n=0}^{\infty} z^n P'_n$$

$$\therefore \quad \frac{\partial}{\partial x}\left\{(1-x^2)\frac{\partial v}{\partial x}\right\} = \frac{\partial}{\partial x}\left[(1-x^2)\sum_{n=0}^{\infty} z^n P'_n\right]$$

$$= (1-x^2)\sum_{n=0}^{\infty} z^n P''_n - 2x\sum_{n=0}^{\infty} z^n P'_n$$

Substituting this in the L.H.S. of the given equation, we get

$$z.\frac{\partial^2(zv)}{\partial z^2} + \frac{\partial}{\partial x}\left\{(1-x^2)\frac{\partial v}{\partial x}\right\}$$

$$= \sum_{n=0}^{\infty} [(n+1)nz^n P_n + (1-x^2)z^n P''_n - 2xz^n P'_n]$$

$$= \sum_{n=0}^{\infty} z^n[(1-x^2)P''_n - 2xP'_n + n(n+1)P_n]$$

$= 0$ since P_n is a solution of Legendre's equation.

Ex. 8. *Show that*

$$\frac{1-z^2}{(1-2xz+z^2)^{3/2}} = \sum_{n=0}^{\infty} (2n+1)P_n(x)z^n.$$

Solution. We have

$$(1-2xz+z^2)^{-1/2} = \sum_{n=0}^{\infty} z^n P_n(x) \qquad \text{...(i)}$$

Differentiating w.r.t. z, we have

$$(x-z)(1-2xz+z^2)^{-3/2} = \sum_{n=0}^{\infty} nz^{n-1} P_n(x)$$

$$\therefore \qquad 2(x-z)z(1-2xz+z^2)^{-3/2} = \sum_{n=0}^{\infty} 2nz^n P_n(x) \qquad \text{...(ii)}$$

Adding (i) and (ii), we have

$$\frac{1-2xz+z^2+2(x-z)z}{(1-2xz+z^2)^{3/2}} = \sum_{n=0}^{\infty} (2n+1)z^n P_n(x)$$

or
$$\frac{1-z^2}{(1-2xz+z^2)^{3/2}} = \sum_{n=0}^{\infty} (2n+1)z^n P_n(x).$$

EXERCISE 2(A)

1. Define Legendre's polynomial $P_n(x)$. Show that it satisfies $(1-x^2)P_n''(x) - 2xP_n'(x) + n(n+1)P_n(x) = 0$.
2. Show that the general solution of Legndre's equation $(1-x^2)y'' - 2xy' + n(n+1)y = 0$, where n is a positive integer is $y = A\,P_n(x) + B\,Q_n(x)$ where $P_n(x)$ and $Q_n(x)$ have their usual meanings.

3. Prove that

$$P_{2n}(0) = (-1)^n \frac{(2n)!}{2^{2n}(n!)^2} \text{ and } P_{2n+1}(0) = 0.$$

4. Prove that

$$P_n\left(-\frac{1}{2}\right) = P_0\left(-\frac{1}{2}\right) P_{2n}\left(\frac{1}{2}\right) + P_1\left(-\frac{1}{2}\right) P_{2n-1}\left(\frac{1}{2}\right) + \ldots - P_{2n}\left(-\frac{1}{2}\right) P_0\left(\frac{1}{2}\right).$$

5. Prove that

$$\frac{1+z}{3\sqrt{[(1-2xz+z^2)]}} - \frac{1}{z} \sum_{n=0}^{\infty} \left[p_n(x) + P_{n+1}(x)\right] z^n.$$

2·6. Laplace's First Integral for $P_n(x)$: when n is a positive integer

Show that

$$\mathbf{P_n(x) = \frac{1}{\pi}\int_0^\pi [x \pm \sqrt{[(x^2-1)]} \cos\phi\,]^n d\phi.}$$

Proof. From integral calculus, we have

$$\int_0^\pi \frac{d\phi}{a \pm b\cos\phi} = \frac{\pi}{\sqrt{[(a^2-b^2)]}}, \text{ where } a^2 > b^2 \quad \ldots\text{(i)}$$

Putting $a = 1 - hx$ and $b = h\sqrt{(x^2-1)}$

so that $a^2 - b^2 = (1-hx)^2 - h^2(x^2-1) = 1 - 2xh + h^2$

Thus, we have from (i)

$$\pi(1-2xh+h^2)^{-1/2} = \int_0^\pi [1 - hx \pm h\sqrt{[(x^2-1)]}\cos\phi]^{-1} d\phi$$

$$= \int_0^\pi [1 - h(x \mp \sqrt{(x^2-1)}\cos\phi)]^{-1} d\phi$$

$$= \int_0^\pi [1 - ht\,]^{-1} d\phi.$$

where $t = x \mp \sqrt{\{(x^2-1)\}}\cos\phi$

$$\text{or } \pi \sum_{n-0}^{\infty} h^n P_n(x) = \int_0^\pi (1 + ht + h^2t^2 + \ldots + h^n t^n + \ldots)\, d\phi$$

Equating the coefficient of h^n, we have

$$\pi P_n(x) = \int_0^\pi t^n\, d\phi = \int_0^\pi [x \mp \sqrt{[(x^2-1)]}\cos\phi]^n\, d\phi$$

$$\therefore \quad P_n(x) = \frac{1}{\pi}\int_0^\pi [x \pm \sqrt{[(x^2-1)}\cos\phi]^n\, d\phi.$$

Deductions

(i) Putting $x = \cos\theta$ in above relation, we get

$$P_n(\cos\theta) = \frac{1}{\pi}\int_0^\pi (\cos\theta + i\sin\theta\cos\phi)^n\, d\phi.$$

(ii) If we take $n = 1$ and + ve sign, then we get

$$P_1(x) = \frac{1}{\pi}\int_0^\pi [x + \sqrt{[(x^2-1)]}\cos\phi]\, d\phi.$$

2·7. Laplace's Second Integral for $P_n(x)$: When n is a positive integer

Show that

$$\mathbf{P_n(x) = \frac{1}{\pi}\int_0^{\pi} \frac{d\phi}{[x \pm \sqrt{[(x^2-1)]} \cos\phi]^{n+1}}}$$

Proof. From integral calculus, we have

$$\int_0^{\pi} \frac{d\phi}{a \pm b\cos\phi} = \frac{\pi}{\sqrt{[(a^2-b^2)]}}, \text{ where } a^2 > b^2. \qquad ...(i)$$

Let $a = xh - 1$ and $b = h\sqrt{\{x^2-1)\}}$

so that $a^2 - b^2 = 1 - 2xh + h^2.$

By putting these values in (i) we have

$$\pi(1 - 2xh + h^2)^{-1/2} = \int_0^{\pi} [-1 + xh \pm h\sqrt{\{(x^2-1)\}} \cos\phi]^{-1} d\phi$$

or
$$\frac{\pi}{h}\left[1 - 2x \cdot \frac{1}{h} + \frac{1}{h^2}\right]^{-1/2}$$
$$= \int_0^{\pi} [h\{x \pm \sqrt{\{(x^2-1)\}} \cos\phi\} - 1]^{-1} d\phi$$

or
$$\frac{\pi}{h}\sum_{n=0}^{\infty} \frac{1}{h^n} P_n(x) = \int_0^{\pi} (t-1)^{-1} d\phi$$

where $t = h\{x \pm \sqrt{[x^2-1)]} \cos\phi\}$

$$= \int_0^{\pi} \frac{1}{t}\left[1 - \frac{1}{t}\right]^{-1} d\phi$$

$$= \int_0^{\pi} \frac{1}{t}\left[1 + \frac{1}{t} + \frac{1}{t^2} + \ldots + \frac{1}{t^n} + \ldots\right] d\phi$$

$$= \int_0^{\pi} \left[\frac{1}{t} + \frac{1}{t^2} + \frac{1}{t^3} + \ldots + \frac{1}{t^{n+1}}\right] d\phi$$

$$= \int_0^{\pi} \sum_{n=0}^{\infty} \frac{1}{t^{n+1}} d\phi$$

$$= \sum_{n=0}^{\infty} \int_0^{\pi} \frac{d\phi}{h^{n+1}[x \pm \sqrt{(x^2-1)} \cos\theta]^{n+1}}$$

Equating the coefficient of $\frac{1}{h^{n+1}}$, we get

$$\pi P_n(x) = \int_0^{\pi} \frac{d\phi}{\{x \pm [(x^2-1)] \cos\phi\}^{n+1}}$$

$$P_n(x) = \frac{1}{\pi}\int_0^{\pi} \frac{d\phi}{\{x \pm \sqrt{[(x^2-1)]} \cos\phi\}^{n-1}}.$$

Deductions. Replacing n by $-(n+1)$ in above relation, we get

$$P_{-(n+1)}(x) = \frac{1}{\pi}\int_0^{\pi} \frac{d\phi}{\{x \pm \sqrt{[(x^2-1)]} \cos\phi\}^{-n}}$$

$$= \frac{1}{\pi}\int_0^{\pi} \{x \pm \sqrt{(x^2-1)} \cos \phi\}^n \, d\phi$$

$$= P_n(x) \text{ by § 2.6.}$$

Thus $$P_n(x) = P_{-(n+1)}(x)$$

2·8. Orthogonal Properties of Legendre's Polynomials.

(i) $$\int_{-1}^{+1} P_m(x)\ P_n(x)\ dx = 0 \text{ if } m \neq n.$$

(ii) $$\int_{-1}^{+1} [P_n(x)]^2\ dx = \frac{2}{(2n+1)} \text{ if } m = n.$$

Proof. Legendre's equation may be written as

$$\frac{d}{dx}\left\{(1-x^2)\frac{dy}{dx}\right\} + n\,(n+1)\,y = 0$$

$$\therefore \quad \frac{d}{dx}\left\{(1-x^2)\frac{dP_n}{dx}\right\} + n\,(n+1)\,P_n = 0 \qquad (\because\ y = P_n) \quad ...(i)$$

and $$\frac{d}{dx}\left\{(1-x^2)\frac{dP_m}{dx}\right\} + m\,(m+1)\,p_m = 0 \qquad ...(ii)$$

Multiplying (i) by P_m and (ii) by P_n and then substracting, we have

$$P_m\frac{d}{dx}\left\{(1-x^2)\frac{dP_n}{dx}\right\} - P_n\frac{d}{dx}\left\{(1-x^2)\frac{dP_m}{dx}\right\} + \{n\,(n+1) - m\,(m+1)\}\,P_nP_m = 0.$$

Integrating between the limits –1 to 1, we get

$$\int_{-1}^{+1} P_m\frac{d}{dx}\left\{(1-x^2)\frac{dP_n}{dx}\right\}dx$$

$$\int_{-1}^{+1} P_n\frac{d}{dx}\left\{(1-x^2)\frac{dP_m}{dx}\right\}dx$$

$$+ \{n\,(n+1) - m\,(m+1)\}\int_{-1}^{+1} P_mP_n\,dx = 0$$

Integrating by parts

$$\left[P_m(1-x^2)\frac{dP_n}{dx}\right]_{-1}^{+1} - \int_{-1}^{+1}\frac{dP_m}{dx}\left\{(1-x^2)\frac{dP_n}{dx}\right\}dx$$

$$-\left[P_n(1-x^2)\frac{dP_m}{dx}\right]_{-1}^{+1} + \int_{-1}^{+1}\frac{dP_n}{dx}\left\{(1-x^2)\frac{dP_m}{dx}\right\}dx$$

$$+\left[n\,(n+1) - m\,(m+1)\int_{-1}^{+1} P_mP_n\,dx = 0\right.$$

$$\therefore \quad \{n\,(n+1) - m\,(m+1)\}\int_{-1}^{+1} P_mP_n\,dx = 0$$

Hence $$\int_{-1}^{+1} P_m(x)\,P_n(x)\,dx = 0, \text{ since } m \neq n.$$

(ii) We have

$$(1 - 2xh + h^2)^{-1/2} = \sum_{n=0}^{\infty} h^n P_n(x)$$

Squaring both sides, we get

$$(1 - 2xh + h^2)^{-1} = \sum_{n=0}^{\infty} h^{2n} \{P_n(x)\}^2 + 2 \sum_{\substack{m=0 \\ m-0 \\ m \neq u}}^{\infty} h^{m+n} P_m(x) P_n(x)$$

Integrating between the limits –1 to +1, we get

$$\sum_{n=0}^{\infty} \int_{-1}^{+1} h^{2n} [P_n(x)]^2 \, dx + 2 \sum_{\substack{n=0 \\ m-0 \\ m \neq n}}^{\infty} h^{m+n} P_m(x) P_n(x) \, dx$$

$$= \int_{-1}^{+1} \frac{dx}{(1 - 2xh + h^2)}$$

or
$$\sum_{n=0}^{\infty} \int_{-1}^{+1} h^{2n} [P_n(x)]^2 \, dx = \int_{-1}^{+1} \frac{dx}{(1 - 2xh + h^2)}$$

since other integral of the L.H.S. is zero (as shown in prop. (i),) as $m \neq n$.

$$\therefore \quad \sum_{n=0}^{\infty} \int_{-1}^{+1} h^{2n} [P_n(x)]^2 \, dx$$

$$= -\frac{1}{2h} \left\{\log (1 - 2xh + h^2)\right\}_{-1}^{+1}$$

$$= -\frac{1}{2h} \{\log (1 - h)^2 - \log (1 + h)^2\}$$

$$= \frac{1}{2h} \left[\log \left\{\frac{1 + h}{1 - h}\right\}^2\right] = \frac{1}{h} \log \left\{\frac{1 + h}{1 - h}\right\}$$

$$= \frac{2}{h} \left\{h + \frac{h^3}{3} + \frac{h^5}{5} + \ldots\right\}$$

$$= 2 \left\{1 + \frac{h^2}{3} + \frac{h^4}{5} + \ldots + \frac{h^{2n}}{2n + 1} + \ldots\right\}$$

$$= \sum_{n=0}^{\infty} \frac{2h^{2n}}{2n + 1}.$$

Equating the coefficient of h^{2n}, we get

$$\int_{-1}^{+1} [P_n(x)]^2 \, dx = \frac{2}{2n + 1}.$$

2·9. Recurrent formulae

(I) Prove that

$$(2n + 1)\, xP_n = (n + 1)\, P_{n+1} + nP_{n-1}$$

Proof. We have

$$(1 - 2x\,h + h^2)^{-1/2} = \sum_{n=0}^{\infty} h^n P_n(x)$$

Differentiating both sides w.r.t. 'h' we have

$$-\frac{1}{2}(1 - 2x\,h + h^2)^{-3/2}(-2x + 2h) = \sum_{n=0}^{\infty} nh^{n-1} P_n(x)$$

or $$(x - h)(1 - 2xh + h^2)^{-1/2} = (1 - 2x\,h + h^2) \sum_{n=0}^{\infty} nh^{n-1} P_n(x)$$

or $$(x - h) \sum_{n=0}^{\infty} h^n P_n(x) = (1 - 2x\,h + h^2) \sum_{n=0}^{\infty} nh^{n-1} P_n(x)$$

or $$(x - h)[P_0(x) + hP_1(x) + \ldots + h^{n-1} P_{n-1}(x) + h^n P_n(x) + \ldots]$$
$$= (1 - 2x\,h + h^2)[P_1(x) + 2hP_2(x) + \ldots + (n-1)\,h_{n-1} P_{n-1}(x) + nh^{n-1} P_n(x) + (n+1)\,h^n P_{n+1}(x) + \ldots] \quad \ldots(i)$$

Equating the coefficients of h^n from two sides, we have

$$x\,P_n(x) - P_{n-1}(x) = (n+1)\,P_{n+1}(x) - 2xn\,P_n(x) + (n-1)\,P_{n-1}(x)$$

or $$(2n + 1)\,x\,P_n(x) = (n + 1)\,P_{n+1}(x) + n\,P_{n-1}(x)$$

i.e. $$\mathbf{(2n + 1)\,xP_n = (n + 1)\,P_{n+1} + nP_{n-1}}$$

Note. Equating the coefficients of h^{n-1} from the two sides in (i), we get

$$x\,P_{n-1}(x) - P_{n-2}(x) = n\,P_n(x) - 2x\,(n-1).$$

or $$\mathbf{nP_n = (2n - 1)\,xP_{n-1} - (n - 1)\,P_{n-2}}.$$

(II) Prove that

$nP_n = xP'_n - P'_{n-1}$ where dashes denote differential w.r.t. x.

Proof. We have

$$(1 - 2x\,h + h^2)^{-1/2} = \sum_{n=0}^{\infty} h^n P_n(x) \quad \ldots(i)$$

Differentiating (i) w.r.t. h, we have

$$(x - h)\,(1 - 2x\,h + h^2)^{-3/2} = \sum_{n=0}^{\infty} nh^{n-1} P_n(x) \quad \ldots(ii)$$

Again differentiating (i) w.r.t. x, we get

$$h\,(1 - 2x\,h + h^2)^{3/2} = \sum_{n=0}^{\infty} h^n P_n'(x)$$

or $$h\,(x - h)\,(1 - 2x\,h + h^2)^{-3/2} = (x - h) \sum_{n=0}^{\infty} h^n P_n'(x) \quad \ldots(iii)$$

From (ii) and (iii), we get

$$h \sum_{n=0}^{\infty} nh^{n-1} P_n(x) = (x - h) \sum_{n=0}^{\infty} h^n P_n'(x)$$

or $$h\,[P_1(x) + 2h\,P_2(x) + \ldots + nh^{n-1} P_n(x) + \ldots]$$

$$= (x - h)\,[P_0'(x) + hP_1'(x) + \ldots + h^{n-1} P'_{n-1}(x) + h^n P_n'(x) + \ldots]$$

Equating the coefficients of h^n on both sides, we get

$$nP_n(x) = xP'_n(x) - P'_{n-1}(x)$$

i.e. $$\mathbf{nP_n = xP'_n - P'_{n-1}}.$$

(III) Prove that

$$\mathbf{(2n + 1)\, P_n = P'_{n+1} - P^1_{n-1}}.$$

Proof. From recurrence formula (I), we have

$$(2n + 1)\, xP_n = (n + 1)\, P_{n+1} + nP_{n-1}$$

Differentiating w.r.t. x, we have

$$(2n + 1)\, xP'_n + (2n + 1)\, P_n = (n + 1)\, P'_{n+1} + nP'_{n-1} \quad \text{...(i)}$$

From recurrence formula II, we have

$$xP'_n = nP_n + P'_{n-1} \quad \text{...(ii)}$$

Putting the value of xP'_n from (ii) into (i), we get

$$(2n + 1)\, (nP_n + P'_{n-1}) + (2n + 1)\, P_n = (n + 1)\, P'_{n+1} + nP'_{n-1}$$

or $$(2n + 1)\, (n + 1)\, P_n = (n + 1)\, P'_{n+1} + nP'_{n-1} - (2n + 1)\, P'_{n-1}$$

or $$(2n + 1)\, (n + 1)\, P_n = (n + 1)\, P'_{n+1} - (n + 1)\, P'_{n-1}$$

$\therefore$ $$\mathbf{(2n + 1)\, P_n = P'_{n+1} - P'_{n-1}},$$

(IV) Prove that

$$\mathbf{(n + 1)\, P_n = P'_{n+1} - xP'_n}).$$

Proof. From recurrence formulae II and III, we have

$$nP_n = xP'_n - P'_{n-1} \quad \text{...(i)}$$

and $$(2n + 1)\, P_n = P'_{n+1} - P'_{n-1} \quad \text{...(ii)}$$

Substracting (i) from (ii), we have

$$\mathbf{(n + 1)\, P_n = P'_{n+1} - xP'_n}$$

(V) Prove that

$$\mathbf{(1 - x^2)\, P'_n = n\, (P_{n-1} - xP_n)}$$

Proof. In recurrence formula IV, replacing n by $(n-1)$, we get

$$n\, P_{n-1} = P'_n - x\, P'_{n-1} \quad \text{...(i)}$$

From recurrence formula II

$$n\, P_n = x\, P'_n - P'_{n-1} \quad \text{...(ii)}$$

multiplying (ii) by x and then substracting from (i), we get

$$n\, (P_{n-1} - x\, P_n) = (1 - x^2)\, P'_n$$

i.e., $$\mathbf{(1 - x^2)\, P'_n = n\, (P_{n-1} - x\, P_n)}$$

Aliter. From Laplace's first integral, we have

$$P_n\,(x) = \frac{1}{\pi}\int_0^\pi [x + \sqrt{\{(x^2 - 1)\}}\cos\phi]^n\, d\phi$$

Replacing n by $(n-1)$, we get

$$P_{n-1}\,(x) = \frac{1}{\pi}\int_0^\pi [x + \sqrt{\{(x^2 - 1)\}}\cos\phi]^{n-1}\, d\phi$$

$$\therefore \quad P_{n-1} - xP_n = \frac{1}{\pi}\int_0^\pi [x + \sqrt{\{(x^2 - 1)\}}\cos\phi]^{n-1}$$
$$- x\,\{x + \sqrt{\{(x^2-1)\}}\cos\phi\}^n]\, d\phi$$

$$= \frac{1}{\pi}\int_0^\pi \{x + \sqrt{[(x^2 - 1)]}\cos\phi\}^{n-1}\, [1 - x\,\{x + \sqrt{\{(x^2-1)\}}\cos\phi\}]\, d\phi$$

$$= \frac{1}{\pi}\int_0^\pi \{x + \sqrt{[(x^2-1)]}\cos\phi\}^{n-1}[(1-x^2)-x\sqrt{\{(x^2-1)\}}\cos\phi]\,d\phi$$

$$= -\frac{(x^2-1)}{\pi}\int_0^\pi \{x+\sqrt{[(x^2-1)]}\cos\phi\}^{n-1}\left\{1+\frac{x}{\sqrt{[(x^2-1)]}}\cos\phi\right\}d\phi$$

$$= -\frac{(x^2-1)}{\pi}\int_0^\pi [\{x+\sqrt{[(x^2-1)]}\cos\phi\}^{n-1}\times\frac{d}{dx}\{x+\sqrt{[(x^2-1)]}\cos\phi\}]\,d\phi$$

$$= -\frac{(x^2-1)}{\pi}\int_0^\pi\left[\frac{1}{n}\cdot\frac{d}{dx}\{x+\sqrt{[(x^2-1)]}\cos\phi\}^n\right]d\phi$$

$$= \frac{(1-x^2)}{n\pi}\frac{d}{dx}\int_0^\pi \{x+\sqrt{[(x^2-1)]}\cos\phi\}^n\,d\phi$$

$$= \frac{(1-x^2)}{n\pi}\frac{d}{dx}\{\pi P_n(x)\} \qquad \text{[from Laplace's first integral]}$$

$$= \frac{(1-x^2)}{n}\cdot P'_n(x)$$

$\therefore$ $\mathbf{(1-x^2)\,P'_n = n\,(P_{n-1} - xP_n)}$

(VI) $(1-x^2)\,P'_n = (n+1)\,(xP_n - P_{n+1})$

Proof. From recurrence formula I, we have

$$(2n+1)\,xP_n = (n+1)\,P_{n+1} + nP_{n-1} \qquad \text{...(i)}$$

this may be written as

$$(n+1)\,xP_n + nxP_n = (n+1)\,P_{n+1} + nP_{n-1}$$

or

$$(n+1)\,(xP_n - P_{n+1}) = n\,(P_{n-1} - xP_n)$$

From recurrence formula (V), we have

$$(1-x^2)\,P'_n = n\,(P_{n-1} - xP_n) \qquad \text{...(ii)}$$

From (i) and (ii) we have

$$\mathbf{(1-x^2)\,P'_n = (n+1)\,(xP_n - P_{n+1})}$$

Aliter. From Laplace's second integral, we have

$$P_n(x) = \frac{1}{\pi}\int_0^\pi \frac{d\phi}{[x+\sqrt{\{x^2-1\}}\cos\phi]^{n+1}}$$

$$\therefore \quad xP_n - P_{n+1} = \frac{x}{\pi}\int_0^\pi \frac{d\phi}{[x+\sqrt{\{(x^2-1)\}}\cos\phi]^{n+1}} - \frac{1}{\pi}\int_0^\pi \frac{d\phi}{\{x+\sqrt{[(x^2-1)]}\cos\phi\}^{n+2}}$$

$$= \frac{1}{\pi}\int_0^\pi [\{x+\sqrt{[(x^2-1)]}\cos\phi\}]^{-n-2}[x\{x+\sqrt{[(x^2-1)]}\cos\phi\}-1]\,d\phi$$

$$= \frac{1}{\pi}\int_0^\pi [\{x+\sqrt{[(x^2-1)]}\cos\phi\}]^{-n-2}\times\{(x^2-1)+x\sqrt{[(x^2-1)]}\cos\phi\}]\,d\phi$$

$$= \frac{1}{\pi}\int_0^\pi [\{x+\sqrt{[(x^2-1)]}\cos\phi\}^{-n-2}\times\{(x^2-1)+x\sqrt{[([x^2-1)]}\cos\phi\}]\,d\phi$$

$$= \frac{(x^2-1)}{\pi}\int_0^\pi [\{x+\sqrt{[(x^2-1)]}\cos\phi\}^{-n-2}\times\left\{1+\frac{x}{\sqrt{[(x^2-1)]}}\cos\phi\right\}]\,d\phi$$

$$= \frac{(x^2-1)}{\pi}\int_0^{\pi} [\{x + \sqrt{[(x^2-1)]}\cos\phi\}^{-n-2} \times \frac{d}{dx}\{x + \sqrt{[(x^2-1)]}\cos\phi\}]\,d\phi$$

$$= \frac{(x^2-1)}{\pi}\int_0^{\pi}\left[\frac{1}{(n+1)}\frac{d}{dx}\{x+\sqrt{[(x^2-1)]}\cos\phi\}\right]^{-n-1} d\phi$$

$$= \frac{(1-x^2)}{\pi(n+1)}\frac{d}{dx}\int_0^{\pi}\{x+\sqrt{[\{x^2-1)]}\cos\phi\}^{-n-1}\,d\phi$$

$$= \frac{(1-x^2)}{\pi(n+1)}\frac{d}{dx}\{\pi P_n(x)\} \qquad \text{[from Laplace's first integral]}$$

$$= \frac{(1-x^{2)}p'_n}{n+1}$$

$\therefore$ **$(1-x^2)\, P'_n = (n+1)(xP_n - P_{n+1})$.**

2·10. Beltrami's results

Prove that **$(2n+1)(x^2-1)\,P'_n = n(n+1)(P_{n+1} - P_{n-1})$**

Proof. From recurrence formulae V and VI, we have

$$(1-x^2)\,P'_n = n\,(P_{n-1} - xP_n) \qquad \text{...(i)}$$

and

$$(1-x^2)\,P'_n = (n+1)\,(xP_n - P_{n+1}) \qquad \text{....(ii)}$$

Substituting for xP_n from (i) in (ii), we get

$$(1-x^2)\,P'_n = (n+1)\left[P_{n-1} - \frac{(1-x^2)}{n}P'_n - P_{n+1}\right]$$

or

$$(1-x^2)\left\{1 + \frac{(n+1)}{n}\right\}P'_n = (n+1)(P_{n-1} - P_{n+1})$$

or

$$-(x^2-1)(2n+1)\,P'_n = n(n+1)(P_{n-1} - P_{n+1})$$

or

$$\mathbf{(2n+1)(x^2-1)\,P'_n = n(n+1)(Pn+1 - Pn-1)}$$

This result is known as **Beltrami's results.**

2·11. Christoffel's Expansion

Prove that

$P'_n = (2n-1)\,P_{n-1} + (2n-5)\,P_{n-2} + (2n-9)\,P_{n-5} + \ldots$

the last term of the series being $3P_1$ or P_0 according as n is even or odd.

Proof. From recurrence formula III, we have

$$P'_{n+1} = (2n+1)\,P_n + P'_{n-1} \qquad \text{...(i)}$$

Replacing n by $(n-1)$, we get

$$P'_n = (2n-1)\,P_{n-1} + P'_{n-2} \qquad \text{... (ii)}$$

Replacing n by $(n-2)$, $(n-4)$, ... in (ii), we have

$$P'_{n-2} = (2n-5)\,P_{n-3} + P'_{n-4} \qquad \text{.... (iii)}$$

$$P'_{n-4} = (2n-9)\,P_{n-5} + P'_{n-6} \qquad \text{.... (iv)}$$

... ...

... ...

$$P'_2 = 3P_1 + P'_0$$

where n is even.

Adding (i), (ii), (iii) etc., we get

$$P_n' = (2n-1)P_{n-1} + (2n-5)P_{n-3} + (2n-9)P_{n-5} + \ldots + 3P_1 + P_0'$$
$$= (2n-1)P_{n-1} + (2n-5)P_{n-3} + (2n-9)P_{n-5} + \ldots + 3P_1 \qquad [\because P_0' = 0]$$

when n is odd.

$$P_n' = (2n-1)P_{n-1} + (2n-5)P_{n-2} + \ldots + P_2 + P_1'$$
$$= (2n-1)P_{n-1} + (2n-5)P_{n-2} + \ldots + P_0 \qquad [\because P_1' = 1 = P_0]$$

Hence $P_n' = (2n-1)P_{n-1} + (2n-5)P_{n-3} + \ldots$

the last term of the series being $3P_1$ or P_0 according as n is even or odd.

2.12 Christoffel's Summation Formula

Prove that

Proof. From recurrence formula I, we have

$$(2r+1)xP_r(x) = (r+1)P_{r+1}(x) + rP_{r-1}(x) \qquad \ldots\text{(i)}$$
$$(2r+1)xP_r(y) = (r+1)P_{r+1}(y) + rP_{r-1}(y) \qquad \ldots\text{(ii)}$$

Multiplying (i) by $P_r(y)$ and (ii) by $P_r(x)$ and then subtracting, we have

$$(2r+1)(x-y)P_r(x)P_r(y) = (r+1)[P_{r+1}(x)P_r(y) - P_{r+1}(y)P_r(x)] - r[P_{r-1}(y)P_r(x) - P_{r-1}(x)P_r(y)]$$

Putting $r = 0, 1, 2, 3, \ldots, (n-1), n$, we have

$$(x-y)P_0(x)P_0(y) = [P_1(x)P_0(y) - P_1(y)P_0(x)] + 0 \ldots (A_0)$$
$$3(x-y)P_1(x)P_1(y) = 2.[P_2(x)P_1(y) - P_2(y)P_1(x)] - 1.[P_0(y)P_1(x) - P_0(x)P_1(y)] . (A_1)$$
$$5(x-y)P_2(x)P_2(y) = 3[P_3(x)P_2(y) - P_3(y)P_2(x)] - 2.[P_1(y)P_2(x) - P_1(x)P_2(y)] \ldots (A_2)$$

....

....

$$(2n-1)(x-y)P_{n-1}(x)P_{n-1}(y) = n.[P_n(x).P_{n-1}(y) - P_n(y).P_{n-1}(x)] - (n-1)[P_{n-2}(y)P_{n-1}(x) - P_{n-2}(x)P_{n-1}(y)] \ldots (A_{n-1})$$
$$(2n+1)(x-y)P_n(x).P_n(y) = (n+1)]P_{n+1}(x)P_n(y) - P_{n+1}(y)P_n(x)] - n.[P_{n-1}(y)P_n(x) - P_{n-1}(x)P_n(y)] \ldots (A_n)$$

Adding $(A_0), (A_1), (A_2) \ldots (A_{n-1})$ and (A_n), we get

$$(x-y)\sum_{r=0}^{n}(2r+1)P_r(x)P_r(y)$$
$$= (n+1)[P_{n+1}(x)P_n(y) - P_{n+1}(y)P_n(x)]$$

$$\text{Hence } \sum_{r=0}^{n}(2r+1)P_r(x)P_r(y) =$$

$$= (n+1) \frac{P_{n+1}(x) P_n(y) - P_{n+1}(y) P_n(x)}{(x-y)}$$

This is **Christoffel's Summatioa Formula.**

2·13. Rodrigue's Formula

Prove that

$$\mathbf{P_n(x) = \frac{1}{n!\,2^n} \cdot \frac{d^n}{dx^n} (x^2-1)^n}.$$

Proof. Let $y = (x^2-1)^n$

Differentiating,

$$\frac{dy}{dx} = n\,(x^2-1)^{n-1} \,.\, 2x$$

$$\therefore \qquad (x^2-1) \frac{dy}{dx} = 2nxy.$$

Differentiating $(n+1)$ times by Leibnitz Theorem, we get

$$(x^2-1) \times \frac{d^{n+2}y}{dx^{n+2}} + (n+1) \,.\, \frac{d^{n+1}y}{dx}{}^{n+1} \,.\, 2x - \frac{(n+1)n}{2\,!} \,.\, \frac{d^n y}{dx^n} \,.\, 2$$

$$= 2n \left[x \, \frac{d^{n+1}y}{dx}{}^{n+1} + (n+1) \frac{d^n y}{dx}{}^{n} \,.\, 1 \right]$$

or $$(x^2-1) \frac{d^{n+2}y}{dx^{n+2}} + 2x \,.\, \frac{d^{n+1}y}{dx^{n+1}} - n\,(n+1) \frac{d^n y}{dx^n} = 0$$

or $$(1-x^2) \frac{d^{n+2}y}{dx^{n+1}} - 2x \, \frac{d^{n+1}y}{dx^{n+1}} + n\,(n+1) \frac{d^n y}{dx^n} = 0$$

Let us put $$Z = \frac{d^n y}{dx^n}$$

$$\therefore \ (1-x^2) \frac{d^2 Z}{dx^2} - 2x \frac{dZ}{dx} + n(n+1)\,Z = 0$$

which is Legendre's equation.

Hence its solution will be

$$Z = cP_n(x)$$

where c is a constant.

or $$\mathbf{\frac{d^n y}{dx^n} = c\,P_n(x)}.$$

Putting $x = 1$, we get

$$\left(\frac{d^n y}{dx^n}\right)_{x=1} = c \qquad [\because P_n(1) = 1]$$

Now, $$y = (x^2-1)^n = (x+1)^n \,.\, (x-1)^n.$$

Differentiating n times by Leibnitz's theorem, we get

$$\frac{d^n y}{dx^n} = (x-1)^n \cdot \frac{d^n}{dx^n}(x+1)^n + n \left\{ \frac{d^{n-1}}{dx^{n-1}} (x+1)^n \right\}.$$

$$+ n(x-1)^{n-1} + \ldots + n\left\{\frac{d}{dx}(x+1)^n\right\}\frac{d^{n-1}}{dx^{n-1}}(x-1)^n$$
$$+ (x+1)^n \cdot \frac{d^n}{dx^n}(x-1)^n.$$

$$= (x-1)^n . n! + n . \frac{n!}{1!}(x+1)\, n(x-1)^{n-1} + \ldots$$
$$+ n . n(x+1)^{n-1}\frac{n!}{1!}(x-1) + (x+1)^n\, n!.$$

Putting $x = 1$, $\left(\frac{d^n y}{dx^n}\right)_{x-1} = (1+1)^n . n! = 2^n . n! = c$

∴ From (i), we have

$$P_n(x) = \frac{1}{c}\frac{d^n y}{dx^n}$$

or
$$\mathbf{P_n(x) = \frac{1}{2^n . n!}\frac{d^n(x^2-1)^n}{dx^n}}$$

This is Rodrigue's Formula.

ILLUSTRATIVE EXAMPLES

Ex. 9. *If $P_n(x)$ is a Legendre polynomial of degree n and α is such that $P_n(\alpha) = 0$. Show that $P_{n-1}(\alpha)$ and $P_{n+1}(\alpha)$ are of opposite signs.*

Solution. From recurrence formula I, we have

$$(2n+1)\, xP_n(x) = (n+1)\, P_{n+1}(x) + nP_{n-1}(x) \quad \text{...(i)}$$

Given that

$$P_n(\alpha) = 0 \quad \text{...(ii)}$$

Putting $x = \alpha$ in (i) and using (ii), we have

$$(2n+1)\, \alpha . 0 = (n+1)\, P_{n+1}(\alpha) + n\, P_{n-1}(\alpha)$$

or
$$\frac{P_{n+1}(\alpha)}{P_{n-1}(\alpha)} = -\frac{n}{(n+1)} \quad \text{...(iii)}$$

Since n is a positive integer, so that R.H.S. of (iii) is negative. Hence (iii) shows that $P_{n+1}(\alpha)$ and $P_{n-1}(\alpha)$ must be of opposite signs.

Ex. 10. *Prove that*

$$P'_{n+1} + P'_n = P_0 + 3P_1 + 5P_2 + \ldots + (2n+1)P_n$$
$$= \sum_{r=1} (2r+1)\, P_r(x).$$

Solution. From recurrence formula III, we have

$$(2n+1)\, P_n = P'_{n+1} - P'_{n-1}.$$

Putting $n = 1, 2, 3, \ldots\ldots\ldots$, we get

$$3P_1 = P'_2 - P'_0$$
$$5P_2 = P'_3 - P'_1$$
$$7P_3 = P'_4 - P'_2$$

$$\ldots \quad \ldots \quad \ldots$$
$$\ldots \quad \ldots \quad \ldots$$
$$(2n-3)\,P_{n-2} = P'_{n-1} - P'_{n-3}$$
$$(2n-1)\,P_{n-1} = P'_{n} - P'_{n-2}$$
$$(2n+1)\,P_{n} = P'_{n+1} - P'_{n-1}$$

Adding all, we get

$$3P_1 + 5P_2 + \ldots + (2n+1)\,P_n = P'_n + P'_{n+1} - P'_0 - P'_1$$
$$= P'_n + P'_{n+1} - 0 - P_0$$

Since $P_0 = 1$, and $P_1 = x$ [By Ex. 1]

$\therefore$ $$P'_1 = 1 = P_0$$

Hence

$$P_0 + 3P_1 + 5P_2 + \ldots + (2n+1)\,P_n = P'_{n+1} + P'_n,$$

Ex. 11. *Prove that*

$$P_0^2(x) + 3P_1^2(x) + 5P_2^2(x) + \ldots + (2n+1).\,P_n^2(x)$$
$$= (n+1)\,[P_n(x)\,P'_{n+1}(x) - P_{n+1}(x)\,P'_n(x)]$$
$$= (n+1)^2\,P_n^2(x) + (1-x^2)\,\{P'_n(x)\}^2.$$

Solution. From Christoffel's summation-formula, we have

$$(x-y)\sum_{r=0}^{n}(2r+1)\,P_r(x)\,P_r(y)$$
$$= (n+1)\,[P_{n+1}(x)\,P_n(y) - P_{n+1}(y)\,P_n(x)].$$

Let $y = x + h,$

where h is a small quantity. Then

$$-h\sum_{r=0}^{n}(2r+1)\,P_r(x)\,P_r(x+h)$$
$$= (n+1)\,[P_{n+1}(x)\,P_n(x+h) - P_{n+1}(x+h)\,P_n(x)]$$

Expanding by Taylor's Theorem, we get

$$-h\sum_{r=0}^{n}(2r+1)\,P_r(x)\,\{P_r(x) + h\,P'_r(x) + \ldots\}$$
$$= (n+1)\left[P_{n+1}(x)\left\{P_n(x) + P'_n(x) + \frac{h^2}{2!}P''_n(x)\right.\right.$$
$$\left.\left. + \ldots\right\} - \left\{P_{n+1}(x) + h\,P'_{n+1}(x) + \frac{h^2}{2!}P''_{n+1}(x) + \ldots\right\}P_n(x)\right]$$
$$= -h\,(n+1)\,[P_n(x)\,P'_{n+1}(x) - P'_n(x)\,P_{n+1}(x) + h(\ldots) + \ldots]$$

or $$\sum_{r=0}^{n}(2r+1)\,P_r(x)\,\{P_r(x) + h\,P'_r(x) + \ldots +\}$$
$$= (n+1)\,[P_n(x).\,P'_{n+1} - P'_n(x)\,P_{n+1}(x) + h\,(\ldots) + \ldots]$$

Taking limit as $h \to 0$, we have

$$\sum_{r=0}^{n} (2r+1) P^2{}_r(x) = (n+1) [P_n(x) P'_{n+1}(x) - P'_n(x) P_{n+1}(x)]$$

or
$$P_0^2(x) + 3P_1^2(x) + 5P^2{}_2(x) + \dots + (2n+1) P_n^2(x)$$
$$= (n+1) [P_n(x) P'_{n+1}(x) - P_{n+1}(x) P'_n(x)]$$

Again,
$$(n+1)^2 P_n^2(x) + (1-x^2) P'_n{}^2(x)$$
$$= (n+1) P_n(x) [(n+1) P_n(x)] + P'_n(x) [(1-x^2) P'_n(x)]$$
$$= (n+1) P_n(x) [P'_{n+1}(x) - x P'_n(x)] + P'_n(x) [(n+1) \{x P_n(x) - P_{n+1}(x)\}]$$

[from recurrence formula IV and VI]

$$= (n+1) [P_n(x) P'_{n+1}(x) - P_{n+1}(x) P'(x)],$$

Ex. 12. *Prove that*

$$\int_{-1}^{+1} (x^2-1) P_{n+1} P'_n \, dx = \frac{2n(n+1)}{(2n+1)(2n+3)}$$

Solution. From recurrence formula V, we have

$$(x^2-1) P'_n = n (x P_n - P_{n-1})$$

$$\therefore \int_{-1}^{+1} (x^2-1) P_{n+1} P'_n \, dx$$
$$= \int_{-1}^{+1} n (x P_n - P_{n+1}) P_{n+1} \, dx$$
$$= n \int_{-1}^{+1} x P_n P_{n+1} \, dx,$$

the other integral being zero, because

$$\int_{-1}^{+1} P_m P_n \, dx = 0, \text{ if } m \neq n$$

$$= n \int_{-1}^{+1} \frac{(n+1) P_{n+1} + n P_{n-1}}{2n+1} P_{n+1} \, dx$$

[from Recurrence formula I]

$$= \frac{n(n+1)}{2n+1} \int_{-1}^{+1} P^2{}_{n+1} \, dx + \frac{n^2}{2n+1} \int_{-1}^{+1} P_{n-1} P_{n+1} \, dx$$
$$= \frac{n(n+1)}{(2n+1)} \cdot \frac{2}{2(n+1)+1} + 0$$

[By § 2.8 (i) and (ii)]

$$= \frac{2n(n+1)}{(2n+1)(2n+3)}.$$

Ex. 13. *Prove that*

(i) $\int_{-1}^{+1} P_n(x) \, dx = 0, \quad n \neq 0$

and *(ii)* $\int_{-1}^{+1} P_0(x) \, dx = 2.$

Solution. From Rodrigue's formula (§ 2.13], we have

$$P_n(x) = \frac{1}{2^n \text{ n!}} \cdot \frac{dn}{dxn} (x2 - 1)n$$

$$\therefore \quad \int_{-1}^{+1} P_n(x)\, dx = \frac{1}{2_n\, n!} \int_{-1}^{+1} \frac{d^n}{dx^n} (x^2 - 1)^n\, dx$$

$$= \frac{1}{2n^n\, n!} \left[\frac{d^{n-1}}{dx^{n-1}} (x^2 - 1)^n \right]_{-1}^{+1}$$

Now $\frac{d^{n-1}}{dx^{n-1}} (x^2 - 1)^n = \frac{d^{n-1}}{dx^{n-1}} (x+1)^n (x-1)^n$

$$= (x+1)^n \frac{d^{n-1}}{dx^{n-1}} (x-1)^n$$

$$+ (n-1).\, n\, (x+1)^{n-1} \frac{d^{n-2}}{dx^{n-2}} (x-1)^n$$

$$+ .. + (x-1)^n \frac{d^{n-1}}{dx^{n-1}} (x+1)^n$$

$$= (x+1)^n \frac{n!}{1!} (x-1)$$

$$+ n(n-1)(x+1)^{n-1} \frac{n!}{2!} (x-1)^2 + ...$$

$$= 0,$$

$\therefore$ From (i), $\int_{-1}^{+1} dx = 0.$

(ii) We known that $P_0(x) = 1$.

$$\therefore \quad \int_{-1}^{+1} P_0(x)\, dx = \int_{-1}^{+1} dx = [x]_{-1}^{+1} = 2.$$

Ex. 14. *Prove that if m is a integer less than n.*

$$\int_{-1}^{+1} x^m P_n(x)\, dx = 0$$

and
$$\int_{-1}^{+1} x^n P_n(x) = \frac{2^{n+1} (n!)^2}{(2n+1)!}$$

Solution. Let

$$I = \int_{-1}^{+1} x^m P_n(x)\, dx$$

$$= \int_{-1}^{+1} x^m \frac{1}{2^n .n!} \frac{d^n}{dx^n} \{x^2 - 1\}^n\, dx$$

[By Rodrigue's formula]

$$= \frac{1}{2^n .n!} \int_{-1}^{+1} x^m \cdot \frac{d^n}{dx^n} (x^2 - 1)^n\, dx$$

$$= \frac{1}{2^n \cdot n!}\left[\left\{x^m \int \frac{d^{n-1}}{dx^{n-1}}(x^2-1)^n\,dx\right\}_{-1}^{+1} - \int_{-1}^{+1} mx^{m-1}\frac{d^{n-1}}{dx^{n-1}}(x^2-1)^n\,dx\right]$$

$$= \frac{(-1)\,m}{2^n \cdot n!}\int_{-1}^{+1} x^{m-1}\,\frac{d^{n-1}}{dx^{n-1}}(x^2-1)^n\,dx$$

$$\left[\text{since}\left\{\frac{d^{n-1}}{dx^{n-1}}(x^2-1)^n\right\}_{-1}^{+1} = 0,\ \text{see example 13}\right]$$

Proceeding similarly, we have

$$I = \frac{(-1)^m m!}{2^n \cdot n!}\int_{-1}^{+1} x^0\,\frac{d^{n-m}}{dx^{n-m}}(x^2-1)^n\,dx$$

$$= \frac{(-1)^m m!}{2^n \cdot n!}\left[\frac{d^{n-m-1}}{dx^{n-m-1}}(x^2-1)^n\right]_{-1}^{+1}$$

$= 0,$ [can be shown easily as $n > m + 1$]

Again, if $m = n$, then

$$\int_{-1}^{+1} x^n P_n(x)\,dx = \frac{(-1)^n \cdot n!}{2^n \cdot n!}\int_{-1}^{+1}\frac{d^{n-n}}{dx^{n-n}}(x^2-1)^n\,dx$$

$$= \frac{(-1)^n}{2^n}\cdot\int_{-1}^{+1}(x^2-1)^n\,dx$$

$$= \frac{2}{2^n}\int^{1}(1-x)^n\,dx$$

Put $x = \sin\theta$, $dx = \cos\theta\,d\theta$

$$= \frac{2}{2^n}\int_0^{\pi/2}\cos^{2n+1}\theta\,d\theta$$

$$= \frac{2}{2^n}\,\frac{\Gamma(n+1)\,\Gamma\frac{1}{2}}{2\,\Gamma\frac{(2n+3)}{2}}$$

$$= \frac{2}{2^n}\cdot\frac{n!\,\sqrt{(\pi)}}{2\left\{\frac{2n+1}{2}\right\}\left\{\frac{2n-1}{2}\right\}\ldots-\frac{5}{2}\cdot\frac{3}{2}\cdot\frac{1}{2}\sqrt{(\pi)}}$$

$$= \frac{2.\,(n!)^2}{2^n.2.\left\{\frac{2n+1}{2}\right\}\left\{\frac{2n}{2}\right\}\left\{\frac{2n-1}{2}\right\}\ldots-\frac{3}{2}\cdot\frac{2}{2}\cdot\frac{1}{2}}$$

$$= \frac{(n!)^2}{2^n\cdot\frac{(2n+1)!}{2^{2n+1}}} = \frac{2^{n+1}.\,(n!)^2}{(2n+1)!}$$

Ex. 15. *Prove that*

$$\int_{-1}^{+1} (P'_n)^2\, dx = n\,(n+1)$$

Solution. From Christoffel's expansion, we have

$$P'_n = (2n-1)\,P_{n-1} + (2n-5)\,P_{n-3} + (2n-9)\,P_{n-5} + \ldots \qquad \ldots(i)$$

the last term is P_0, *i.e.*, 1 or $3P_1$, *i.e.*, $3x$ according as n is odd or even. When n is odd, let m be the number of terms on the R.H.S. of (i) then last coeff.1 = $(2n-1) + (m-1).(-4)$

$$\therefore \quad m = \frac{n+1}{2}$$

and when n is even, let m' be the number of terms on the R.H.S. of (i) then last coeff.

$$3 = (2n-1) + (m'-1)\,(-4).$$
$$\therefore \quad m' = n/2$$

Now,

$$(P'_n)^2 = (2n-1)^2\, P^2_{n-1} + (2n-5)^2\, P^2_{n-3} + \ldots$$
$$+\, 2\,(2n-1)\,(2n-5)\,P_{n-1}\,P_{n-3} + \ldots$$

$$\therefore \int_{-1}^{+1} (P'_n)^2\, dx = (2n-1)^2 \int_{-1}^{+1} (P_{n-1})^2\, dx + (2n-5)^2 \int_{-1}^{+1} P^2_{n-3}\, dx \ldots\ldots$$

other integrals are zero by § 2·8 (i)

$$= (2n-1)^2 \cdot \frac{2}{2\,(n-1)+1} + (2n-5)^2 \frac{2}{2\,(n-3)+1}$$
$$+\, (2n-9)^2 \cdot \frac{2}{2\,(n-5)+1} + \ldots$$

$$= 2\,[(2n-1) + (2n-5) + (2n-9) + \ldots] \qquad \ldots(ii)$$

the last term being 1 or 3 according as n is odd or even.

Case I. When n is even, number of terms on the R.H.S. of (ii) is $n/2$

$$\therefore \int_{-1}^{+1} (P'_n)^2\, dx = 2 \cdot \frac{1}{2} \cdot \frac{n}{2} \left[2\,(2n-1) + \left(\frac{n}{2} - 1\right)(-4) \right] = n\,(n+1)$$

Case II. When n is odd, number of terms on the R.H.S. of (ii) is $\dfrac{n+1}{2}$

$$\therefore \int_{-1}^{+1} (P'_n)^2\, dx = 2.\frac{1}{2} \left(\frac{n+1}{2}\right) \left[2.\,(2n-1) + \left\{\frac{n+1}{2} - 1\right\} \left(-4\right) \right]$$

$$= n\,(n+1).$$

Hence $$\int_{-1}^{+1} (P'_n)^2\, dx = n\,(n+1).$$

Ex. 16. *Prove that*

$$\int_{-1}^{+1} x^2\, P_{n+1}\, P_{n-1}\, dx = \frac{2n\,(n+1)}{(2n-1)\,(2n+1)\,(2n+3)}$$

Solution. From recurrence formula I, we have

$$(2n+1)\, xP_n = (n+1)\, P_{n+1} + nP_{n-1}$$

Replacing n by $(n-1)$ and $(n+1)$ respectively, we get

$$(2n-1)\, xP_{n-1} = nP_n + (n-1)\, P_{n-2}$$

and $(2n+3)xP_{n+1} = (n+2)P_{n+2} + (n+1)P_n$.

Multiplying $(2n-1)(2n+3)x^2 P_{n+1} P_{n-1} = n(n+1)P_n^2 + n(n+2)P_n P_{n+2}$
$+ (n-1)(n+2)P_{n-2} P_{n+2} + (n-1)(n+1)P_{n-2} P_n$

Integrating between the limits – 1 to + 1, we get

$$(2n-1)(2n+3)\int_{-1}^{+1} x^2 P_{n+1} P_{n-1}\, dx$$

$$= n(n+1)\int_{-1}^{+1} P^2\, dx \qquad \text{all other integrals being zero}$$

$$= n(n+1).\frac{2}{(2n+1)}$$

$$\therefore \int_{-1}^{+1} x^2 P_{n+1}.P_{n-1}\, dx = \frac{2n(n+1)}{(2n-1)(2n+1)} \cdot (2n+3)$$

Ex. 17. *Prove that*

$$\int_{-1}^{+1} (1-x^2)(P_n')^2\, dx = \frac{2n(n+1)}{2n+1}$$

Solution. From Christoffel's result, we have

$$P_n' = (2n-1)P_{n-1} + (2n-5)P_{n-3} + (2n-9)P_{n-5} + \cdots \qquad \text{...(i)}$$

Also from Beltrami's result, we have

$$(1-x^2)P_n' = \frac{n(n+1)}{2n+1}(P_{n-1} - P_{n+1}) \qquad \text{...(ii)}$$

Multiplying (i) and (ii) and then integrating between the limits – 1 to + 1, we have

$$\int_{-1}^{+1} (1-x^2)(P_n')^2\, dx$$

$$= \frac{n(n+1)}{(2n+1)}\int_{-1}^{+1} [(2n-1)P_{n-1}^2 - (2n-1)P_{n-1}P_{n+1} + (2n-5)P_{n-1}P_{n+1} + \ldots]\, dx$$

$$= \frac{n(n+1)(2n-1)}{(2n+1)}\int_{-1}^{+1} P_{n-1}^2\, dx$$

$$\left[\text{since all other integrals are zero by the property } \int_{-1}^{+1} P_m P_n\, dx = 0 \;\; m \neq n\right]$$

$$= \frac{n(n+1)(2n-1)}{(2n+1)} \cdot \frac{2}{2(n-1)+1}$$

$$= \frac{2n(n+1)}{(2n+1)}.$$

Ex. 18. *Prove that* $\int_{-1}^{+1} (1-x^2)\, P_m'\, P_n'\, dx = 0,$

where m and n are distinct positive integers.

where m and n are distinct positive integers.

Solution. $\int_{-1}^{+1} (1-x^2) P'_m P'_n \, dx$

$$= \left[\left(1-x^2\right) P'_m P_n \right]_{-1}^{+1} - \int_{-1}^{+1} \left[P_n \frac{d}{dx} \left\{ \left(1-x^2\right) P'_m \right\} \right] dx$$

(integrating by parts taking P_n as second function)

$$= -\int_{-1}^{+1} \left[P_n \frac{d}{dx} \{(1-x^2) P'_m\} \right] dx \qquad ...(i)$$

Now, since P_m is the solution of the Legendre's equation.

$\therefore \ (1-x^2) P''_m - 2x P'_m + m(m+1) P_m = 0$

or $$\frac{d}{dx} [(1-x^2) P'_m] = -m(m+1) P_m$$

Hence, from (i), we get

$$\int_{-1}^{+1} (1-x^2) P'_m P'_n \, dx = -\int_{-1}^{+1} [-P_n . m(m+1) P_m] \, dx$$

$$= m(m+1) \int_{-1}^{+1} P_n P_m \, dx$$

$$= 0. \qquad \text{Since } m \neq n.$$

Ex. 19. *Prove that all the roots of $P_n(x) = 0$ are distinct.*

Solution. If the roots of $P_n(x) = 0$ are not all different, then at least two of them must be equal.

Let α be their common value.

Hence, $$P_n(\alpha) = 0 \qquad ...(i)$$

and $$P'_n(\alpha) = 0 \qquad ...(ii)$$

But $P_n(x)$ is the solution of Legendre's equation.

$$\therefore \ (1-x^2) \frac{d^2}{dx^2} P_n(x) - 2x \frac{d}{dx} P_n(x) + n(n+1) P_n(x) = 0$$

Differentiating r times by Leibnitz's theorem, we get

$$(1-x^2) \frac{d^{r+2}}{dx^{r+2}} P_n(x) - 2x . {}^rc_1 \frac{d^{r+1}}{dx^{r+1}} P_n(x)$$

$$- 2 \ {}^rc_2 \frac{d^r}{dx^r} [P_n(x)] - 2 \left[x . \frac{d^{r+1}}{dx^{r+1}} P_n(x) \right.$$

$$\left. + 1 / {}^rc_1 \frac{d^r}{dx^r} P_n(x) \right] + n(n+1) \frac{d^r}{dx^r} P_n(x) = 0$$

or $$(1-x^2) \frac{d^{r+2}}{dx^{r+2}} P_n(x) - 2x ({}^rc_1 + 1) \frac{d^{r+1}}{dx^{r+1}} P_n(x)$$

$$- \{2 . {}^rc_2 + 2 . {}^rc_1 - n(n+1)\} \frac{d^r}{dx^r} P_n(x) = 0 \qquad ...(iii)$$

Putting $r = 0$ and $x = \alpha$, we get

$$(1-\alpha^2) \left[\frac{d^2}{dx^2} P_n(x) \right]_{x=\alpha} - 2\alpha \left[\frac{d}{dx} P_n(x) \right]_{x=\alpha}$$

$$+ n(n+1) P_n(\alpha) = 0$$

or $\quad P_n''(\alpha) = 0$ by (i) and (ii).

Similarly, writing $r = 1, 2, 3, \ldots$ in (iii) and simplifying stepwise, we have

$$P_n'''(\alpha) = 0 = P_n^{\text{iv}}(\alpha) = \ldots = P_n^n(\alpha)$$

But, since

$$P_n(x) = \frac{1.3\ldots.(2n-1)}{n!}\left[x^n - \frac{n(n-1)}{2.(2n-1)}x^{n-2} - \ldots\right]$$

$$\therefore \quad P_n^n(\alpha) = \frac{1.3\ldots.(2n-1)}{n!}\cdot n!$$

$$\therefore \quad P_n^n(\alpha) \neq 0.$$

Therefore, our assumption that $P_n(x) = 0$ has a repeated root is not correct. Hence all the roots of $P_n(x) = 0$ are distinct.

Ex. 20. *Show that all the roots of $P_n(x) = 0$ are real and lie between -1 and $+1$.*

Solution. We know that

$$P_n(x) = \frac{1}{2^n \cdot n!}\frac{d^n}{dx^n}(x^2-1)^n$$

Now, $\quad (x^2-1)^n = (x-1)^n \cdot (x+1)^n.$

Hence $(x^2-1)^n$ vanishes n times at $x = +1$ and n times at $x = -1$.

Therefore, by the theory of equations $\frac{d^n}{dx^n}(x^2-1)$ will have n roots, all real and lying between -1 and $+1$.

Hence, $P_n(x) = \frac{1}{2^\mu \cdot n!}\frac{d^n}{dx^n}(x^2-1)^n = 0$ has n roots all real and lying between -1 and $+1$.

Exercise 2 (B)

1. Prove that

$$P_n' - P_{n-2}' = (2n-1)P_{n-1}.$$

2. Prove that

$$x P_9' = P_8' - 2P_9.$$

3. Show that

$$11(x^2-1)P_5' = 30(P_6 - P_4)$$

4. Show that

$$\int_{-1}^{1} x P_n(x) P_{n-1}(x)\, dx = \frac{2}{4n^2-1}.$$

5. Prove

$$\int_{-1}^{+1} x^2 P_n^2\, dx = \frac{1}{8(2n-1)} + \frac{3}{4(2n+1)} + \frac{1}{8(2n+3)}$$

6. Prove that $\int_0^1 P_n(x)\,dx = \frac{(-1)^{(n-1)/2}(n-1)!}{2^n\{(n+1)/2\}!\{(n-1)/2\}!}$

when n is odd.

7. Prove that $\int_0^1 P_n(x)\,dx = \frac{1}{(2n+1)}[P_{n-1}(x) - P_{n+1}(x)]$.

8. Evaluate $\int_{-1}^{+1} x^4 P_6(x)\,dx$.

9. Prove that $x P_n' = n P_n + (2n-3) P_{n-2} - (2n-7) P_{n-4} + \ldots$
and hence or otherwise show that

(a) $\int_{-1}^{1} P_n P_n'\,dx = (2n)/(2n+1)$

(b) $\int_{-1}^{1} x P_n P_m'\,dx =$ either 0 or 2 or $(2n)/(2n+1)$

2.14 Even and Odd Function

Even function: $f(x)$ is said to be an even function of x if $f(-x) = f(x)$.
If an even function $f(x)$ is expressed as series of functions so that

$$f(x) = f_1(x) + f_2(x) + \ldots + f_n(x) + \ldots$$

Then all $f_1(x), f_2(x)$ ... etc. must be even function of x.

Odd function. $f(x)$ is said to be an odd function of x, if

$$f(-x) = -f(x).$$

If an odd function $f(x)$ is expressed as a series of functions so that

$$f(x) = f_1(x) + f_2(x) + \ldots + f_n(x) + \ldots$$

none of f_n's may be an even function of x.

2.15 Expansion of x^n in Legendre's Polynomials

Let
$$x^n = a_n P_n(x) + a_{n-2} P_{n-2}(x) + a_{n-4} P_{n-4}(x) + \ldots a_r P_r(x) + \ldots \quad \ldots(i)$$

where $P_n(x)$, $P_{n-2}(x)$ are all even or odd functions of x according as x^n is an even or odd function.

Since $P_n(x)$ contains terms of degree n and lower, we can not have in the expansion of x^n any P with suffix higher than n.

Also, $P_{n-1}(x)$, $P_{n-3}(x)$ ... can not occur in this expansion as they are odd or even function of x if x^n is even and odd function of x respectively.

Now, we have to determine the values of the coefficients a_n, a_{n-1} ... etc. For this let us multiply both sides of (i) by $P_r(x)$ and then integrate between the limits – 1 to + 1.

Thus we get $\int_{-1}^{+1} x^n \cdot P_r(x) = a_r \int_{-1}^{+1} P_r^2(x)\,dx$

All other integrals on the L.H.S. are zero by the property

$$\int_{-1}^{+1} P_m P_n \, dx = 0, \text{ if } m \neq n.$$

$$\therefore \int_{-1}^{+1} x^n . P_r(x) = a_r \int_{-1}^{+1} P_r^2(x)\, dx = a_r \cdot \frac{2}{(2r+1)}$$

or

$$a_r = \frac{2r+1}{2} \int_{-1}^{+1} x^n P_r(x)\, dx \qquad \text{...(ii)}$$

$$= \frac{(2r+1)}{2} \int_{-1}^{+1} x^n . \frac{1}{2^r . r!} \frac{d^r}{dx^r} (x^2-1)^r \, dx$$

[by Rodrigue's formula]

$$= \frac{(2r+1)}{2^{r+1} r!} \int_{-1}^{+1} x^n \frac{d^r}{dx^r} (x^2-1)^r \, dx.$$

Integrating by parts taking x^n as first function

$$= \frac{(2r+1)}{2^{r+1} r!} \left[\left\{ x^n \frac{d^{r-1}}{dx^{r-1}} (x^2-1)^r \right\}_{-1}^{+1} - n \int_{-1}^{+1} x^{n-1} \frac{d^{r-1}}{dx^{r-1}} (x^2-1)^r \, dx \right]$$

$$= (-1) \frac{(2r+1)}{2^{r+1} r!} n \int_{-1}^{+1} x^{n-1} \frac{d^{r-1}}{dx^{r-1}} (x^2-1)^r \, dx$$

$$= (-1)^2 \frac{(2r+1)}{2^{r+1} r!} n(n-1) \int_{-1}^{+1} x^{n-2} \frac{d^{r-2}}{dx^{r-2}} (x^2-1)^r \, dx$$

[Repeating the same process again].

$$= (-1)^r \frac{(2r+1)}{2^{r+1} r!} n(n-1)...(n-r+1) \int_{-1}^{+1} x^{n-r} (x^2-1)^r \, dx$$

$$= (-1)^r (-1)^r \frac{(2r+1)\, n!}{2^{r+1} r!\, (n-r)} \int_{-1}^{+1} x^{n-r} (1-x^2)^r \, dx \qquad \text{...(iii)}$$

But r is one of the integers $n, n-2, n-4$... Therefore, $(n-r)$ is one of the numbers 0, 2, 4, 6,...etc., *i.e.*, $(n-r)$ is an even integer including zero. So $x^{n-r}(1-x^2)^r$ is an even function of x.

Hence from (iii), we get

$$a_r = \frac{(2r+1)}{2^{r+1} r!} \frac{n!}{(n-r)!} 2 \int_0^1 x^{n-r} (1-x^2)^r \, dx$$

Putting $x^2 = t$, so that $2x\, dx = dt$

$$= \frac{(2r+1)}{2^{r+1} . r!} \cdot \frac{n!}{(n-r)!} \int_0^1 t^{(n-r-1)/2} (1-t)^r \, dt$$

$$= \frac{(2r+1)}{2^{r+1} . r!} \cdot \frac{n!}{(n-r)!} \int_0^1 t^{\{(n-r+1)/2-1\}} (1-t)^{(r+1)-1} . \, dt$$

$$= \frac{(2r+1)}{2^{r+1}.\, r\,!} \cdot \frac{n\,!}{(n-r)\,!} \cdot \frac{\Gamma\left(\frac{n-r+1}{2}\right)\Gamma(r+1)}{\Gamma\left(\frac{n-r+1}{2}+r+1\right)}$$

$$\left[\because \quad B(l, m) = \int_0^1 x^{l-1}(1-x)^{m-1}\,dx = \frac{\Gamma(l)\,\Gamma(m)}{\Gamma(l+m)}\right]$$

$$= \frac{(2r+1)}{2^{r+1}.\, r\,!} \cdot \frac{n\,!}{(n-r)\,!} \cdot \frac{\Gamma\left(\frac{n-r+1}{2}\right) r\,!}{\Gamma\left(\frac{n+r+3}{2}\right)}$$

$$= \frac{(2r+1)}{2^{r+1}} \cdot \frac{n\,!}{(n-r)\,!}$$

$$\times \frac{\Gamma\left(\frac{n-r+1}{2}\right)}{\left(\frac{n+r+1}{2}\right)\left(\frac{n+r-1}{2}\right)\cdots\left(\frac{n-r+3}{2}\right)\left(\frac{n-r+1}{2}\right)\Gamma\left(\frac{n-r+1}{2}\right)}$$

$$= (2r+1)\cdot\frac{n(n-1)(n-2)\ldots(n-r+1)(n-r)\,!}{(n+r+1)(n+r-1)(n+r-3)\ldots(n-r+3)(n-r+1)(n-r)\,!}$$

$$\therefore \quad a_r = (2r+1)\,\frac{n(n-1)(n-2)\ldots(n-r+2)}{(n+r+1)(n+r-1)\ldots(n-r+3)} \qquad \text{...(iv)}$$

Putting $r = n, (n-2), (n-4), \ldots$, in (iv) we get

$$a_n = (2n+1)\,\frac{n(n-1)\ldots 2}{(2n+1)(2n-1)\ldots 3}$$

i.e.,

$$a_n = \frac{2.3.4\ldots n}{3.5\ldots(2n+1)}(2n+1)$$

$$a_{n-2} = \frac{4.5\ n}{5.7\ldots.(2n-1)}(2n-3)$$

$$= \frac{2.3.4\ldots n}{3.5.7\ldots(2n+1)} \cdot \frac{(2n+1)}{2} \cdot (2n-3)$$

$$a_{n-4} = \frac{2.3\ldots n}{3.5.7\ldots(2n+1)} \cdot \frac{(2n+1)(2n+1)}{2.4} \cdot (2n-7) \text{ etc.}$$

Substituting these values in eqn. (i), we get

$$x^n = \frac{n\,!}{1.3.5\ldots(2n+1)}\Bigg[(2n+1)P_n(x) + (2n-3)\frac{(2n+1)}{2}$$

$$P_{n-2}(x) + (2n-7)\frac{(2n+1)(2n-1)}{2.4}P_{n-4}(x) + \ldots$$

$$+ \frac{1}{n+1}P_0(x) \text{ or } \frac{3}{n+2}P_1(x)\Bigg] \qquad \text{...(v)}$$

according as n is even or odd.

ILLUSTRATIVE EXAMPLES

Ex. 21. *Prove that, for all x*

(a) $x^4 = 8/35\, P_4(x) + 4/7\, P_2(x) + 1/5\, P_0(x)$

and (b) $x^5 = 8/63\, P_5(x) + 4/9\, P_3(x) + 3/7\, P_1(x)$

Solution. (a) We know that

$$x^n = \frac{n\,!}{3.5...(2n+1)}\left[(2n+1)\,P_n(x) + \frac{(2n-3)}{3}(2n+1)\right.$$
$$\left. P_{n-2}(x) - (2n-7)\frac{(2n+1)(2n-1)}{2.4}P_{n-4}(x) + ...\right]$$

Hence $n = 4$,

$$\therefore\quad x^4 = \frac{4\,!}{3.5.7.9}\left[9.P_4(x) + \frac{59}{2}\cdot P_2(x) + 1\cdot\frac{9.7}{2.4}P_0(x)\right]$$

$$= 8/35\, P_4(x) + 4/7\, P_2(x) + 1/5\, P_0(x).$$

(b) When $n = 5$

$$x^5 = \frac{4\,!}{3.5.7.9.11}\left[11.P_5(x) + 7.\frac{11}{2}P_3(x). + 3.\frac{11.9}{2.4}P_1(x)\right]$$

$$= \frac{8}{63}P_5(x) + \frac{4}{9}P_3(x) + \frac{3}{7}P_1(x).$$

Ex. 22. *Expand f(x) in the form* $\sum_{r=0}^{\infty} C_r\, P_r(x)$

where $$f(x) = \begin{cases} 0, & -1 < x < 0 \\ 1, & 0 < x < 1 \end{cases} \qquad ...(i)$$

Solution. We know that $f(x) = \sum_{r=1}^{\infty} C_r\, P_r(x)$ ...(ii)

where $$C_r = \left(r + \frac{1}{2}\right)\int_{-1}^{+1} f(x)\, P_r\,(x)\, dx$$

$$= \frac{(2r+1)}{2}\left[\int_{-1}^{0} f(x)\, P_r(x)\, dx + \int_0^1 f(x)\, P_r(x)\; x\right]$$

$$\therefore\quad C_r = \frac{(2r+1)}{2}\int_0^1 P_r(x)\, dx, \text{ by (i)} \qquad ...(iii)$$

Putting $r = 0, 1, 2, ...$ successively in (iii), we get

$$C_0 = \frac{1}{2}\int_0^1 P_0(x)\, dx = \frac{1}{2}\int_0^1 (1)\, dx = \frac{1}{2}$$

$$C_1 = \frac{3}{2}\int_0^1 P_1(x)\, dx = \frac{3}{2}\int_0^1 x\, dx = \frac{3}{4}$$

$$C_2 = \frac{5}{2}\int_0^1 P_2(x)\, dx = \frac{5}{2}\int_0^1 \frac{3x^2-1}{2}\, dx = 0$$

$$C_3 = \frac{7}{2}\int_0^1 P_3(x)\,dx = \frac{7'}{2}\int_0^1 \frac{5x^3 - 2x}{2}\,dx = -\frac{7}{16}$$

and so on. Using these values in (ii), we get

$$f(x) = \frac{1}{2}P_0(x) + \frac{3}{4}P_1(x) - \frac{7}{16}P_3(x) + ... + C_r P_r(x) + ...$$

where $$C_r = (r + \tfrac{1}{2})\int_0^1 P_r(x)\,dx.$$

Ex. 23. *Obtain the first three terms in the expansion of the following function in terms of Legendre's polynomials :*

$$\left.\begin{aligned} f(x) &= 0, \text{ if } -1 < x < 0, \\ &= x, \text{ if } \ 0 < x < 1. \end{aligned}\right\}$$

Solution. Let

$$f(x) = a_0 P_0(x) + a_1 P_1(x) + a_2 P_2(x) + ...$$

where we obtain a_0, a_1, a_2 ... as follows :

$$a_0 = \frac{1}{2}\int_0^1 x P_0(x)\,dx = \frac{1}{2}\int_0^1 x.1\,dx = \frac{1}{4}$$

$$a_1 = \frac{1}{2}\int_0^1 x P_1(x)\,dx = \frac{1}{2}\int_0^1 x.x\,dx = \frac{1}{2}\int_0^1 x^2\,dx = \frac{1}{6}$$

$$a_3 = \frac{1}{2}\int_0^1 x P_2(x)\,dx = \frac{1}{2}\int_0^1 x.\frac{1}{2}(3x^2 - 1)\,dx$$

$$= \frac{1}{4}\int_0^1 (3x^3 - x\}\,dx = \frac{1}{4}\left[\frac{3}{4} - \frac{1}{2}\right] = \frac{1}{16}.$$

Hence

$$f(x) = \frac{1}{4}P_0(x) + \frac{1}{6}P_1(x) + \frac{1}{16}P_2(x) + ...$$

EXERCISE 2 (C)

Expand $f(x)$ In a series of Legendre's polynomials, if

1. $f(x) = x, \quad 0 < x < 1 \; ; f(x) = 0, \quad -1 < x < 0$
2. $f(x) = 0, \quad -1 \le x < \alpha \; ; f(x) = 1, \alpha < x \le 1$
3. $f(x) = \frac{1}{2}, \quad 0 < x < 1 \; ; f(x) = -\frac{1}{2}, \quad -1 < x < 1$
4. $f(x) = 2x + 1, 0 < x \le 1 \; ; f(x) = 0, \quad -1 \le x < 0.$
5. $f(x) = |x|$ for $-1 \le x \le 1$.
6. Obtain the first few terms in the representation of the function $f(x) = x$ over the interval $0 \le x < 1$ in series of Legendre polynomials of even degree to show that

   $x = \frac{1}{2}P_0(x) + 5/8\,P_2(x) - 3/16\,P_4(x) + ... \; (0 \le x < 1)$
7. Expand $f(x) = x^2$ in a series of the form $\Sigma\, C_r\, P_0(x)$ or find series of Legendre's polynomials for x^2.
8. Expand $x^4 - 3x^2 + x$ in a series of form $\Sigma\, C_r\, P_r(x)$.

ANSWERS

1. $f(x) = \frac{1}{4} + \frac{1}{2} P_1(x) + \frac{5}{16} P_2(x) + ... + C_r P_r(x) + ...$

   where $C_r = (r + \frac{1}{2}) \int_0^1 x P_r(x) \, dx$

2. $f(x) = \frac{1}{2}(1 - \alpha) - \sum_{r=1}^{\infty} [P_{r+1}(\alpha) - P_{r-1}(\alpha)] P_r(x)$

3. $C_r = 0$ if r is even, and

   $$C_r = (-1)^{r-\frac{1}{2}} \frac{(r + \frac{1}{2})(r - 1)!}{2^r \{(r + 1)/2\}! \{(r - 1)/2\}!} \text{; if } r \text{ is odd}$$

4. $f(x) = P_0(x) + \frac{7}{4} P_2(x) + \frac{5}{8} P_2(x) - \frac{7}{16} P_3(x) + \ldots$

5. $f(x) = \sum_{r=0}^{\infty} \frac{(-1)^{n+1}(4n + 1)(2n - 2)!}{2_2{}^n (n + 1)!(n - 1)!} P_{2n}(x)$

7. $x^2 = \frac{1}{3} P_0(x) + \frac{2}{3} P_2(x).$

3

Legendre's Functions of the Second kind

3·1. Legendre's function of the second kind

In § 2·3, we have defined the Legendre's function of the second kind, Q_n, such that

$$Q_n(x) = \frac{n!}{1.3...(2n+1)}\left[x^{-n-1} + \frac{(n+1)(n+2)}{2.(2n+3)} \cdot x^{-n-3} + \frac{(n+1)(n+2)(n+3)(n+4)}{2.4.(2n+3)(2n+5)} x^{-n-5} \ldots\right]$$

or
$$Q_n(x) = \frac{2^n n!}{(2n+1)!} \sum_{r=0}^{\infty} \frac{(n+2r)\, x^{-(n+2r+1)}}{2^r r!(2n+3)(2n+5)\ldots(2n+2r+1)}$$

3·2. Prove : $\dfrac{1}{(y-x)} = \sum\limits_{m=0}^{\infty} (2m+1) P_m(x) Q_m(y)$

Proof. Let
$$f(x) = \frac{1}{(y-x)} = \frac{1}{y(1-x/y)}$$
$$= \frac{1}{y}\left\{1 - \frac{x}{y}\right\}^{-1}$$
$$= \frac{1}{y}\left\{1 + \frac{x}{y} + \frac{x^2}{y^2} + \ldots + \frac{x^m}{y_m} + \frac{x^{m+1}}{y^{m+1}} + \ldots\right\}$$
$$= y^{-1} + xy^{-2} + y^{-3}x^2 + y^{-4}x^3 + \ldots + y^{-(m+1)}x^m + y^{-(m+2)}x^{m+1} + \ldots \quad \ldots(i)$$

Let
$$f(x) = A_0 + A_1 x + A_2 x^2 + \ldots \quad \ldots(ii)$$
where A's are constants. Further suppose that $f(x)$ is also expressed as
$$f(x) = \sum_{m=0}^{\infty} B_m P_m(x) \quad \ldots(iii)$$
then we know that
$$B_m = \frac{1.2.3...m}{1.3.5...(2m-1)}\left[A_m + \frac{(m+1)(m+2)}{2(2m+3)} A_{m+2}\right.$$

$$+ \frac{(m+1)(m+2)(m+3)(m+4)}{2.4.(2m+3)(2m+5)} A_{m+4} + \ldots \Bigg]$$

Comparing (i) and (ii), we have

$$A_0 = y^{-1}, A_1 = y^{-2}, \ldots A_m = y^{-(m+1)}$$

$$A_{m+1} = y^{-(m+2)}, \ldots$$

$$\therefore \quad B_m = \frac{m!}{1.3.5\ldots(2m-1)}$$

$$\times \left[y^{-(m+1)} + \frac{(m+1)(m+2)}{2(2m+3)} y^{-(m+3)} + \ldots \right]$$

$$= (2m+1)\, Q_m(y), \text{ by definition}$$

$$\therefore \quad f(x) = \frac{1}{y-x} \sum_{m=0}^{\infty} B_m P_m(x)$$

$$= \sum_{m=0}^{\infty} (2m+1).\, P_m(x)\, Q_m(y).$$

3.3. Neumann's Integral. If n is zero or a positive integer, then prove that

$$\mathbf{Q_n(y) = \frac{1}{2} \int_{-1}^{+1} \frac{P_n(x)}{(y-x)} dx}$$

where $y > 1$ and $-1 \le x \le 1$.

In § 3·2, we have proved that

$$\frac{1}{y-x} = \sum_{n=0}^{\infty} (2n+1)\, Q_n(y)\, P_n(x)$$

Multiplying both sides by $P_n(x)$ and then integrating w.r.t. 'x' between the limits -1 to $+1$, we get

$$\int_{-1}^{+1} \frac{P_n(x)}{y-x} dx = Q_n(y) \int_{-1}^{+1} \left\{ P_n(x) \sum_{n=0}^{\infty} (2n+1) P_n(x) \right\} dx$$

$$= (2n+1)\, Q_n(y) \int_{-1}^{+1} P_n^{\,2}(x)\, dx$$

$$\text{since} \int_{-1}^{+1} P_n(x)\, P_m(x)\, dx = 0 \text{ if } m \neq n.$$

$$= (2n+1)\, Q_n(y) \cdot \frac{2}{(2n+1)} = 2Q_n(y)$$

[from § 2·8]

$$\therefore \quad Q_n(y) = \frac{1}{2} \int_{-1}^{+1} \frac{P_n(x)}{y-x} dx.$$

3·4. Recurrence formulae for $Q_n(x)$

(I) $Q'_{n+1}(x) - Q'_{n-1}(x) = (2n+1)\, Q_n(x)$

We know that

$$Q'_n(x) = \frac{2^n n!}{(2n+1)!} \sum_{r=0}^{\infty} \frac{(n+2r)!\, x^{-(n+2r+1)}}{2^r r!\,(2n+3)(2n+5)......(2n+2r+1)}$$

Differentiating w.r.t. 'x', we get

$$Q'_n(x) = \frac{2^n n!}{(2n+1)!} \sum_{r=0}^{\infty} \frac{(n+2r+1)!\, x^{-(n+2r+2)}}{2^r r!\,(2n+3)(2n+5)...(2n+2r+1)} \quad ...(i)$$

Replacing n by $(n-1)$ and $(n+1)$, we get

$$Q'_{n-1}(x) = -\frac{2^{n-1}(n-1)!}{(2n+1)!} \sum_{r=0}^{\infty} \frac{(n+2r)!\, x^{-(n+2r+1)}}{2^r r!\,(2n+1)(2n+3)...(2n+2r-1)}$$

$$= -\frac{2^n.n!}{(2n)!} \sum_{r=0}^{\infty} \frac{(n+2r)!\, x^{-(n+2r+1)}}{2^r r!\,(2n+1)(2n+3)...(2n+2r-1)} \quad ...(ii)$$

and

$$Q'_{n+1}(x) = -\frac{2^{n-1}(n+1)!}{(2n+3)!} \sum_{r=0}^{\infty} \frac{(n+2r+2)!\, x^{-(n+2r+3)}}{2^r r!\,(2n+5)(2n+7)...(2n+2r+3)}$$

$$= -\frac{2^n.n!}{(2n)!} \sum_{r=0}^{\infty} \frac{(n+2r+2)!\, x^{-(n+2r+3)}}{2^r r!\,(2n+1)(2n+3)...(2n+2r+3)} \quad ...(iii)$$

Now,

$$(2n+1)\, Q_n(x) + Q'_{n-1}(x)$$

$$= \frac{2^n n!}{2n!} \sum_{r=0}^{\infty} \frac{(n+2r)!\, x^{-(n+2r+1)}}{2^r r!\,(2n+3)(2n+5)...(2n+2r+1)}$$

$$- \frac{2^n n!}{2n!} \sum_{r=0}^{\infty} \frac{(n+2r)!\, x^{-(n+2r+1)}}{2^r r!\,(2n+1)(2n+3)...(2n+2r-1)}$$

$$= \frac{2^n n!}{2n!} \sum_{r=0}^{\infty} \frac{(n+2r)!\,\{(2n+1)-(2n+2r+1)\}\, x^{-(n+2r+1)}}{2^r r!\,(2n+1)(2n+3)...(2n+2r+1)}$$

$$= \frac{2^n n!}{2n!} \sum_{r=0}^{\infty} \frac{(n+2r)!\,(-2r)\, x^{-(n+2r+1)}}{2^r r!\,(2n+1)(2n+3)...(2n+2r+1)}$$

$$= -\frac{2^n n!}{2n!} \sum_{r=0}^{\infty} \frac{(n+2r)!\, x^{-(n+2r+1)}}{2^r r!\,(r-1)!\,(2n+1)(2n+3)...(2n+2r+1)}$$

[$\because$ term corresponding to $r = 0$ is zero]

$$= -\frac{2^n n!}{2n!} \sum_{r=0}^{\infty} \frac{(n+2s+2)!\, x^{-(n+2s+3)}}{2^s s!\,(r-1)!\,(2n+1)(2n+3)...(2n+2s+3)}$$

Putting $r - 1 = s$.

$= Q'_{n+1}(x)$

$\therefore$ $\mathbf{Q'_{n+1}(x) - Q'_{n-1}(x) = (2n+1)\, Q_n(x)}$

II. $\mathbf{Q'_{n+1}(x) - xQ'_n(x) = (n+1)\, Q_n(x)}$

We know that

$$Q_n(x) = \frac{2^n n!}{(2n+1)!} \sum_{r=0}^{\infty} \frac{(n+2r)!\, x^{-(n+2r+1)}}{2^r r!\,(2n+3)(2n+5)...(2n+2r+1)}$$

Also, from equations (i) and (iii) of I, we have

$$Q'_n(x) = \frac{2^n n!}{(2n-1)!} \sum_{r=0}^{\infty} \frac{(n+2r+1)!\, x^{-(n+2r+2)}}{2^r r!\,(2n+3)(2n+5)\ldots(2n+2r+5)}$$

and $$Q'_{n+1}(x) = \frac{2^n n!}{2n!} \sum_{r=0}^{\infty} \frac{(n+2r+2)!\, x^{-(n+2r+3)}}{2^r r!\,(2n+1)(2n+3)\ldots(2n+2r+3)}$$

$\therefore \quad (n+1)\, Q_n(x) + x\, Q'_n(x)$

$$= \frac{2^n n!}{(2n+1)!} \sum_{r=0}^{\infty} \frac{(n+1)(n+2r)!\, x^{-(n+2r+1)}}{2^r r!\,(2n+3)(2n+5)\ldots(2n+2r+1)}$$

$$- \frac{2^n n!}{(2n+1)!} \sum_{r=0}^{\infty} \frac{(n+2r+1)!\, x^{-(n+2r+1)}}{2^r r!\,(2n+3)(2n+5)\ldots(2n+2r+1)}$$

$$= \frac{(2^n n!)}{(2n+1)!} \sum_{r=0}^{\infty} \frac{(n+2r)!\,\{(n+1)-(n+2r+1)\}\, x^{-(n+2r+1)}}{2^r r!\,(2n+3)(2n+5)\ldots(2n+2r+1)}$$

$$= \frac{2^n n!}{2n!} \sum_{r=0}^{\infty} \frac{(n+2r)!(-2r)\, x^{-(n+2r+1)}}{2^r r!\,(2n+1)!\,(2n+3)\ldots(2n+2r+1)}$$

$$= -\frac{2^n n!}{2n!} \sum_{r=1}^{\infty} \frac{(n+2r)!\, x^{-(n+2r+1)}}{2^r - 1\,(r-1)!\,(2n+1)(2n+3)\ldots(2n+2r+1)}$$

[$\because$ term corresponding to $r = 0$ is zero]

$$= \frac{2^n n!}{2n!} \sum_{s=0}^{\infty} \frac{(2+2s+2)!\, x^{-(n+2s+3)}}{2^s s!\,(2n+1)(2n+3)\ldots(2n+2s+3)}$$

Putting $r - 1 = s$.

$= Q'_{n+1}(x)$.

$\therefore$ **$Q'_{n+1}(x) - x\, Q'_n(x) = (n+1)\, Q_n(x)$**

III. $n\, Q'_{n+1}(x) + (n+1)\, Q'_{n-1}(x) = (2n+1)\, x\, Q_n'(x)$

We know that

$$Q_n(x) = \frac{2^n n!}{(2n+1)!} \sum_{r=0}^{\infty} \frac{(n+2r)!\, x^{-(n+2r+1)}}{2^r r!\,(2n+3)(2n+5)\ldots(2n+2r+1)}$$

By eqns. (i), (ii) and (iii) of I, we have

$$Q_n'(x) = -\frac{2^n n!}{(2n+1)!} \sum_{r=0}^{\infty} \frac{(n+2r+1)!\, x^{-(n+2r+2)}}{2^r r!\,(2n+3)(2n+5)\ldots(2n+2r+1)}$$

$$Q'_{n-1}(x) = -\frac{2^n n!}{(2n)!} \sum_{r=0}^{\infty} \frac{(n+2r)!\, x^{-(n+2r+1)}}{2^r r!(2n+1)(2n+3)\ldots(2n+2r+1)}$$

and $$Q'_{n+1}(x) = -\frac{2^n n!}{(2n)!} \sum_{r=0}^{\infty} \frac{(n+2r+2)!\, x^{-(n+2r+3)}}{2^r r!(2n+1)(2n+3)\ldots-(2n+2r+3)}$$

$\therefore \quad (2n+1)\, x\, Q'_n(x) - (n+1)\, Q'_{n-1}(x)$

$$= -\frac{2^n n!}{(2n)!} \sum_{r=0}^{\infty} \frac{(n+2r+1)!\, x^{-(n+2r+1)}}{2^r r!\,(2n+3)(2n+5)\ldots(2n+2r+1)}$$

$$+ \frac{2^n n!}{(2n)!} \sum_{r=0}^{\infty} \frac{(n+1)(n+2r)!\, x^{-(n+2r+1)}}{2^r r!\,(2n+1)(2n+3)\ldots(2n+2r-1)}$$

$(n+2r)!\,\{(n+2r+1)(2n+1)-(n+1)$

$$= \frac{2^n n!}{(2n)!} \sum_{r=0}^{\infty} \frac{(2n+2r+1)\} x^{-(n+2r+1)}}{2^r r! (2n+1)(2n+3)\ldots(2n+2r+1)}$$

$$= -\frac{2^n n!}{(2n)!} \sum_{r=0}^{\infty} \frac{(n+2r)!\, 2r \,.\, x^{-(n+2r+1)}}{2^r r! (2n+1)(2n+3)\ldots(2n+2r+1)}$$

$$= -n \,.\, \frac{2^n n!}{(2n)!} \sum_{r=0}^{\infty} \frac{(n+2r)!\, x^{-(n+2r+1)}}{2^r r! (r-1)! (2n+1)(2n+3)\ldots(2n+2r+1)}$$

$$= -\mathrm{n} \,.\, \frac{2^n n!}{(2n)!} \sum_{s=0}^{\infty} \frac{(n+2s+2)!\, x^{-(n+2s+3)}}{2^s \,.\, s! (2n+1)(2n+3)\ldots(2n+2s+3)}$$

$$= n\, Q'_{n+1}(x).$$

$\therefore$ **$n\, Q'_{n+1}(x) + (n+1)\, Q'_{n-1}(x) = (2n+1)\, x\, Q'_n(x)$.**

IV. $x\, Q'_n(x) - Q'_{n-1}(x) = n\, Q_n(x)$

We have

$$Q_n(x) = \frac{2^n n!}{(2n+1)!} \sum_{r=0}^{\infty} \frac{(n+2r)!\, x^{-(n+2r+1)}}{2^r r! (2n+3)(2n+5)\ldots(2n+2r+1)}$$

By equations (i) and (iii) of I, we have

$$Q_n'(x) = \frac{2^n n!}{(2n+1)!} \sum_{r=0}^{\infty} \frac{(n+2r+1)!\, x^{-(n+2r+2)}}{2^r r! (2n+3)(2n+5)\ldots(2n+2r+1)}$$

and $$Q'_{n-1}(x) = -\frac{2^n n!}{(2n)!} \sum_{r=0}^{\infty} \frac{(n+2r)!\, x^{-(n+2r+1)}}{2^r r! (2n+1)(2n+3)\ldots(2n+2r-1)}$$

$\therefore\ x\, Q_n'(x) - n\, Q_n(x)$

$$= -\frac{2^n n!}{(2n+1)!} \sum_{r=0}^{\infty} \frac{n(n+2r+1)!\, x^{-(n+2r+1)}}{2^r r! (2n+3)(2n+5)\ldots(2n+2r+1)}$$

$$-\frac{2^n n!}{(2n+1)!} \sum_{r=0}^{\infty} \frac{n\,(n+2r)!\, x^{-(n+2r+1)}}{2^r r! (2n+3)(2n+5)\ldots(2n+2r+1)}$$

$$= -\frac{2^n n!}{2n\,!} \sum_{r=0}^{\infty} \frac{(n+2r)!\,(n+2r+1+n)\, x^{-(n+2r+1)}}{2^r r! (2n+1)(2n+3)\ldots(2n+2r+1)}$$

$$= -\frac{2^n n!}{(2n)!} \sum_{r=0}^{\infty} \frac{(n+2r)!\, x^{-(n+2r+1)}}{2^n r! (2n+1)(2n+3)\ldots(2n+2r-1)}$$

$$= Q'_{n-1}(x).$$

$\therefore$ **$x\, Q'_n(x) = nx Q_n(x) - n\, Q_{n-1}(x)$.**

V. $(x^2-1)\, Q_n'(x) = nx\, Q_n(x) - n\, Q_{n-1}(x)$.

Replacing n by $(n-1)$ in recurrence formula II, we get

$$Q'_n(x) - x\, Q'_{n-1}(x) = n\, Q'_{n-1}(x) \quad \ldots(i)$$

From recurrence formula IV

$$x\, Q'_n(x) - Q'_{n-1}(x) = n\, Q_n(x) \quad \ldots(ii)$$

Multiplying (ii) by x and then subtracting from (i), we get

$$(1-x^2)\, Q_n'(x) = n\, Q_{n-1}(x) - nx\, Q_n(x)$$

$\therefore$ **$(x^2-1)\, Q_n'(x) = nx\, Q_n(x) - n\, Q_{n-1}(x)$.**

VI. $(n+1)\, Q_{n+1}(x) - (2n+1)x\, Q_n(x) + n\, Q_{n-1}(x) = 0$.

We have

$$Q_n(x) = \frac{2^n n!}{(2n+1)!} \sum_{r=0}^{\infty} \frac{(n+2r)!\, x^{-(n+2r+1)}}{2^r r! (2n+3)(2n+5)\ldots(2n+2r+1)}.$$

Replacing n by $(n-1)$ and $(n+1)$, we get

$$Q_{n-1}(x) = \frac{2^{n-1}(n-1)!}{(2n+1)!} \sum_{r=0}^{\infty} \frac{(n+2r-1)\, x^{-(n+2r)}}{2^r\, r!\,(2n+1)(2n+3)\ldots(2n+2r-1)}$$

and $$Q_{n+1}(x) = \frac{2^{n+1}(n+1)!}{(2n+3)!} \sum_{r=0}^{\infty} \frac{(n+2r+1)!\, x^{-(n+2r+2)}}{2^r\, r!\,(2n+5)(2n+7)\ldots(2n+2r+3)}$$

$\therefore$ $$-n\,Q_{n-1}(x) + (2n+1)\,x\,Q_n(x)$$

$$= \frac{2^n\, n!}{(2n-1)!} \sum_{r=0}^{\infty} \frac{(n+2r-1)!\, x^{-(n+2r)}}{2^r\, r!\,(2n+1)(2n+3)\ldots(2n+2r-1)}$$

$$+ \frac{2^n . n}{2n!} \sum_{r=0}^{\infty} \frac{(n+2r)!\, x^{-(n+2r)}}{2^r\, r!\,(2n+3)(2n+5)\ldots(2n+2r+1)}$$

$$= \frac{2^{n+1}\, n!}{(2n+3)!} \sum_{r=0}^{\infty} \frac{(n+2r-1)!\, x^{-(n+2r)} . 2n . (2n+2)}{2^r\, r!\,(2n+5)(2n+7)\ldots(2n+2r-1)}$$

$$+ \frac{2^n\, n!}{(2n+3)!} \sum_{r=0}^{\infty} \frac{(n+2r)!\,(2n+1)\, x^{-(n+2r)}\,(n+2)}{2^r\, r!\,(2n+5)(2n+7)\ldots(2n+2r+1)}$$

$$= \frac{2^{n+1}(n+1)!}{(2n+3)!}$$

$$\times \sum_{r=0}^{\infty} \frac{(n+2r-1)!\,\{-(2n+2r+1)\,n + (n+2r)(2n+1)\}\, x^{-(n+2r)}}{2^r\, r!\,(2n+5)(2n+7)\ldots(2n+2r+1)}$$

$$= \frac{2^{n+1}(n+1)!}{(2n+3)} \sum_{r=0}^{\infty} \frac{(n+2r-1)!\,(2nr+2r)\, x^{-(n+2r)}}{2^r\, r!\,(2n+5)(2n+7)\ldots(2n+2r+1)}$$

$$= (n+1)\,\frac{2^{n+1}(n+1)!}{(2n+3)}$$

$$\times \sum_{r=0}^{\infty} \frac{(n+2r-1)!\, x^{-(n+2r)}}{2^{r-1}\,(r-1)\,(2n+5)(2n+7)\ldots(2n+2r+1)}$$

$$= (n+1)\,\frac{2^{n+1}(n+1)!}{(2n+3)} \sum_{s=0}^{\infty} \frac{(n+2s+1)!\, x^{-(n+2s+2)}}{2^s\, s!\,(2n+5)(2n+7)\ldots(2n+2s+3)}$$

Putting $r-1=s$

$$= (n+1)\,Q_{n+1}(x)$$

$\therefore$ $$\mathbf{(n+1)\,Q_{n+1}(x) - (2n+1)\,x\,Q_n(x) + n\,Q_{n-1}(x) = 0.}$$

3·5. Relations between $P_n(x)$ and $Q_n(x)$

(I) $$(x^2-1)(Q_n P_n' - P_n Q_n') = C$$

From Legendre's equation, we have

$$(1-x^2)\frac{d^2y}{dx^2} - 2x\frac{dy}{dx} + n(n+1)\,y = 0 \qquad \text{...(i)}$$

Since $P_n(x)$ and $Q_n(x)$ are solution of (i), hence

$$(1-x^2)\frac{d^2P_n}{dx^2} - 2x\frac{dP_n}{dx} + n(n-1)\,Q_n = 0 \qquad \text{...(ii)}$$

and $$(1-x^2)\frac{d^2Q_n}{dx^2} - 2x\frac{dQ_n}{dx} + n(n+1)\,Q_n = 0. \qquad \text{...(iii)}$$

Multiplying (ii) by Q_n, (iii) by P_n and then subtracting, we get

$$(1-x^2)\left[\frac{d^2P_n}{dx}Q_n - P_n\cdot\frac{d^2Q_n}{dx^2}\right] - 2x\left[\frac{dP_n}{dx}Q_n - P_n\cdot\frac{dQ_n}{dx}\right] = 0$$

or
$$\frac{\dfrac{d^2P_n}{dx^2}\cdot Q_n - P_n\cdot\dfrac{d^2Q_n}{dx^2}}{\dfrac{dP_n}{dx}Q_n - P_n\cdot\dfrac{dQ_n}{dx}} = \frac{2x}{1-x^2}$$

or
$$\frac{\dfrac{d}{dx}\left(\dfrac{dP_n}{dx}\cdot Q_n - P_n\cdot\dfrac{dQ_n}{dx}\right)}{\dfrac{dP_n}{dx}\cdot Q_n - P_n\cdot\dfrac{dQ_n}{dx}} = \frac{\dfrac{d}{dx}(x^2-1)}{-(x^2-1)}$$

Integrating, we get

$$\log\left(Q_n\frac{dP_n}{dx} - P_n\cdot\frac{dQ_n}{dx}\right) = -\log(x^2-1) + \log c$$

or
$$Q_n P'_n - P_n Q'_n = \frac{c}{(x^2-1)}$$

or
$$(x^2-1)(Q_n P'_n - P_n Q'_n) = c.$$

(II) $$\frac{Q_n(x)}{P_n(x)} = \int_x^\infty \frac{dx}{(x^2-1)P_n{}^2(x)}$$

hence deduce that

(i) $Q_0(x) = \frac{1}{2}\log\frac{x+1}{x-1}$ and **(ii)** $Q_1(x)$

$$= \frac{x}{2}\log\frac{x+1}{x-1} - 1.$$

In (I), we have proved that

$$Q_n P_n' - P_n Q_n' = \frac{c}{x^2-1} = \frac{c}{x^2}\left(1-\frac{1}{x^2}\right)^{-1}$$

$$= \frac{c}{x^2}\left(1+\frac{1}{x^2}+\frac{1}{x^4}+\ldots\right)$$

$$= c\left(\frac{1}{x^2}+\frac{1}{x^4}+\frac{1}{x^6}+\ldots\right) \qquad \ldots\text{(i)}$$

Further, we know that

$$P_n(x) = \frac{1.3\ldots(2n+1)}{n!}\left[x^n - \frac{n(n-1)}{2(2n-1)}x^{n-2}\ldots\right]$$

$$Q_n(x) = \frac{n!}{1.3\ldots(2n+1)}\left[x^{-n-1} + \frac{(n+1)(n+1)}{2.(2n+3)}x^{-n-3}\ldots\right]$$

Substituting the values of $P_n(x)$, $Q_n(x)$ and their derivatives $P_n'(x)$, $Q_n'(x)$ in (i), we have

$$Q_n P_n' - P_n Q_n'$$

$$= \frac{n!}{1.3...(2n+1)}\left[x^{-n-1} + \frac{(n+1)(n+2)}{2.(2n+3)}x^{-n-3} + ...\right]$$

$$\times \frac{1.3\,(2n-1)}{n!}\left[nx^{n-1} - \frac{n(n-1)(n-2)}{2.(2n-1)}x^{n-3}...\right]$$

$$-\frac{1.3...(2n-1)}{n!}\left[x^{n} - \frac{n(n-1)}{2(2n-1)}x^{n-2}...\right]$$

$$\times \frac{n!}{1.3...(2n+1)} \times \left[-(n+1)\,x^{-n-2} - \frac{(n+1)(n+2)(n+3)}{2(2n+3)}x^{-n-4}...\right]$$

$$= -c\left[\frac{1}{x^2} + \frac{1}{x^4} + ...\right]$$

Equating the coefficients of $\frac{1}{x^2}$ from the two sides we have

$$\frac{n!}{1.3...(2n+1)} \cdot \frac{1.3...(2n-1)}{n!}n + \frac{1.3...(2n-1)}{n!} \cdot \frac{n!\,(n+1)}{1.3...(2n+1)} = c$$

or
$$c = \frac{n}{2n+1} + \frac{n+1}{2n+1} = 1.$$

$$\therefore \quad Q_n P_n' - P_n Q_n' = \frac{1}{x^2-1}.$$

Dividing both sides by $P_n^{\,2}$, we have

$$\frac{P_n' Q_n - Q_n' P_n}{P_n^2} = \frac{1}{(x^2-1)\,P_n^{\,2}}$$

or
$$\frac{d}{dx}\left(\frac{Q_n}{P_n}\right) = \frac{1}{(x^2-1)\,P_n^{\,2}}$$

Integrating both sides between the limits x to ∞, we have

$$\left(-\frac{Q_n}{P_n}\right)_x^{\infty} \int_x^{\infty} \frac{dx}{(x^2-1)\,P_n^{\,2}}$$

or
$$-\left(\frac{Q_n}{P_n}\right)_{x=\infty} + \frac{Q_n}{P_n} = \int_x^{\infty} \frac{dx}{(x^2-1)\,P_n^{\,2}}$$

or
$$\frac{Q_n(x)}{P_n(x)} = \int_x^{\infty} \frac{dx}{(x^2-1)\,P_n^{\,2}(x)}$$

Since $\lim\limits_{x\to\infty} \frac{Q_n(x)}{P_n(x)} = \lim\limits_{x\to\infty} \frac{n\text{th derivative of } Q_n(x)}{n\text{th derivative of } P_n(x)}$

$$\lim_{x\to\infty} \frac{\frac{n!}{1.3...(2n+1)}\left[(-1)^n (n+1)(n+2)...(n+n)\,x^{-(n+n+1)} + ...\right]}{\frac{1.3...(2n-1)}{n!}\,[n! + 0]}$$

$$= 0.$$

Hence $$\frac{Q_n(x)}{P_n(x)}=\int_x^{\infty}\frac{dx}{(x^2-1)\,P_n{}^2(x)} \qquad ...(ii)$$

Deductions :

(i) Putting $n = 0$ in (ii), we get

$$\frac{Q_0(x)}{P_0(x)}=\int_x^{\infty}\frac{dx}{(x^2-1)\,P_0{}^2(x)}$$

or $$Q_0(x)=\int_x^{\infty}\frac{dx}{x^2-1} \text{ since } P_0(x) = 1$$

or $$Q_0(x)=\frac{1}{2}\left(\log\frac{x-1}{x+1}\right)_x^{\infty}$$

or $$Q_0(x)=\frac{1}{2}\underset{x\to\infty}{Lim}\log\frac{x-1}{x+1}-\frac{1}{2}\log\frac{x-1}{x+1}$$

$$=\frac{1}{2}\underset{x\to\infty}{Lim}\log\frac{1-\dfrac{1}{x}}{1+\dfrac{1}{x}}-\frac{1}{2}\log\frac{x-1}{x+1}$$

$$=0-\frac{1}{2}\log\frac{x-1}{x+1}=\frac{1}{2}\log\frac{x+1}{x-1}$$

(ii) Putting $n = 1$ in (ii), we get

$$\frac{Q_1(x)}{P_1(x)}=\int_x^{\infty}\frac{dx}{(x^2-1)\,P_1{}^2(x)}$$

or $$Q_1(x)=x\int_x^{\infty}\frac{dx}{(x^2-1)\,x^2}$$

Since $P_1(x) = x$.

$$=x\int_0^{\infty}\left(\frac{1}{(x^2-1)}-\frac{1}{x^2}\right)dx$$

$$=x\left[\frac{1}{2}\log\frac{x-1}{x+1}+\frac{1}{x}\right]_x^{\infty}$$

$$=x\left[\frac{1}{2}\left(\log\frac{x-1}{x+1}\right)_{x=\infty}+\frac{1}{\infty}-\frac{1}{2}\log\frac{x-1}{x+1}-\frac{1}{x}\right]$$

$$=\frac{x}{2}\log\left(\frac{x+1}{x-1}\right)-1.$$

(III) $P_n\,Q_{n-1}-Q_n\,P_{n-1}=\frac{1}{n}$.

From recurrence formula I for $P_n(x)$ and recurrencre formula VI for $Q_n(x)$, we have

$$(2n+1)\,x\,P_n=(n+1)\,P_{n+1}+n\,P_{n-1} \qquad ...(i)$$

and $$(2n+1)\,x\,Q_n=(n+1)\,Q_{n+1}+n\,Q_{n-1} \qquad ...(ii)$$

Replacing n by $(n-1)$, both in (i) and (ii), we get

$$(2n-1)\,x\,P_{n-1} = n\,P_n + (n-1)\,P_{n-2} \quad ...(iii)$$
$$(2n-1)\,x\,Q_{n-1} = n\,Q_n + (n-1)\,Q_{n-2} \quad ...(iv)$$

Multiplying (iii) by Q_{n-1} and (iv) by P_{n-1} and then subtracting, we have

$n\,(P_n\,Q_{n-1} - Q_n\,P_{n-1}) = (n-1)\,(P_{n-1}\,Q_{n-2} - Q_{n-1}\,P_{n-2})$

Hence

$$f_n = f_{n-1} \text{ where } f_n = n\,(P_n\,Q_{n-1} - Q_n\,P_{n-1})$$

Similarly $\quad f_n = f_{n-1} = f_{n-2} = \ldots = f_1 = P_1Q_0 - Q_1P_0$

$$\therefore \quad n\,(P_n\,Q_{n-1} - Q_n\,P_{n-1}) = P_1\,Q_0 - Q_1\,P_0 \quad ...(v)$$

But $\quad P_0 = 1, P_1 = x$

$$\therefore \quad Q_0 = P_0 \int_x^\infty \frac{dx}{(x^2-1)\,P_0^{\,2}} \quad \text{(from II)}$$

$$= \int_x^\infty \frac{dx}{(x^2-1)} \quad \text{since } P_0 = 1$$

and

$$Q_1 = P_1 \int_x^\infty \frac{dx}{(x^2-1)\,P_1^{\,2}} = x \int_x^\infty \frac{dx}{(x^2-1)\,x^2}$$

$$= x \int_x^\infty \left(\frac{1}{(x^2-1)} - \frac{1}{x^2}\right) dx$$

$$= x\,Q_0 - x \int_x^\infty \frac{dx}{x^2}$$

$$= x\,Q_0 + x \cdot \left(\frac{1}{x}\right)_x^\infty = x\,Q_0 + x\left(0 - \frac{1}{x}\right)$$

$$= x\,Q_0 - 1.$$

$\therefore$ From (v), we have

$n\,(P_n\,Q_{n-1} - Q_n\,P_{n-1}) = x\,Q_0 - (x\,Q_6 - 1),\ 1 = 1.$

or

$$P_n\,Q_{n-1} - Q_n\,P_{n-1} = \frac{1}{n}.$$

(IV) $\quad \mathbf{P_n\,Q_{n-2} - Q_n\,P_{n-2} = \dfrac{(2n-1)}{n\,(n-1)}\,x.}$

From recurrence formula I for P_n, we have

$$(2n+1)\,x\,P_n = (n+1)\,P_{n+1} + n\,P_{n-1} \quad ...(i)$$

Also, from recurrence formula VI for $Q_n(x)$, we get

$$(2n+1)\,x\,Q_n = (n+1)\,Q_{n+1} + n\,Q_{n-1} \quad ...(ii)$$

Replacing n by $(n-1)$ in both the eqns. (i) and (ii), we get

$$(2n-1)\,x\,P_{n-1} = n\,P_n + (n-1)\,P_{n-2} \quad ...(iii)$$

and

$$(2n-1)\,x\,Q_{n-1} = n\,Q_n + (n-1)\,Q_{n-2} \quad ...(iv)$$

Multilplying (iv) by P_n and (iii) by Q_n and then subtracting, we get

$(n-1)\,x\,(Q_{n-1}\,P_n - P_{n-1}\,Q_n) = (n-1)\,(Q_{n-2}\,P_n - Q_n\,P_{n-2})$

or

$$\mathbf{P_n\,Q_{n-2} - Q_n\,P_{n-2} = \frac{(2n-1)\,x}{n\,(n-1)}}$$

$$\because \quad P_n\,Q_{n-1} - Q_n\,P_{n-1} = \frac{1}{n} \quad \text{from (III)}$$

3·6. Christoffel's Second Summation Formula

Prove that

$$\sum_{r=0}^{n} (2r+1) P_r(x) Q_r(y) = \frac{1+(n+1)[P_{n+1}(x) Q_n(y) - P_n(x) Q_{n+1}(y)]}{y-x}$$

From Recurrence formula I for $P_n(x)$ and VI for $Q_n(x)$, we have

$$(2r+1)\, x\, P_r(x) = (r+1) P_{r+1}(x) + r P_{r-1}(x) \quad \text{...(i)}$$

and

$$(2r+1)\, y\, Q_r(y) = (r+1) Q_{r+1}(y) + r Q_{r-1}(y) \quad \text{...(ii)}$$

Multiplying (i) by by $Q_r(y)$ and (ii) by $P_r(x)$ and then subtracting, we get

$$(2r+1)(x-y) P_r(x) Q_r(y)$$
$$= (r+1)[P_{r+1}(x) Q_r(y) - P_r(x) Q_{r+1}(y)]$$
$$- r\,[P_r(x) Q_{r-1}(y) - P_{r-1}(x) Q_r(y) \quad \text{...(iii)}$$

Putting $r = 1, 2, 3, ...(n-1), n$ in (iii), we get

$$3\,(x-y) P_1(x) Q_1(y) = 2\,[P_2(x) Q_1(y) - P_1(x) Q_2(y)]$$
$$- 1.\,[P_1(x) Q_0(y) - P_0(x) Q_1(y)] \text{...}(A_1)$$

$$5\,(x-y) P_2(x) Q_2(y) = 3\,[P_3(x) Q_2(y) - P_2(x) Q_3(y)]$$
$$- 2.\,[P_2(x) Q_1(y) - P_1(x) Q_2(y)] \text{...}(A_2)$$

....

....

$$(2n-1)(x-y) P_{n-1}(x) Q_{n-1}(y) = n\,[P_n(x) Q_{n-1}(y)$$
$$- P_{n-1}(x) Q_n(y)] - (n-1)\,[P_{n-1}(x) Q_{n-2}(y)$$
$$- P_{n-2}(x) Q_{n-1}(Y)] \text{ ... } (A_{n-1})$$

$$(2n+1)(x-y) P_n(x) Q_n(y) = (n+1)\,[P_{n+1}(x) Q_n(y)$$
$$- P_n(x) Q_{n+1}(y)]$$
$$- n\,[P_n(x) Q_{n-1}(y) - P_{n-1}(x) Q_n(y)] \text{...}(A_n)$$

Adding (A_1), (A_2), ...(A_n), we get

$$\sum_{r=0}^{n} (2r+1)(x-y) P_r(x) Q_r(y)$$
$$= (n+1)\,[P_{n+1}(x) Q_n(y) - P_n(x) Q_{n+1}(y)]$$
$$- [P_1(x) Q_0(y) - P_0(x) Q_1(y)]$$
$$= (n+1)\,[P_{n+1}(x) Q_n(y) - P_n(x) Q_{n+1}(y)]$$
$$- [x\, Q_0(y) - 1, \quad \{y\, Q_0(y) - 1\}]$$

since $Q_1(y) = y$, $Q_0(y) = 1$,
$P_1(x) = x$, $P_0(x) = 1$.

$$= -1 + (n+1)\,[P_{n+1}(x) Q_n(y) - P_n(x) Q_{n+1}(y)]$$
$$- (x-y) P_0(x) P_0(y) \qquad \text{since } P_0(x) = 1.$$

or

$$\sum_{r=0}^{n} (2r+1)(y-x) P_r(x) Q_r(y)$$
$$= 1 - (n+1)\,[P_{n+1}(x) Q_n(y) - P_n(x) Q_{n+1}(y)]$$

or

$$\sum_{r=0}^{n} (2r+1) P_r(x) Q_r(y)$$
$$= \frac{1-(n+1)\,[P_{n+1}(x) Q_n(y) - P_n(x) Q_{n+1}(y)}{(x-y)}$$

3.7 A Property: Assuming P_n as a solution of Legendre's equation, show that the complete solution of the Legendre's equation is given by

$$A P_n + B Q_n, \text{ where } Q_n = cP_n \int \frac{dx}{(1-x^2) P_n^2}, \text{ c being a constant.}$$

From Legendre's equation, we have

$$(1-x^2)\frac{d^2y}{dx^2} - 2x\frac{dy}{dx} + n(n+1)y = 0$$

Let $y = uP_n$ be the complete solution of the equation (i), where u is a function of x, so that

$$\frac{dy}{dx} = u\frac{dP_n}{dx} + \frac{du}{dx}$$

and
$$\frac{d^2y}{dx^2} = u\frac{d^2p}{dx^2} + 2\frac{du}{dx}\cdot\frac{dP_n}{dx} + Pn\cdot\frac{d^2u}{dx^2}.$$

Substituting these values in (i), we get

$$(1-x^2)\left[u\frac{d^2P_n}{dx^2} + 2\frac{du}{dx}\cdot\frac{dP_n}{dx} + P_n\cdot\frac{d^2u}{dx^2}\right]$$

$$-2x\left[u\cdot\frac{dP_n}{dx} + P_n\cdot\frac{du}{dx}\right] + n(n+1)uP_n = 0$$

or
$$(1-x^2)\left(P_n\frac{d^2u}{dx^2} + 2\frac{du}{dx}\cdot\frac{dP_n}{dx}\right)$$

$$+u\cdot\left[(1-x^2)\frac{d^2P_n}{dx^2} + 2x\frac{dP_n}{dx} + n(n+1)P_n\right]$$

$$-2xP_n\frac{du}{dx} = 0$$

or
$$(1-x^2)\left[P_n\frac{d^2u}{dx^2} + 2\frac{du}{dx}\cdot\frac{dP_n}{dx}\right] - 2xP_n\frac{du}{dx} = 0$$

$\because P_n$ is the solution of (i)

or
$$P_n\frac{d^2u}{dx^2} + 2\frac{du}{dx}\cdot\frac{dP_n}{dx} = \frac{2x}{1-x^2}P_n\cdot\frac{du}{dx}$$

or
$$\frac{\frac{d^2u}{dx^2}}{\frac{du}{dx}} + 2\frac{\frac{dP_n}{dx}}{P_n} = \frac{2x}{1-x^2}$$

Integrating w.r.t. x, we get

$$\log\frac{du}{dx} + 2\log P_n = -\log(1-x^2) + \log D$$

where D is a constant.

or
$$\frac{du}{dx}P_n^2(1-x^2) = D$$

or $$\frac{du}{dx} = \frac{D}{(1-x^2)\,P_n^2}$$

Integrating, we get

$$u = D\int \frac{dx}{(1-x^2)\,P_n^2} + A$$

where A is a constant.

Hence the complete solution of (i) is given by

$$y = \left[D\int \frac{dx}{(1-x^2)\,P_n^2} + A\right] P_n$$

$$= AP_n + \frac{D}{C}\cdot CP_n \int \frac{dx}{(1-x^2)\,P_n^2} = AP_n + BQ_n$$

where $B = \dfrac{D}{C}$ = constant, and $Q_n = CP_n \displaystyle\int \frac{dx}{(1-x^2)\,P_n^2}$

ILLUSTRATIVE EXAMPLES

Ex. 1. *Show that*

$$Q_2(x) = \frac{1}{2}P_2(x)\log\frac{x+1}{x-1} - \frac{3x}{2}.$$

Solution. From recurrence formula VI for $Q_n(x)$, we have

$$(n+1)\,Q_{n+1}(x) - (2n+1)\,xQ_n(x) + nQ_n{-1}(x) = 0$$

Putting $n = 1$, we get

$$2Q_2 = 3x\,Q_1 - Q_0$$

$$= 3x\left[\frac{x}{2}\log\frac{x+1}{x-1} - 1\right] - \frac{1}{2}\log\frac{x+1}{x-1}$$

[substituting the values of Q_0 and Q_1]

$$= \frac{(3x^2-1)}{2}\log\frac{x+1}{x-1} - 3x$$

$$= P_2(x)\log\frac{x+1}{x-1} - 3x$$

$$\left[\because\ P_2(x) = \frac{(3x^2-1)}{2}\right]$$

$$\therefore\quad Q_2(x) = \frac{1}{2}P_2(x)\log\frac{x+1}{x-1} - \frac{3x}{2}.$$

Ex. 2. *Prove that*

$$(2n+1)(1-x^2)\,Q_n'(x) = n(n+1)\,[Q_{n-1}(x) - Q_{n+1}(x)]$$

We know that $Q_n(x)$ is the solution of Legendre's equation

$$\frac{d}{dx}\left[(1-x^2)\frac{dy}{dx}\right] + n(n+1)\,y = 0 \qquad \text{...(i)}$$

$$\therefore\quad \frac{d}{dx}[(1-x^2)\,Q_n'] = -n(n+1)\,Q_n \qquad \text{...(ii)}$$

Integrating both sides between the limits ∞ to x, we get

$$\left[(1-x^2)\,Q'_n\right]_\infty^x = -\,n(n+1)\int_\infty^x Q_n\,dx$$

or
$$(1-x^2)\,Q'_n - (Q'_n - x^2Q'_n)_{x=\infty}$$
$$= -\,n(n+1)\int_\infty^x Q_x\,dx$$

or
$$(1-x^2)\,Q'_n = -\,n(n+1)\int_\infty^x Q_n\,dx \qquad \text{...(iii)}$$

Since $(Q'_n)_{x=\infty} = 0$ and $(x^2\,Q'_n)_{x=\infty} = 0$.

By recurrence formula I for $Q_n(x)$, we have

$$Q'_{n+1} - Q'_{n-1} = (2n+1)\,Q_n \qquad \text{...(iv)}$$

Integrating both sides between the limits ∞ to x, we have

$$Q_{n+1} - Q_{n-1} = (2n+1)\int_\infty^x Q_n\,dx \qquad \text{...(v)}$$

Since $(Q_{n+1})_{x=\infty} = 0$ and $(Q_{n-1})_{x=\infty} = 0$.

Eliminating $\int_\infty^x Q_n\,dx$ from (iii) and (v) ; we have

$$(1-x^2)\,Q_n' = -\,\frac{n(n+1)}{(2n+1)}\,(Q_{n+1} - Q_{n-1})$$

or
$$(2n+1)\,(1-x^2)\,Q_n'(x) = n(n+1)\,[Q_{n-1}(x) - Q_{n+1}(x)].$$

Ex. 3. *Prove that*

$$\frac{d^{n+1}Q_n}{dx^{n+1}} = -\,\frac{(-2)^n\,n\,!}{(x^2-1)^{n+1}}$$

We know that

$$Q_n(x) = \frac{n\,!}{1.3.5...(2n+1)}\left[x^{-n-1} + \frac{(n+1)\,(n+2)}{2\,(2n+3)}\,x^{-n-3} + \frac{(n+1)\,(n+2)\,(n+3)\,(n+4)}{2.4(2n+3)\,((2n+5)}\,x^{-n-5} + \ldots\right]$$

Differentiating both sides $(n+1)$ times w.r.t. 'x' we get

$$\frac{d^{n+1}Q_n}{dx^{n+1}} = \frac{n\,!}{1.3...(2n+1)}\Bigg[(-1)^{n+1}\,(n+1)\,(n+2)\,\ldots$$
$$(2n+1)\,x^{-2n-2} + (-1)^{n+1}\,\frac{(n+1)\,(n+2)\,(n+3)...(2n+3)}{2\,(2n+3)}$$
$$x^{-2n-4} + (-1)^{n+1}\,\frac{(n+1)\,(n+2)...(2n+5)}{2.4\,(2n+3)\,(2n+5)}\,x^{-2n-5} + \ldots\Bigg]$$
$$= \frac{(-1)^{n+1}\,(2n+1)\,!\,x^{-2n-2}}{1.3...(2n+1)}\left[1 + \frac{(2n+2)}{3}\cdot x^{-2} + \frac{(2n+2)\,(2n+3)\,(2n+4)\,(2n+5)}{2.4.(2n+3)\,(2n+5)}\,x^{-4} + \ldots\right]$$

$$= (-1)^{n+1}\, 2.4.6...(2n)\, x^{-2n-2} \left[1 + (n+1) \cdot \frac{1}{x^2} + \frac{(n+1)(n+2)}{2!} \cdot \frac{1}{x^4} + \ldots \right]$$

$$= (-1)^{n+1} \quad 2^n\, n!\, x^{-2n-2} \left(1 - \frac{1}{x^2} \right)^{-n-1}$$

$$= (-1)(-2)^n\, n!\, (x^2-1)^{-n-1} = -\frac{(-2)^n \cdot n!}{(x^2-1)^{n+1}}.$$

Ex. 4. *Prove that*

$$Q_n(x) = 2^n\, n! \int_x^\infty dx \int_x^\infty dx ... \int_x^\infty (x^2-1)^{-n-1} dx$$

We have,

$$(x^2-1)^{-n-1} = x^{-2n-2} \left(1 - \frac{1}{x^2} \right)^{-n-1}$$

$$= x^{-2n-2} \left[1 + (n+1) \cdot \frac{1}{x^2} + \frac{(n+1)(n+2)}{2!} \frac{1}{x^4} + \ldots \right]$$

$$= x^{-(2n+2)} + (n+1)\, x^{-(2n+4)} + \frac{(n+1)(n+2)}{2!} x^{-(2n+2)} + \ldots$$

Integrating both sides w.r.t. 'x', between the limits x to ∞. we have

$$\int_x^\infty (x^2-1)^{-n-1} dx = \left[-\frac{x^{-(2n+1)}}{(2n+1)} - \frac{(n+1)}{(2n+3)} x^{-(2n+3)} - \frac{(n+1)((n+2)}{2!\,(2n+5)} \cdot x^{-(2n+5)} \right]_x^\infty$$

$$= \frac{x^{-(n+1)}}{(2n+1)} + \frac{(n+1)}{(2n+3)} x^{-(2n+3)} + \frac{(n+1)(n+2)}{2!\,(2n+5)} x^{-(2n+5)} \ldots \qquad ...(i)$$

Integrating (i) n times, w.r.t. 'x' between the same limits x to ∞, we get

$$\int_x^\infty dx \int_x^\infty dx \ldots \int_x^\infty (x^2-1)^{-n-1} dx$$

$$= \frac{x^{-(n+1)}}{(2n+1)(2n)...(n+1)} + \frac{(n+1)\, x^{-(n+3)}}{(2n+3)(2n+2)...(n+3)} + \frac{(n+1)(n+2)\, x^{-(n+5)}}{2!\,(2n+5)(2n+3)...(n+5)} + \ldots$$

$$= \frac{n!\, x^{-n-1}}{\{1.3...(2n+1)\}\{2.4...2n\}} + \frac{n!\,(n+1)(n+2)(n+1)\, x^{-n-3}}{\{1.3...(2n+1)(2n+3)\}\{2.4...2n\,(2n+2)\}}$$

$$+ \frac{n!\,(n+1)\,(n+2)\,x^{-n-5}\,(n+4)\,(n+3)\,(n+2)\,(n+1)}{2!\,\{1.3...(2n+1)\,(2n+3)\,(2n+5)\}\,\{2.4...(2n)\,(2n+2)\,(2n+4)\} + ...}$$

$$\therefore \quad 2^n\, n!\int_x^\infty dx \int_x^\infty dx ... \int_x^\infty (x^2-1)^{-n-1}\, dx$$

$$= \frac{n!}{1.3...(2n+1)} x^{-n-1} + \frac{(n+1)\,(n+2)}{2\,(2n+3)} x^{-n-3}$$

$$+ \frac{(n+1)\,(n+2)\,(n+3)\,(n+4)}{2.4\,(2n+3)\,(2n+5)} x^{-n-5} + ... = Q_n\,(x).$$

i.e.

$$Q_n(x) = 2^n\, n!\int_x^\infty dx. \int_x^\infty dx ... \int_x^\infty (x^2-1)^{-n-1}\, dx.$$

EXERCISE 3

1. By using the definition of $Q_n(x)$, find value of $Q_0(x)$ and $Q_1(x)$.
2. Prove that
$n\,(Q_n\,P_{n-1} - P_{n-1}\,Q_n) = (n-1)\,(Q_{n-1}\,P_{n-2} - Q_{n-2}\,P_{n-1})$ and deduce that
$$n\,(Q_n\,P_{n-1} - Q_{n-1}\,P_n) = -1.$$
3. Prove that
$$P_n\,Q_{n-2} - Q_n\,P_{n-2} = \frac{(2n-1)\,x}{n\,(n-1)}$$

4 Associated Legendre's Polynomials

4.1 Associated Legendre Equation

The differential equation

$$(1 - x^2)\frac{d^2y}{dx^2} - 2x\frac{dy}{dx} + \left\{n(n+1) - \frac{m^2}{1-x^2}\right\}y = 0$$

is known as the **Associated Legendre equation.**

4.2. If v is a solution of Legendre equation

$$(1 - x^2)\frac{d^2y}{dx^2} - 2x\frac{dy}{dx} + n(n+1)y = 0$$

then $$y_1 = (1 - x^2)^{m/2}\frac{d^m v}{dx^m}$$

is a solution of associated Legendre Equation

$$(1 - x^2)\frac{d^2y_1}{dx^2} - 2x\frac{dy_1}{dx} + \left\{n(n+1) - \frac{m^2}{1-x^2}\right\}y_1 = 0$$

Proof. Since v is the solution of Legendre's equation, we have

$$(1 - x^2)\frac{d^2v}{dx^2} - 2x\frac{dv}{dx} + n(n+1)v = 0 \qquad ...(i)$$

Differentiating (i) m times with respect to x by Leibnitz theorem, we have

$$(1 - x^2)\frac{d^{m+2}v}{dx^{m+2}} - m.2x\frac{d^{m+1}v}{dx^{m+1}} - \frac{m(m+1)}{2!}\cdot 2\cdot\frac{d^m v}{dx^m}$$
$$- 2\left\{x\frac{d^{m+1}v}{dx^{m+1}} + m\cdot\frac{d^m v}{dx^m}\right\} + n(n+1)\frac{d^m v}{dx^m} = 0$$

or $$(1 - x^2)\frac{d^{m+2}v}{dx^{m+2}} - 2(m+1)x\cdot\frac{d^{m+1}v}{dx^{m+1}}$$
$$+ [n(n+1) - m(m+1)]\frac{d^m v}{dx^m} = 0$$

writing v_1 for $\frac{d^m v}{dx^m}$, we have

$$(1-x^2)\frac{d^2v_1}{dx^2}-2(m+1)x\frac{dv_1}{dx}$$

$$+\{n(n+1)-m(m+1)\}v_1=0 \qquad \text{...(ii)}$$

Now, let $z=(1-x^2)^{m/2}\dfrac{d^m y}{dx^m}=(1-x^2)^{m/2}v_1$

So that $v_1=(1-x^2)^{-m/2}z$,

$$\frac{dv_1}{dx}-(1-x^2)^{-m/2}\frac{dz}{dx}+m(1-x^2)^{-\left(\frac{m}{2}\right)^{-1}}xz$$

and $\dfrac{d^2v_1}{dx^2}=(1-x^2)^{-m/2}\dfrac{d^2z}{dx^2}+2m(1-x^2)^{\left(-\frac{m}{2}\right)-1}x\dfrac{dz}{dx}$

$$+mz(1-x^2)^{-(m/2)-1}+m(m+2)x^2z.(1-x^2)^{-(m/2)-2}=0$$

Putting in equation (ii), we have

$$(1-x2)\left\{(1-x^2)^{-m/2}\frac{d^2z}{dx^2}+2m(1-x^2)^{-\left(\frac{m}{2}\right)-1}x\frac{dz}{dx}\right.$$

$$\left.+mz(1-x^2)^{-(m/2)-1}+m(m+2)x^2z(1-x^2)^{-(m/2)-2}\right\}$$

$$-2(m+1)x\left\{(1-x^2)^{-m/2}\frac{dz}{dx}+mxz(1-x^2)^{-(m/2)-1}\right\}$$

$$+\{n(n+1)-m(m+1)\}(1-x^2)^{-\left(\frac{m}{2}\right)}\cdot z=0$$

or $\quad (1-x^2)^{-m/2}\left[(1-x^2)\dfrac{d^2z}{dx^2}-2x\dfrac{dz}{dx}+\left\{n(n+1)-\dfrac{m^2}{1-x^2}\right\}z\right]=$

or $\quad (1-x^2)\dfrac{d^2z}{dx^2}-2x\dfrac{dz}{dx}+\left\{n(n+1)-\dfrac{m^2}{1-x^2}\right\}z=0$.

Hence $z=(1-x^2)^{m/2}\dfrac{d^m v}{dx^m}$ is the solution of associated Legendre equation.

$$(1-x^2)\frac{d^2z}{dx^2}-2x\frac{dz}{dx}+\left\{n(n+1)-\frac{m^2}{1-x^2}\right\}z=0$$

4.3 Associated Legendre Function

The associated Legendre function $P_n^m(x)$ is defined by

$$P_n^m(x)=(1-x^2)^{m/2}\frac{d^m}{dx^m}P_n(x) \qquad \text{...(i)}$$

$P_n^m(x)$ thus defined satisfy the associated Legendre equation.

Using Rodrigue's formula, we have

$$P_n^m(x) = (1-x^2)^{m/2} \cdot \frac{1}{2^n . n!} \frac{d^{m+n}}{dx^{m+n}} (x^2-1)^n \qquad ...(ii)$$

Here right hand side is well defined for negative values of m such that $m + n \geq 0$, i.e., $m \geq -n$.

Thus form (i) is used to define $P_n^m(x)$ for $m \geq 0$ while the form (ii) may be used to define $P_n^m(x)$ for values $m \geq -n$.

4.4. Properties of the Associated Legendre Functions

(i) $P_n^0(x) = P_n(x)$

and (ii) $P_n^m(x) = 0$ if $m > n$.

Proof (i) We have $P_n^m(x) = (1-x^2)^{m/2} \dfrac{d^m}{dx^m} P_n(x)$

Taking $m = 0$, We have

$$P_n^0(x) = P_n(x)$$

(ii) We have

$$P_n^m(x) = (1-x^2)^{m/2} \frac{d^m}{dx^m} P_n(x) \qquad ...(i)$$

$P_n(x)$ is a polynomial of degree n. If $m > n$, then

$$\frac{d^m}{dx^m} P_n(x) = 0.$$

from (i), $P_n^m(x) = 0$ if $m > n$.

4.5 Orthagonal properties of associated Legendre's functions

Prove that

$$\int_{-1}^{1} P_{n'}^m(x)\, P_n^m(x)\, dx = \frac{2\,(n+m)!}{(2n+1)\,(n-m)}\, \delta_{nn'}$$

whose $\delta_{nn'}$ *is Kronecker delta*

Proof

Case I when $n \neq n'$

$P_n^m(x)$ and $P_{n'}^m(x)$ satisfy the corresponding associated Legendre equation. Now associated Legendre equation may be written as

$$\frac{d}{dx}\left\{(1-x^2)\frac{dy}{dx}\right\} + \left\{n(n+1) - \frac{m^2}{1-x^2}\right\} y = 0$$

$$\therefore \quad \frac{d}{dx}\left\{(1-x^2)\frac{d}{dx} P_n^m(x)\right\}$$

$$+ \left\{n(n+1) - \frac{m^2}{1-x^2}\right\} P_n^m(x) = 0 \qquad ...(i)$$

and
$$\frac{d}{dx}\left\{(1-x^2)\frac{d}{dx}P_{n'}^m(x)\right\} + \left\{n'(n'+1) - \frac{m^2}{1-x^2}\right\} P_{n'}^m(x) = 0 \qquad \text{...(ii)}$$

Multiplying (i) by $P_{n'}^m(x)$ and (ii) by $P_n^m(x)$ and then subtracting, we have

$$P_{n'}^m(x)\cdot\frac{d}{dx}\left\{(1-x^2)\frac{d}{dx}P_n^m(x)\right\} - P_n^m(x)\cdot\frac{d}{dx}\left\{(1-x^2)\frac{d}{dx}P_{n'}^m(x)\right\} + \left\{n(n+1) - n'(n'+1)\right\} P_n^m(x) P_{n'}^m(x) = 0$$

Integrating between the limits –1 to 1, we get

$$\{n(n+1) - n'(n'+1)\}\int_{-1}^{1} P_n^m(x) P_{n'}^m(x)\, dx = 0$$

$$\therefore \quad \int_{-1}^{1} P_n^m(x) P_{n'}^m(x)\, dx = 0 \text{ since } n \neq n'$$

Case II When $n = n'$

Since $P_n^m(x) = (1-x^2)^{m/2}\dfrac{d^m}{dx^m}P_n(x)$ if $m > 0$

$$\therefore \quad \int_{-1}^{1} P_n^m(x) P_n^m(x)\, dx = \int_{-1}^{1} \{P_n^m(n)\}^2\, dx$$

$$= \int_{-1}^{1} (1-x^2)^m \left[\frac{d^m}{dx^m}P_n(x)\right] \left\{\frac{d^m}{dx^m}P_n(x)\right\} dx$$

Integrating by parts, taking $\dfrac{d^m}{dx^m}P_n(x)$ as the second function, we get

$$= \left[\left\{(1-x^2)^m \frac{d^m}{dx^m}P_n(x)\right\}\left\{\frac{d^{m-1}}{dx^{m-1}}P_n(x)\right\}\right]_{-1}^{1} - \int_{-1}^{1}\left\{\frac{d^{m-1}}{dx^{m-1}}P_n(x)\right\}\frac{d}{dx}\left\{(1-x^2)^m\frac{d^m}{dx^m}P_n(x)\right\}$$

$$= -\int_{-1}^{1}\left\{\frac{d^{m-1}}{dx^{m-1}}P_n(x)\right\}\frac{d}{dx}\left\{(1-x^2)\frac{d^m}{dx^m}P_n(x)\right\} dx. \qquad \text{...(iii)}$$

Now $P_n(x)$ satisfy Legendre equation

$$\therefore \quad (1-x^2)\frac{d^2 Pn(x)}{dx^2} - 2x\frac{d}{dx}P_n(x) + n(n+1)P_n(x) = 0$$

Differentiating (m–1) times with respect to x by Leibritz's theorem, we have

$$(1-x^2)\frac{d^{m+1}}{dx^{m+1}}P_n(x) - 2mx\frac{d^m}{dx^m}P_n(x)$$

$$+\{n(n+1)-(m-1)m\}\frac{d^{m-1}}{dx^{m-1}}P_n(x) = 0$$

Multiplying by $(1-x^2)^{m-1}$, we have

$$(1-x^2)^m\frac{d^{m+1}}{dx^{m+1}}P_n(x) - 2xm(1-x^2)^{m-1}\frac{d^m P_n(x)}{dx^m}$$

$$+[n(n+1)-(m-1)m](1-x^2)^{m-1}.\frac{d^{m-1}P_n(x)}{dx^{m-1}} = 0$$

or

$$\frac{d}{dx}\left[(1-x^2)^m\frac{d^m}{dx^m}P_n(x)\right]$$

$$= -(n+m)(n-m+1)(1-x^2)^{m-1}\frac{d^{m-1}}{dx^{m-1}}P_n(x)$$

Putting in (iii), we have

$$\int_{-1}^{1}[P_n^m(x)]^2\,dx$$

$$=\int_{-1}^{1}\left[\frac{d^{m-1}}{dx^{m-1}}P_n(x)\right].(n+m)(n-m+1)$$

$$(1-x^2)^{m-1}\times\frac{d^{m-1}}{dx^{m-1}}P_n(x)\,dx$$

$$=(n+m)(n-m+1)\int_{-1}^{1}(1-x^2)^{m-1}\left[\frac{d^{m-1}}{dx^{m-1}}P_n(x)\right]^2 dx$$

$$=(n+m)(n-m+1)\int_{-1}^{1}[P_n^{m-1}(x)]^2\,dx$$

Repeating the same process again and again m times, we have

$$\int_{-1}^{1}[P_n^m(x)^2\,dx = [(n+m)(n-m+1)][(n+m-1)(n-m+1)]$$

$$\ldots[(n+1)n]\int_{-1}^{1}[P_n^o(x)]^2\,dx$$

$$=(n+m)(n+m-1) \text{ — } (n+1).\ n(n-1)$$

$$(n-m+2)(n-m+1)\times\int_{-1}^{1}[P_n(x)]^2\,dx$$

$$[\because P_n^o(x)=Pn(x)]$$

$$=\left\{\frac{(n+m)!}{(n-m)!}\right\}\frac{2}{2n+1} \quad \text{......(iv)}$$

since $\int_{-1}^{1}\left[P_n(x)\right]^2 dx = \frac{2}{2n+1}$

Now if $m < 0$, Say $m = -l$ when $l > 0$

$$\text{then} \int_{-1}^{1} \{P_n^m(x)\}^2\,dx = \int_{-1}^{1} \{P_n^{-l}(x)\}^2\,dx$$

$$= \int_{-1}^{1} \left((-1)^n \frac{[(n-l)]!}{[(n+l)]!}\right)^2 [P_n^l(x)]^2\,dx$$

$$\left[\text{Since } P_n^{-m}(x) = (-1)^m \frac{(n-m)!}{(n+m)!} P_n^m(x)\right]$$

$$= \left[\frac{(n-l)!}{(n+l)!}\right]^2 \int_{-1}^{1} \{P_n^l(x)\}^2\,dx$$

$$= \left[\frac{(n-l)!}{(n+l)!}\right]^2 \left[\frac{(n+l)!}{(n-l)!}\right] \cdot \frac{2}{2n+1}$$

from the last derived result (iv) for $m > o$

Here $l > 0$

$$= \frac{(n-l)!}{(n+l)!} \cdot \frac{2}{2n+1} = \frac{(n+m)!}{(n-m)!} \cdot \frac{2}{2n+1}$$

$$\text{Hence} \int_{-1}^{1} P_{n'}^m(x) \,.\, P_{n'}^m(x)\,dx$$

$$= \frac{2(n+m)}{(2n+1)(n-m)!}\,\delta n'n$$

4.6 Recurrence Formulae for Associated Legendre's Function

(I) $\quad \mathbf{P_n^{m+1}(x) - \dfrac{2mx}{\sqrt{\{(1-x^2)\}}} P_n^m(x) + \{n(n+1) - m(m-1)\,P_n^{m-1}(x)\} = 0}$

Proof. Since $P_n(x)$ is the solution of Legendre's equation, hence

$$(1-x^2)\frac{d^2}{dx^2}P_n(x) - 2x\frac{d}{dx}P_n(x) + n(n+1)P_n(x) = 0$$

Differentiating $(m-1)$ times, with respect to x by Liebritz's theorem, we have

$$\left\{(1-x^2)\frac{d^{m+1}}{dx^{m+1}}P_n(x) - 2x(m-1)\frac{d^m}{dx^m}P_n(x)\,P_n(x) - 2\frac{(m-1)(m-2)}{2}!\,\frac{d^{m-1}}{dx^{m-1}}P_n(x)\right\}$$

$$-2\left\{x\frac{d^m}{dx^m}P_n(x) + (m-1).1.\frac{d^{m-1}}{dx^{m-1}}P_n(x)\right\}$$

$$+ n(n+1)\frac{d^{m-1}}{dx^{m-1}}P_n(x) = 0$$

or
$$(1-x^2)\frac{d^{m+1}}{dx^{m+1}}P_n(x) - 2xm\frac{d^m}{dx^m}P_n(x) +$$
$$\{n(n+1)-(m-1)m\}\frac{d^{m-1}}{dx^{m-1}}P_n(x) = 0$$

Multiplying by $((1-x^2)^{(m-1)/2}$, we have

$$(1-x^2)^{(m+1)/2}\frac{d^{m+1}}{dx^{m+1}}P_n(x) - 2xm(1-x^2)^{-1/2}$$
$$(1-x^2)^{m/2}\cdot\frac{d^m}{dx^m}P_n(x)$$
$$+\{n(n+1)-(m-1)m\}(1-x^2)^{(m-1)/2}$$
$$\frac{d^{m-1}}{dx^{m-1}}P_n(x) = 0$$

or
$$P_n^{m+1}(x) - \frac{2mx}{\sqrt{(1-x^2)}}P_n^m(x) + \{n(n+1)$$
$$-(m-1)m\}P_n^{m-1}(x) = 0$$

$\{$since $P_n^m(x) = (1-x^2)^{m/2}\frac{d^m}{dx^m}P_n(x)\}$

(II) $$(2n+1)xP^m_n(x) = (n+m)P_{n-1}^m(x) - (n-m+1)P_{n+1}^m(x)$$

Proof From recurrence formula (I) and (III) for Legendre's polynomial, we have

$$(2n+1)xP_n(x) = (n+1)P_{n+1}(x) + nP_{n-1}(x) \qquad \text{...(i)}$$

and
$$(2n+1)P_n(x) = \frac{d}{dx}P_{n+1}(x) - \frac{d}{dx}P_{n-1}(x) \qquad \text{...(ii)}$$

Differentiating (i) m times with respect to x by Leibritz's theorem, we have

$$(2n+1)\left\{x\frac{d^m}{dx^m}P_n(x) + m\cdot 1\cdot\frac{d^{m-1}}{dx^{m-1}}P_n(x)\right\}$$
$$= (n+1)\frac{d^m}{dx^m}P_{n+1}(x) + n\frac{d^m}{dx^m}P_{n-1}(x) \qquad \text{...(iii)}$$

Differenting (ii) $(m-1)$ times w.r.t.x. by Leitbritz's theorem, we have

$$(2n+1)\frac{d^{m-1}}{dx^{m-1}}P_n(x) = \frac{d^m}{dx^m}P_{n+1}(x) - \frac{d^m}{dx^m}P_{n-1}(x) \qquad \text{...(iv)}$$

Substituting the value of $(2n+1)\frac{d^{m-1}}{dx^{m-1}}P_n(x)$

from (iii) in (ii), we have

$$(2n+1)x\frac{d^m}{dx^m}P_n(x) + m\left\{\frac{d^m}{dx^m}P_{n+1}(x) - \frac{d^m}{dx^m}P_{n-1}(x)\right\}$$
$$= (n+1)\frac{d^m}{dx^m}P_{n+1}(x) + n\frac{d^m}{dx^m}P_{n-1}(x)$$

or
$$(2n+1)\,x \frac{d^m}{dx^m} P_n(x) = (n+m) \frac{d^m}{dx^m} P_{n-1}(x)$$
$$+ (n-m+1) \frac{d^m}{dx^m} P_{n+1}(x)$$

Multiplying by $(1-x^2)^{m/2}$, we have

$$(2n+1)\,x\,.\,(1-x^2)^{m/2} \frac{d^m}{dx^m} P_n(x) = (n+m)\,(1-x^2)^{m/2} \frac{d^m}{dx^m} P_{n-1}(x)$$
$$+ (n-m+1)\,(1-x^2)^{m/2} \frac{d^m}{dx^m} P_{n+1}(x)$$

or
$$(2n+1)\,x\,P^m_n(x) = (n+m)\,P^m_{n-1}(x) + (n-m+1)\,P^m_{n+1}(x)$$

$\{$ since $P^m_n(x) = (1-x^2)^{m/2} \frac{d^m}{dx^m} P_n(x)$ $\}$

(III)
$$\sqrt{\{(1-x^2)\}}\,P_n^m(x) = \frac{1}{(2n+1)} \left\{P_{n+1}^{m+1}(x) - P_{n-1}^{m+1}(x)\right\}$$

Proof We have for Legendre's function

$(2n+1)\,P_n = P'_{n+1} - P'_{n-1}$

Differentiating it m times with respect to 'x' we have

$$(2n+1) \frac{d^m}{dx^m} P_n(x) = \frac{d^{m+1}}{dx^{m+1}} P_{n+1}(x) - \frac{d^{m+1}}{dx^{m+1}} P_{n-1}(x)$$

Multiplying by $(1-x^2)^{(m+1)/2}$, we have

$$(2n+1)\,(1-x^2)^{1/2}\,(1-x^2)^{m/2} \frac{d^m}{dx^m} P_n(x)$$
$$= (1-x^2)^{(m+1)/2} \frac{d^{m+1}}{dx^{m+1}} P_{n+1}(x) - (1-x^2)^{(m+1)/2} \frac{d^{m+1}}{dx^{m+1}} P_{n-1}(x)$$

or
$$\{\,(2n+1)\,\sqrt{(1-x^2)}\,\}\,P_n^m(x) = P_{n+1}^{m+1}(x) - P_{n-1}^{m+1}(x)$$

or
$$\sqrt{(1-x^2)}\,P_n^m(x) = \frac{1}{2n+1} \{P_{n+1}^{m+1}(x) - P_{n-1}^{m+1}(x)\}$$

(IV)
$$\sqrt{\{(1-x^2)\}}\,P_n^m(x) + \frac{1}{(2n+1)}\{\,(n+m)\,(n+m-1)P_{n-1}^{m-1}(x)$$
$$-\,(n-m+1)\,(n-m-2)\,P_{n+1}^{m-1}(x)\}$$

Proof From recurrence formula II, we have

$$P^m_n(x) = \frac{1}{(2n+1)} \left\{(n+m)\,P^m_{n-1}(x) + (n-m+1)\,P^m_{n+1}(x)\right\}$$

Putting this value of $x\,P^m_n(x)$ in recurrence formula I, we have

$$P_n^{m+1}(x) - \frac{2m}{\sqrt{(1-x^2)}} \frac{1}{(2n+1)} \{(n+m)\,P^m_{n-1}(x)$$
$$+ (n-m+1)\,P^m_{n+1}(x)\}$$
$$+ \{\,n\,(n+1) - m\,(m-1)\,P_n^{m-1}(x) = 0 \qquad \text{... (i)}$$

Now in recurrence formula III replacing m by $(m-1)$ we have

$$\sqrt{\{(1-x^2)\}}\,P_n^{m-1}(x) = \frac{1}{(2n+1)} \left\{P^m_{n+1}(x) - P^m_{n-1}(x)\right\} \qquad \text{...(ii)}$$

Putting the value of $P_n^{m-1}(x)$ from (ii) in (i) we have

$$P_n^{m+1}(x) - \frac{2m}{(2n+1)\sqrt{\{(1-x^2)\}}}\{(n+m)\ P_{n-1}^m(x)$$

$$+ (n-m-1)\ P_{n+1}^m(x)\} + \{n(n+1) - m(m-1)\}$$

$$\times \frac{1}{(2x+1)\sqrt{(1-x^2)}}\left\{P_{n+1}^m(x) - P_{n-1}^m(x)\right\} = 0$$

or $$\sqrt{(1-x^2)}\ P_n^{m+1}(x) = \frac{1}{(2n+1)}\ [\{2m(n+m) + n(n+1)$$

$$- m(m-1)\}\ P_{n-1}^m(x)$$

$$+ \{2m(n-m+1) - n(n+1) - m(m-1)\}\ P_{n+1}^m(x)]$$

or $$\sqrt{\{(1-x^2)\}}\ P_n^{m+1}(x) = \frac{1}{(2n+1)}\left[(n+m)(n+m+1)\ P_{n-1}^m(x) - (n-m)(n-m+1)\ P_{n+1}^m(x)\right]$$

Writing $(m-1)$ for m, we have

$$\sqrt{\{(1-x^2)\}}\ P_n^m(x) = \frac{1}{(2n+1)}\ [(n+m-1)(n+m)P_{n-1}^{m-1}(x)$$

$$- (n-m+1)(n-m+2)P_{n+1}^{m-1}(x)$$

5

Bessel Functions

5·1. Bessel's Equation

Originally introduced by Bessel, in 1824, while discussing a problem in astronomy, the Bessel functions have received the most extensive treatment among all the special functions.

The differential equation of the form

$$\frac{d^2y}{dx^2} + \frac{1}{x}\frac{dy}{dx} + \left(1 - \frac{n^2}{x^2}\right) y = 0$$

is called **Bessel's differential equation.**

Remark. In what follows, we shall use the following results of Gamma function $\Gamma(n)$ and Beta function $B(m, n)$:

(i) $\Gamma(n) = \int_0^\infty e^{-x} x^{n-1}\, dx,\ n > 0$

(ii) $\Gamma(n) = 2\int_0^\infty e^{-x2} x^{2n-1}\, dx$

(iii) $\Gamma(1) = 1$

(iv) $\Gamma\left(\frac{1}{2}\right) = \sqrt{\pi}$

(v) $\Gamma(n+1) = n\,\Gamma(n),\ n > 0$

(iv) $\Gamma(n+1) = n\,!$, n is a + ve integer

(vii) $B(m, n) = B(n, m)$

(viii) $\Gamma(n)\,\Gamma(1-n) = \pi/\sin n\pi$

(ix) $\Gamma(m) = \infty$, if $m = 0$ or – ve integer

(x) $B(m, n) = \int_0^1 x^{m-1}(1-x)^{n-1}\, dx$

$$= \int_0^1 x^{n-1}(1-x)^{m-1}\, dx,$$

where $m > 0,\ n > 0$

(xi) $B(m, n) = \dfrac{\Gamma(m)\,\Gamma(n)}{\Gamma(m+n)}$

(xii) $\Gamma(2n) = \dfrac{2^{2n-1}}{\sqrt{\pi}}\,\Gamma(n)\,\Gamma(n + \frac{1}{2})$.

5·2. Solution of Bessel's differential equation

The Bessel's differential equation is

$$\frac{d^2y}{dx^2} + \frac{1}{x}\frac{dy}{dx} + \left(1 - \frac{n^2}{x^2}\right) y = 0 \qquad \text{...(i)}$$

We can integrate (i) in a series of ascending powers of x. Let us assume that its solution is

$$y = \sum_{r=0}^{\infty} a_r x^{k+r}$$

$$\therefore \quad \frac{dy}{dx} = \sum_{r=0}^{\infty} a_r (k + r) x^{k+r-1}$$

and

$$\frac{d^2y}{dx^2} = \sum_{r=0}^{\infty} a_r (k + r)(k + r - 1) x^{k+r-2}$$

Substituting these values in (i), we get

$$\sum_{r=0}^{\infty} a_r \left[(k + r)(k + r - 1) x^{k+r-2} + \frac{1}{x}(k + r) x^{k+r-1} + \left(1 - \frac{n^2}{x^2}\right) x^{k+r} \right] = 0$$

or

$$\sum_{r=0}^{\infty} \left[a_r \left\{ \left(k + r \right)^2 - n^2 \right\} x^{k+r-2} + x^{k+r} \right] = 0 \qquad \text{...(ii)}$$

Since relation (ii) is an identity, the coefficients of various powers of x must be zero.

$\therefore$ Equating to zero the coefficient of lowest power of x, *i.e.*, of x^{n-2} in (ii), we have

$$a_0 (k^3 - n^2) = 0.$$

Now, $a_0 \neq 0$ as it is the coefficient of the first term with which we begin the series

$$\therefore \; k^2 - n^2 = 0$$

or

$$k = \pm n \qquad \text{...(iii)}$$

Now, equating to zero the coefficient of x^{k-1} in (ii), we get

$$a_1 \{(k + 1)^2 - n^2\} = 0$$

But $(k + 1)^2 - n^2 \neq 0$ for $k = \pm n$ given by (iii)

$$\therefore \quad a_1 = 0.$$

Again equating to zero the coefficient of general term, *i.e.*, of x^{k+r} in (ii), we get

$$a_{r+2} \{(k + r + 2)^2 - n^2\} + a_r = 0$$

or

$$a_{r+2} (k + r + n + 2)(k + r - n + 2) = - a_r.$$

$$\therefore \quad a_{r+2} = - \frac{a_r}{(k + r + n + 2)(k + r - n + 2)} \qquad \text{...(iv)}$$

Putting $r = 1$ in (iv), we get

$$a_3 = \frac{a_1}{(k + n + 3)(k - n + 3)}$$

$= 0$ since $a_1 = 0$.

Similarly putting $r = 3, 5$, etc. in (iv), we get

$$a_1 = a_3 = a_5 \ldots = 0$$

Now, two cases arise.

Case I. When $k = n$, from (iv), we get

$$a_{r+2} = -\frac{a_r}{(2n + r + 2)(r + 2)}$$

Putting $r = 0, 2, 4 \ldots$etc.

$$a_2 = \frac{a_0}{(2n + 2)(2)} = -\frac{a_0}{2^2 . 1 ! (n + 1)}$$

$$a_4 = \frac{a_2}{(2n + 4)(4)} = -\frac{a_2}{2^2 . 2 ! (n + 2)}$$

$$= -\frac{a_0}{2^4 . 2 ! (n + 1)(n + 2)} \text{ etc.}$$

$$\therefore \quad y = a_0 \left[x^n - \frac{x^{n+2}}{2^2 . 1 ! (n + 1)} + \frac{x^{x+4}}{2^4 . 2 ! (n + 1)(n + 2)} - \ldots \right]$$

$$= a_0 x^n . \left[1 + (-1) \frac{x^2}{2^2 . 1 ! (n + 1)} + (-1)^2 \frac{x^4}{2^4 . 2 ! (n + 1)(n + 2)} + \ldots \right]$$

If $a_0 = \dfrac{1}{2^n \Gamma(n + 1)}$, this solution is called $J_n(x)$, known as **Bessel's Function of the first kind of order n.**

$$\therefore \quad J_n(x) = \frac{x^n}{2^n \Gamma n + 1} \left[1 + (-1) \frac{x^2}{2^2 . 1 ! (n + 1)} + (-1)^2 \frac{x^4}{2^4 . 2 ! (n + 1)(n + 2)} + \ldots \right]$$

$$= \frac{x^n}{2^n \Gamma(n + 1)} \times \sum_{r=0}^{\infty} (-1)^r \frac{x^{2r}}{2^r r ! (n + 1)(n + 2) \ldots (n + r)}$$

$$= \sum_{r=0}^{\infty} (-1)^r \left(\frac{x}{2} \right)^{n+2r} \frac{1}{r ! \Gamma(n + r + 1)}$$

Case II. When $k = -n$.

In this case the solution is obtained by replacing n by $-n$ in the value of J_n.

$$\therefore \quad J_{-n}(x) = \sum_{r=0}^{\infty} (-1)^r \left(\frac{x}{2} \right)^{-n+2r} \frac{1}{r ! (-n + r + 1) !}$$

when n is not integer $J_{-n}(x)$ is distinct from $J_n(x)$.

The solution of Bessel's equation are called **Bessel's functions.**

5·3. General Solution of Bessel's Equation

The most general solution of Bessel's equation is

$$y = A J_{-n}(x) + B J_n(x),$$

where A, B are two arbitrary constants.

5·4. Integration of Bessel's equation in series for n = 0.

The differential equation

$$\frac{d^2y}{dx^2} + \frac{1}{x}\frac{dy}{dx} + y = 0 \qquad \text{...(i)}$$

is known as Bessel's equation for $n = 0$.

Let us assume that its solution is

$$y = \sum_{r=0}^{\infty} a_r x^{k+r}$$

$$\therefore \quad \frac{dy}{dx} = \sum_{r=0}^{\infty} a_r (k+r) x^{k+r-1}$$

and $$\frac{d^2y}{dx^2} = \sum_{r=0}^{\infty} a_r (k+r)(k+r-1) x^{k+r-2}.$$

Substituting these values in (i), we get

$$\sum_{r=0}^{\infty} a_r \left[(k+r(k+r-1) x^{k+k-2} + \frac{1}{x}(k+r) x^{k+r-1} + x^{k+r} \right] = 0$$

or $$\sum_{r=0}^{\infty} a_r \left[(k+r)^2 x^{k+r-2} + x^{k+r} \right] = 0 \qquad \text{...(ii)}$$

which is an identity. Equating to zero the coefficient of lowest power of x, *i.e.*, x^{k-2}, we have

$a_0 k^2 = 0$. Since $a_0 \neq 0$ as it is the coefficient of the first term with which we begin the series

$$\therefore \quad k^2 = 0, \qquad \therefore \quad k = 0 \qquad \text{...(iii)}$$

Now, equating to zero the coefficient of next power of x, *i.e.*, x^{k+1}, we get

$$a_1 (k+1)^2 = 0.$$

Since $k + 1 \neq 0$ by virtue of (iii), we get

$$a_1 = 0.$$

Again equating to zero the coefficient of the general term, *i.e.*, x^{k-r}, we get

$$a_{r+2} (k+r+2)^2 + a_r = 0$$

$$\therefore \quad a_{r+2} = -\frac{a_r}{(k+r+2)^2}.$$

When $$k = 0$$

$$a_{r+2} = -\frac{a_r}{(r+2)^2}$$

Putting $$r = 1, 3, 5, \ldots \text{etc.}$$

we have $$a_1 = a_3 = a_5 = \ldots = 0.$$

Again putting $r = 0, 2, 4$ etc., we get

$$a_2 = -\frac{a_0}{2^2}$$

$$a_4 = -\frac{a_2}{4^2} = \frac{a_0}{2^2 . 4^2} \text{ etc.}$$

Since $y = \sum_{r=0}^{\infty} a_r x^r$, when $k = 0$

$$\therefore \quad y = a_0 \left(1 - \frac{x^2}{2^2} + \frac{x^4}{2^2.4^2} - \frac{x^6}{2^2.4^2.6^2} \cdots \right)$$

If $a_0 = 1$, this solution is denoted by $J_0(x)$.

$$\therefore \quad \mathbf{J_0(x) = 1 - \frac{x^2}{2^2} + \frac{x^4}{2^2.4^2} - \frac{x^6}{2^2.4^2.6^2} + \ldots} \text{[Kanpur 85]}$$

where $J_0(x)$ is called **Bessel's function of zeroeth order.**

5·5. Recurrence Formulae of $J_n(x)$

(I) $x.\ J_n'(x) = n.\ J_n(x) - x.J_{n+1}(x)$.

Proof: We know that

$$J_n(x) = \sum_{r=0}^{\infty} (-1)^r \left(\frac{x}{2}\right)^{n+2r} \frac{1}{r!\,\Gamma(n+r+1)}$$

where n is a positive integer.

Differentiating w.r.t. x, we get

$$J_n'(x) = \sum_{r=0}^{\infty} (-1)^r \frac{(n+2r)}{r!\,\Gamma(n+r+1)} \cdot \frac{1}{2}\left(\frac{x}{2}\right)^{n+2r-1}$$

$$\therefore \quad x J_n'(x) = \sum_{r=0}^{\infty} (-1)^r \frac{(n+2r)}{r!\,\Gamma(n+r+1)} \left(\frac{x}{2}\right)^{n+2r}$$

$$= \sum_{r=0}^{\infty} (-1)^r \frac{n}{r!\,\Gamma(n+r+1)} \left(\frac{x}{2}\right)^{n+2r}$$

$$+ \sum_{r=0}^{\infty} (-1)^r \frac{2r}{r!\,\Gamma(n+r+1)} \cdot \frac{x}{2}\left(\frac{x}{2}\right)^{n+2r-1}$$

$$= n J_n(x) + x \sum_{r=1}^{\infty} (-1)^r \cdot \frac{1}{(r-1)!\,\Gamma(n+r+1)} \left(\frac{x}{2}\right)^{n+2r-1}$$

Putting $(r - 1) = s$

$$= n J_n(x) - x \sum_{s=0}^{\infty} (-1)^s \frac{1}{s!\,\Gamma(n+1-s+1)} \left(\frac{x}{2}\right)^{n+1+2s}$$

$$= n J_n(x) - x J_{n+1}(x).$$

Hence $\mathbf{xJ'_n = nJ_n(x) - xJ_{n+1}(x)}$

which may also be written as

$$\frac{d}{dx}(x^{-n} J_n) = -x^{-n} J_{n+1}.$$

(II) $x\ J'_n(x) = -n\ J_n(x) + x\ J_{n-1}(x)$

As in I, we have

$$x J'_n(x) = \sum_{r=0}^{\infty} (-1)^r \frac{(n+2r)}{r!\,\Gamma(n+r+1)} \left(\frac{x}{2}\right)^{n+2r}$$

$$= \sum_{r=0}^{\infty} (-1)^r \frac{(2n+2r-n)}{r!\,\Gamma(n+r+1)} \left(\frac{x}{2}\right)^{n+2r}$$

$$= -n \sum_{r=0}^{\infty} (-1)^r \frac{1}{r!\,\Gamma(n+r+1)} \left(\frac{x}{2}\right)^{n+2r}$$

$$+ \sum_{r=0}^{\infty} (-1)^r \frac{(2n+2r)}{r!\,\Gamma(n+r+1)} \left(\frac{x}{2}\right)^{n+2r}$$

$$= -n J_n(x) \sum_{r=0}^{\infty} (-1)^r \frac{2(n+r)}{r!\,(n+r+1)} \cdot \left(\frac{x}{2}\right)^{n+2r-1} \cdot \left(\frac{x}{2}\right)$$

$$= -n J_n(x) + x \sum_{r=0}^{\infty} (-1)^r \frac{1}{r!\,\Gamma\,\overline{n-1+r+1}} \cdot \left(\frac{x}{2}\right)^{\overline{n-1}+2r}$$

$$= -n J_n(x) + x J_{n-1}(x).$$

$\therefore$ $\mathbf{x\, J'_n(x) = -n\, J_n(x) + x\, J_{n-1}(x).}$

This way also be written as

$$\frac{d}{dx}(x^n J^n) = x^n J_{n-1}.$$

(III). $2\, J'_n(x) = J_{n-1}(x) - J_{n+1}(x).$

From recurrence formulae I and II, we have

$$x\, J'_n(x) = n\, J_n(x) - x\, J_{n+1}(x)$$

and $$x\, J'_n(x) = -n\, J_n(x) + x\, J_{n-1}(x)$$

Adding, we get

$$2x\, J'_n(x) = x\, [J_{n-1}(x) - J_{n+1}(x)]$$

$\therefore$ $\mathbf{2J'_n(x) = J_{n-1}(x) - J_{n+1}(x)}$

Aliter. $$J_n(x) = \sum_{r=0}^{\infty} (-1)^r \frac{1}{r!\,\Gamma(n+r+1)} \left(\frac{x}{2}\right)^{n+2r}$$

$$2J'_n(x) = \sum_{r=0}^{\infty} (-1)^r \frac{2\,(n+2r)}{r!\,\Gamma(n+r+1)} \frac{1}{2} \left(\frac{x}{2}\right)^{n+2r-1}$$

$$= \sum_{r=0}^{\infty} (-1)^r \frac{(n+r+r)}{r!\,\Gamma(n+r+1)} \left(\frac{x}{2}\right)^{n+2r-1}$$

$$= \sum_{r=0}^{\infty} (-1)^r \frac{(n+r)}{r!\,\Gamma(n+r+1)} \cdot \left(\frac{x}{2}\right)^{n+2r-1}$$

$$+ \sum_{r=0}^{\infty} (-1)^r \frac{r}{r!\,\Gamma(n+r+1)} \left(\frac{x}{2}\right)^{n+2r-1}$$

$$= \sum_{r=0}^{\infty} (-1)^r \frac{1}{r!\,\Gamma(n+r)} \left(\frac{x}{2}\right)^{n+2r-1} -$$

$$- \sum_{r=0}^{\infty} (-1)^{r-1} \frac{1}{(r-1)!\,\Gamma(n+r+1)} \left(\frac{x}{2}\right)^{n+2r-1}$$

$$= \sum_{r=0}^{\infty} (-1)^r \frac{1}{r!\Gamma\{(n-r)+r+1\}} \left(\frac{x}{2}\right)^{\{(n-1)+2r\}}$$

$$- \sum_{s=0}^{\infty} (-1)^s \frac{1}{s!\Gamma\{n+1)+s+1\}} \left(\frac{x}{2}\right)^{n+1+2s}$$ Putting $r-1=s$.

$$= J_{n-1}(x) - J_{n+1}(x)$$

$\therefore$ $\mathbf{2J'_n(x) = J_{n-1}(x) - J_{n+1}(x).}$

(IV) $\mathbf{2n\, J_n(x) = x\, [J_{n-1}(x) + J_{n+1}(x)]}$

From recurrence formula I and II, we have

$$x J'_n(x) = n J_n(x) - x J_{n+1}(x)$$

and $$x J'_n(x) = -n J_n(x) + x J_{n-1}(x)$$

Subtracting, we get $0 = 2_n J_n(x) - x\,[J_{n+1}(x) + J_{n-1}(x)]$

$\therefore$ $\mathbf{2n\, J_n(x) = x\, [J_{n+1}(x) + J_{n-1}(x)]}$

Aliter. $$J_n(x) = \sum_{r=0}^{\infty} (-1)^r \frac{1}{r!\Gamma(n+r+1)} \left(\frac{x}{2}\right)^{n+2r}$$

$$\therefore \quad 2n\, J_n(x) = \sum_{r=0}^{\infty} (-1)^r \frac{(2n+2r-2r)}{r!\Gamma(n+r+1)} \left(\frac{x}{2}\right)^{n+2r}$$

$$= \sum_{r=0}^{\infty} (-1)^r \frac{2(n+r)}{r!\Gamma(n+r+1)} \left(\frac{x}{2}\right)^{n+2r}$$

$$- \sum_{r=0}^{\infty} (-1)^r \frac{2r}{r!\Gamma(n+r+1)} \left(\frac{x}{2}\right)^{n+2r}$$

$$= x \sum_{r=0}^{\infty} (-1)^r \frac{1}{r!\Gamma(n-r)+r-1)} \left(\frac{x}{2}\right)^{\overline{n-1}+2r}$$

$$+ x \sum_{r=0}^{\infty} (-1)^{r-1} \frac{1}{(r-1)!\Gamma(n+r+1)} \left(\frac{x}{2}\right)^{n+2r-1}$$

$$= x\, J_{n-1}(x) + x \sum_{s=0}^{\infty} (-1)^s \frac{1}{s!\Gamma(n+1+s+1)} \left(\frac{x}{2}\right)^{\overline{n+1}+2s}$$

Putting $r-1=s$

$$= x\, J_{n-1}(x) + x\, J_{n+1}(x)$$

$\therefore$ $\mathbf{2n\, J_n(x) = x\, [J_{n-1}(x) + J_{n+1}(x)]}$

(v) $\mathbf{\frac{d}{dx} [x^{-n} J_n(x)] = -x^{-n} J_{n+1}(x).}$

We have $$\frac{d}{dn}[x^{-n} J_n(x)] = -n x^{-n-1} J_n(x) + x^{-n} J'_n(x)$$

$$= x^{-n-1} [-n J_n(x) + x J'_n(x)]$$

$$= x^{-n-1} [-n J_n(x) + \{n J_n(x) - x J_{n+1}(x)\}]$$

From reccurence formula I.

$$= x^{-n-1} [-x J_{n+1}(x)]$$

$$= -x^{-n} J_{n+1}(x).$$

$$\therefore \quad \frac{d}{dx}[x^{-n} J_n(x)] = -x^{-n} J_{n+1}(x).$$

(VI) $\frac{d}{dx}[x^n J_n(x)] = x^n J_{n-1}(x).$

We have

$$\frac{d}{dx}[x^n j_n(x)] = n x^{n-1} J_n(x) + x^n J'_n(x)$$

$$= x^{n-1}[n J_n(x) + x J'_n(x)]$$

$$= x^{n-1}[n J_n(x) + \{-n J_n(x) + x J_{n-1}(x)\}]$$

From recurrence formula II

$$= x - n[x J_{n-1}(x)]$$

$$= x^n J_{n-1}(x).$$

$$\therefore \quad \frac{d}{dx}[x^n J_n(x)] = x^n J_{n-1}(x)$$

5·6. Show that when n is

(i) Positive integer, $J_{-n}(x) = (-1)^n J_n(x)$

(ii) any integer, $J_n(-x) = (-1)^n J_n(x)$

(i) we know that

$$J_{-n}(x) = \sum_{r=0}^{\infty} (-1)^r \left(\frac{x}{2}\right)^{-n+2r} \frac{1}{r!\,\Gamma(-n+r+1)}$$

Since if p is an integer, then $\Gamma(-p)$ is infinity for $p > 0$, $\therefore$ we get terms in J_{-n} equal to zero till $-n+r+1 < 1$, *i.e.*, $r < n$. Hence we can write

$$J_{-n}(x) = \sum_{r=0}^{\infty} \frac{(-1)^r}{r!\,\Gamma(-n+r+1)} \left(\frac{x}{2}\right)^{-n+2r}$$

$$= \sum_{s=0}^{\infty} \frac{(-1)^{n+s}}{(n+s)!\,\Gamma(s+1)} \left(\frac{x}{2}\right)^{n+2r} \qquad \text{Putting } r = n+s$$

$$= (-1)^n \sum_{s=0}^{\infty} \frac{(-1)^s}{\Gamma(n+s+1).s!} \left(\frac{x}{2}\right)^{n+2r}$$

$$= (-1)^n J_n(x).$$

(ii) We know that

$$J_n(x) = \sum_{r=0}^{\infty} (-1)^r \frac{(-1)^r}{r!\,\Gamma(-n+r+1)} \left(\frac{x}{2}\right)^{n+2r}$$

Case I. Let n be a positive integer. Replacing x by $-x$, we get

$$J_n(-x) = \sum_{r=0}^{\infty} (-1)^r \frac{1}{r!\,\Gamma(n+r+1)} \left(-\frac{x}{2}\right)^{n+2r}$$

$$= (-1)^n \sum_{r=0}^{\infty} (-1)^r \frac{1}{r!\,\Gamma(n+r+1)} \left(\frac{x}{2}\right)^{n+2r}$$

$$= (-1)^n J_n(x) \qquad [\because \ (-1)^{2r} = 1]$$

Case II. If n is a negative integer

Let $n = -m$ where m is a postive integer,

$$\therefore \ J_n(x) = J_{-m}(x)$$
$$= (-1)^m J_m(x) \qquad \text{[as in (i) part]}$$

Replacing x by $-x$

$$J_n(-x) = (-1)^m J_m(-x)$$
$$= (-1)^m (-1)^m J_m(x) \qquad \text{[as in case I]}$$
$$= (-1)^{2m} J_m(x)$$
$$= (-1)^{-m} J_{-m}(x) \qquad [\because \ (-1)^{2m} = 1]$$
$$= (-1)^n J_n(x)$$

Hence $J_n(-x) = (-1)^n J_n(x)$ for positive or negative integer.

5·7. Generating function for $J_n(x)$.

Prove that when n is a positive integer $J_n(x)$ is the coefficient of z^n in the expansion of $e^{x\left(z-\frac{1}{z}\right)/2}$ in ascending and descending powers of z. Also prove that $J_n(x)$ is the coefficient of z^{-n} multiplied by $(-1)^n$ in the expansion of above expression.

$$e^{x\left(z-\frac{1}{z}\right)/2}$$

$$= e^{xz/2} e^{-x/2z}$$

$$= \left[1 + \frac{xz}{2} + \frac{1}{2!}\left(\frac{xz}{2}\right)^2 + \ldots + \frac{1}{n!}\left(\frac{xz}{2}\right)^n + \frac{1}{(n+1)!}\left(\frac{xz}{2}\right)^{n+1} + \frac{1}{(n+2)}\left(\frac{xz}{2}\right)^{n+2} + \ldots\right] \times$$

$$\times \left[1 - \frac{x}{2z} + \frac{1}{2!}\left(\frac{x}{2z}\right)^2 + \ldots + \frac{(-1)^n}{n!}\left(\frac{x}{2z}\right)^n + \frac{(-1)^{n+1}}{(n+1)!}\left(\frac{x}{2z}\right)^{n+1} + \frac{(-1)^{n+2}}{(n+2)!}\left(\frac{x}{2z}\right)^{n+2} + \ldots\right]$$

Coefficient of z^n in this product

$$= \frac{1}{n!}\left(\frac{x}{2}\right)^n - \frac{1}{(n+1)!}\left(\frac{x}{2}\right)\left(\frac{x}{2}\right)^{n+1} + \frac{1}{(n+2)!}\frac{1}{2!}\left(\frac{x}{2}\right)^2 \times$$
$$\times \left(\frac{x}{2}\right)^{n+2} + \ldots$$

$$= \frac{1}{n!}\left(\frac{x}{2}\right)^n - \frac{1}{(n+1)!}\left(\frac{x}{2}\right)^{n+2} + \frac{1}{2!(n+2)!}\cdot\left(\frac{x}{2}\right)^{n+1} + \ldots$$

$$= \frac{(-1)^0}{\Gamma(n+1)}\left(\frac{x}{2}\right)^n + \frac{(-1)}{1\,!\,\Gamma(n+2)}\cdot\left(\frac{x}{2}\right)^{n+2}$$

$$= \frac{(-1)^2}{2\,!\,\Gamma(n+3)}\left(\frac{x}{2}\right)^{n+4} + \ldots$$

$$= \sum_{r=0}^{\infty} (-1)^r \frac{1}{r\,!\,\Gamma(n+r+1)}\cdot\left(\frac{x}{2}\right)^{n+2r}$$

Similarly, the coefficient of z^{-n} in the product

$$= \frac{(-1)^n}{n\,!}\left(\frac{x}{2}\right)^n + \frac{(-1)^{n+1}}{(n+1)\,!}\cdot\frac{x}{2}\cdot\left(\frac{x}{2}\right)^{n+1}$$

$$+ \frac{(-1)^{n+2}}{(n+2)\,!}\cdot\frac{1}{2\,!}\left(\frac{x}{2}\right)^2\left(\frac{x}{2}\right)^{n+2} + \ldots$$

$$= (-1)^n\left[\frac{1}{n\,!}\left(\frac{x}{2}\right)^n + \frac{(-1)}{\Gamma(n+2)}\left(\frac{x}{2}\right)^{n+2}\right.$$

$$\left. + \frac{(-1)^2}{2\,!\,\Gamma(n+3)}\left(\frac{x}{2}\right)^{n+4} + \ldots\right]$$

$$= (-1)^n J_n(x).$$

Remark. In the above product the term independent of z is

$$1 - \frac{x^2}{2^2} + \frac{x^4}{2^2.\,4^2} - \frac{x^6}{2^2.\,4^2.\,6^2} + \ldots = J_0(x).$$

Hence

$$e^{x\left(z-\frac{1}{z}\right)/2} = J_0 + \left(z - \frac{1}{z}\right)J_1$$

$$+ \left(z^2 + \frac{1}{z^2}\right)J_2 + \ldots + \left[z^n - (-1)^n\frac{1}{z^n}\right]J_n + \ldots$$

$$= \sum_{-\infty}^{\infty} z^n J_n(x)\,.$$

Since $J_{-n}(x) = (-1)^n J_n(x)$ [by § 5·6]

Illulstrative Examples

Ex. 1. *Show that*

(i) $J_{-1/2}(x) = \sqrt{\left\{\left(\frac{2}{\pi x}\right)\right\}}\,.\cos x$

(ii) $J_{1/2}(x) = \sqrt{\left\{\left(\frac{2}{\pi x}\right)\right\}}\,.\sin x$

and (iii) $[J_{1/2}(x)]^2 + [J_{-1/2}(x)]^2 = \frac{2}{\pi x}$

(i) We know that

$$J_n(x) = \frac{x^n}{2^n\,\Gamma(n+1)}\left[1 - \frac{x^2}{2\,(2n+2)} + \frac{x^4}{2.4\,(2n+2)\,(2n+4)} + \ldots\right]$$

Putting $n = -\frac{1}{2}$

$$J_{-\frac{1}{2}}(x) = \frac{x^{-\frac{1}{2}}}{2^{-\frac{1}{2}}\left(\frac{1}{2}\right)!}\left[1 - \frac{x^2}{2\,(-1+2)} + \frac{x^4}{2.4.\,(-1+2)(-1+4)} - \ldots\right]$$

$$= \sqrt{\left\{\left(\frac{2}{\pi x}\right)\right\}}\left[1 - \frac{x^2}{2\,!} + \frac{x^4}{4\,!} - \ldots\right]$$

$$= \sqrt{\left\{\left(\frac{2}{\pi x}\right)\right\}}\,.\,\cos x.$$

(iii) Square and add (i) and (ii).

Ex. 2. *(i) Prove that* $J_n J'_{-n} - J_n{}' J_{-n}$

$$= -\frac{2\sin nx}{\pi x}$$

(ii) Prove that

$$\frac{d}{dx}\left(\frac{J_{-n}}{Jn}\right) = -\frac{2\sin n\pi}{\pi x J_n^{\,2}}$$

Solution. (i) We know that J_n and J_{-n} are solutions of Bessel's equation.

$$y'' + \left(\frac{1}{x}\right)y' + \left(1 - \frac{n^2}{x^2}\right)y = 0$$

(iii) Square and add (i) and (ii).

Ex. 2. *(i) Prove that* $J_n J'_{-n} - J_n' J_{-n}$

$$= -\frac{2\sin n\pi}{\pi x}$$

(ii) Prove that

$$\frac{d}{dx}\left(\frac{J_{-n}}{J_n}\right) = -\frac{2\sin n\pi}{\pi x J_n^{\,2}}$$

(iii) Prove that $J_n'(x)\,J_{-n}(x) - j_n\,(x)\,J'_{-n}(x) = c/x$ *whese c is a constant, by considering the behaviour for the large values of x, show that* $c = (2\sin n\pi)/\pi$.

Solution. (i) We know that J_n and J_{-n} are solutions of Bessel's equation.

$$y'' + \left(\frac{1}{x}\right)y' + \left(1 - \frac{n^2}{x^2}\right)y = 0$$

$$\therefore \quad J_n'' + \left(\frac{1}{x}\right) J_n' + \left(1 - \frac{n^2}{x^2}\right) J_n = 0 \quad \text{...(i)}$$

and
$$J_{-n}'' + \left(\frac{1}{x}\right) J_{-n}' + \left(1 - \frac{n^2}{x^2}\right) J_{-n} = 0 \quad \text{...(ii)}$$

Multiplying (i) by J_{-n} and (ii) by J_n and then subtracting gives

$$J_n'' J_{-n} - J''_{-n} J_n + (1/x)(J_n' J_{-n} - J_{-n}' J_n) = 0 \quad \text{...(iii)}$$

Let
$$J_n' J_{-n} - J_{-n}' J_n = v \quad \text{...(iv)}$$

Differentiating w.r.t. 'x', (iv) gives

$$J_n'' J_{-n} + J_n' J_{-n}' - (J_{-n}'' J_n + J_{-n}' J_n') = v'$$

or
$$J_n'' J_{-n} - J_{-n}'' J_n = v' \quad \text{...(v)}$$

Using (iv) and (v), (iii) becomes

$$v' + \left(\frac{1}{x}\right) v = 0 \quad \text{or} \quad \frac{dv}{dx} + \left(\frac{1}{x}\right) v = 0$$

or
$$\frac{dv}{v} + \frac{dx}{x} = 0$$

Integrating $\log n + \log x = \log c$ or $v = c/x$

or
$$J_n' J_{-n} - J'_{-n} J_n = c/x \text{ by (iv)} \quad \text{...(vi)}$$

$$\because \quad J_n(x) = \frac{1}{2^n \Gamma(n+1)} \left[x^n - \frac{x^{n+2}}{4(n+1)} + \frac{x^{n+4}}{4.8(n+1)(n+2)} - \dots \right]$$

$$J_{-n}(x) = \frac{1}{2^{-n} \Gamma(-n+1)} \left[x^{-n} - \frac{x^{2-n}}{4(1-n)} + \frac{x^{4-n}}{4.8.(1-n)(2-n)} - \dots \right]$$

$\therefore$ Using the above values of J_n and J_{-n}, (vi) gives

$$\frac{1}{2\,\Gamma(n+1)} \left[n\,x^{n-1} - \frac{(n+2)\,x^{n+1}}{4(n+1)} + \frac{(n+4)\,x^{n+3}}{4.8.(n+1)(n+2)} - \dots \right]$$

$$\times \frac{1}{2^{-n} \Gamma(-n+1)} \left[n\,x^{n-1} - \frac{x^{n+1}}{4(n+1)} + \frac{(n+4)\,x^{n+3}}{4.8.(n+1)(n+2)} - \dots \right]$$

$$\times \frac{1}{2^{-n} \Gamma(-n+1)} \left[-n\,x^{-n-1} - \frac{(2-n)\,x^{1-n}}{4(1-n)} + \frac{(4-n)\,x^{3-n}}{4.8(1-n)(2-n)} - \dots \right]$$

$$\times \frac{1}{2^{-n} \Gamma(n+1)} \left[x^n - \frac{x^{n+2}}{4(n+1)} + \frac{x^{n+4}}{4.8.(n+1)}(n+2) - \dots \right] = \frac{c}{x}.$$

Now, comparing the coefficients of $1/x$ from both sides gives

$$\frac{n}{2^n \Gamma(n+1) \,.\, 2^n \Gamma(-n+1)} + \frac{n}{2^{-n} \Gamma(-n+1) \,.\, 2^n \Gamma(n+1)} = c$$

or
$$c = \frac{2n}{n\,\Gamma(n)\,\Gamma(1-n)} \qquad [\because \Gamma(n+1) = n\,\Gamma(n)]$$

$$= \frac{2}{(\pi/\sin n\pi)} - \frac{2 \sin n\pi}{\pi} \left[\because \quad \Gamma(n)\,\Gamma(1-n) = \frac{\pi}{\sin n\pi} \right]$$

Putting these values of c in (vi) and then multiplying both sides by (– 1), we get

$$J_n J'_{-n} - J' J_{-n} = -\frac{2 \sin n\pi}{\pi x} \qquad \text{...(vii)}$$

Part (ii) : Dividing both sides of (vii) by J_n^2, we get

$$\frac{J_n J'_{-n} - J_n' J_{-n}}{J_n^{\ 2}} = -\frac{2 \sin n\pi}{\pi x J_n^{\ 2}}$$

or

$$\frac{d}{dx}\left(\frac{J_{-n}}{J_n}\right) = -\frac{2 \sin n\pi}{\pi x J_n^{\ 2}}$$

Ex. 3. *Prove that*

$$\sqrt{\left\{\left(\frac{\pi x}{2}\right)\right\}} J_{3/2}(x) = \frac{1}{x} \sin x - \cos x.$$

We know that

$$J_n(x) = \frac{x^n}{2^n \Gamma(n+1)} \left[1 - \frac{x^2}{2(n+2)} + \frac{x^4}{2.4\,(2n+2)\,(2n+4)} \cdots \right]$$

Putting $n = \frac{3}{2}$, we get

$$J_{3/2}(x) = \frac{x^{3/2}}{2^{3/2}\,\Gamma(5/2)} \left[1 - \frac{x^2}{2.5} + \frac{x^4}{2.4.5.6.7.9.} \cdots \right]$$

$$= \frac{x\sqrt{x}}{2\sqrt{2}.\frac{3}{2}.\frac{1}{2}\sqrt{\pi}} \left[1 - \frac{x^2}{2.5} + \frac{x^4}{2.4.5.7} - \frac{x^6}{2.4.5.6.7.9} + \cdots \right]$$

$$\therefore \quad \sqrt{\left\{\left(\frac{\pi x}{2}\right)\right\}} J_{3/2}(x) = \frac{1}{3} \left[x^2 - \frac{x^4}{2.5} + \frac{x^6}{2.4.5.7} - \frac{x^8}{2.4.5.6.7.9} + \cdots \right]$$

$$= \frac{2x^2}{3\,!} - \frac{4x}{5\,!} + \frac{6x^6}{7\,!} - \frac{8x^8}{9\,!} + \cdots$$

$$= \left(\frac{1}{2\,!} - \frac{1}{3\,!}\right) x^2 - \left(\frac{1}{4\,!} - \frac{1}{5\,!}\right) x^4 + \left(\frac{1}{6\,!} - \frac{1}{7\,!}\right) x^6 - \left(\frac{1}{8\,!} - \frac{1}{9\,!}\right) x^8 \ldots$$

$$= \left(\frac{x^2}{2\,!} + \frac{x^4}{4\,!} + \frac{x^6}{6\,!} \cdots\right) + \left(-\frac{x^2}{3\,!} + \frac{x^4}{5\,!} - \frac{x^6}{7\,!} \cdots\right)$$

$$= -\left(1 - \frac{x^2}{2\,!} + \frac{x^4}{4\,!} - \frac{x^6}{6\,!}\right) + \frac{1}{x}\left[x - \frac{x^3}{3\,!} + \frac{x^5}{5\,!} - \frac{x^7}{7\,!} \cdots \right]$$

$$= -\cos x + \frac{1}{x}\sin x.$$

Hence $$\sqrt{\left\{\left(\frac{\pi x}{2}\right)\right\}}\, J_{3/2}(x) = \frac{1}{x}\sin x - \cos x$$

Ex. 4. *Prove that* $J_n(x) = (-2)^n \cdot x^n \dfrac{d^n}{d(x^2)^n} J_0(x)$.

Bessel's equation for zeroth order is

$$y_2 + \frac{1}{x} y_1 + y = 0 \qquad \text{where } y_1 = \frac{dy}{dx}, \quad y_2 = \frac{d^2y}{d_x 2}, \qquad \text{...(i)}$$

whose solution is $J_0(x)$.

Changing the independent variable from x to X, by the relation $x^2 = X$, so that

$$y_1 = \frac{dy}{dx} = \frac{dy}{dx} \cdot \frac{dX}{dx} = 2x\frac{dy}{dX} = 2\sqrt{X}\frac{dy}{dX}$$

and $$y_2 = \frac{d^2y}{dx^2} = \frac{d}{dx}\left(2\sqrt{X}\frac{dy}{dX}\right)$$

$$= \frac{d}{dX}\left(2\sqrt{X}\frac{dy}{dX}\right) \cdot \frac{dX}{dx}$$

$$= \left(2\sqrt{X}\frac{d^2y}{dX^2} + \frac{1}{\sqrt{x}}\frac{dy}{dX}\right) \cdot 2\sqrt{X}$$

$$= 4X\frac{d^2y}{dX^2} + 2\frac{dy}{dX}$$

Substituting in (i), we get

$$\left(4X\frac{d^2y}{dX^2} + 2\frac{dy}{dX}\right) + \frac{1}{\sqrt{X}} \cdot 2\sqrt{X} \cdot \frac{dy}{dX} + y = 0,$$

or $$4X\frac{d^2y}{dX^2} + 4\frac{dy}{dX} + y = 0 \qquad \text{...(ii)}$$

Differentiating (ii) n times w.r.t. X, by Leibnitz theorem, we have

$$4\left[X\frac{d^{n+2}y}{dX^{n+2}} + n.1.\frac{d^{n+1}y}{dX^{n+1}}\right] + 4\frac{d^{n+1}y}{dX^{n+1}} + \frac{d^ny}{dX^n} = 0$$

or $$4X\frac{d^{n+2}y}{dX^{n+2}} + 4.(n+1)\frac{d^{n+1}y}{dX^{n+1}} + \frac{d^ny}{dX^n} = 0$$

Putting $Y = \dfrac{d^ny}{dX^n} = \dfrac{d^n J_0(x)}{dX^n}$, it becomes

$$4X\frac{d^2Y}{dX^2} + 4(n+1) + \frac{dY}{dX} + Y = 0. \qquad \text{...(iii)}$$

Again, $J_n(x)$ is the solution of the Bessel's equation

$$\frac{d^2Y}{dX^2} + \frac{1}{x}\frac{dy}{dx} + \left(1 - \frac{n^2}{x^2}\right)y = 0 \qquad \text{...(iv)}$$

Putting $y = x^n Z$,

so that $$\frac{dy}{dx} = x^n \frac{dZ}{dx} + nx^{n-1} Z$$

and $$\frac{d^2y}{dx^2} = x^n \frac{d^2Z}{dx^2} + 2n\, x^{n-1} \frac{dZ}{dx} + n\,(n-1)\, x^{n-2}\, Z = 0$$

Substituting in (iv), we get

$$x^n \frac{d^2Z}{dx^2} + 2n\, x^{n-1} \frac{dZ}{dx} + n\,(n-1)\, x^{n-2}\, Z$$

$$+ \frac{1}{x}\left[x^n \frac{dZ}{dx} + nx^{n-1} Z \right] + \left[1 - \frac{n^2}{x^2} \right] . x^n Z = 0$$

or $$x^n \frac{d^2Z}{dx^2} + (2n+1)\, x^{n-1} \frac{dZ}{dx} + x^n Z = 0$$

or $$\frac{d^2Z}{dx^2} + (2n+1) \frac{1}{x} \frac{dZ}{dx} + Z = 0.$$

Putting $x^2 = X$, it becomes

$$\left[4X \frac{d^2Z}{dX^2} + 2 \frac{dZ}{dX} \right] + (2n+1) . \frac{1}{\sqrt{X}} , 2\sqrt{X} \frac{dZ}{dX} + Z = 0$$

or $$4X \frac{d^2 Z}{dX^2} + n\,(n+1) \frac{dZ}{dX} + Z = 0 \qquad \text{...(v)}$$

Comparing (iii) and (v), we get

$$Z = Y = \frac{d^n J_0(x)}{dX^n} = \frac{d^n J_0(x)}{d\,(x^2)^n}.$$

But $$y = x^n Z.$$

Hence $$J_n(x) = cx^n \frac{d^n J_0(x)}{d(x^2)^n}$$

whose c is a constant to be determined.

We know that $$J_0(x) = \sum_{r=0}^{\infty} \frac{(-1)^r x^{2r}}{(2^r . r!)^2}$$

$$\therefore \frac{d^2 J_0(x)}{d\,(x^2)^n} = \frac{d^n}{d(x^2)^n} \sum_{r=0}^{\infty} \frac{(-1)^r x^{2r}}{(2^r . r!)^2}$$

$$= \frac{d^n}{d(x^2)^n} \sum_{r=0}^{\infty} \frac{(-1)^{n+r} (x^2)^{n+r}}{[2^{n+r} (n+r)!]^2}$$

[Since all the terms in which the index of x is less than $2n$ will vanish on differentiation n times w.r.t. x^2]

$$= \sum_{r=0}^{\infty} \frac{(-1)^{n+r} (n+r)(n+r-1)...(r+1)(x^2)^r}{[2^{n+r} (n+r)!]^2}$$

$$= (-1)^n \sum_{r=0}^{\infty} (-1)^r . \frac{(n+r)!}{(r!\, 2^{2(n+r)} . [(n+r)!]^2} . x^{2r}$$

$$\therefore \quad J_n(x) = cx^n . (-1)^n \sum_{r=0}^{\infty} (-1)^r \frac{1}{r!\, 2^{2n+2r} . (n+r)!} . x^{2r}$$

$$= \frac{c\,(-1)^r}{2^n} \sum_{r=0}^{\infty} (-1)^r \frac{1}{r!\, \Gamma(n+r+1)} \left[\frac{x}{2}\right]^{n+2r}$$

$$= \frac{c}{(-2)^n} J_n(x)$$

$$\therefore \quad c = (-2)^n$$

$$\therefore \quad J_n(x) = (-2)^n . x^n . \frac{d^n J_0(x)}{d(x^2)^n}$$

Ex. 5. *Prove that*

(i) $J_0' = -J_1$

(ii) $J_2 = J_0'' - x^{-1} J_0'$

and (iii) $J_2 - J_0 = 2J_0''$

(i) From recurrence formula I, we have

$$x J'_n = n J_n - x J_{n+1}$$

Putting $n = 0$, we get

$$x J'_0 = -x J_1$$

$$\therefore \quad J_0' = -J_1.$$

(ii) From recurrence formula I

$$x J'_n = n J_n - x J_{n+1}$$

Putting $n = 1$, we get

$$x J'_1 = J_1 - x J_2 \qquad \text{...(A)}$$

But from (i) $J_0' = -J_1$

Differentiating, $J_0'' = -J_1'$

Substituting these results in (A), we get

$$-x J_0'' = -J_0' - x J_2$$

or

$$x J_2 = x J_0'' - J_0'$$

$$\therefore \quad J_2 = J_0'' - x^{-1} J_0'$$

(iii) From recurrence formula III, we have

$$2 J'_n = J_{n-1} - J_{n+1} \qquad \text{...(B)}$$

Differentiating both sides w.r.t. x as multiplying by 2, we get

$$2^2 J''_n = 2J'_{n-1} - 2J'_{n+1} \qquad \text{...(C)}$$

From (B), replacing n by $(n-1)$ and $(n+1)$ respectively, we get

$$2 J'_{n-1} = J_{n-2} - J_n$$

and

$$2 J'_{n+1} = J_n - J_{n+2} .$$

Substituting these values in *(C)*, we get

$$2^2 J''_n = (J_{n-2} - J_n) - (J_n - J_{n+2})$$

$$= J_{n-2} - 2 J_n + J_{n+2}$$

Putting $n = 0$,

$$2^2 J_0'' = J_{-2} - 2 J_0 + J_2$$

$$= (-1)^2 J_2 - 2 J_0 + J_2$$

$$= 2J_2 - 2J_0 \qquad [\because J_{-n} = (-1)^n J_n]$$

$$\therefore\ 2J_0'' = J_2 - J_0$$

Ex. 6. *Prove that*

$$J_{n-1} = \frac{2}{x}[nJ_n - (n+2)J_{n+2} + (n+4)J_{n+4} \ldots]$$

and hence deduce that

$$\frac{1}{2}xJ_n = (n+1)J_{n+1} - (n+3)J_{n+3} + (n+5)J_{n+5} + \ldots$$

From recurrence formula IV, we have

$$x(J_{n-1} + J_{n+1}) = 2nJ_n$$

$$\therefore J_{n-1} + J_{n+1} = \frac{2}{x}nJ_n \qquad \ldots(i)$$

Replacing n by $(n + 2)$, and changing sign, we have

$$-J_{n+1} - J_{n+3} = -\frac{2}{x}(n+2)J_{n+2} \qquad \ldots(ii)$$

Again replacing n by $(n + 4)$ in (i), we get

$$J_{n+3} + J_{n+5} = \frac{2}{x}(n+4)J_{n+4} \qquad \ldots(iii)$$

Again replacing n by $(n + 6)$ in (i) and changing sign,

$$-J_{n+5} - J_{n+7} = \frac{2}{x}(n+6)J_{n+6} \qquad \ldots(iv)$$

....

....

Adding (i), (ii), (iii), (iv) etc., we have

$$J_{n-1} = \frac{2}{x}[nJ_n - (n+2)J_{n+2} + (n+4)J_{n+4} - (n+6) J_{n+6} \ldots]$$

Since $J_n \to 0$ as $n \to \infty$

Deduction. Replacing n by $(n + 1)$, we get

$$\frac{x}{2}J_n = (n+1)J_{n+1} - (n+3)J_{n+3} + (n+5)J_{n+5} \ldots$$

Ex. 7. *Express $J_4(x)$ in terms of J_0 and J_1.*

Recurrence relation VI is

$$J_{n+1}(x) = (2n/x)J_n(x) - J_{n-1}(x) \qquad \ldots(i)$$

Replacing n by 3 in (i), we get

$$J_4(x) = (6/x)J_3(x) - J_2(x) \qquad \ldots(ii)$$

Now, replacing n by 2 in (i), we get

$$J_3(x) = (4/x)J_2(x) - J_1(x) \qquad \ldots(iii)$$

Using (iii), (ii) becomes

$$J_4(x) = \frac{6}{x}\left[\frac{4}{x}J_2(x) - J_1(x)\right] - J_2(x)$$

or $$J_4(x) = \left(\frac{24}{x^2} - 1\right) J_2(x) - \frac{6}{x} J_1(x) \qquad \text{...(iv)}$$

Next, replacing n by 1 in (i) gives

$$J_2(x) = (2/x)\, J_1(x) - J_0(x) \qquad \text{...(v)}$$

Using (v), (iv) becomes

$$J_4(x) = \left(\frac{24}{x^2} - 1\right)\left[\frac{2}{x} J_1(x) - J_0(x)\right] - \frac{6}{x} J_1(x)$$

or $$J_4(x) = \left(\frac{48}{x^3} - \frac{8}{x}\right) J_1(x) - \left(\frac{24}{x^2} - 1\right) J_0(x).$$

Ex. 8. *Prove that*

$$\frac{d}{dx}\left[J_n{}^2 + J_{n+1}{}^2\right] = 2\left(\frac{n}{x} J_n{}^2 - \frac{n+1}{x} J_{n+1}{}^2\right)$$

or $$J_n J_n' + J_{n+1} J'_{n+1} = \frac{1}{x}\left[n J_n{}^2 - (n+1) J_{n+1}{}^2\right]$$

We have

$$\frac{d}{dx}(J_n{}^2 + J_{n+1}{}^2) = 2 J_n J_n' + 2J_{n+1} J'_{n+1} \qquad \text{...(i)}$$

From recurrence formula I, we have

$$J_n' = \frac{n}{x} J_n - J_{n+1} \qquad \text{...(ii)}$$

Also from recurrence formula II, we have

$$J_n' = -\frac{n}{x} J_n + J_{n+1}$$

Replacing n by $(n+1)$, we get

$$J'_{n+1} = -\frac{n+1}{x} J_{n+1} + J_n \qquad \text{...(iii)}$$

Substituting the values of J_n' and J'_{n+1} from (ii) and (iii) in (i), we get

$$\frac{d}{dx}(J_n{}^2 + J^2{}_{n+1}) = 2 J_n\left(\frac{n}{x} J_n - J_{n+1}\right) + 2 J_{n+1}\left(-\frac{n+1}{x} J_{n+1} + J_n\right)$$

$$= 2\left(\frac{n}{x} J_n{}^2 - \frac{n+1}{x} J^2{}_{n+1}\right)$$

Ex. 9. *Prove that*

$$J_0^2 + 2\,(J_1^2 + J_2^2 + J_3^2 ...) = 1$$

Deduce that

$$|\, J_0(x)\,| \le 1,\ |\, J_n(x)\,| \le 2^{-1/2} (n \ge 1)$$

In the last example 8, we have proved that

$$\frac{d}{dx}(J_n{}^2 + J_{n+1}{}^2) = 2\left(\frac{n}{x} J_n{}^2 - \frac{n+1}{x} J^2{}_{n+1}\right)$$

Putting $n = 0, 1, 2, 3, ...$ etc., we get

$$\frac{d}{dx}(J_0{}^2 + J_1{}^2) = 2\left(0 - \frac{1}{x}J_1{}^2\right)$$

$$\frac{d}{dx}(J_1{}^2 + J_2{}^2) = 2\left(\frac{1}{x}J_1{}^2 - \frac{2}{x}J_2{}^2\right)$$

$$\frac{d}{dx}(J_2{}^2 + J_3{}^2) = 2\left(\frac{2}{x}J_2{}^2 - \frac{3}{x}J_3{}^2\right)$$

....

....

etc.

Adding, we get

$$\frac{d}{dx}[J_0{}^2 + 2(J_1{}^2 + J_2{}^2 + J_3{}^2 + \ldots)] = 0$$

Since $\qquad J_n \to \infty$

as $\qquad n \to \infty$

Integrating, we get

$$J_0^2 + 2(J_1^2 + J_2^2 + J_3^2 + \ldots) = \text{constet} = c \text{ (say)}$$

Putting $x = 0$

$$(J_0^2)x_0 = c \qquad \text{since } (J_1)_{x=0} = 0,\ (J_2)_{x=0} = 0 \text{ etc.}$$

or $\qquad 1 = c$

Hence $\qquad J_0^2 + 2(J_1^2 + J_2^2 + J_3^2 + \ldots) = 1.$

Deduction. We have proved that

$$J_0^2 + 2(J_1^2 + J_2^2 + J_3^2 + \ldots + J_n^2 + \ldots) = 1$$

Since $\quad J_1^2\ J_2^2 J_3^2\ldots$ are all positive or zero

$\therefore J_0^2 \le 1 \qquad$ hence $|J_0| \le 1$

i.e., $\qquad |J_0(x)| \le 1$

Also $\qquad |2J_n^2| \le 1$

or $\qquad |J_n| \le \frac{1}{\sqrt{2}}$

Hence $|J_n| \le 2^{-1/2}$, *i.e.*, $|J_n(x)| \le 2^{-1/2} \qquad$ (for $n \ge 1$)

Ex. 10. *Prove that*

$$\frac{d}{dx}(xJ_nJ_{n+1}) = x(J_n{}^2 - J^2{}_{n+1})$$

We have

$$\frac{d}{dx}(xJ_nJ_{n+1}) = J_nJ_{n+1} + x(J'_nJ_{n+1} + J_nJ'_{n+1})$$

$$= J_nJ_{n+1} + x(J'_n)J_{n+1} + J_n(xJ'_{n+1}) \qquad \ldots\text{(i)}$$

From recurrence formulae I and II; we have

$$xJ'_n = nJ_n - xJ_{n+1} \qquad \ldots\text{(ii)}$$

and

$$xJ'_n = -nJ_n - xJ_{n-1} \qquad \ldots\text{(iii)}$$

Replacing n by $(n + 1)$ in (iii), we get

$$xJ'_{n+1} = -(n+1)J_{n+1} + xJ_{n+2} \qquad \ldots\text{(iv)}$$

Substituting the values of $x\,J'_n$ and $x\,J'_{n+1}$ from (ii) and (iv) in (i), we have

$$\frac{d}{dx}(x J_n J_{n+1}) = J_n J_{n+1} + (n J_n - x J_{n+1}) J_{n+1}$$
$$+ J_n \{-(n+1) J_{n+1} + x J_n\}$$
$$= x (J_n^2 - J_{n+1}^2)$$

Ex. 11. *Prove that*

$$J_n' = \frac{2}{x}\left[\frac{n}{2} J_n (n+2) J_{n+2} + (n+4) J_{n+4} \cdots\right]$$

From recurrence formula II, we have

$$J_n' = -\frac{n}{x} J_n + J_{n-1}$$

Substituting the value of J_{n-1} from. Example 6, we get

$$J_n' = -\frac{n}{x} J_n + \frac{2}{x}\left[n J_n - (n+2) J_{n+2} + (n+4) J_{n+4 \ldots}\right]$$

$$= \frac{2}{x}\left[\frac{n}{2} J_n - (n+2) J_{n+2} + (n+4) J_{n+4} \cdots\right]$$

Ex. 12. *Prove that*

$x = 2 J_0 J_1 + 6 J_1 J_2 + \ldots + 2(2n+1) J_n J_{n+1} \ldots$

In example 10, above we have already proved that

$$\frac{d}{dx}(x J_n J_{n+1}) = x (J_n^2 - J_{n+1}^2)$$

Putting $n = 0, 1, 2, 3\ldots$ we have

$$\frac{d}{dx}(x J_0 J_1) = x (J_0^2 - J_1^2) \quad \ldots\text{(i)}$$

$$\frac{d}{dx}(x J_1 J_2) = x (J_1^2 - J_2^2) \quad \ldots\text{(ii)}$$

$$\frac{d}{dx}(x J_2 J_3) = x (J_2^2 - J_3^2) \quad \ldots\text{(iii)}$$

....

....

Multiplying (i), (ii), (iii),... by 1, 3, 5,... respectively and adding, we get

$$\frac{d}{dx}[x (J_0 J_1 + 3 J_1 J_2 + 5 J_2 J_3 + \ldots)]$$
$$= x [(J_0^2 - J_1^2) + 3 (J_1^2 - J_2^2) + 5 (J_2^2 - J_3^2) + \ldots]$$
$$= x [J_0^2 + 2 (J_1^2 + J_2^2 + \ldots)]$$
$$= x . 1 = x \qquad \text{[From § 4·6]}$$

Integrating both sides, we get

$$x (J_0 J_1 + 3 J_1 J_2 + 5 J_2 J_3 + \ldots) = \frac{x^2}{2} + c$$

Putting $x = 0$, $0 = 0 + c$ $\therefore c = 0$.

Hence $x (J_0 J_1 + 3 J_1 J_2 + 10 J_2 J_3 + \ldots$

$$+ 2. (2n + 1) J_n J_{n+1} + \ldots = \frac{x^2}{2}$$

or $$2 J_0 J_1 + 6 J_1 J_2 + 10 J_2 J_3 + \ldots + 2 (2n + 1) J_n J_{n+1} + \ldots = x.$$

Ex. 13. *Establish the formula*

$$x^2 J_n''(x) = (n^2 - n - x^2) J_n(x) + x J_{n+1}(x) \ (n = 0, 1, 2, \ldots).$$

Writing recurrence formula I, we have

$$x J'_n(x) = n J_n(x) - x J_{n+1}(x) \qquad \ldots(i)$$

Differentiating both sides w.r.t. x, we get

$$x J''_n(x) + J'_n(x) = n J'_n(x) - x J'_{n+1}(x) + J_{n+1}(x)$$

or $$x^2 J_n''(x) = (n - 1) x J_n'(x) - x.x J'_{n+1}(x) - x J_{n+1}(x) \qquad \ldots(ii)$$

From recurrence formula II

$$x J_n'(x) = - n J_n(x) + x J_{n-1}(x).$$

Writing $(n + 1)$ for n, we get

$$x J'_{n+1}(x) = - (n + 1) J_{n+1}(x) + x J_n(x) \qquad \ldots(iii)$$

Substituting for $xJ'_n(x)$ from (i) and for $x J_{n+1}(x)$ from (iii) in (ii), we get

$$x^2 J_n''(x) = (n - 1) [n J_n(x) - x J_{n+1}(x)] - x [- (n + 1) J_{n+1}(x) + x J_n(x)] - x J_{n+1}(x)$$

$$= (n^2 - n - x^2) J_n(x) + x J_{n+1}(x).$$

Ex. 14. *From the recurrence formula*

$$2J_n' = J_{n-1} - J_{n+1}$$

deduce the result

$$2^r J_n' = J_{n-1} - r J_{n-r+2} + \frac{r (r - 1)}{2 !} J_{n-r+4} - \ldots + (- 1)^r J_{n+r}.$$

The given recurrence formula is

$$2J_n' = J_{n-1} - J_{n+1} \qquad \ldots(i)$$

Differentiating w.r.t. x, we get

$$2J_n'' = J'_{n-1} - J'_{n+1}$$

$$\therefore \ 2^2 J_n'' = 2 J'_{n-1} - 2 J'_{n+1} \qquad \ldots(ii)$$

Substituting the values of $2 J'_{n-1}$ and $2 J'_{n+1}$ from (i) obtained by replacing n by $(n - 1)$ and $(n + 1)$ respectively.

$$= (J_{n-4} - J_n) - (J_n - J_{n+2})$$

$$= J_{n-2} - 2 J_n + J_{n+2}$$

Differentiating (ii) again and multiplying by 2, we get

$$2^3 J_n''' = 2 J'_{n-2} - 2^2 J_n' + 2 J'_{n+2}$$

Substituting the values of $2 J'_n$, $2 J'_{n-2}$, $2J'_{n+2}$ from (i), the last two obtained by replacing n by $(n - 2)$ and $(n + 2)$ respectively in (i)

$$= (J_{n-2} - J_{n-1}) - 2 (J_{n-1} - J_{n+1}) + (J_{n+1} - J_{n+3})$$

$$= J_{n-3} - 3 J_{n-1} + 3 J_{n+1} - J_{n+3}$$

$$= J_{n-3} - {}^3c_1 J_{n-1} + {}^3c_2 J_{n+1} - {}^3c_3 J_{n+3}$$

Applying the same process again and again, we get

$$2^r J_n{}^r = J_{n-r} - {}^rc_1 J_{n-r+2} + {}^rc_2 J_{n-r+4} + \ldots$$

$$+ (-1)^r \, {}^rc_r J_{n+r}$$

$$= J_{n-r} - r J_{n-r+2} + \frac{r(r-1)}{2!} J_{n-r+4} + \ldots + (-1)^r J_{n+r}.$$

Exercise 5 (A)

1. Show that $y = x^{-n/2} J_n (2\sqrt{x})$ satisfies the equation

$$x y'' + (n+1) y' + y = 0.$$

2. Show that $\int_0^{\pi/2} \sqrt{\{(\pi x)\}} J_{1/2}(2x)\, dx = 1.$

3. Prove that

$$[J_{1/2}(x)]^2 + [J_{-1/2}(x)]^2 = 2/(\pi x)$$

4. Prove that

$$J_2 + 3J_0' + 4J_0'' = 0$$

5. Establish the relation

$$2J'_n(x) = J_{n-1}(x) - J_{n+1}(x)$$

for the Bessel's function $J_n(x)$

Hence deduce that

$$J_n''(x) = \tfrac{1}{4}[J_{n-2}(x) - 2J_n(x) + J_{n+2}(x)].$$

6. Prove that

$$\tfrac{1}{2} x J_n = (n+1) J_{n+1} - (n+3) J_{n+3} + (n+5) J_{n+5} \cdots$$

7. Prove that

$$J_0^2 + 2(J_1^2 + J_2^2 + J_3^2 + \ldots) = 1.$$

8. Prove that

$$J_n' = \frac{2}{x}\left[\frac{n}{2} J_n - (n+2) J_{n+2} + (n+4) J_{n+4} - \ldots\right]$$

9. Prove that

(a) $x J_n''(x) + J_n'(x) = (x^2/x) J_n(x) - x J_n(x)$

(b) $4 \dfrac{d^2}{dx^2}\left[J_n(x)\right] = J_{n-2}(x) - 2J_n(x) + J_{n+2}(x)$

(c) $\int J_{n+1}(x)\, dx = \int J_{n-1}(x)\, dx - 2J_n(x)$

10. Evaluate $J_3(x)$ in terms of $J_0(x)$ and $J_1(x)$.

[**Ans.** $J_3(x) = \{(8 - x^2)/x^2\} J_1(x) - (4/x) J_0(x)$]

5·8. Trigonometric expansions involving Bessel's Functions

Show that

(a) $\cos(x \sin\phi) = J_0 + 2\cos 2\phi . J_2 + 2\cos 4\phi . J_4 \ldots$

(b) $\sin(x \sin\phi) = 2\sin\phi . J_1 + 2\sin 3\phi . J_3 + \ldots$

(c) $\cos(x \cos\phi) = J_0 - 2\cos 2\phi . J_2 + 2\cos 4\phi . J_4 - \ldots$

(d) $\sin(x \cos\phi) = 2\cos\phi . J_1 - 2\cos 3\phi\, J_3 + 2\cos 5\phi . J_5 \ldots$

(e) $\cos x = J_0 - 2J_2 + 2J_3 + 2J_4 - \ldots$

(f) $\sin x = 2J_1 - 2J_3 + 2J_5 - \ldots$

We know that

$$e^{\left(\frac{1}{2}\right)x\left(z-\frac{1}{z}\right)} = J_0 + (z - z^{-1}).\, J_1 + (z^2 + z^{-2})\, J_2 + (z^3 - z^{-3})\, J_3 + \ldots \quad \ldots(i)$$

Let $z = e^{i\phi}$, so that $z^n = e^{in\phi}$ and $z^{-n} = e^{-in\phi}$.

Then from (i) we get

$$e^{\left(\frac{1}{2}\right)x\cdot(e^{i\phi} - e^{-i\phi})} = J_0 + (e^{i\phi} - e^{-i\phi})\, J_1 + (e^{2i\phi} + e^{-2i\phi})\, J_2 + (e^{3i\phi} - e^{-3i\phi})\, J_3 + \ldots \quad \ldots(ii)$$

Since $\cos n\phi = \frac{1}{2}(e^{ni\phi} + e^{-ni\phi})$, $\sin n\phi = \frac{1}{2i}(e^{ni\phi} - e^{-ni\phi})$, (ii) may be written as

$$e^{xi \sin \phi} = J_0 + 2i \sin \phi\, J_1 + 2 \cos 2\phi.\, J_2 + 2i \sin 3\phi.\, J_3 + \ldots$$

or

$$\cos(x \sin n\phi) + i \sin(x \sin \phi) = (J_0 + 2 \cos 2\phi\, J_2 + \ldots) + 2i(\sin \phi.\, J_1 + \sin 3\phi.\, J_2 + \ldots) \quad \ldots(iii)$$

(a) Equating real parts in (iii), we get

$$\cos(x \sin \phi) = J_0 + 2 \cos 2\phi\, J_2 + 2 \cos 4\phi\, J_4 + \ldots \quad \ldots(iv)$$

(b) Equating imaginary parts in (iii), we get

$$\sin(x \sin \phi) = 2 \sin \phi.\, J_1 + 2 \sin 3\phi.\, J_3 + 2 \sin 5\phi\, J_5 + \ldots \quad \ldots(v)$$

(c) Replacing ϕ by $\pi/2 - \phi$ in (iv) and simplifying, we get

$$\cos(x \cos \phi) = J_0 - 2 \cos 2\phi\, J_2 + 2 \cos 4\phi\, J_4 - \ldots \quad \ldots(vi)$$

(d) Replacing ϕ by $(\pi/2 - \phi)$ in (v) and simplifying, we get

$$\sin(x \cos \phi) = 2 \cos \phi\, J_1 - 2 \cos 3\phi\, J_3 + 2 \cos 5\phi\, J_5 - \ldots \quad \ldots(vii)$$

(e & f) Replacing ϕ by 0 in (vi) and (vii), we get

$$\cos x = J_0 - 2\, J_2 + 2\, J_3 - \ldots$$

and

$$\sin x = 2\, J_0 - 2\, J_3 + 2\, J_5 - \ldots$$

Illustrative Examples

Ex. 15. *Show that*

(i) $x \sin x = 2\,(2^2 J_2 - 4^2 J_4 + 6^2 J_6 - \ldots)$

(ii) $x \cos x = 2\,(1^2 J_1 - 3^2 J_3 + 5^2 J_5 - \ldots)$

Solution. (i) We know that

$$\cos(x \sin \phi) = J_0 + 2\, J_2 \cos 2\phi + 2\, J_4 \cos 4\phi + \ldots \quad \ldots(i)$$

Differentiating w.r.t. 'ϕ' we get

$$-\sin(x \sin \phi).\, x \cos \phi = 0 - 2.2\, J_2 \sin 2\phi - 2.4\, J_4 \sin 4\phi \ldots \quad \ldots(ii)$$

Differentiating (ii) w.r.t. 'ϕ', we have

$$-\cos(x\sin\phi)\,.\,(x\cos\phi)^2+\sin(x\sin\phi)(x\sin\phi)$$
$$=-2.2^2.J_2\cos 2\phi-2.4^2 J_4\cos 4\phi-2.6^2 J_0\cos 6\phi... \quad ...(iii)$$

Replacing ϕ by $\pi/2$ in (iii), we get

$$x\sin x=2\,(2^2 J_2-4^2 J_4+6^2 J_6...)$$

(ii) Start with

$$\sin(x\sin\phi)=2J_1\sin\phi+2J_3\sin 3\phi+...$$

Differentiate this twice w.r.t. 'ϕ' as in part (i) and then replace ϕ by $\pi/2$. Thus we can get the required answer.

Ex. 16. *Show that when n is integral*

(a) $\pi J_n=\int_0^{\pi}\cos(n\theta-x\sin\theta)\,d\theta$

(b) $\pi J_0=\int_0^{\pi}\cos(x\cos\phi)\,d\phi$

$$=\int_0^{\pi}\cos(x\sin\phi)\,d\phi$$

and hence deduce that

$$J_n(x)=1-\frac{x^2}{2^2}+\frac{x^4}{2^2.4^2}-\frac{x^6}{2^2.4^2.6^2}+\ldots$$
$$=\sum_{r=0}^{\infty}\frac{(-1)^r x^{2r}}{(2^r.r\,!)^2}.$$

Solution. We know that

$$\cos(x\sin\theta)=J_0+2J_2\cos 2\theta+...+2J_{2m}\cos 2m\theta+... \quad ...(i)$$

and $\sin(x\sin\theta)=2\sin\theta.J_1+2\sin 3\theta\,J_3+...$

$$+2J_{2m+1}\sin(2m+1)\,\theta+... \quad ...(ii)$$

(a) Multiplying both sides of (i) by $\cos 2m\theta$ and then integrating between the limits 0 to π, we get

$$\int_0^{\pi}\cos(x\sin\theta)\cos 2m\theta\,d\theta$$
$$=J_0\int_0^{\pi}\cos 2m\theta\,d\theta+2J_2\int_0^{\pi}\cos 2\theta\cos 2m\theta\,d\theta+\ldots$$
$$+2J_{2m}\int_0^{\pi}\cos^2 2m\theta\,d\theta+\ldots$$
$$=0+0+\ldots+J_{2m}\int_0^{\pi}(1+\cos 4m\theta)\,d\theta+\ldots$$
$$=\pi J_{2m}.$$

Similarly, we can prove that

$$\int_0^{\pi}\cos(x\sin\theta)\cos(2m+1)\,\theta\,d\theta=0$$

Again multiplying both sides of (ii) by $\sin(2m+1)\theta$ and then integrating between the limits 0 to π, we get

$$\int_0^{\pi} \sin(x\sin\theta)\sin(2m+1)\theta\, d\theta$$

$$= 2J_1\int_0^{\pi} \sin\theta.\sin(2m+1)\theta\, d\theta$$

$$+ 2J_2\int_0^{\pi} \sin 3\theta\sin(2m+1)\theta d\theta +$$

$$+ \ldots + 2J_{2m+1}\int_0^{\pi} \sin^2(2m+1)\theta\, d\theta + \ldots$$

$$= 0 + 0 + \ldots + J_{2m+1}\int_0^{\pi} \{1-\cos 2(2m+1)\theta\}\, d\theta + \ldots$$

$$= J_{2m+1}\Big[\ \theta\ \Big]_0^{\pi} = \pi J_{2m+1}$$

Similarly,

$$\int_0^{\pi} \sin(x\sin\theta)\sin 2m\theta\, d\theta = 0.$$

Therefore

$$\int_0^{\pi} \cos(2m\theta - x\sin\theta)\, d\theta = \int_0^{\pi} \cos 2m\theta.\cos(x\sin\theta)\, d\theta$$

$$+ \int_0^{\pi} \sin 2m\theta.\sin(x\sin\theta)\, d\theta$$

$$= \pi\, J_{2m}.$$

Also,

$$\int_0^{\pi} \cos[(2m+1)\theta - x\sin\theta]\, d\theta$$

$$= \int_0^{\pi} \cos(2m+1)\theta.\cos(x\sin\theta)\, d\theta$$

$$+ \int_0^{\pi} \sin(2m+1)\theta\sin(x\sin\theta)\, d\theta$$

$$= \pi J_{2m+1}$$

Hence for all positive integral n, we get

$$\int_0^{\pi} \cos(n\theta - x\sin\theta)\, d\theta = \pi J_n.$$

If n is negative, say $n = -m$, where m is positive, then

$$\int_0^{\pi} \cos(n\theta - x\sin\theta)\, d\theta$$

$$= \int_0^{\pi} \cos(-m\theta - x\sin\theta)\, d\theta$$

$$= -\int_{\pi}^{0} \cos\{-m(\pi-\phi) - x\sin(\pi-\phi)\}\, d\pi$$

Putting $\theta = \pi - \phi$

$$= \int_0^\pi \cos\{-m\pi + (m\phi - x\sin\phi)\}\, d\phi$$

$$= \int_0^\pi \{\cos m\pi \cos(m\phi - x\sin\phi) + \sin m\pi \sin(m\phi - x\sin\phi)\}\, d\phi$$

$$= (-1)^m \int_0^\pi \cos(m\phi - x\sin\phi)\, d\phi$$

$$= (-1)^m \pi J_m(x)$$

Since $J_{-m}(x) = (-1)^m J_m(x)$.

$$= \pi J_n(x)$$

Hence for all integral values of n

$$\int_0^\pi \cos(n\theta - x\sin\theta)\, d\theta = \pi J_n$$

(b) Putting $\theta = \pi/2 + \phi$ in the value of $\cos(x\sin\theta)$ from (i), we have

$$\cos(x\cos\phi) = J_0 - 2J_2\cos 2\phi + 2J_4\cos 4\phi - ...$$

$$\therefore \int_0^\pi \cos(x\cos\phi)\, d\phi = J_0\int_0^\pi d\theta - 2J_2\int_0^\pi \cos 2\phi\, d\phi + \ldots$$

$$= \pi J_0$$

From (i) we have

$$\cos(x\sin\phi) = J_0 + 2J_2\cos 2\phi + 2J_4\cos 4\phi + \ldots$$

$$\therefore \int_0^\pi \cos(x\sin\phi)\, d\phi = J_0\int_0^\pi d\phi + 2J_2\int_0^\pi \cos 2\phi\, d\phi + \ldots$$

$$= \pi J_0.$$

Deduction. We have to prove that

$$J_0(x) = \frac{1}{\pi}\int_0^\pi \cos(x\cos\phi)\, d\phi$$

$$= \frac{1}{\pi}\int_0^\pi \left(1 - \frac{x^2\cos^2\phi}{2!} + \frac{x^4\cos^4\phi}{4!} - \frac{x^6\cos^6\phi}{6!} + \ldots\right) d\phi \quad \text{...(iii)}$$

Since $\int_0^\pi \cos^{2r}\phi\, d\phi = \dfrac{1.3.5...(2r-1)}{2.4.6...(2r)}\cdot\pi$

from definite integrals.

$\therefore$ from (iii), we get

$$J_0(x) = \frac{1}{\pi}\left[\pi - \frac{x^2}{2!}\cdot\tfrac{1}{2}\pi + \frac{x^4}{4!}\cdot\frac{1.3}{2.4}\pi - \frac{x^6}{6!}\cdot\frac{1.3.5}{2.4.6}\pi + \ldots\right]$$

$$= 1 - \frac{x^2}{2^2} + \frac{x^4}{2^2.4^2} - \frac{x^6}{2^2.4^2.6^2} + \ldots$$

$$= 1 - \frac{x^2}{2^2} + \frac{x^4}{2^4.(2!)^2} - \frac{x^6}{2^6.(3!)^2} + \ldots$$

$$= \sum_{r=0}^{\infty} \frac{(-1)^r x^{2r}}{(2^r.r!)^2}$$

Ex. 17. *Verify directly from the representation*

$$J_0(x) = \frac{1}{\pi}\int_0^{\pi} \cos (x \sin \phi)\, d\phi$$

that $J_0(x)$ satisfies Bessel's equation in which $n = 0$

Let $y = J_0(x) = \frac{1}{\pi}\int_0^{\pi} \cos (x \sin \phi)\, d\phi$ ...(i)

$$\therefore \quad \frac{dy}{dx} = -\frac{1}{\pi}\int_0^{\pi} \sin (x \sin \phi) \sin \phi \, d\phi \quad \text{...(ii)}$$

and $$\frac{d^2y}{dx^2} = -\frac{1}{\pi}\int_0^{\pi} \cos (x \sin \phi) \sin^2 \phi \, d\phi \quad \text{...(iii)}$$

From (ii), we get

$$\frac{dy}{dx} = -\frac{1}{\pi}\left[\left\{ -\sin (x \sin \phi) \cos \phi \right\}_0^{\pi} + \int_0^{\pi} \cos (x \sin \phi) . x \cos^2 \phi \, d\phi \right]$$

$$= -\frac{x}{\pi}\int_0^{\pi} \cos (x \sin \phi) . \cos^2 \phi \, d\phi$$

$$= -\frac{x}{\pi}\int_0^{\pi} \cos (x \sin \phi) . (1 - \sin^2 \phi)\, d\phi$$

$$= -\frac{x}{\pi}\int_0^{\pi} \cos (x \sin \phi)\, d\phi + \frac{x}{\pi}\int_0^{\pi} \cos (x \sin \phi) \sin^2 \phi \, d\phi$$

$$= -xy - x\frac{d^2y}{dx^2} \text{ from (i) and (iii)}$$

$$\therefore \quad \frac{d^2y}{dx^2} + \frac{1}{x}\frac{dy}{dx} + y = 0$$

which is Bessel's equation for $n = 0$

$$\therefore \quad J_0(x) = \frac{1}{x}\int_0^{\pi} \cos (x \sin \phi)\, d\phi$$

satisfies the Bessel's equation of zeroeth order.

Ex. 18. *Prove that $J_n(x) = 0$ has no repeated roots except at $x = 0$.*

Solution. If possible let α be a repeated root of $J_n(x) = 0$

$\therefore \quad J_n(\alpha) = 0$ and $J'_n(\alpha) = 0$ ...(i)

From recurrence formula I and II, we have,

$$J_{n+1}(x) = \frac{n}{x}J_n - J'_n(x)$$

and $$J_{n-1}(x) = \frac{n}{x}J_n + J'_n(x).$$

$\therefore J_{n+1}(\alpha) = 0$ and $J_{n-1}(\alpha) = 0$

with the help of (i), *i.e.*, for the same value of x, $J_n(x)$, $J_{n+1}(x)$ and $J_{n-1}(x)$ are all zero, which is absurd as we can not have two power series having the same sum function. Thus $J_n(x) = 0$ can not have repeated roots except at $x = 0$.

Ex. 19. *Prove*

$$\int_0^\infty e^{-ax} J_0(bx)\, dx = \frac{1}{\sqrt{\{(a^2+b^2)\}}},\ a > 0.$$

Solution. From example 16 above, we have

$$J_0(x) = \frac{1}{\pi}\int_0^\pi \cos(x\sin\phi)\, dx$$

$$\therefore \int_0^\infty e^{-ax} J_0(bx)\, dx = \int_0^\infty e^{-ax}\left\{\frac{1}{\pi}\int_0^\pi \cos(bx\sin\phi)\, d\phi\right\} dx$$

$$= \frac{1}{\pi}\int_0^\pi\left[\int_0^\infty e^{-ax}\cos(bx\sin\phi)\, dx\right] d\phi$$

$$= \frac{1}{\pi}\int_0^\pi\left[\int_0^\infty e^{-ax}\,.\,\frac{e^{i(bx\sin)} + e^{-i(bx\sin\phi)}}{2}\, dx\right] dx$$

$$= \frac{1}{2\pi}\int_0^\pi\left[\int_0^\infty\left\{e^{-(a-ib\sin\phi)x} + e^{-(a+ib\sin\phi)x}\right\} dx\right]$$

$$= \frac{1}{2\pi}\int_0^\pi\left[\frac{e^{-(a-ib\sin\phi)x}}{-(a-ib\sin\phi)} - \frac{e^{-(a+ib\sin\phi)x}}{a+ib\sin\phi}\right]_0^\infty d\phi$$

$$= \frac{1}{2\pi}\int_0^\pi\left[\frac{1}{a-ib\sin\phi} + \frac{1}{a+ib\sin\phi}\right] d\phi$$

$$= \frac{1}{2\pi}\int_0^\pi \frac{2a\, d\phi}{a^2+b^2\sin^2\phi}$$

$$= 2.\frac{a}{\pi}\int_0^{\pi/2}\frac{\operatorname{cosec}^2\phi\, d\phi}{b^2+a^2\operatorname{cosec}^2\phi}$$

$$= 2.\frac{a}{\pi}\int_0^{\pi/2}\frac{\operatorname{cosec}^2\phi\, d\phi}{(a^2+b^2)+a^2\cot^2\phi}$$

$$= 2.\frac{a}{\pi}\left[\frac{1}{a\sqrt{\{(a^2+b^2)\}}}\cot^{-1}\frac{a\cot\phi}{\sqrt{\{(a^2+b^2)\}}}\right]_0^{\pi/2}$$

$$= \frac{2}{\pi\sqrt{\{(a^2+b^2)\}}}\left[\cot^{-1}0 - \cot^{-1}\infty\right]$$

$$= \frac{1}{\sqrt{\{(a^2+b^2)\}}}.$$

Ex. 20. *Prove that*

$$(i)\ J_n(x) = \frac{1}{\sqrt{\pi}\,\Gamma(n+\frac{1}{2})}\left(\frac{x}{2}\right)^n\int_0^\pi \cos(x\sin\phi)\cos^{2n}\phi\, d\phi.$$

(i) $J_n(x) = \dfrac{1}{\sqrt{\pi}\,\Gamma(n+\frac{1}{2})}\left(\dfrac{x}{2}\right)^n \displaystyle\int_0^{\pi} \cos(x \sin\phi)\cos^{2n}\phi\, d\phi.$

(ii) $J_n(x) = \dfrac{1}{\sqrt{\pi}\,\Gamma(n+\frac{1}{2})}\left(\dfrac{x}{2}\right)^n \displaystyle\int_0^{\pi} \cos(x \cos\phi)\sin^{2n}\phi\, d\phi.$

Solution. Let

$$I = \int_0^{\pi} \cos(x\sin\phi)\cos^{2n}\phi\, d\phi \qquad \text{...(i)}$$

$$\therefore \qquad I = 2\int_0^{\pi/2} \cos(x\sin\phi)\cos^{2n}\phi\, d\phi$$

or

$$I = 2\int_0^{\pi/2} \cos^{2n}\phi\left[1 - \frac{x^2\sin^2\phi}{2!} + \frac{x^4\sin^4\phi}{4} - \dots\right] d\phi \qquad \text{...(ii)}$$

But

$$\int_0^{\pi/2} \cos^m\phi\,\sin^n\phi\, d\phi = \frac{\left(\frac{m+1}{2}\right)\Gamma\left(\frac{n+1}{2}\right)}{2\Gamma\left(\frac{m+n+2}{2}\right)} \qquad \text{...(iii)}$$

Using (iii), (ii) may be written as

$$I = 2\left[\frac{\Gamma(n+\frac{1}{2})\Gamma\left(\frac{1}{2}\right)}{2\Gamma(n+1)} - \frac{x^2}{2!}\frac{\Gamma(n+\frac{1}{2})\Gamma\left(\frac{3}{2}\right)}{2\Gamma(n+2)} + \frac{x^4}{4!}\frac{\Gamma(n+\frac{1}{2})\Gamma(5/2)}{2\Gamma(n+3)} - \dots\right]$$

$$= \Gamma(n+\tfrac{1}{2})\left[\frac{\sqrt{\pi}}{\Gamma(n+1)} - \frac{x^2}{2!}\times\frac{\frac{1}{2}\sqrt{\pi}}{(n+1)\Gamma(n+1)} + \frac{x^4}{4!}\frac{\frac{3}{2}\cdot\frac{1}{2}\sqrt{\pi}}{(n+2)(n+1)\Gamma(n+1)} - \dots\right]$$

$$= \frac{\Gamma(n+\frac{1}{2})\sqrt{\pi}}{\Gamma(n+1)}\left[1 - \frac{x^2}{4(n+1)} + \frac{x^4}{4.8(n+1)(n+2)} - \dots\right] \qquad \text{...(iv)}$$

We known that [by definition]

$$J_n(x) = \frac{x_a}{2^n\Gamma(n+1)}\left[1 - \frac{x^2}{4(n+1)} + \frac{x^4}{4.8(n+1)(n+2)} - \dots\right] \qquad \text{...(v)}$$

Multiplying both sides of (iv) by $\dfrac{x^n}{2^n\Gamma(n+\frac{1}{2})\sqrt{\pi}}$, we get

$$\frac{x^n}{2^n\Gamma(n+\frac{1}{2})\sqrt{\pi}}\times I = \frac{x^n}{2^n\Gamma(n+1)} \times\left[1 - \frac{x^2}{4(n+1)} + \frac{x^4}{4.8(n+1)(n+2)} - \dots\right] \qquad \text{...(vi)}$$

Using (i) and (v), (vi) becomes

$$\frac{x^n}{2^n \Gamma(n+\frac{1}{2})\sqrt{\pi}} \int_0^{\pi} \cos(x \sin\phi)\cos^{2n}\phi \, d\phi.$$

(ii) Proceed as above.

Ex. 21. *Prove that*

$$\int_0^x t\{J_n(t)\}^2 \, dt = \frac{x^2}{2}\{J_n{}^2(x) - J_{n-1}(x) J_{n+1}(x)'\}$$

$$= \frac{x^2}{2}\{J_n{}^2(x) - J_{n-1}(x) J_{n+1}(x)\}$$

Solution. We know that

$$\frac{d}{dt}\left[\frac{t^2}{2}\left\{J_n{}^2(t) - J_{n-1}(t) J_{n+1}(t)\right\}\right]$$

$$= t\,(J_n^2 - J_{n-1} J_{n+1} + \frac{t^2}{2}[2 J_n J_n' - J'_{n-1} J_{n+1} - J_{n-1} J'_{n+1}]$$

[writing $J_n(t)$ as J_n in short]

$$= t\,(J_n^2 - J_{n-1} J_{n+1}) + \frac{t^2}{2}[J_n (J_{n-1} - J_{n+1})$$

$$-\left(\frac{n-1)}{t}J_{n-1} - J_n\right) J_{n+1} - J_{n-1}\left(-\frac{n+1}{t}J_{n+1} + J_n\right)\Bigg]$$

[Substituting the value of $2J_n'$ from recurrence formula III and the value of $2J'_{n-1}$ and J'_{n+1} obtained by replacing n by $n-1$ and $n+1$ in recurrence formulae I and II respectively].

$$\therefore \frac{d}{dt}\left[\frac{t^2}{2}\{J_n{}^2(t) - J_{-1}(t) J_{n+1}(t)\}\right] = t J_n{}^2(t)$$

Integrating both sides from 0 to x, we get

$$\int_0^x t\{J_n(t)\}^2 \, dt$$

$$= \left[\frac{t^2}{2}\{J_n{}^2(t) - J_{n-1}(t) J_{n+1}(t)\right]_0^x$$

$$= \frac{x^2}{2}\left\{J_n{}^2(x) - J_{n-1}(x) J_{n+1}(x)\right\}$$

Ex. 22. *Using generating function or otherwise, show that*

$$J_n(-x) = (-1)^n J_n(x)$$

Solution. We have

$$\sum_{n=-\infty}^{\infty} J_n(x) z^n = e^{\frac{x}{2}\left(z - \frac{1}{z}\right)} \quad \text{...(i)}$$

Replacing x by $-x$ in (i), we get

$$\sum_{n=-\infty}^{\infty} J_n(-x) x^n = e^{-\frac{x}{2}\left(z - \frac{1}{z}\right)} = e^{\frac{x}{2}\left(-z - \frac{1}{-z}\right)}$$

$$= \sum_{n=-\infty}^{\infty} J_n(x) \cdot (-z)^n \qquad \text{[by (i)]}$$

$$\therefore \sum_{n=-\infty}^{\infty} J_n(-x) z^n = \sum_{n=-\infty}^{\infty} J_n(x) \cdot (-1)^n z^n \qquad \text{...(ii)}$$

Equating the coefficients of z^n from both sides of (ii) gives

$$J_n(-x) = (-1)^n J_n(x).$$

Ex. 23. *If $n > -1$, show that*

$$\int_0^x x^{n+1} J_n(x)\, dx = x^n J_{n-1}(x)$$

Solution. From recurrence formula I, we have

$$\frac{d}{dx}\{x^n J_n(x)\} = x^n J_{n-1}(x) \qquad \text{...(i)}$$

Replacing n by $(n + 1)$ in (i), we get

$$\frac{d}{dx}\{x^{n+1} J_{n+1}(x)\} = x^{n+1} J_n(x) \qquad \text{...(ii)}$$

Integrating (i) w.r.t. 'x' between the limits 0 and x, we get

$$\Big[x^{n+1} J_{n+1}(x) \Big]_0^x = \int_0^x x^{n+1} J_n(x)\, dx$$

or

$$\int_0^x x^{n+1} J_n(x)\, dx = x^{n+1} J_{n+1}(x).$$

Ex. 24. *Show that*

(*a*) $\int_0^x x^{-n} J_{n+1}(x)\, dx = \dfrac{1}{2^n \Gamma(n+1)} - x^{-n} J_n,\ n > 1.$

(*b*) $\int_0^\infty x^{-n} J_{n+1}(x)\, dx = \dfrac{1}{2^n \Gamma(n+1)},\ n > -\frac{1}{2}.$

Solution.

(*a*) From recurrence formula II, we have

$$\frac{d}{dx}[x^{-n} J_n(x)] = -x^{-n} J_{n+1}(x) \qquad \text{...(i)}$$

Integrating (i) w.r.t. 'x' between the limits 0 and x, we get

$$\Big[x^{-n} J_n(x) \Big]_0^x = -\int_0^x x^{-n} J_{n+1}(x)\, dx$$

$$\therefore\ x^{-n} J_n(x) - \lim_{x \to 0} \frac{J_n(x)}{x^n} = -\int_0^x x^{-n} J_{n+1}(x)\, dx \qquad \text{...(ii)}$$

But $\lim_{x \to 0} \dfrac{J_n(x)}{x^n} = \lim_{x \to 0} \dfrac{1}{x^n} \cdot \dfrac{x^n}{2^n \Gamma(n+1)} \left[1 - \dfrac{x^2}{2.2.(n+1)} + \dots \right]$

$$= \frac{1}{2^n \Gamma(n+1)}.$$

Hence (ii) may be written as

$$\int_0^x x^{-n} J_{n+1}(x)\, dx = \frac{1}{2^n \Gamma(n+1)} - x^{-n} J_n(x)$$

(b) Integrating (i) w.r.t. 'x' from 0 to ∞, we get

$$\left[x^{-n} J_n(x) \right]_0^\infty = -\int_0^\infty x^{-n} J_{n+1}(x)\, dx$$

$$\therefore \quad \lim_{x \to 0} \frac{J_n(x)}{x^n} - \lim_{x \to 0} \frac{J_n(x)}{x^n} = -\int_0^\infty x^{-n} J_{n+1}(x)\, dx \qquad \text{...(iii)}$$

As in part *(a)*, $\lim_{x \to 0} \frac{J_{n+1}(x)}{x^n} = \frac{1}{2^n \Gamma(n+1)}$ ...(iv)

We know that for large values of x the approximate value of $J_n(x)$ is given by

$$J_n(x) \sim \left(\frac{2}{\pi x} \right)^{1/2} \cos \left\{ x - \left(n + \frac{1}{2} \right) \frac{\pi}{2} \right\}, n > -\frac{1}{2} \qquad \text{...(v)}$$

Using (v), $\lim_{x \to \infty} \frac{J_n(x)}{x^n} = 0$ ...(vi)

Using (iv) and (vi), (iii) reduces to

$$\int_0^\infty x^{-n} J_{n+1}(x)\, dx = \frac{1}{2^n \Gamma(n+1)}.$$

Ex. 25. *Evaluate* $\int x^3 J_3(x)\, dx$.

Solution. Since $\frac{d}{dx} \{x^{-n} J_n\} = -x^n J_{n+1}$,

$$\therefore \quad \int x^{-n} J_{n+1}\, dx = -x^{-n} J_n \qquad \text{...(i)}$$

Now, $\int x^3 J_3(x)\, dx = \int x^5 (x^{-2} J_3)\, dx$

$$= x^5 (-x^{-2} J_2) - \int 5x^4 (-x^{-2} J_2)\, dx$$

[On integration by parts and using (i) for $n = 2$]

$$= x^3 J_2 + 5 \int x^2 J_2\, dx$$

$$= x^3 J_2 + 5 \int x^3 (x^{-1} J_2)\, dx$$

$$= -x^3 J_2 + 5 \left[x^3 (-x^{-1} J_1) - \int 3x^2 (-x^{-1} J_1)\, dx \right]$$

[on integration by parts and using (i) for $n = 1$]

$$= -x^3 J_2 - 5x^2 J_1 + 15 \int x J_1\, dx$$

$$= -x^3 J_2 - 5x^2 J_1 + 15 \int x(-J_0')\, dx \; [\because J_1 = -J_0']$$

$$= -x^3 J_2 - 5x^2 J_1 - 15 \int x J_0'\, dx$$

$$= -x^3 J_2 - 5x^2 J_1 - 15 \left[x J_0 - \int 1 . J_0\, dx \right]$$

$$= -x^3 J_2 - 5x^2 J_1 - 15x J_0 + 15 \int J_0\, dx.$$

Ex. 26. *Express* $\int x^{-3} J_4(x)\, dx$ *in terms of* J_0 *and* J_1.

Solution. Recurrence formula II is

$$\frac{d}{dx}\{x^{-n} J_n\} = -x^{-n} J_{n+1}$$

Put $n = 3$,

$$\frac{d}{dx}\{x^{-3} J_2\} = -x^{-3} J_4$$

Integrating,

$$\int x^{-3} J_4(x)\, dx = -x^{-3} J_3 + c \quad \text{...(i)}$$

Recurrence formula VI is

$$J_{n+1} = (2n/x) J_n - J_{n-1} \quad \text{...(ii)}$$

Replacing n by 2 and 1 successively in (i) gives

$$J_3 = (6/x) J_2 - J_1 \quad \text{...(iii)}$$

and

$$J_2 = (4/x) J_1 - J_3 \quad \text{...(iv)}$$

Using (iv), (iii) becomes

$$J_3 = (6/x)\,[(4/x) J_1 - J_0] - J_1$$
$$= (24\, x^{-2} - 1) J_1 - (6/x) J_0 \quad \text{...(v)}$$

Using (v), (i) becomes

$$\int x^{-3} J_4(x)\, dx = -x^{-3}\,[(24\, x^{-2} - 1) J_1 - 6x^{-1} J_0] + c.$$

5·9. Second solution of Bessel's Equation

To show that $\gamma_0(x)$, the Bessel's function of the second kind, can be expressed as

$$\gamma_0(x) = J_0 \log x - 2\,[J_2 - \frac{1}{2} J_4 + \frac{1}{3} J_6 - \frac{1}{4} J_8 + \ldots \infty\,].$$

when n = 0, *the Bessel's equation reduces to*

$$\frac{d^2y}{dx^2} + \frac{1}{x}\frac{dy}{dx} + y = 0 \quad \text{...(i)}$$

Again when $n = 0$, the two solutions J_n and J_{-n} become identical, but (*i*) being an equation of second order must have two solutions, one of them is J_0.

Let the other solution be $y = uJ_0(x) + v$.

$$\therefore \quad \frac{dy}{dx} = J_0 \frac{du}{dx} + u\frac{dJ_0}{dx} + \frac{dv}{dx},$$

and

$$\frac{d^2y}{dx^2} = J_0 \frac{d^2u}{dx^2} + \frac{2\,du}{dx}\cdot\frac{dJ_0}{dx}\, u\, \frac{d^2J_0}{dx^2} + \frac{d^2u}{dx^2}$$

Putting the values of y, $\dfrac{dy}{dx}$, $\dfrac{d^2y}{dx^2}$ in (*i*), we get

$$\left(J_0\frac{d^2u}{dx^2} + 2\frac{du}{dx}\cdot\frac{d\,J_0}{dx} + u\frac{d^2J_0}{dx^2} + \frac{d^2v}{dx^2}\right) + \frac{1}{x}\left(J_0\frac{du}{dx} + u\frac{d\,J_0}{dx} + \frac{dv}{dx}\right) + u\,J_0(x) + v = 0$$

or

$$\left(\frac{d^2v}{dx^2} + \frac{1}{x}\frac{dv}{dx} + v\right) + J_0\left(\frac{d^2u}{dx^2} + \frac{1}{x}\frac{du}{dx}\right) + 2\frac{du}{dx}\cdot\frac{d\,J_0}{dx} + u\left(\frac{d^2J_0}{dx^2} + \frac{1}{x}\frac{d\,J_0}{dx} + J_0\right) = 0$$

as J_0 being the solution of (*i*) hence $\dfrac{d^2J_0}{dx^2} + \dfrac{1}{x}\dfrac{dJ_0}{dx} + J_0 = 0$

$$\therefore \quad \left(\frac{d^2u}{dx^2} + \frac{1}{x}\frac{du}{dx} + \text{v}\right) + J_0\left(\frac{d^2u}{dx^2} + \frac{1}{x}\frac{du}{dx}\right) + 2\frac{du}{dx}\cdot\frac{dj_0}{dx} = 0 \quad \text{...(ii)}$$

Putting $u = \log x$, i.e., $\dfrac{du}{dx} = \dfrac{1}{x}, \dfrac{d^2u}{dx^2} = -\dfrac{1}{x^2}$ ..(iii)

becomes

$$\frac{d^2v}{dx^2} + \frac{1}{x}\frac{dv}{dx} + v = -\frac{2}{x}\frac{dJ_0}{dx} = -\frac{2}{x}J_0'$$

$$= -\frac{2}{x}(-J_1) = \frac{2J_1}{x}$$

$$(\because J_0' = -J_1)$$

$$= \frac{2}{x}\left[\frac{2}{x}(2J_2 - 4J_4 + 6J_6 ...)\right]$$

$$= \frac{4}{x^2}\Sigma\,(-1)^{(n/2)-1}\,nJ_n\,,$$

where n is an even integer

$$= \Sigma\,\frac{n^2}{x^2}\left[\frac{4(-1)^{(n/2)-1}}{n}\right]J_n$$

$$= \Sigma\,k_n\frac{n^2}{x^2}J_n\,,\ \text{where } k_n = \left\{\frac{4(-1)^{(n/2)-1}}{n}\right\}.$$

$$\therefore \quad \frac{d^2v}{dx^2} + \frac{1}{x}\frac{dv}{dx} + v = \Sigma k_n\frac{n^2}{x^2}J_n \quad \text{...(iii)}$$

Again J_n is a solution of $\dfrac{d^2y}{dx^2} + \dfrac{1}{x}\dfrac{dy}{dx} + \left\{1 - \dfrac{n^2}{x^2}\right\}y = 0$

Therefore $k_n J_n$ is also a particular solution of above

$$\therefore \quad \frac{d^2y}{dx^2} + \frac{1}{x}\frac{dy}{dx} + y = \left(\frac{n^2}{x^2}\right)k_n J_n \quad \text{...(iv)}$$

Comparing (iii) and (iv) a solution of (iii) is given by

$$\text{v} = \sum k_n J_n = \sum\frac{4}{n}(-1)^{(n/2)-1}J_n\,,\ n \text{ is an even integer}$$

$$= \left[2J_2 - J_4 + \frac{2}{3}J_6 - \frac{1}{4}J_8 + ...\right]$$

Hence the solution of (i) is

$$y = u\,J_0 + \text{v} = J_0(x)\log x + 2\left[J_2 - \frac{1}{2}J_4 + \frac{1}{3}J_6 - \frac{1}{4}J_8 + ...\right]$$

which is denoted by $\gamma_0(x)$.

In case of Bessel's equation of nth order, the second solution is $Y_n(x)$ and the complete primitive is given by

$$\gamma = A J_n(x) + B Y_n(x).$$

5·10. Bessels Function of the third kind (Hankel functions)

Hankel functions are defined as

$$H_n^{(1)}(x) = J_n(x) + i\,\gamma_n(x),\ H_n^{(2)}(x) = J_n(x) - i\,\gamma_n(x)$$

Addition and subtraction of these gives $J_n(x) = \frac{1}{2}\left\{H_n^{(1)}(x) + H_n^{(2)}(x)\right\}$ and

$\gamma_n(x) = -\frac{1}{2}\,i\left\{H_n^{(1)}(x) - H_n^{(2)}(x)\right\}$.

5·11. The modified Bessels's Function

Bessel's differential equation of nth order is

$$\frac{d^2y}{dx^2} + \frac{1}{x}\frac{dy}{dx} + \left(1 - \frac{n^2}{x^2}\right)y = 0 \qquad \text{...(i)}$$

Put $x = iz$, so that $\frac{dx}{dz} = i$, i.e., $\frac{dz}{dx} = \frac{1}{i}$

$$\therefore \quad \frac{dy}{dx} = \frac{dy}{dz}\cdot\frac{dz}{dx} = \frac{1}{i}\frac{dy}{dz}$$

and

$$\frac{d^2y}{dx^2} = \frac{d}{dx}\left(\frac{1}{i}\frac{dy}{dz}\right) = \frac{1}{i}\frac{d^2y}{dz^2}\cdot\frac{dz}{dx}$$

with these substitutions, eqn. (i) becomes

$$-\frac{d^2y}{dz^2} + \frac{1}{iz}\cdot\frac{1}{i}\frac{dy}{dz} + \left\{1 - \frac{n^2}{(iz)^2}\right\}y = 0$$

i.e.,

$$\frac{d^2y}{dz^2} + \frac{1}{z}\frac{dy}{dz} - \left\{1 + \frac{n^2}{z^2}\right\}y = 0 \qquad \text{...(ii)}$$

Since the complete primitive of (i) is $y = A J_n(x) + B \gamma_n(x)$, therefore the solution of (ii) is obtained by putting $x = iz$ and that is

$$y = A J_n(iz) + B Y_n(iz) \qquad \text{...(iii)}$$

Now, we know that

$$J_n(x) = \sum_{r=0}^{\infty} (-1)^r \frac{(x/2)^{n+2r}}{r!(n+r)!}$$

Putting $x = iz$, this becomes

$$J_n(iz) = \sum_{r=0}^{\infty} (-1)^r \frac{(iz)^{n+2r}}{2^{n+2r}\, r!(n+r)!}$$

$$= i^n \sum_{r=0}^{\infty} \frac{z^{n+2r}}{2^{n+2r}\, r!(n+r)!}$$

$\because \quad i^{2r} = (i^2)^r = (-1)^r$ and

therefore $(-1)^r\, i^{2r} = (-1)^{2r} = 1.$

or
$$i^{-n} J_n(iz) = \sum_{r=0}^{\infty} \frac{z^{n+2r}}{2^{n+2r}\, r!\,(n+r)!}$$

Here $i^{-n} J_n(iz)$ is denoted by $I_n(z)$ which is known as the *modified function of the first kind of order n.* Thus replacing z by x, we get

$$I_n(z) = i^{-n} J_n(ix) = \sum_{r=0}^{\infty} \frac{s^{n+2r}}{2^{n+2r}\, r!\,\Gamma(n+r+1)}$$

$$\because \quad (n+r)! = \Gamma(n+r+1)$$

If we put $n = 0$, its particular case is found as

$$I_0(x) = \sum_{r=0}^{\infty} \frac{(x/2)^{2r}}{(r!)^2}$$

$$= 1 + \left(\frac{x}{2}\right)^2 + \frac{(x/2)^4}{(21)^2} + \frac{(x/2)^6}{(31)^2} + \ldots\ldots$$

when n is integer, the *modified function of the second kind,* i.e., $K_n(x)$ is related with this modified function as

$$K_n(x) = \frac{1}{2} \sum_{r=0}^{n-1} (-1)^r \frac{(n-r-1)!}{r!} \left(\frac{2}{x}\right)^{n-2r}$$

$$+ (-1)^{n+1} \sum_{r=0}^{\infty} \frac{(x/2)^{n+2r}}{r!\,(n+r)!}$$

$$\left[\log\frac{x}{2} - \frac{1}{2}\{\Psi(r+1) + \Psi(r+1)\}\right] \qquad \ldots\text{(iv)}$$

where $\psi(r+1) = \left(1 + \frac{1}{2} + \frac{1}{3} + \ldots\ldots + \frac{1}{r}\right) - \gamma$

and $\psi(n+r+1) = \left(1 + \frac{1}{2} + \frac{1}{3} + \ldots\ldots + \frac{1}{n+r}\right) - \gamma$

But if n is not an integer, then

$$K_n(x) = \frac{\pi}{2} \frac{[I_{-n}(x) - I_n(x)]}{\sin n\pi} \qquad \ldots\text{(v)}$$

In particular when n is an integer, we have

$$K_0(x) = -\left\{Y + \log\frac{x}{2}\right\} I_0(x) + \sum_{r=0}^{\infty} \frac{\left(\frac{1}{2}x\right)^{2r}}{(2!)^2} \left\{1 + \frac{1}{2} + \frac{1}{3} + \ldots. + \frac{1}{r}\right\}$$

Hence the complete primitive of the equation (ii) is

$$y = A\, I_n(x) + B\, K_n(x).$$

5·12 The Ber, Bei, Ker, Kei Functions

Suppose we have an equation of the form

$$x \frac{d^2y}{dx^2} + \frac{dy}{dx} - ip^2 xy = 0 \qquad \ldots\text{(i)}$$

This may be written as

$$\frac{d^2y}{dx^2} + \frac{1}{x}\frac{dy}{dx} - (p\sqrt{i})^2\, y = 0$$

Obviously, this is a modified Bessel's equation of the order zero. Hence its solution will be

$$y = A\, I_0\,(x\,p\sqrt{i}) + B\, K_0\,(x\,p\sqrt{i})$$

In order to express this solution in terms of real and imaginery parts, we introduce four new functions namely *Ber* (i.e., Bessel real), *Bei* (i.e., Bessel imaginary), *Ker* and *Kei* are their analogues. These are defined as

$$I_0\,(x\sqrt{i}) = Ber\,(x) + i\,Bei\,(x) \qquad \text{...(ii)}$$

$$K_0\,(x\sqrt{i}) = Ker\,(x) + i\,Kei\,(x) \qquad \text{...(iii)}$$

where

$$Ber\,(x) = \frac{\left(\frac{1}{2}x\right)^4}{(2\,!)^2} + \frac{\left(\frac{1}{2}x\right)^8}{(4\,!)^2} + \ldots \qquad \text{...(iv)}$$

$$Bei\,(x) = \left(\frac{x}{2}\right)^2 - \frac{\left(\frac{1}{2}x\right)^6}{(3\,!)^2} + \frac{\left(\frac{1}{2}x\right)^{10}}{(5\,!)^2} + \ldots \qquad \text{...(v)}$$

5·13. Spherical Bessel Functions

Spherical Bessel functions are defined as solution of differential equation

$$r^2\frac{d^2R}{dr^2} + 2r\frac{dR}{dr} + [\,k^2 r^2 - n\,(n+1)\,]\,R = 0 \qquad \text{...(i)}$$

Equation (i) is the radial equation obtained by seperating the spherical polar coordinates of Helmholtz equation, constant k occurs in Helmholtz equation and the integer n is a seperation constant. This equation (i) can be reduced to Bessels equation by the substitution

$$R\,(kr) = \frac{Z_{n+\frac{1}{2}}\,(kr)}{\sqrt{(kr)}} \qquad \text{...(ii)}$$

Then equation (i) reduces to

$$r^2\frac{d^2Z}{dr^2} + r\frac{dZ}{dr} + \left[k^2 r^2 - \left(n+\frac{1}{2}\right)^2\right] Z = 0 \qquad \text{...(iii)}$$

which is Bessel's equation where Z is Bessel function of $\left(n+\frac{1}{2}\right)^{th}$ order of integer n.

Functions (ii) are called **Spherical Bessel Functions** which are defined as follows in terms of Bessel functions of different kinds:

(a) $j_n\,(x) = \sqrt{\left(\frac{\pi}{2x}\right)}\, J_{n+\frac{1}{2}}\,(x)$

(b) $y_n\,(x) = \sqrt{\left(\frac{\pi}{2x}\right)}\, Y_{n+\frac{1}{2}}\,(x)(-1)^{n+1}\sqrt{\left(\frac{\pi}{2x}\right)}.(x)\,J_{-n-1/2}$

(c) $h_n^{(1)}(x) = \sqrt{\left(\frac{\pi}{2x}\right)} H^{(i)}_{n+\frac{1}{2}} = j_n(x) + i\, y_n(x)$

(d) $h_n^{(2)}(x) = \sqrt{\left(\frac{\pi}{2x}\right)} H^{(2)}_{n+\frac{1}{2}}(x) = j_n(x) + i\, y_n(x)$

We know that

$$j_n(x) = \sum_{r=0}^{\infty} \frac{(-1)^r}{r!\,\Gamma(n+r+1)} \left(\frac{x}{2}\right)^{n+2r}$$

Replacing n by $n + \frac{1}{2}$, we get

$$J_{n+\frac{1}{2}}(x) = \sum_{r=0}^{\infty} \frac{(-1)^r}{r!\,\Gamma(n+r+3/2)} \left(\frac{x}{2}\right)^{n+2r\frac{1}{2}} \qquad \text{...(iv)}$$

Again $$\Gamma\, n + r\, 3/2 = \frac{2^{-2n-2r-1}\pi^{1/2}\,\Gamma(2n+2r+2)}{\Gamma(n+r+1)}$$

$$[\because \Gamma(3+1)\,\Gamma(3+3/2) = 2^{-2z-1}\sqrt{\pi}\,\Gamma\ 2z+2\,]$$

Putting this value in (iv), we have

$$J_{n+\frac{1}{2}}(x) = \sum_{r=0}^{\infty} (-1)^r \frac{(n+r)!\,2^{2n+2r+1}}{\sqrt{\pi}\,(2n+2r+1)!\,r!} \left(\frac{x}{2}\right)^{n+2r+\frac{1}{2}}$$

Putting this expression in (a), we get

$$j_n(x) = \sqrt{\left(\frac{\pi}{2x}\right)} \sum_{r=0}^{\infty} \frac{(-1)^r (n+r)!\,2^{2n+2r+1}}{\sqrt{\pi}\,(2n+2r+1)!\,r!} \left(\frac{x}{2}\right)^{n+2r+\frac{1}{2}}$$

$$= 2^n x^n \sum_{r=0}^{\infty} (-1)^r \frac{(n+r)!}{r!\,(2n+2r+1)!} x^{2r} \qquad \text{...(v)}$$

which is series expansion for $j_n(x)$. In the same manner expansions can be derived for the Spherical Bessel Function of other kinds.

Putting $n = 0$ in (v), we get shperical Bessel functions of zeroeth order

$$j_0(x) = \sum_{r=0}^{\infty} \frac{(-1)^r}{(2r+1)!} x^{2r} = \frac{1}{x} \sum_{r=0}^{\infty} (-1)^r \frac{x^{2r+1}}{(2r+1)!}$$

$$= \frac{\sin x}{x}$$

Recurrence Relations for Spherical Bessel Functions – Recurrence relations for sperical Bessel's function of first kind can be obtained from those of Bessel's function of first kind by putting $n + \frac{1}{2}$ for n and then multiplying with $\sqrt{\left[\frac{\pi}{2x}\right]}$, thus we have

$$J_{n-1}(x) + J_{n+1}(x) = \frac{2n+1}{x} J_n(x) \qquad \text{...(vi)}$$

$$n\,J_{n-1}(x)-(n+1)\,J_{n+1}(x)=(2n+1)\,J_n{}'(x) \quad \text{...(vii)}$$

$$\frac{d}{dx}\left[x^{n+2}\,J_n(x)\right]=x^{n+1}\,J_{n-1}(x) \quad \text{...(viii)}$$

and
$$\frac{d}{dx}\left[x^{-n}\,J_n(x)\right]=x^{-n}\,J_{n+1}(x) \quad \text{...(ix)}$$

Similarly recurrence relations for $y_n(x)$, $h_n^{(1)}(x)$ and $h_n^{(2)}(x)$ can be obtained Again putting $n = 0$ in (ix) we have]

$$\frac{d}{dx}[\,J_0(x)\,]=-J_1(x) \text{ or } J_1(x)=-\frac{d}{dx}\left[\frac{\sin x}{x}\right]$$

$$\left(\because\ J_0(x)=\frac{\sin x}{x}\right)$$

$$=\frac{\sin x}{x^2}-\frac{\cos x}{x} \quad \text{...(x)}$$

Similarly, putting $n = 1$ in (ix), we get

$$x^{-1}\,J_2(x)=-\frac{d}{dx}\left[x^{-1}\,J_1(x)\right]$$

or
$$J_2(x)=\left(\frac{3}{x^3}-\frac{1}{x}\right)\sin x-\frac{3}{x^2}\cos x \quad \text{...(xi)}$$

Repeating this again and again, we get

$$J_n(x)=(-1)^n\,x^n\left(\frac{d}{x\,dx}\right)^n\left(\frac{\sin x}{x}\right) \quad \text{...(xii)}$$

Similarly, we can prove that

$$y_n(x)=-(-1)^n\,x^n\left(\frac{d}{x\,dx}\right)^n\left(\frac{\cos x}{x}\right) \quad \text{...(xiii)}$$

$$h_n^{(1)}(x)=-i\,(-1)^n\,x^n\left(\frac{d}{x\,dx}\right)^n\left(\frac{e^{ix}}{x}\right) \quad \text{...(xiv)}$$

and
$$h_n^{(2)}(x)=i\,(-1)^n\,x^n\left(\frac{d}{x\,dx}\right)^n\left(\frac{e^{ix}}{x}\right) \quad \text{...(xv)}$$

6

Hermite Polynomials

6.1 Hermite's equation and its solution

The differential equation

$$\frac{d^2y}{dx^2} - 2x\frac{dy}{dx} + 2\lambda y = 0, \qquad \text{...(i)}$$

where λ is constant, is called *Hermite's differential equation.*

Let the series solution of (i) is

$$y = \sum_{r=0}^{\infty} a_r x^{k+r} \qquad \text{...(ii)}$$

$$\therefore \quad \frac{dy}{dx} = \sum_{r=0}^{\infty} a_r (k+r) x^{k+r-1}$$

and $$\frac{d^2y}{dx^2} = \sum_{r=0}^{\infty} a_r (k+r)(k+r-1) x^{k+r-2}$$

Substituting in (i), we have

$$\sum_{r=0}^{\infty} a_r [(k+r)(k+r-1) x^{k+r-2} - 2(k+r) x^{k+r} + 2\lambda x^{k+r}] = 0,$$

or $$\sum_{r=0}^{\infty} a_r [(k+r)(k+r-1) x^{k+r-2} - 2(k+r-\lambda) x^{k+r}] = 0 \qquad \text{...(iii)}$$

Now (iii) being an identity, we can equate to zero the coefficients of various powers of x.

Equating to zero the coefficient of lowest power of x, i.e., of x^{k-2}, we get

$$a_0 k (k-1) = 0.$$

Now $a_0 \neq 0$, as it is the coefficient of the first term with which the series is started.

$$\therefore \quad \text{either } k = 0$$
$$\text{or } k = 1 \qquad \text{...(iv)}$$

Equating the coefficient of x^{k-1} in (iii) to zero, we get

$$a_1 (k+1) k = 0 \qquad \text{...(v)}$$

which implies that $a_1 = 0$ or $k = 0$ or both are zero, since $k+1 \neq 0$ for any value of k given by (iv).

Now equating to zero the coefficient of general term, i.e., x^{k+r} in (iii), we get

$$a_{r+2} (k+r+2)(k+r+1) 2a_r (k+r-\lambda) = 0$$

or $$a_{r+2} = \frac{2\,(k+r-\lambda)}{(k+r+2)\,(k+r+1)}\,.\,a_r$$

or $$a_{r+2} = \frac{2\,(k+r)-2\lambda}{(k+r+2)\,(k+r+1)}\,.\,a_r \qquad \text{...(vi)}$$

Now two cases arise—

Case I. when $k = 0$, from (vi), we have

$$a_{r+2} = \frac{2r-2\lambda}{(r+2)\,(r+1)}\,a_r \qquad \text{...(vii)}$$

Putting $r = 0, 2, 4$, etc. in (vii), we have

$$a_2 = \frac{-2\lambda}{2.1}\,a_0 = -\frac{2\lambda}{2\,!}\,a_0$$

$$a_4 = \frac{4-2\lambda}{4.3}\,a_2 = -\frac{(4-2\lambda)\,.\,2\lambda}{4.3.2\,!}\,a_0$$

$$= \frac{2^2\,(-2+\lambda)\,\lambda}{4\,!}\,a_0 = \frac{2^2\,\lambda\,(\lambda-2)}{4\,!}\,a_0$$

and so on.

$$\therefore \qquad a_{2m} = \frac{(-2)^m\,\lambda\,(\lambda-2)\,\ldots\,(\lambda-2m+2)}{(2m)\,!}\,a_0.$$

Again putting $r = 1, 3, 5$, etc.

$$a_3 = \frac{2-2\lambda}{3.2}\,a_1 = -\frac{2\,(\lambda-1)}{3\,!}\,a_1$$

$$a_5 = \frac{6-2\,\lambda}{5.4}\,a_3$$

$$= \frac{-2\,(6-2x)\,(\lambda-1)}{5.4.3}\,a_1$$

$$(-2)^2\,\frac{(\lambda-1)\,(\lambda-3)}{5\,!}\,a_1$$

and so on.

$$\therefore \qquad a_{2m+1} = \frac{(-2)^m\,(\lambda-1)\,(\lambda-3)\,\ldots\,(\lambda-2m+1)}{(2m+1)\,!}\,a_1$$

Now if $a_1 \neq 0$, then we have

$$y = \sum_{r=0}^{\infty} a_r\,x^r$$

$$= a_0 + a_1 x + a_2\,x^2 + a_3\,x^3 + \ldots$$

$$= a_0\left[1 - \frac{2\lambda}{2\,!}\,x^2 + \frac{2^2\lambda\,(\lambda-2)}{4\,!}\,x^4 + \ldots + \frac{(-2)^m\,\lambda\,(\lambda-2)\,\ldots\,(\lambda-2m+2)}{(2m)\,!}\,x^{2m} + \ldots\right]$$

$$+ a_1\left[x - \frac{2\,(\lambda-1)}{3\,!}\,x^3 + \frac{2^2\,(\lambda-1)\,(\lambda-3)}{5\,!}\,x^5 + \ldots + \frac{(-2)^m\,(\lambda-1)\,(\lambda-3)\,\ldots\,(\lambda-2m+1)}{(2m+1)\,!}\,x^{2m+1} + \ldots\right] \qquad \text{...(viii)}$$

and if $a_1 = 0$, then we have

$$y = a_0 \left[1 - \frac{2\lambda}{2!}x^2 + \frac{2^2 \lambda(\lambda-2)}{4!}x^4 + \dots + \frac{(-2)^m \lambda(\lambda-2)\dots(\lambda-2m+2)}{(2m)!}x^{2m} + \dots\right] \quad \dots(ix)$$

$$= y_1 \text{ (say)}.$$

Case II. When $k = 1$, from (vi), we have

$$a_{r+2} = \frac{2(r+1) - 2\lambda}{(r+3)(r+2)} a_r.$$

Putting $r = 1, 3, \dots$ etc.

$$a_3 = a_5 = \text{- - -} = 0 \text{ (each)}.$$

Since in this case from (iv), $a_1 = 0$

Putting $r = 0, 2, 4, \dots$ etc.

$$a_2 = \frac{2 - 2\lambda}{3.2} a_0 = -\frac{2(\lambda-1)}{3!} a_0$$

$$a_4 = \frac{6 - 2\lambda}{5.4} a_2 = \frac{2(\lambda-1)(\lambda-3)}{3!} a_0$$

and so on.

$$\therefore \quad a_{2m} = \frac{(-2)^m (\lambda-1)(\lambda-3)\dots(\lambda-2m+1)}{(2m+1)!} a_0$$

$\therefore$ we have

$$y = \sum_{r=0}^{\infty} a_r x^{r+1}$$

$$= a_0 x + a_2 x^3 + a_4 x^5 + \dots + a_{2m} x^{2m+1} + \dots$$

$$= a_0 \left[x - \frac{2(\lambda-1)}{3!}x^3 + \frac{2^2(\lambda-1)(\lambda-3)}{5!}x^5 + \dots + \frac{(-2)^m (\lambda-1)(\lambda-3)\dots(\lambda-2m+1)}{(2m+1)!}x^{2m+1} + \dots\right]$$

$$= y_2 \text{ (say)} \quad \dots(x)$$

From (viii) and (x) it is obvious that (x) is the part of solution, given by (viii). But as the two are the solutions of the same equations so (x) must not be the part of solution (viii).

$\therefore$ $a_1 = 0$ and the solution in the case $k = 0$ must be given by (ix).

Hence the general solution of Hermite's equation is

$$y = Ay_1 + By_2,$$

where A and B are arbitrary constants and y_1, y_2 are given by (ix) and (x).

6.2 Hermite's Polynomials

When λ is an even integer, equation (ix) gives an even polynomial of degree n.

Let $\lambda = n$, n is an even integer

and $$a_0 = (-1)^{n/2} \frac{n!}{\left(\frac{n}{2}\right)!}$$

$\therefore$ Coefficient of x^n in (ix) is

$$(-1)^{n/2} \frac{n!}{\left(\frac{n}{2}\right)!} \cdot \frac{(-2)^{n/2} n(n-2) \dots (n-n+2)}{n!}$$

$$= \frac{2^n \cdot \frac{n}{2}\left(\frac{n}{2}-1\right) \dots 1}{(n/2)!} = 2^n .$$

Similarly coefficient of x^{n-2}

$$= (-1)^{n/2} \frac{n!}{(n/2)!} \frac{(-2)^{(n-2)/2} n(n-2) \dots (n-n+2+2)}{(n-2)!}$$

$$= -\frac{2^{n-2} n(n-1)\, n/2\, (n/2-1) \dots 2}{(n/2)!}$$

$$= -\frac{n(n-1)}{1!} 2^{n-2}$$

and so on.

So value of y is given by

$$y_n = (2x)^2 - \frac{n(n-1)}{1!}(2x)^{n-2} + \frac{n(n-1)(n-2)(n-3)}{2!}(2x)^{n-4} + \dots + (-1)^{n/2} \frac{n!}{(n/2)!}$$

This value of y is known as the *Hermite's polynomial* of degree n and is written as

$$H_n(x) = (2x)^n - \frac{n(n-1)}{1!}(2x)^{n-2} + \frac{n(n-1)(n-2)(n-3)}{2!}(2x)^{n-4} + \dots + (-1)^{n/2} \frac{n!}{(n/2)!}.$$

or $$H_n(x) = \sum_{r=0}^{(n/2)} (-1)^r \frac{n!}{r!(n-2r)!}(2x)^{n-2r}$$

where $$\left(\frac{n}{2}\right) = \begin{cases} n/2 & \text{if } n \text{ is even} \\ \frac{1}{2}(n-1) & \text{if } n \text{ is odd} \end{cases}$$

6.3 Generating Functions

To prove $$e^{2tx-t^2} = \sum_{n=0}^{\infty} \frac{t^n}{n!} H_n(x).$$

We have

$$e^{2tx-t^2} = e^{2tx} e^{-t^2}$$

$$= \sum_{r=0}^{\infty} \frac{(2tx)^r}{r!} \cdot \sum_{s=0}^{\infty} \frac{(-t^2)^s}{s!}$$

$$= \sum_{r=0,\, s=0}^{\infty} (-1)^s \frac{(2x)^r}{r!\,s!} \cdot t^{r+2s}$$

Coefficient of t^n (for fixed value of s)
[obtained by putting $r+2s = n$, i.e., $r = n-2s$]

$$= (-1)^s \frac{(2x)^{n-2s}}{(n-2s)!\,s!}$$

The total value of coefficient of t^n is obtained by summing over all allowed values of s, and since $r = n - 2s$

$\therefore \quad n - 2s \geq 0$ or $s \leq n/2$

Thus if n is even s goes from 0 to $n/2$ and if n is odd, s goes from 0 to $(n-1)/2$.

$$\therefore \text{ Coefficient of } t^n = \sum_{s=0}^{(n/2)} (-1)^s \frac{(2x)^{n-2s}}{(n-2s)!\,s!}$$

$$= \frac{H_n(x)}{n!}$$

$$\text{Hence } e^{2tx-t^2} = \sum_{n=0}^{\infty} \frac{t^n}{n!} H_n(x)$$

$$\text{or } e^{x^2-(t-x)^2} = \sum_{n=0}^{\infty} \frac{t^n}{n!} H_n(x)$$

6.4 Other form for the Hermite Polynomials

$$\mathbf{H}_n(x) = 2^n \left\{ \exp\left(-\frac{1}{4}\frac{d^2}{dx^2}\right) x^n \right\}$$

We have

$$\frac{1}{2}\frac{d}{dx} e^{2tx} = t\, e^{2tx} \quad \text{...(i)}$$

$$\frac{d}{dx}\left(\frac{1}{2}\frac{d}{dx} e^{2tx}\right) = 2t^2 e^{2tx}$$

$$\therefore \quad \frac{1}{2}\frac{d}{dx}\left(\frac{1}{2}\frac{d}{dx} e^{2tx}\right) = t^2 e^{2tx}$$

$$\text{or} \quad \left(\frac{1}{2}\frac{d}{dx}\right)^2 e^{2tx} = t^2 e^{2tx}$$

$$\therefore \quad \left(\frac{1}{2}\frac{d}{dx}\right)^n e^{2tx} = t^2 e^{2tx} \quad \text{...(ii)}$$

Hence

$$\left\{ \exp\left(-\frac{1}{4}\frac{d^2}{dx^2}\right) \right\} e^{2tx}$$

$$= \left[\sum_{n=0}^{\infty} \frac{1}{n!} \left(-\frac{1}{4}\frac{d^2}{dx^2}\right)^n \right] e^{2tx}$$

$$= \left[\sum_{n=0}^{\infty} \frac{1}{n!}\left(-\frac{1}{4}\frac{d^2}{dx^2}\right)^n\right] e^{2tx}$$

$$= \sum_{n=0}^{\infty} \frac{(-1)^n}{n!}\left(\frac{1}{2}\frac{d}{2x}\right)^{2n} e^{2tx}$$

$$= \sum_{n=0}^{\infty} \frac{(-1)^n}{n!} t^{2n} e^{2tx} \text{ [from (ii)]}$$

$$= e^{2tx} \sum_{n=0}^{\infty} \frac{(-1)^n}{n!} t^{2n}$$

$$= e^{2tx} . e^{-t^2} = e^{-t^2+2tx}$$

or

$$\left\{\exp.\left(-\frac{1}{4}\frac{d^2}{dx^2}\right)\right\} \sum_{n=0}^{\infty} \frac{1}{n!}(2tx)^n$$

$$= \sum_{n=0}^{\infty} \frac{t^n}{n!} H_n(x)$$

Equating the coefficient of t^n from the two sides, we have

$$\left\{\exp.\left(-\frac{1}{4}\frac{d^2}{dx^2}\right)\right\} \frac{1}{n!} 2^n x^n = \frac{1}{n!} H_n(x)$$

or

$$H_n(x) = 2^n \left\{\exp.\left(-\frac{1}{4}\frac{d^2}{dx^2}\right)\right\} x^n.$$

6.5 The Rodrigues Formula for $H_n(x)$

$$H_n(x) = (-1)^n e^{x^2} \frac{d^n}{dx^n}\left(e^{-x^2}\right)$$

We have $e^{2tx-t^2} = \sum_{n=0}^{\infty} \frac{H_n(x)}{n!} t^n$

or

$$e^{x^2-(t-x)^2} = \frac{H_0(x)}{0!} t^0 + \frac{H_1(x)}{1!} t + \frac{H_2(x)}{2!} t^2 + \ldots + \frac{H_n(x)}{n!} t^n + \frac{H_{n+1}(x)}{(n+1)!} t^{n+1} + \ldots$$

Differentiating both sides, partially with respect to t, n times and then putting $t = 0$, we have

$$\frac{H_n(x)}{n!} n! = \left[\frac{\partial^n}{\partial t^n} e^{-(t-x)^2}\right]_{t=0} e^{x^2}$$

Now let $t - x = \mu$, i.e., at $t = 0$, $x = -\mu$

$$\therefore \quad \frac{\partial}{\partial t} \equiv \frac{\partial}{\partial \mu}$$

or $$\left[\frac{\partial^n}{\partial t^n} e^{-(t-x)^2}\right]_{t=0} = \frac{\partial^n}{\partial \mu^n}\left(e^{-\mu^2}\right)$$

$$= (-1)^n \frac{\partial^n}{\partial x^n}\left(e^{-x^2}\right) = (-1)^n \frac{d^n}{dx^n}\left(e^{-x^2}\right) \qquad \left(\because \mu = -x \text{ at } t = 0\right)$$

$$\therefore \quad H_n(x) = (-1)^n . e^{x^2} \frac{d^n}{dx^n}\left(e^{-x^2}\right)$$

6.6 First few Hermite Polynomids

From Rodrigues Formula for $H_n(x)$

$$H_n(x) = (-1)^n e^{x^2} . \frac{d^n}{dx^n}\left(e^{-x^2}\right)$$

Putting $n = 0, 1, 2, 3, \ldots$ we get

$$H_0(x) = e^{x^2} . e^{-x^2} = 1$$

$$H_1(x) = (-1) e^{x^2} \frac{d}{dx}\left(e^{-x^2}\right) = 2x$$

$$H_2(x) = (-1)^2 e^{x^2} \frac{d^2}{dx^2}\left(e^{-x^2}\right) = e^{x^2} \frac{d}{dx}\left(-2xe^{-x^2}\right)$$

$$= e^{x^2}\left(4x^2 e^{-x^2} - 2e^{-x^2}\right)$$

$$= (4x^2 - 2).$$

$$H_3(x) = (-1)^3 e^{x^2} \frac{d^3}{dx^3}\left(e^{-x^2}\right)$$

$$= -e^{x^2} \frac{d}{dx}\left\{(4x^2-2)\, e^{-x^2}\right\}$$

$$= -e^{x^2}\left\{-2x\,(4x^2-2)\, e^{-x^2} + 8xe^{-x^2}\right\}$$

$$= -e^{x^2}\left\{(-8x^3 + 12x)e^{-x^2}\right\} = 8x^3 - 12x.$$

Similarly, $$H_4(x) = 16x^4 - 48x^2 + 12 \text{ etc.}$$

6.7 Orthogonal Properties of Hermite Polynomials

$$\int_{-\infty}^{\infty} e^{-x^2} \mathbf{H}_n(x)\, \mathbf{H}_m(x)\, dx = \begin{cases} \mathbf{0}, & \text{if } m \neq n \\ \sqrt{\pi}\, 2^2\, (n)\,! & \text{if } m = n \end{cases}$$

We have $$e^{-t^2 + 2tx} = \sum_{n=0}^{\infty} H_n(x) \frac{t^n}{n!}$$

and $$e^{-s^2+2sx} = \sum_{m=0}^{\infty} H_m(x) \frac{s^m}{m!}$$

$$\therefore \quad e^{-t^2 + 2tx}\, e^{-s^2+2sx} = \sum_{n=0}^{\infty} H_n(x) \frac{t^n}{n!} \sum_{m=0}^{\infty} H_m(x) \frac{s^m}{m!}$$

$\therefore \quad \frac{1}{n!\,m!} H_n(x) H_m(x)$=Coeff. of $t^n s^m$ in the expansion of $e^{-t^2 + 2tx}\, e^{-s^2 + 2sx}$

$\therefore \quad \int_{-\infty}^{\infty} e^{-x^2} H_n(x) H_m(x)\,dx$ is equal to n ! m ! times the coefficient of $t^n s^m$ in the expansion of

$$\int_{-\infty}^{\infty} e^{-x^2} . e^{-t^2+2tx} . e^{-s^2+2sx}\,dx$$

Now,

$$\int_{-\infty}^{\infty} e^{-x^2} . e^{-t^2+2tx} . e^{-s^2+2sx}\,dx$$
$$= e^{-t^2-s^2} \int_{-\infty}^{\infty} e^{-x^2+2tx+2sx}\,dx$$
$$= e^{-t^2-s^2} \int_{-\infty}^{\infty} e^{-\left[x^2-(t+s)^2+(t+s)^2\right]}dx$$
$$= e^{2ts} \int_{-\infty}^{\infty} e^{-[x-(t+x)]^2}\,dx$$
$$= e^{2ts} \int_{-\infty}^{\infty} e^{-u^2}\,du, \qquad \text{putting } x-(t+s)=u$$
$$= e^{2ts}\sqrt{\pi},$$

$$\text{since} \int_{-\infty}^{\infty} e^{-u^2}\,du = \sqrt{\pi}$$

$$= \sqrt{\pi}\left[1+2ts+\frac{(2ts)^2}{2!}+\ldots+\frac{(2ts)^n}{n!}+\ldots\right]$$

Coefficient of $t^n s^m$ in the expansion of

$$\int_{-\infty}^{\infty} e^{-x^2} e^{-t2+2tx} e^{-s^2+2sx}\,dx$$

is $\quad 0 \qquad$ if $m \neq n$

and $\quad \dfrac{2n\sqrt{\pi}}{n!} \qquad$ if m = n.

We can also write is an follows

$$\int_{-\infty}^{\infty} e^{-x^2} H_n(x) H_m(x)\,dx = \sqrt{\pi}\, 2^n\, n!\,\delta_{mn},$$

where δ_{nm} is Kronecker delta defined as

$$\partial_{mn} = \begin{cases} 0, & \text{if } m \neq n \\ 1, & \text{if } m = n \end{cases}$$

6.8 Recurrence formulae for Hermite Polynomials

(I) $\qquad H_n'(x) = 2n\,H_{n-1}(x) \qquad$ for $n \geq 1$

We have
$$\sum_{n=0}^{\infty} \frac{H_n(x)}{n!} t^n = e^{-t2+2tx}$$

Differentiating both sides with respect to x, we have

$$\sum_{n=0}^{\infty} \frac{H_n'(x)}{n!} t^n = e^{-t2+2tx}\, 2t$$

$$= 2t \sum_{n=0}^{\infty} \frac{H_n(x)}{n!} t^n$$

$$= 2 \sum_{n=0}^{\infty} \frac{H_{n-1}(x)}{(n-1)!} t^{n+1}$$

$$= 2 \sum_{n=1}^{\infty} \frac{H_{n-1}(x)}{(n-1)!} t^n$$

Equating the coeffiicient of t^n, on both the sides, we have

$$\frac{H'_n(x)}{n!} = 2 \frac{H_{n-1}(x)}{(n-1)!}$$

i.e., $H'_n(x) = 2n H_{n-1}(x)$

(II) $2x H_n(x) = 2n H_{n-1}(x) + H_{n+1}(x)$

We have $\sum_{n=0}^{\infty} \frac{H'_n(x)}{n!} t^n = e^{-t^2+2tx}$

Differentiating both sides with respect to t, we get

$$\sum_{n=0}^{\infty} \frac{H_n(x)}{n!} nt^{n-1} = e^{-t^2+2tx}(-2t+2x)$$

or $$\sum_{n=1}^{\infty} \frac{H_n(x)}{(n-1)!} t^{n-1} = -2t\, e^{-t^2+2tx} + 2x\; e^{-t^2+2tx}$$

or $$\sum_{n=1}^{\infty} \frac{H_n(x)}{(n-1)!} t^{n-1} = -2t \sum_{n=0}^{\infty} \frac{H_n(x)}{n!} t^n + 2x \sum_{n=0}^{\infty} \frac{H_n(x)}{n!} t^n$$

(Since term of L.H.S. Corresponding to $n = 0$ is zero)

or $$2x \sum_{n=0}^{\infty} \frac{H_n(x)}{n!} t^n = 2 \sum_{n=0}^{\infty} \frac{H_n(x)}{n!} t^{n+1} \sum_{n=1}^{\infty} \frac{H_n(x)}{(n-1)!} t^{n-1}$$

or $$2x \sum_{n=0}^{\infty} \frac{H_n(x)}{n!} t^n = 2 \sum_{n=1}^{\infty} \frac{H_{n-1}(x)}{(n-1)!} t^n \sum_{n=0}^{\infty} \frac{H_{n+1}(x)}{n!} t^n$$

Equating the coefficient of t^n, on the two sides, we have

$$2x \frac{H_n(x)}{n!} = 2 \frac{H_{n-1}(x)}{(n-1)!} + \frac{H_{n+1}(x)}{n!}$$

or $\mathbf{2x\, H_n(x) = 2n\, H_{n-1}(x) + H_{n+1}(x)}$

(III) $\mathbf{H'_n(x) = 2x\, H_n(x) - H_{n+1}(x)}$

Writing recurrence formulae I and II, we have

$$H'_n(x) = 2n H_{n-1}(x) \quad \text{...(i)}$$

and $$2x H_n(x) = 2n H_{n-1}(x) + H_{n+1}(x) \quad \text{...(ii)}$$

Subtracting (ii) from (i), we have

$\mathbf{H_n'(x) = 2x\, H_n(x) - H_{n+1}(x)}$

(IV) $\mathbf{H_n''(x) - 2x\, H_n'(x) + 2n\, H_n(x) = 0}$

Hermite's differential equation is

$$\frac{d^2y}{dx^2} - 2x \frac{dy}{dx} + 2ny = 0 \quad \text{...(i)}$$

Since $H_n(x)$ is the solution of (i), hence, we have

$$\mathbf{H_n''(x) - 2x\, H_n'(x) + 2n\, H_n(x) = 0}$$

Illustrative Examples

Ex. 1. *Evaluate*

$$\int_{-\infty}^{\infty} x\, e^{-x^2} H_n(x)\, H_m(x)\, dx$$

Solution. From recurrence formula II, we have

$$x\, H_n(x) = n\, H_{n-1}(x) + \frac{1}{2} H_{n+1}(x)$$

$$\therefore \quad \int_{-\infty}^{\infty} x\, e^{-x^2} H_n\, H_m(x)\, dx$$

$$= \int_{-\infty}^{\infty} e^{-x^2} \left\{ nH_{n-1}(x) + \frac{1}{2} H_{n+1}(x) \right\} H_m(x)\, dx$$

$$= n \int_{-\infty}^{\infty} e^{-x^2} H_{n-1}(x)\, H_m(x)\, dx + \frac{1}{2} \int_{-\infty}^{\infty} e^{-x^2} H_{n+1}(x)\, H_m(x)\, dx$$

$$= n\sqrt{\pi}\, 2^{n-1} (n-1)!\, \delta_{n-1,m} + \frac{1}{2} \sqrt{\pi}\, 2^{n+1} (n+1)!\, \delta_{n+1,m}$$

$$= \sqrt{\pi}\, 2^{n-1}\, n!\, \delta_{n-1,m} + \sqrt{\pi}\, 2n\, (n+1)!\, \delta_{n+1,m}$$

where δ is Kronecker delta.

Ex. 2. *Prove that* $H_n'' = 4n(n-1) H_{n-1}$

Solution From recurrence formula I, we have

$$H_n' = 2n\, H_{n-1} \qquad \text{...(i)}$$

Differentiating with respect to x, we have

$$H_n'' = 2n\, H_{n-1}' \qquad \text{...(ii)}$$

Replacing n by $(n-1)$ in (i), we have

$$H'_{n-1} = 2(n-1)\, H_{n-2} \qquad \text{...(iii)}$$

$\therefore$ From (ii) and (iii), we have

$$H_n'' = 4n(n-1)\, H_{n-1}$$

Ex. 3. *Prove that, if* $m < n$

$$\frac{d^m}{dx^m}\{H_n(x)\} = \frac{2^m\, n!}{(n-m)!} H_{n-m}(x)$$

Solution We have

$$\sum_{n=0}^{\infty} \frac{t^n}{n!} H_n(x) = e^{-t^2 + 2tx} \qquad \text{...(i)}$$

$$\therefore \quad \sum_{n=0}^{\infty} \frac{t^n}{n!} \frac{d^m}{dx^m}\{H_n(x)\} = \frac{d^m}{dx^m} e^{-t^2 + 2tx}$$

$$= (2t)^m e^{-t^2 + 2tx}$$

$$= (2t)^m \sum_{n=0}^{\infty} \frac{t^n}{n!} H_n(x) \text{ from (i)}$$

$$= 2m \sum_{n=0}^{\infty} \frac{1}{n\,!} t^{n+m} H_n(x)$$

Putting $n+m = r$, $n = r-m$, for $n = 0$;
$r = m$, for $n = \infty$, $r = \infty$

$$= 2^m \sum_{r=m}^{\infty} \frac{1}{(r-m)\,!} t^r H_{r-m}(x)$$

Equating the coefficient of t^n from the two sides, we have

$$\frac{1}{n\,!} \frac{d^m}{dx^m} \{H_n(x)\} = 2^m \frac{1}{(n-m)\,!} H_{n-m}(x)$$

$$\therefore \quad \frac{d^m}{dx^m} \{H_n(x)\} = \frac{2^m\, n\,!}{(n-m)\,!} H_{n-m}(x)$$

Ex. 4. *Prove that (i)* $H_{2n}(o) = (-1)^n \cdot \frac{(2n)\,!}{n\,!}$ *and (ii)* $H_{2n+1}(o) = 0$

Solution We have

$$\sum_{n=0}^{\infty} \frac{t^n}{n\,!} H_n(x) = e^{-t^2 + 2tx}$$

Putting $x = 0$

$$\sum_{n=0}^{\infty} \frac{t^n}{n\,!} H_n(o) = e^{-t^2}$$

$$= \left[1 - t^2 + \frac{(t^2)^2}{2\,!} + \ldots + (-1)^n \frac{(t^2)^n}{n\,!} + \ldots\right] \quad \ldots(i)$$

(i) Equating the coefficients of t^{2n}, on the two sides, we have

$$\frac{1}{(2n)\,!} H_{2n}(o) = (-1)^n \frac{1}{n\,!}$$

$$\therefore \quad H_{2n}(o) = (-1)^n \frac{(2n)\,!}{n\,!}$$

(ii) Again equating the coefficients of t^{2n+1}, on the two sides of (i), we have

$$\frac{1}{(2n+1)\,!} H_{2n+1}(o) = 0$$

[Since R.H.S. of (i) do not involve odd powers of t]

Hence $H_{2n+1}(o) = 0$

Ex. 5. *Show that*

$$\sum_{k=0}^{n} \frac{H_k(x) H_k(y)}{2^k\, k!} = \frac{H_{n+1}(y) H_n(x) - H_{n+1}(x) H_n(y)}{2^{n+1}\, n\,!\,(y-x)}$$

Solution. From recurrence formula II, we have

$$x H_n(x) = n H_{n-1} + \frac{1}{2} H_{n+1}(x) \quad \ldots(i)$$

$$\therefore \quad y H_n(y) = n H_{n-1}(y) + \frac{1}{2} H_{n+1}(y) \quad \ldots(ii)$$

Multiplying (ii) by $H_n(x)$ and (i) by $H_n(y)$ and then subtracting, we have

$$(y-x)\,H_n(x)\,H_n(y) = \frac{1}{2}\,[\,H_{n+1}(y)\,H_n(x) - H_{n+1}(x)\,H_n(y)]$$
$$-n\,[H_{n-1}(x)\,H_n(y) - H_{n-1}(y)\,H_n(x)] \quad ...(iii)$$

Putting $n = 0, 1, 2, 3, ..., (n-1), n$ in (iii), we have

$$(y-x)\,H_0(x)\,H_0(y) = \frac{1}{2}\,(H_1(y)\,H_0(x) - H_1(x)\,H_0(y)] = 0 \quad ...(1)$$

$$(y-x)\,H_1(x)\,H_1(y) = \frac{1}{2}\,[H_2(y)\,H_1(x) - H_2(x)\,H_1(y)]$$
$$-1\,[H_0(x)\,H_1(x) - H_0(y)\,H_1(x)] \quad ...(2)$$

$$(y-x)\,H_2(x)\,H_2(y) = \frac{1}{2}\,[H_3(y)\,H_2(x) - H_3(x)\,H_2(y)]$$
$$-2\,[H_1(x)\,H_2(y) - H_1(y)\,H_2(x)] \quad ...(3)$$

$$(y-x)\,H_3(x)\,H_3(y) = \frac{1}{2}\,[H_4(y)\,H_3(x) - H_4(x)\,H_3(y)]$$
$$-3\,[H_2(x)\,H_3(y) - H_2(y)\,H_3(x)] \quad ...(4)$$

- -

- -

- -

$$(y-x)\,H_{n-1}(x)\,H_{n-1}(y) = \frac{1}{2}\,[H_n(y)\,H_{n-1}(x) - H_n(x)\,H_{n-1}(y)]$$
$$-(n-1)\,[H_{n-2}(x)\,H_{n-1}(y) - H_{n-2}(y)\,H_{n-1}(x)] \quad ...(n-1)$$

$$(y-x)\,H_n(x)\,H_n(y) = \frac{1}{2}\,[\,H_{n+1}(y)\,H_n(x) - H_{n+1}(x)\,H_n(y)]$$
$$-n\,[H_{n-1}(x)\,H_n(y) - H_{n-1}(y)\,H_n(x)] \quad ...(n)$$

Multiplying (1), (2), (3), ... $(n-1)$, (n) by

$$1, \frac{1}{2.1\,!}, \frac{1}{2^2.2\,!}, \frac{1}{2^3.3\,!}, \ldots \frac{1}{2^{n-1}\,(n-1)}, \frac{1}{2^n.n\,!}$$

respectively and adding, we have

$$(y-x)\sum_{k=0}^{n} \frac{H_k(x)\,H_k(y)}{2^k\,k\,!} = \frac{H_{n+1}(y)\,H_n(x) - H_{n+1}(x)\,H_n(y)}{2^{n+1}\,n\,!}$$

$$\therefore \quad \sum_{k=0}^{n} \frac{H_k(x)\,H_k(y)}{2^k\,k\,!} = \frac{H_{n+1}(y)\,H_n(x) - H_{n+1}(x)\,H_n(y)}{2^{n+1}\,n\,!}$$

Ex. 6. *Prove that* $P_n(x) = \frac{2}{\sqrt{\pi}\,.\,n\,!}\int_0^\infty t^n\,e^{-t^2}\,H_n(xt)\,dt$

Solution. We have

$$H_n(x) = \sum_{r=0}^{(n/2)} (-1)^r \frac{n\,!}{r\,!\,(n-2r)}\,(2x)^{n-2r}$$

$$\therefore \quad H_n(xt) = \sum_{r=0}^{(n/2)} (-1)^r \frac{n\,!}{r\,!\,(n-2r)\,!}\,(2xt)^{n-2r}$$

$$\therefore \quad \frac{2}{\sqrt{\pi}\,n\,!}\int_0^\infty t^n\,e^{-t^2}\,H_n(xt)\,dt$$

$$= \frac{2}{\sqrt{\pi}\,.\,n\,!}\int_0^{\infty} t^n e^{-t^2} \sum_{r=0}^{(n/2)} (-1)^r \frac{n\,!}{r\,!\,(n-2r)\,!}(2xt)^{n-2r}.dt$$

$$= \sum_{r=0}^{(n/2)} \frac{2^{n-2r+1}\,(1)^r\,x^{n-2r}}{\sqrt{\pi}\;r\,!\,(n-2r)\,!}\int_0^{\infty} e^{-t^2}\, t^{2\left(n+r+\frac{1}{2}\right)-1}\,dt$$

$$= \sum_{r=0}^{(n/2)} \frac{2^{n-2r+1}\,(1)^r\,x^{n-2r}}{\sqrt{\pi}\;r\,!\,(n-2r)\,!}\,\frac{1}{2}\,\Gamma\left(n-r+\frac{1}{2}\right)$$

$$\left[\text{Since } 2\int_0^{\infty} e^{-t^2}\, t^{(2n-1)}\,dt = \Gamma(n)\right]$$

$$= \sum_{r=0}^{(n/2)} \frac{2^{n-2r}\,(-1)^r\,x^{n-2r}\,[2\,(n-r)]\,!}{\sqrt{\pi}\;r\,!\,(n-2r)\,!\,2^{2(n-r)}\,(n-r)\,!}\sqrt{\pi}$$

$$\left[\text{Since } \Gamma\left(x+\frac{1}{2}\right) = \frac{(2x)\,!}{2^{2x}\,x\,!}\sqrt{\pi}\right]$$

$$= \sum_{r=0}^{(n/2)} (-1)^r \frac{(2n-2r)\,!}{2^n\,(r)\,!\,(n-2r)\,!\,(n-r)\,!} = P_n(x)$$

Hence,

$$P_n(x)\,\frac{2}{\sqrt{\pi}\;n\,!}\int_0^{\infty} t^n e^{-t^2} H_n(xt)\,dt.$$

EXERCISE–6

1. Prove that

$$H_n(x) = 2^{n+1} e^{x^2}\int_x^{\infty} e^{-t^2}\, t^{n+1}\, P_n\left(\frac{x}{t}\right) dt.$$

2. Show that $H_1(x) = 2x\,H_0(x)$.
3. Prove that $H_5(x) = 32x^5 - 160\,x^3 + 120x$.
4. Show that

$$\int_{-\infty}^{\infty} x^2 e^{-x^2}\{H_n(x)\}^2\,dx$$

$$= \sqrt{\pi}\;2^n\,n\,!\,\left(n+\frac{1}{2}\right).$$

5. For what value of n, $H_n(o) = 0$.

7

Laguerre and Chebyshev Polynomials

7.1 Laguerre's Differential Equation and its solution

The differential equation

$$x\frac{d^2y}{dx^2}+(1-x)\frac{dy}{dx}+\lambda y=0 \qquad \text{...(i)}$$

Where λ is a constant, is called *Laguerre's differential equation.*

To solve this equation, let

$$y=\sum_{r=0}^{\infty} a_r\, x^{k+r} \qquad \text{...(ii)}$$

be the solution of the equation (i).

$$\therefore \qquad \frac{dy}{dx}=\sum_{r=0}^{\infty} a_r\,(k+r)\,x^{k+r-1}$$

and

$$\frac{d^2y}{dx^2}=\sum_{r=0}^{\infty} a_r\,(k+r)\,(k+r-1)\,x^{k+r-2}$$

Substituting in (i), we get

$$\sum_{r=0}^{\infty} a_r\,[(k+r)\,(k+r-1)\,x^{k+r-1}+(1-x)\,(k+r)\,x^{k+r-1}+\lambda x^{k+r}]=0$$

or

$$\sum_{r=0}^{\infty} a_r[\,(k+r)^2\,x^{k+r-1}-(k+r-\lambda)\,x^{k+r}]=0 \qquad \text{...(iii)}$$

Now (iii) being an identity, we can equate the coefficients of various powers of x to zero.

Equating to zero the coefficient of lowest power of x, i.e., of x^{k-1}, we have

$$a_0\,k^2=0$$

Now, $a_0 \neq 0$, as it is the coefficient of the first term with which the series is started.

$$\therefore \qquad k=0.$$

Equating to zero the coefficient of general term, i.e., of x^{k+r}, we have

$$a_{r+1}\,(k+r+1)^2-a_r\,(k+r-\lambda)=0$$

$$\therefore \qquad a_{r+1}=\frac{(k+r-\lambda)}{(k+r+1)^2}\,a_r$$

for $k=0$

$$a_{r+1}=\frac{r-\lambda}{(r+1)^2}\,a_r \qquad \text{....(iv)}$$

Putting $r = 0, 1, 2, \ldots$, in (iv), we have

$$a_1 = -\frac{\lambda}{1} a_0 = (-1)\,\lambda a_0$$

$$a_2 = \frac{1-\lambda}{2^2} a_1 = (-1)^2 \frac{\lambda(\lambda-1)}{(2\,!)^2} a_0$$

$$a_3 = \frac{2-\lambda}{3^2} \cdot a_2 = (-1)^3 \frac{\lambda(\lambda-1)(\lambda-2)}{(3\,!)^2} a_0 \text{ etc.}$$

Hence $$a_r = (1)^r \frac{\lambda(\lambda-1)(\lambda-2)\ldots(\lambda-r+1)}{(r\,!)^2} a_0$$

$\therefore$ From (ii), we have

$$y = \sum_{r=0}^{\infty} a^r x^r = a_0 + a_1 x + a_2 x^2 + \ldots + a_r x^r + \ldots$$

$$= a_0 \left[1 - \lambda x + \frac{\lambda(\lambda-1)}{(2\,!)^2} x^2 - \frac{\lambda(\lambda-1)(\lambda-2)}{(3\,!)^2} x^3 + \ldots + (-1)^r \frac{\lambda(\lambda-1)\ldots(\lambda-r+1)}{(r\,!)^2} x^r + \ldots\right] \quad \ldots(\text{v})$$

If $\lambda = n$

$$y = a_0 \left[1 - \frac{n}{1^2} \cdot x + \frac{n(n-1)}{(2\,!)^2} x^2 + \ldots + (-1)^2 \frac{n(n-1)\ldots(n-r+1)}{(r\,!)^2}\right]$$

$$= a_0 \sum_{r=0}^{n} (-1)^r \frac{n(n-1)\ldots(n-r+1)}{(r\,!)^2} x^r$$

$$= a_0 \sum_{r=0}^{n} (-1)^r \frac{n\,!}{(n-r)\,!\,(r\,!)^2} x^r$$

7.2 Laguerre Polynomials

The standard solution of Laguerre equation for which $a_0 = 1$ is called the Laguerre polynomial of order n and is denoted by $L_n(x)$.

$$\therefore \quad L_n(x) = \sum_{r=0}^{n} (-1)^r \frac{n\,!}{(n-r)\,!\,(r\,!)^2} x^r$$

7.3 Generating Function

To prove $$\frac{1}{1-t} e^{-tx/(1-t)} = \sum_{r=0}^{\infty} t^n L_n(x).$$

We have

$$\frac{1}{1-t} e^{-tx/(1-t)} = \frac{1}{1-t} \sum_{r=0}^{\infty} \frac{1}{r!}\left(-\frac{xt}{1-t}\right)^r$$

$$= \sum_{r=0}^{\infty} \frac{(-1)^r}{r!} \frac{x^r t^r}{(1-t)^{r+1}}$$

$$= \sum_{r=0}^{\infty} \frac{(-1)^r}{r!} x^r t^r (1-t)^{-(r+1)}$$

$$= \sum_{r=0}^{\infty} \frac{(-1)^r}{r!} x^r t^r \left[1 + (r+1)\,t + \frac{(r+1)(r+2)}{2!} t^2 + \ldots\right]$$

$$= \sum_{r=0}^{\infty} \left[\frac{(-1)^r}{r!} x^r t^r \sum_{s=0}^{\infty} \frac{(r+s)!}{r!\,s!} . t^s\right]$$

$$= \sum_{r,s=0}^{\infty} (-1)^r \frac{(r+s)!}{(r!)^2 s!} x^r t^{r+s}$$

Putting $s + r = n$, or $s = n - r$, we get the coefficient of t^n, for a fixed value of r as

$$(-1)^r \frac{n!}{(r!)^2 (n-r)!} . x^r$$

Therefore the total coefficient of t^n is obtained by summing over all allowed values of r, since $s = n-r$ and $s \geq 0$

$\therefore$ $\quad n-r \geq 0$ or $r \leq n$.

Hence the coefficient of t^n is

$$\sum_{r=0}^{n} (-1)^r \frac{n!}{(r!)^2 (n-r)!} x^r = L_n(x)$$

Hence $$\frac{1}{(1-t)} e^{-xt/(1-t)} = \sum_{n=0}^{\infty} t_n L_n(x).$$

7.4 Rodrigues Formula

To prove

$$L_n(x) = \frac{e^x}{n!} \frac{d^n}{dx^n} (x^n e^{-x})$$

We have

$$\frac{e^x}{n!} \frac{d^n}{dx^n} (x^n e^{-x}) = \frac{e^x}{n!} \Big[x^n (-1)^n e^{-x} + n.n\,x^{n-1} . (-1)^{n-1} e^{-x}$$

$$+ \frac{n(n-1)}{2} n(n-1) x^{n-2} (-1)^{n-2} e^{-x} + \ldots + n!\,e^{-x}\Big]$$

[Using Leibnitz's theorem]

$$= \frac{e^x}{n!} . e^{-x} \left[(-1)^n x^n + (-1)^{n-1} \frac{n.n!}{(n-i)!} x^{n-1} + \ldots + n!\right]$$

$$= (-1)^n \frac{n!}{(n!)^2} x^n + (-1)^{n-1} \frac{n!}{\{(n-1)!\}^2 .i!} x^{n-1} + \ldots + \frac{n!}{n!}$$

$$= \sum_{r=0}^{n} (-1)^r \frac{n!}{(r!)^2 (n-r)!} x^r = L_n(x)$$

Hence $$L_n(x) = \frac{e^x}{n!} \frac{d^n}{dx^n} (x^n e^{-x}).$$

7.5 First Few Laguerre polynomials

We have from Rodrigue's formula

$$L_n(x) = \frac{e^x}{n!}\frac{d^n}{dx^n}(x^n e^{-x})$$

Putting $n = 0$

$$L_0(x) = \frac{e^x}{o!}(x^o e^{-x}) = 1$$

Putting $n = 1$

$$L_1(x) = \frac{e^x}{1!}\frac{d}{dx}(x e^{-x}) = e^x(e^{-x} - xe^{-x}) = 1-x$$

Putting $n = 2$

$$L_2(x) = \frac{e^x}{2!}\frac{d^2}{dx^2}(x^2 e^{-x}) = \frac{e^x}{2!}\frac{d}{dx}(2xe^{-x} - x^2 e^{-x})$$

$$= \frac{e^x}{2!}(2e^{-x} - 4x e^{-x} + x^2 e^{-x})$$

$$= \frac{1}{2!}(2 - 4x + x^2)$$

Similarly,

$$L_3(x) = \frac{1}{3!}(6 - 18x + 9x^2 - x^3)$$

$$L_4(x) = \frac{1}{4!}(24 - 96x + 72x^2 - 16x^3 + x^4), \text{ .... etc.}$$

7.6 Orthogonality Property

To prove $\int_0^\infty e^{-x} L_n(x) L_m(x)\, dx = \delta_{mn} = \begin{cases} 0 \text{ if } m \neq n \\ 1 \text{ if } m = n \end{cases}$

We have from the generating function of Laguerre polynomial, that

$$\sum_{n=0}^{\infty} t^n L_n(x) = \frac{1}{1-t} e^{-tx/(1-t)}$$

and
$$\sum_{m=0}^{\infty} s^m L_m(x) = \frac{1}{1-s} e^{-xs/(1-s)}$$

$$\therefore \quad \sum_{m,n=0}^{\infty} e^{-x} t^n s^m L_n(x) L_m(x) = e^{-x} \frac{1}{(1-t)(1-s)} e^{-xt/(1-t)} e^{-sx/(1-s)}$$

Thus $\int_0^\infty e^{-x} L_n(x) L_m(x)\, dx$

= Coeff. of $s^m t^n$ in the expansion of

$$\int_0^\infty e^{-x} \frac{1}{(1-t)(1-s)} e^{-tx(1-t)} e^{-sx/(1-s)}\, dx$$

$$= \frac{1}{(1-t)(1-s)} \int_0^\infty e^{-x\left[1 + \frac{t}{1-t} + \frac{s}{1-s}\right]} dx$$

$$= \frac{1}{(1-t)(1-s)} \frac{-1}{1 + \frac{t}{(1-t)} + \frac{s}{(1-s)}} x$$

$$x\left[e^{-x\left(1+\frac{t}{1-t}+\frac{s}{1-s}\right)}\right]_0^{\infty}.$$

$$= -\frac{1}{(1-t)(1-s)}\frac{(1-t)(1-s)}{\{(1-t)(1-s)+t(1-s)+s(1-t)\}}[-1]$$

$$= \frac{1}{1-st} = (1-st)-1 = [1+st+(st)^2+(st)^3+\ldots(st)^n+\ldots]$$

In which coefficient of $s^m\, t^n$

is 0 if $m \neq n$

and is 1 if $m = n$

Hence $$\int_0^{\infty} e^{-x}\, L_n(x)\, L_m(x)\, dx = \begin{cases} 0 & \text{if } m \neq n \\ 1 & \text{if } m = n \end{cases}$$

or $$\int_0^{\infty} e^{-x}\, L_n(x)\, L_m(x)\, dx = \delta_{mn}.$$

7.7 Recurrence Formulae for Lagurre Polynomials

(i) $$\mathbf{(n+1)\, L_{n+1}(x) = (2n+1-x)\, n\, L_n(x) - L_{n-1}(x)}$$

We have $$\sum_{n=0}^{\infty} t^n\, L_n(x) = \frac{1}{(1-t)}\, e^{\frac{-tx}{(1-t)}}$$

Differentiating both sides with respect to t, we have

$$\sum_{n=1}^{\infty} n\, t^{n-1}\, L_n(x) = \frac{1}{(1-t)^2}\left(1-\frac{x}{1-t}\right) e^{\left[-\frac{x}{(1-t)}\right]}$$

or $$(1-t)^2 \sum_{n=1}^{\infty} n\, t^{n-1}\, L_n(x) = (1-t)\frac{e^{-tx/(1-t)}}{(1-t)} - x.\,\frac{1}{1-t}\, e^{-tx/(1-t)}$$

or $$(1-t)^2 \sum_{n=1}^{\infty} n\, t^{n-1}\, L_n(x) = (1-t)\sum_{n=0}^{\infty} t^n\, L_n(x) - x\sum_{n=0}^{\infty} t^n\, L_n(x)$$

or $$(1-2t+t^2)\sum_{n=1}^{\infty} n\, t^{n-1}\, L_n(x) = (1-t)\sum_{n=1}^{\infty} n\, t^{n+1}\, L_n(x)$$

or $$\sum_{n=1}^{\infty} n\, t^{n-1}\, L_n(x) - 2\sum_{n=1}^{\infty} x\, t^n\, L_n(x) + \sum_{n=1}^{\infty} n\, t^{n+1}\, L_n(x)$$

$$= \sum_{n=0}^{\infty} t^n\, L_n(x) - \sum_{n=0}^{\infty} t^{n+1}\, L_n(x) - x\sum_{n=0}^{\infty} t^n\, L_n(x)$$

Equating the coefficient of t^n on the two sides, we have

$$(n+1)\, L_{n+1}(x) - 2n - L_n(x) + (n-1)\, L_{n-1}(x)$$
$$= L_n(x) - L_{n-1}(x) - x\, L_n(x)$$

or $$\mathbf{(n+1)\, L_{n+1}(x) = (2n+1-x)\, L_n(x) - L_{n-1}(x)}$$

II $$\mathbf{x\, L'_n(x) = n\, L_n(x) - n\, L_{n-1}(x)}$$

We have

$$\sum_{n=0}^{\infty} t^n\, L_n(x) = \frac{1}{(1-t)}\, e^{-tx/(1/t)}$$

Differentiating with respect to x, we have

$$\sum_{n=0}^{\infty} t^n L'_n(x) = \frac{1}{(1-t)} e^{-tx/(1-t)} \left(-\frac{t}{1-t}\right)$$

or $$(1-t)\sum_{n=0}^{\infty} t^n L'_n(x) = -t \cdot \frac{1}{1-t} e^{-tx/(1-t)}$$

or $$(1-t)\sum_{n=0}^{\infty} t^n L'_n(x) = -t\sum_{n=0}^{\infty} t_n L_n(x)$$

or $$\sum_{n=0}^{\infty} t^n L'_n(x) - \sum_{n=0}^{\infty} t^{n+1} L'_n(x) - \sum_{n=0}^{\infty} t^{n+1} L'_n(x) = \sum_{n=0}^{\infty} t^{n+1} L_n(x)$$

Equating the coefficients of t^n, on both the sides, we get

$$L'_n(x) - L'_{n-1}(x) = -L_{n-1}(x)$$

or $$L'_n(x) = L'_{n-1}(x) - L_{n-1}(x) \quad \text{...(i)}$$

Differentiating recurrence formula I with respect to x, we get

$$(n+1) L'_{n+1}(x) = (2n+1-x) L'_n(x) - L'_n(x) - n L'_{n-1}(x) \quad \text{...(ii)}$$

Replacing n by $(n+1)$ in (i), we get

$$L'_{n+1}(x) = L'_n(x) - L_n(x)$$

Also from (i) $L'_{n-1}(x) = L'_n(x) + L_{n-1}(x)$

Substituting these values in (ii), we have

$$(n+1)\{L'n(x) - L_n(x)\}$$
$$= (2n+1-x) L'_n(x) - L_n(x) - n\{L'_n(x) + L_{n-1}(x)\}$$

or $$\mathbf{x L'_n(x) = n L_n(x) - n L_{n-1}(x)}$$

III $$\mathbf{L'_n(x) = -\sum_{r=0}^{n-1} L_r(x)}$$

We have $$\sum_{n=0}^{\infty} t^n L_n(x) = \frac{1}{1-t} e^{-tx/(1-t)}$$

Differentiating with respect to x, we have

$$\sum_{n=0}^{\infty} t^n L'_n(x) = \frac{-t}{1-t} \sum_{r=0}^{\infty} t^r L_r(x)$$

(an in II)

$$= -t(1-t)^{-1} \sum_{r=0}^{\infty} t^r L_r(x)$$

$$= -t(1 + tt^2 + \ldots)\sum_{r=0}^{\infty} t^r L_r(x)$$

$$= -t\sum_{s=0}^{\infty} t^s \sum_{r=0}^{\infty} t^r L_r(x)$$

$$= -\sum_{s=0, r=0}^{\infty} t^{r+s+1} L_r(x) \quad \text{...(i)}$$

For fixed value of r, the coefficient of t^n on the R.H.S. is $-L_r(x)$, obtained by putting $r+s+1 = n$ or $s = n-r-1$.

Total Coefficient of t^n is obtained by summing over all allowed values of r.

Since $s = n-r-1$ and $r \geq 0$

Therefore $n-r-1 \geq 0$ or $r \leq (n-1)$.

$\therefore$ Coefficient of t^n on the R.H.S. $= -\sum_{r=0}^{n-1} L_r(x)$

Therefore equating coefficient of t^n, on the two sides of (i), we have

$$L'_n(x) = -\sum_{r=0}^{\infty} L_r(x).$$

Illustrative Examples

Ex. 1. *Prove that $L_n(o) = 1$.*

Solution. We have

$$\sum_{n=0}^{\infty} t^n L_n(x) = \frac{1}{(1-t)} e^{-tx(1-t)}$$

Putting $x = 0$, we have

$$\sum_{n=0}^{\infty} t_n L_n(x) = \frac{1}{(1-t)} = (1-t)^{-1}$$

$$= 1 + t + t^2 + \ldots + t^n + \ldots$$

$$= \sum_{n=0}^{\infty} t^n$$

$\therefore$ $L_n(0) = 1$

Ex. 2. *Expand $x^3 + x^2 - 3x + 2$ in a series of Laguerre polynomials.*

Solution. We know that $L_n(x)$ is a polynomial of degree n. Since $x^3 + x^2 - 3x + 2$ is a polynomial of degree 3, we may write

$$x^3 + x^2 - 3x + 2 = c_0 L_0(x) + c_1 L_1(x) + c_2 L_2(x) + c_3 L_3(x) \quad \ldots(i)$$

Putting values of $L_0(x)$, $L_1(x)$, $L_2(x)$ and $L_3(x)$ from § 7.5, we have

$$x^3 + x^2 - 3x + 2 = c_0 + c_1(1-x) + c_2 \cdot \frac{1}{2!}(2-4 + x^2) + \frac{c_3}{3!}(6-18x + 9x^2 + x^3)$$

or $$x^3 + x^2 - 3x + 2 = (c_0 + c_1 + c_2 + c_3) - (c_1 + 2c_2 + 3c_3) + \left(\frac{c_2}{2} + \frac{3}{2}c_3\right)x^2 - \frac{c_3}{6}x^3$$

Equating coefficients of like powers of x on both sides of (ii), we get

$$c_0 + c_1 + c_2 + c_3 = 2$$

$$c_1 + 2c_2 + 3c_3 = 3$$

$$\frac{1}{2}c_2 + \frac{3}{2}c_3 = 1 \text{ and } -\frac{c_3}{6} = 1$$

Solving these, we get,

$$c_3 = -6,\ C_2 = 20,\ c_1 = -19,\ c_0 = 7$$

Putting these values in (i) we get

$$x^3 + x^2 - 3x + 2 = 7L_0(x) - 19L_1(x) + 20L_2(x) - 6L_3(x).$$

Ex. 3. *Prove that*

$$x L''_n(x) + (1-x) L'_n(x) + n L_n(x) = 0$$

and hence deduce that

$$L'_n(0) = -n$$

Solution. Since $L_n(x)$ satisfies the Laguerre's equation $x\dfrac{d^2y}{dx^2} + (1-x)\dfrac{dy}{dx} + ny = 0$, for $\lambda = n$

$$\therefore \quad x L''_n(x) + (1+x) L'_n(x) + n L_n(x) = 0.$$

Putting $x = 0$, we have

$$L'_n(0) = -n L_n(0)$$

or

$$L'_n(0) = -n$$

(Since $L_n(0) = 1$)

7.8 Associated Laguerre Equation.

The differential equation

$$x\frac{d^2y}{dx^2} + (\alpha + 1 + x)\frac{dy}{dx} + ny = 0$$

is called *associated Laguerre equation.*

7.9 Theorem.

If μ is a solution of Laguerre equation of order $(n + d)$ then $\dfrac{d^\alpha\mu}{dx^\alpha}$ satisfies Laguerre's associated equation.

Laguerre's equation of order $(n + \alpha)$ is

$$x\frac{d^2y}{dx^2} + (1-x)\frac{dy}{dx} + (n + \alpha)\, y = 0 \qquad \text{...(i)}$$

Since μ is the solution of this equation, hence

$$x\frac{d^2\mu}{dx^2} + (1-x)\frac{d\mu}{dx} + (n + \alpha)\,\mu = 0 \qquad \text{...(ii)}$$

Differentiating (ii) α times with respect to x by Leibnitz's theorem, we get

$$\left(x\frac{d^{\alpha+2}\mu}{dx^{\alpha+2}} + \alpha.1\frac{d^{\alpha+1}\mu}{dx^{\alpha+1}}\right) + \left((1-x)\frac{d^{\alpha+1}\mu}{dx^{\alpha+1}} + (-1).\alpha\frac{d^\alpha\mu}{dx^\alpha}\right) + (n + \alpha)\frac{d^\alpha\mu}{dx^\alpha} = 0$$

or

$$\frac{d^{\alpha+2}\mu}{dx^{\alpha+2}} + (\alpha + 1 - x)\frac{d^{\alpha+1}\mu}{dx^{\alpha+1}} + n\frac{d^\alpha y}{dx^\alpha} = 0$$

which shows that

$$y = \frac{d^\alpha\mu}{dx^\alpha}$$

satisfies Laguerre's associated equation

$$x\frac{d^2y}{dx^2} + (a + 1 - x)\frac{dy}{dx} + ny = 0$$

7.10 Associated Laguerre's Polynomials

From § 7.9 we see that if μ is the solution of Laguerre's equation of order $(n + \alpha)$, i.e. $\mu = L_{n+\alpha}(x)$, then $\dfrac{d^\alpha\mu}{dx^\alpha} = \dfrac{d^\alpha}{dx^\alpha} L_{n+\alpha}(x)$ satisfies the associated Laguerre equation.

Thus we define the associated Leguerre polynomial by

$$\mathbf{L}^{\alpha}_{n}(x) = (-1)^{\alpha} \frac{d^{\alpha}}{dx^{\alpha}} \mathbf{L}_{n+\alpha}(x)$$

7.11 Expansion associated Laguerre's Polynomial

To prove that

$$L^{\alpha}_{n}(x) = \sum_{r=0}^{n} (-1)^{r} \frac{(n+\alpha)!}{(n-r)!\,(\alpha+r)!\,(r)!} x^{r}$$

We have

$$L_{n}(x) = \sum_{r=0}^{n} (-1)^{r} \frac{(n+r)!}{(n-r)!\,(r!)^{2}} x^{r}$$

$$\therefore \quad L_{n+\alpha}(x) = \sum_{r=0}^{n+\alpha} (-1)^{r} \frac{(n+\alpha)!}{(n+\alpha-r)!\,(r!)^{2}} x^{r}$$

Differentiating with respect to x, α times, we have

$$\frac{d^{\alpha}}{dx^{\alpha}} L_{n+\alpha}^{(x)} = \frac{d^{\alpha}}{dx^{\alpha}} \sum_{r=0}^{n+\alpha} (-1)^{r} \frac{(n+\alpha)!}{(n+\alpha-r)!\,(r!)^{2}} x^{r}$$

$$= \frac{d^{\alpha}}{dx^{\alpha}} \sum_{r=\alpha}^{n+\alpha} (-1)^{r} \frac{(n+\alpha)!}{(n+\alpha-r)!\,(r!)^{2}} x^{r}$$

$$\left(\text{Since } \frac{d^{\alpha}}{dx^{\alpha}} x^{r} = 0, \text{ where } 0 \leq r < \alpha\right)$$

$$= \sum_{r=\alpha}^{n+\alpha} (-1)^{r} \frac{(n+\alpha)!}{(n+\alpha-r)!\,(r!)^{2}} \cdot r\,(r-1)\,\ldots\,(r-\alpha+1)^{xr-\alpha}$$

$$= \sum_{r=\alpha}^{n+\alpha} (-1)^{r} \frac{(n+\alpha)!}{(n+\alpha-r)!\,(r!)^{2}} \cdot \frac{r!}{(r-\alpha)!} x^{r-\alpha}$$

$$= \sum_{s=0}^{n} (-1)^{\alpha+s} \frac{(n+\alpha)!}{(n-s)!\,(\alpha+s)!} \cdot \frac{1}{(s)!} x^{s}$$

$$(\text{taking } r-\alpha = s)$$

$$= (-1)^{\alpha} \sum_{r=0}^{n} (-1)^{r} \frac{(n+\alpha)!}{(n-r)!\,(\alpha+r)!\,r!} x^{r}$$

$$\therefore \quad L^{\alpha}_{n}(x) = (-1)^{\alpha} \cdot \frac{d^{\alpha}}{dx^{\alpha}} L_{n+\alpha}^{(x)}$$

$$= \sum_{r=0}^{n} (-1)^{r} \frac{(n+\alpha)!}{(n-r)!\,(\alpha+r)!\,r!} x^{r}$$

7.12 Generating Function

To prove

$$\frac{1}{(1-t)^{\alpha+1}} e^{-xt/(1-t} = \sum_{n=0}^{\infty} t^{\alpha} L^{\alpha}_{n}(x).t^{n}$$

Let $L_n(x)$ be the Laguerre polynomial of degree n, then from § 7.3, we have

$$\frac{1}{(1-t)} e^{-xt/(1-t)} = \sum_{n=0}^{\infty} t^n \,.\, L_n(x)$$

Differentiating both sides α times with respect to x, we get

$$\frac{1}{(1-t)} \frac{d^\alpha}{dx^\alpha} e^{-xt/(1-t)} = \frac{d^\alpha}{dx^\alpha} \sum_{n=0}^{\infty} t^n \,.\, L_n(x)$$

or $$\frac{1}{(1-t)} \left\{\frac{-t}{1-t}\right\}^\alpha e^{-xt/(1-t)} = \frac{d^\alpha}{dx^\alpha} \sum_{n=0}^{n} t^{n+\alpha} \,.\, L_{n+\alpha}^{(x)}$$

(Since $\frac{d^\alpha}{dx^\alpha} L_n(x) = 0$

where $0 \leq n < \alpha$ as $L_n(x)$ is a polynomial of order n)

or $$(-1)^\alpha \frac{t^\alpha}{(1-t)^{\alpha+1}} e^{-xt/(1-t)} = \sum_{n=0}^{\infty} t^{n+\alpha} \frac{d^\alpha}{dx^\alpha} L_{n+\alpha}^{(x)}$$

or $$(-1)^{2\alpha} \frac{1}{(1-t)^{\alpha+1}} e^{-xt/(1-t)} = \sum_{n=0}^{\infty} t^n \,.\, (-1)^\alpha \frac{d^\alpha}{dx^\alpha} L_{n+\alpha}^{(x)}$$

or $$\frac{1}{(1-t)^{\alpha+1}} e^{-xt/(1-t)} = \sum_{n=0}^{\infty} t^n L_n^\alpha(x)$$

7.13 Rodrigues formula for associated Laguerre Polynomial

To prove

$$L_n^\alpha(x) = \frac{e^x x^{-\alpha}}{n!} \cdot \frac{d^n}{dx^n} (e^{-x} \,.\, x^{n+\alpha})$$

We have

$$\frac{e^x x^{-\alpha}}{n!} \cdot \frac{d^n}{dx^n} (e^{-x} \,.\, x^{n+\alpha})$$

$$= \frac{e^x \,.\, x^{-\alpha}}{n!} \Big[x^{n+\alpha} \,.\, (-1)^n e^{-x} + n\,(n+\alpha)\, x^{n+\alpha-1} e^{-x}$$

$$+ \frac{n\,(n-1)}{2!} (n+\alpha)\,(n+\alpha-1)\, x^{n+\alpha-2} (-1)^{n-2} e^{-x}$$

$$+ \ldots + n(-1)\, e^{-x} \frac{(n+\alpha)!}{(\alpha+1)!} \,.\, x^{\alpha+1}$$

$$+ e^{-x} \frac{(n+\alpha)!}{\alpha!} x^\alpha\Big]$$

[Using Leibnitz's theorem]

$$= \frac{(-1)^n x^n}{n!} + (-1)^{n-1} \,.\, \frac{(n+\alpha)}{(n-1)} x^{n-1}$$

$$+ (-1)^{n-2} \frac{(n+\alpha)\,(n+\alpha-1)}{2!\,(n-2)!} x^{n-2}$$

$$+ \ldots + (-1) \frac{(n+\alpha)!}{(\alpha+1)!\,(n-1)!} + \frac{(n+\alpha)!}{\alpha!\,n!}$$

$$= (-1)^n \frac{(n+\alpha)!}{(n-n)!\,(\alpha+n)!\,n!} \,.\, x^n$$

$$+ (-1)^{n-1} \frac{(n+\alpha)!}{\{n-(n-1)\}!\ \{\alpha+(n-1)\}!\ (n-1)!} x^{n-1}$$

$$+ \ldots + (-1) \frac{(n+\alpha)!}{(n+1)\ !\ (\alpha+1)!\ 1!} \cdot x$$

$$+ \frac{(n+\alpha)!}{n!\ \alpha!\ .\ 0!}$$

$$= \sum_{r=0}^{n} (-1)^r \cdot \frac{(n+\alpha)!}{(n-r)!\ (\alpha+r)!\ r!} \cdot x^r$$

$$= L_n^{\alpha}(x)$$

7.14 Orthogonal Property of the associated Laguerre Polynomials

To prove

$$\int_0^{\infty} e^{-x} x^{\alpha} L_n^{\alpha}(x) L_m^{\alpha}(x)\, dx = \frac{(n+\alpha)!}{n!} \delta_{mn}.$$

We have

$$\sum_{n=0}^{\infty} t^n L_n^{\alpha}(x) = \frac{1}{(1-t)^{\alpha+1}} e^{-xt/(1-t)}$$

and

$$\sum_{m=0}^{\infty} s^n L_n^{\alpha}(x) = \frac{1}{(1-s)^{\alpha+1}} e^{-xs/(1-s)}$$

$\therefore$

$$\sum_{m,n=0}^{\infty} t^n s^m e^{-x} x^{\alpha} L_n^{\alpha}(x) L_m^{\alpha}(x)$$

$$= \frac{e^{-\alpha} x^{\alpha}}{(1-t)^{\alpha+1} (1-s)^{\alpha+1}} e^{-tx/(1-t)} \cdot e^{-sx/(1-s)}$$

$$= \frac{x^{\alpha}}{(1-t)^{\alpha+1} (1-s)^{\alpha+1}} \cdot e^{-x(1-tx)/(1-t)(1-s)}$$

$\therefore$

$$\int_0^{\infty} e^{-x} x^{\alpha} L_n^{\alpha}(x) L_m^{\alpha}(x)\, dx$$

= Coeff. of $t^n s^m$ in the expansion of

$$\int_0^{\infty} \frac{x^{\alpha}}{(1-t)^{\alpha+1} (1-s)^{\alpha+1}} \cdot e^{-x(1-tx)/(1-t)(1-s)}\, dx$$

Now,

$$\int_0^{\infty} \frac{x^{\alpha}}{(1-t)^{\alpha+1} (1-s)^{\alpha+1}} \cdot e^{\frac{-(1-ts)x}{(1-t)(1-s)}} .dx$$

$$= \frac{1}{(1-t)^{\alpha+1} (1-s)^{\alpha+1}} \int_0^{\infty} x^{\alpha} \cdot e^{\frac{-(1-tx)x}{(1-t)(1-s)}} .dx$$

Integrating by parts taking x^{α} as the first function, we get

$$= \frac{1}{(1-t)^{\alpha+1} (1-s)^{\alpha+1}} \left[\left\{ -x^{\alpha} \frac{(1-t)(1-s)}{(1-ts)} \exp\left(\frac{-(1-ts)x}{(1-t)(1-s)} \right) \right\}_0^{\infty} \right.$$

$$\left. + \frac{\alpha(1-t)(1-s)}{(1-ts)} \int_0^{\infty} x^{\alpha-1} .\exp\left\{ \frac{-(1-ts)x}{(1-t)(1-s)} \right\} dx \right]$$

$$= \frac{1}{(1-t)^{\alpha+1}(1-s)^{\alpha+1}} \cdot \frac{\alpha(1-t)(1-s)}{(1-ts)}$$

$$\times \int_0^\infty x^{\alpha-1} \cdot e^{\frac{-(1-ts)x}{(1-t)(1-s)}} dx$$

Proceeding similarly $(\alpha-1)$ times, we have

$$= \frac{1}{(1-t)^{\alpha+1}(1-s)^{\alpha+1}} \frac{\alpha(\alpha-1)\ldots 2.1\,(1-t)^\alpha(1-s)^\alpha}{(1-ts)^\alpha}$$

$$\times \int_0^\infty e^{\frac{-(1-ts)x}{(1-t)(1-s)}} dx$$

$$= \frac{\alpha\,!}{(1-t)(1-s)(1-ts)^\alpha}\left[-\frac{(1-t)(1-s)}{(1-ts)^\alpha} \cdot e^{\frac{-(1-ts)x}{(1-t)(1-s)}}\right]_0^\infty$$

$$= \frac{\alpha\,!}{(1-ts)^{\alpha+1}}$$

$$= \alpha\,!\,(1-ts)^{-(\alpha+1)}$$

$$= \alpha\,!\left[1+(\alpha+1)ts+\frac{(\alpha+1)(\alpha+2)}{2\,!}t^2s^2+\ldots\right.$$

$$\left.+\frac{(\alpha+1)(\alpha+2)\ldots(\alpha+n)}{n\,!}(ts)^n+\ldots\right]$$

in which coefficient of $t^n s^m$ is 0 if $m \neq n$ and is

$$\alpha\,!\,\frac{(\alpha+1)(\alpha+2)\ldots(\alpha+n)}{n\,!} = \frac{(n+\alpha)\,!}{n\,!} \quad \text{if } m = n.$$

Hence
$$\int_0^\infty e^{-x} x^\alpha L_n^\alpha(x) L_m^\alpha(x)\, dx = \frac{(n+\alpha)\,!}{n\,!}\,\delta_{mn}$$

7.15 Recurrence formulae for associated Laguerre polynomials

(I) $L^\alpha_{n-1}(x) + L_n^{\alpha-1}(x) = L_n^\alpha(x)$

We have

$$L_n\alpha(x) = \sum_{r=0}^{n} (-1)^r \frac{(n+\alpha)!}{(n-r)!(\alpha+r)!r!} x^r$$

$$\therefore\ L^\alpha_{n-1}(x) + L_n^{\alpha-1}(x)$$

$$= \sum_{r=0}^{n-1} (-1)^r \frac{(n-1+\alpha)!}{(n-1+r)!(\alpha+r)!r!} x^r$$

$$+ \sum_{r=0}^{n} (-1)^r \frac{(n+\alpha-1)!x^r}{(n-r)!(\alpha-1+r)!r!}$$

$$= \sum_{r=0}^{n-1} \frac{(-1)^r}{r!}\left[\frac{(n-1+\alpha)!}{(n-1-r)!(\alpha+r)!} + \frac{(n-1+\alpha)!}{(n-r)!(\alpha-1+r)!}\right] x^r + (-1)^n \cdot \frac{x^n}{n!}$$

$$= \sum_{r=0}^{n-1} (-1)^r \frac{(n-1-\alpha)!}{(n-1-r)!(\alpha+r-1)!r!} x$$

$$\times\left[\frac{1}{\alpha+r}+\frac{1}{n-r}\right]\left[x^r+(-1)^n\frac{x^n}{n!}\right]$$

$$=\sum_{r=0}^{n-1}(-1)^r\frac{(n-1-\alpha)!}{(n-1-r)!(\alpha+r-1)!\,r!}$$

$$\times\frac{n+\alpha}{(\alpha+r)(n-r)}x^r+(-1)^n\frac{x^n}{n!}$$

$$=\sum_{r=0}^{n-1}(-1)^r\frac{(n+\alpha)!}{(n-r)!\,(\alpha+r)!\,r!}x^r+(-1)^n\cdot\frac{x^n}{n!}$$

$$=\sum_{r=0}^{n}(-1)^r\frac{(n+\alpha)!}{(n-r)!\,(\alpha+r)!\,r!}x^r=L_n^\alpha(x)^n$$

or $$\mathbf{L^{\alpha}_{n-1}(x)+L^{\alpha-1}_{n}(x)=L^{\alpha}_{n}(x)}$$

(II) $$\mathbf{(n+1)\,L^{\alpha}_{n+1}(x)=(2n+\alpha+1-x)\,L^{\alpha}_{n}(x)-(n+\alpha)L^{\alpha}_{n-1}(x)}$$

From recurrence formula (I) for Laguerre polynomials, we have

$$(n+1)\,L_{n+1}(x)=(2n+1-x)\,L_n(x)-n\,L_{n-1}(x)$$

Replacing n by $(n+\alpha)$, we have

$$(n+\alpha+1)\,L_{n+\alpha+1}{}^{(x)}=(2n+2\alpha+1-x)\,L_{n+\alpha}(x)-(n+\alpha)L_{n+\alpha-1}(x)$$

Differentiating both sides α times with respect to x, we have

$$(n+\alpha-1)\frac{d^\alpha}{dx^\alpha}L_{n+\alpha+1}{}^{(x)}=(2n+2\alpha+1-x)\frac{d^\alpha}{dx^\alpha}L_{n+\alpha}{}^{(x)}$$

$$+\alpha(-1)\frac{d^{\alpha-1}}{dx^{\alpha-1}}L_{n+\alpha}(x)-(n+\alpha)\frac{d^\alpha}{dx^\alpha}L_{n+\alpha-1}(x)$$

or $$(n+\alpha-1)(-1)^\alpha\frac{d^\alpha}{dx^\alpha}L_{n+\alpha+1}{}^{(x)}$$

$$=(2n+2\alpha-1)(-1)^\alpha\frac{d^\alpha}{dx^\alpha}L_{n+\alpha}(x)$$

$$-x(-1)^\alpha\frac{d^\alpha}{dx^\alpha}L_{n+\alpha}{}^{(x)}+\alpha(-1)^{\alpha-1}L_{n+\alpha-1}{}^{(x)}$$

$$-(n+\alpha)(-1)^\alpha\frac{d^\alpha}{dx^\alpha}L_{n+\alpha-1}{}^{(x)}$$

or $$(n+\alpha+1)\,L^\alpha_{n+1}(x)=(2n+2\alpha+1)\,L_n^\alpha(x)$$

$$-x\,L_n^\alpha(x)+\alpha\,L^{\alpha-1}_{n-1}(x)-(n+\alpha)\,L^\alpha_{n-1}(x)$$

$$=(2n+2\alpha+1)\,L_n^\alpha(x)-x\,L_n^\alpha(x)$$

$$+\alpha\{L^\alpha_{n+1}(x)-L_n^\alpha(x)\}-(n+\alpha)\,L^\alpha_{n-1}(x)$$

Since replacing n by $(n+1)$ is I we have

$$L^{\alpha-1}_{n+1}(x)=L^\alpha_{n+1}(x)-L_n^\alpha(x)$$

or $$\mathbf{(n+1)\,L^\alpha_{n+1}(x)=(2n+\alpha+1-x)\,L_n^\alpha(x)-(n+\alpha)\,L^\alpha_{n-1}}$$

III $$\boldsymbol{x\,L_n^{\alpha\prime}(x)=n\,L_n^\alpha(x)-(n+\alpha)\,L^\alpha_{n+1}(x)}$$

From recurrence formula (II) for Laguerre polynomials we have

$$x\,L_n'(x)=n\,L_n(x)-n\,L_{n-1}(x)$$

Replacing n by $(n+\alpha)$, we have

$$x\,L'_{n+\alpha}(x)=(n+\alpha)L_{n+\alpha}{}^{(x)}-(n+\alpha)\,L_{n-1+\alpha}{}^{(x)}$$

Differentiating both sides α times with respect to x, we have

$$x \frac{d^\alpha}{dx^\alpha} L'_{n+\alpha}(x) + \alpha.1. \frac{d^{\alpha-1}}{dx^{\alpha-1}} L'_{n+\alpha}(x)$$

$$= (n+\alpha) \frac{d^\alpha}{dx^\alpha} L_{n+\alpha}(x) - (n+\alpha) \frac{d^\alpha}{dx^\alpha} L^{(x)}_{n-1+\alpha}$$

or
$$x (-1)^\alpha \frac{d^\alpha}{dx^\alpha} L'_{n+\alpha}(x)$$

$$= n (-1)^\alpha \frac{d^\alpha}{dx^\alpha} L_{n+\alpha}(x) - (n+\alpha)(-1)^\alpha \cdot \frac{d^\alpha}{dx^\alpha} L^{(x)}_{n-1-\alpha}$$

or
$$\boldsymbol{x L_n^{\alpha'}(x) = n L_n^\alpha(x) - (n+\alpha) L^\alpha_{n-1}(x).}$$

IV $\quad \boldsymbol{L_n^{\alpha'}(x) = - L_{n-1}^{\alpha+1}(x)}$

We have

$$L^\alpha_n(x) = \sum_{r=0}^{n} (-1)^r \frac{(n+\alpha)!}{(n-r)!(\alpha+r)!r!} x^r$$

$$\therefore \quad L_n^{\alpha'}(x) = \sum_{r=0}^{n} (-1)^r \frac{(n+\alpha)!}{(n-r)!(\alpha+r)!r!} x^{r-1}$$

$$= \sum_{r=1}^{n} (-1)^r \frac{(n+\alpha)!}{(n-r)!(\alpha+r)!r!} x^{r-1}$$

$$= (-1) \sum_{s=0}^{n-1} (-1)^s \frac{(n-1+\alpha+1)!}{(n-1-s)!(\alpha+1+s)!s!} x^s$$

Taking $r-1 = s$

$$= - L_{n-1}^{\alpha+1}(x)$$

or
$$L_n^{\alpha'}(x) = -L_{n-1}^{\alpha+1}(x)$$

V $\quad \boldsymbol{L_n^{\alpha'}(x) = -\sum_{r=0}^{n-1} L_r^\alpha(x)}$

From recurrence formula III for Laguerre polynomial, we have

$$L'_n(x) = -\sum_{r=0}^{n-1} L_r(x)$$

Replacing n by $(n+\alpha)$ and then differentiating both sides α times with respect to x, we have

$$\frac{d^\alpha}{dx^\alpha} L'_{n+\alpha}(x) = -\sum_{r=0}^{n+\alpha-1} \frac{d^\alpha}{dx^\alpha} L_r(x)$$

$$= -\sum_{r=\alpha}^{n+\alpha-1} \frac{d^\alpha}{dx^\alpha} L_r(x)$$

Since $L_r(x)$ is a polynomial of order r, we have $\frac{d^\alpha}{dx^\alpha} L_r(x) = 0$ for $0 \le r < \alpha$

$$= -\sum_{s=0}^{n-1} \frac{d^\alpha}{dx^\alpha} L_{s+\alpha}(x)$$

Taking $r = s+\alpha$

or $$(-1)^{\alpha} \frac{d^{\alpha}}{dx^{\alpha}} L'_{n+\alpha}(x) = -\sum_{r=0}^{n-1} (-1)^{\alpha} \frac{d^{\alpha}}{dx^{\alpha}} L_{r+\alpha}^{(x)}$$

or $$L_n^{\alpha}(x) = -\sum_{r=0}^{n-1} L_n^{\alpha}(x).$$

(VI) $$L_n^{\alpha+1}(x) = \sum_{r=0}^{n} L_r^{\alpha}(x)$$

From recurrence formulae IV and V, we have

$$L_n^{\alpha'}(x) = -L_{n-1}^{\alpha+1}(x)$$

and $$L_n^{\alpha'}(x) = -\sum_{r=0}^{n-1} L^{\alpha}{}_r(x)$$

$\therefore$ $$L_{n-1}^{\alpha+1}(x) = \sum_{r=0}^{n-1} L^{\alpha}{}_r(x)$$

Replacing n by $n+1$, we have

$$L_n^{\alpha+1}(x) = \sum_{r=0}^{n} L^{\alpha}{}_r(x)$$

Illustrative Examples

Ex. 4. *Prove that*

$$\int_x^{\infty} e^{-t} L_n^{\alpha}(t)\, dt = e^{-x} \{L_n^{\alpha}(x) - L_n^{\alpha'}(x)\}$$

Solution. We have

$$\int_x^{\infty} e^{-t} L_n^{\alpha}(t)\, dt = \left[-e^{-t} L_n^{\alpha}(t)\right]_x^{\infty} + \int_x^{\infty} e^{-t} L_n^{\alpha'}(t)\, dt$$

(integrating by parts taking e^{-t} as second function)

$$= e^{-x} L_n^{\alpha}(x) + \int_x^{\infty} e^{-t} \cdot \left[-\sum_{r=0}^{n-1} L_n^{\alpha}(t)\right] dt$$

(from recurrence formula V)

$$= e^{-x} L_n^{\alpha}(x) + \sum_{r=0}^{n-1} \int_x^{\infty} L_r^{\alpha}(t)\, dt$$

or $$\int_x^{\infty} e^{-t} L_n^{\alpha}(t)\, dt + \sum_{r=0}^{n-1} \int_x^{\infty} e^{-t} L_r^{\alpha}(t)\, dt = e^{-x} L_r^{\alpha}(x) \qquad \text{...(i)}$$

$\therefore$ $$\sum_{r=0}^{n} \int_x^{\infty} e^{-t} L_r^{\alpha}(t)\, dt = e^{-x} L_n^{\alpha}(x) \qquad \text{...(ii)}$$

Subtracting (ii) from (i), we have

$$\int_x^{\infty} e^{-t} L_n^{\alpha}(t)\, dt + \sum_{r=0}^{n-1} \int_x^{\infty} e^{-t} L_r^{\alpha}(t)\, dt - \sum_{r=0}^{n} \int_x^{\infty} e^{-t} L_r^{\alpha}(t)\, dt = 0$$

or $$\int_x^\infty e^{-t} L_n^\alpha(t)\, dt = \sum_{r=0}^{n} \int_x^\infty e^{-t} L_r^\alpha(t)\, dt - \sum_{r=0}^{n-1} \int_x^\infty e^{-t} L_r^\alpha(t)\, dt$$

or $$\int_x^\infty e^{-t} L_n^\alpha(t)\, dt = e^{-x} L_n^\alpha(x) - e^{-x} L_n^{\alpha'}(x)$$

or $$\int_x^\infty e^{-t} L_n^\alpha(t)\, dt = e^{-x}\left[L_n^\alpha(x) - L_n^{\alpha'}(x)\right].$$

7.16 Chebyshev's Differential Equation and Polynomials

The differential equation

$$(1-x^2)\frac{d^2y}{dx^2} - x\frac{dy}{dx}\, n^2 y = 0$$

is called *chebyshev's differential equation.*

The chebysheev polynomials of first kind, $T_n(x)$, and second kind $U_n(x)$ are defined by

$$T_n(x) = \text{Cos}\,(n \cos^{-1} x)$$

and $$U_n(x) = \sin\,(n \cos^{-1} x)$$

where n is a non–negative integer.

7.17 To prove that $T_n(x)$ and $U_n(x)$ are independent solutions of Chebyshev's equation

Chebyshev's equation is

$$(1-x^2)\frac{d^2y}{dx^2} - x\frac{dy}{dx} + n^2 y = 0 \qquad \text{...(i)}$$

Now $$T_n(x) = \text{Cos}\,(n \cos^{-1} x)$$

$$\therefore \quad \frac{d}{dx} T_n(x) = -\sin\,(n\cos^{-1} x)\left\{\frac{-n}{\sqrt{(1-x)^2}}\right\}$$

$$= \frac{n}{\sqrt{(1-x)^2}} \sin\,(n \cos^{-1} x)$$

and $$\frac{d^2}{dx^2} T_n(x) = \frac{n\,x}{(1-x^2)^{3/2}} \sin\,(n\cos^{-1} x) - \frac{n^2}{(1-x^2)} \text{Cos}\,(n \cos^{-1} x)$$

$$\therefore \quad (1-x^2)\frac{d^2}{dx^2} T_n(x) - x\frac{d}{dx} T_n(x) + n^2 T_n(x)$$

$$= \frac{n\,x}{\sqrt{(1-x)^2}} \sin\,(n\cos^{-1} x) - n^2\, \text{Cos}\,(n\cos^{-1} x)$$

$$- \frac{n\,x}{\sqrt{(1-x)^2}} \sin\,(n\cos^{-1} x) + n^2\, \text{Cos}\,(n\cos^{-1} x)$$

$$= 0$$

Hence $T_n(x)$ is the solution of (i).

Similarly, we can prove that

$$U_n(x) = \sin\,(n \cos^{-1} x)$$

is also the solution of (i).

Now, we see that $T_n(1) = 1$ and $U_n(1) = 0$.

Hence $U_n(x)$ can not be written as a constant multiple of $T_n(x)$. Hence $T_n(x)$ and $U_n(x)$ are independent solutions of chebyshev differential equation (i).

7.18 To prove that

(i) $$T_n(x) = \sum_{r=0}^{(n/2)} (-1)^r \frac{n!}{(2r)!(n-2r)!} (1-x^2)^r x^{n-2r}$$

and (ii) $$U_n(x) = \sum_{r=0}^{(n-1)/2} (-1)^r \frac{n!}{(2r+1)!(n-2r-1)!} (1-x^2)^{r+\frac{1}{2}} . x^{n-2r-1}$$

(i) We have $T_n(x) = \text{Cos}(n \cos^{-1} x)$

let $$x = \cos\theta$$

$$\cos n\theta = \frac{e^{in\theta} + e^{-in\theta}}{2}$$

$$= \frac{1}{2}[(\cos\theta + i\sin\theta)^n + (\cos\theta - i\sin\theta)^n]$$

$$= \frac{1}{2}\left[\left\{x + i\sqrt{(1-x^2)}\right\}^n + \left\{x - i\sqrt{(1-x^2)}\right\}^n\right]$$

since $x = \cos\theta \therefore \sqrt{1-x^2} = \sin\theta$

$\therefore$ $$T_n(x) = \frac{1}{2}\left[\left\{x + i\sqrt{(1-x^2)}\right\}^n + \left\{x - i\sqrt{(1-x^2)}\right\}^n\right]$$

$$= \frac{1}{2}\left\{\sum_{r=0}^{n} n_{c_r} x^{n-r}\left\{i\sqrt{(1-x^2)}\right\}^r + \sum_{r=0}^{n} n_{c_r} x^{n-r}\left\{-i\sqrt{1-x^{2r}}\right\}^r\right\}$$

by the Binomial theorem.

$$= \frac{1}{2}\sum_{r=0}^{n} {}^nc_r x^{n-r} \{1 + (-1)^r\}. i^r (1-x^r)^{r/2}.$$

when r is odd $(-1)^r = -1 \therefore 1 + (-1)^r = 0$

and when r is even $(-1)^r = 1 \therefore 1 + (-1)^r = 2$

$\therefore$ $$T_n(x) = \frac{1}{2}\sum_{r=0}^{n} {}^nc_r x^{n-r}. 2 i^r (1-x^2)^{r/2}$$

(even $r \le n$)

Taking $r = 2s$, when n is integral, $r \le n$ means that $s \le n/2$, s is integer less than or equal to $n/2$

We have

$$T_n(x) = \sum_{r=0}^{(n/2)} {}^nc_{2s} x^{n-2s} i^{2s} (1-x^2)^s$$

$$= \sum_{r=0}^{(n/2)} (-1)^s . \frac{n!}{(2s)!(n-2s)!} (1-x^2)^s x^{n-2s}$$

$$= \sum_{r=0}^{(n/2)} (-1)^r . \frac{n!}{(2r)!(n-2r)!} (1-x^2)^r x^{n-2r}$$

(ii) We have $U_n(x) = \sin(n\cos^{-1} x)$

$= \sin n\theta$. Putting $x = \cos\theta$

$$= \frac{1}{2i}(e^{in\theta} - e^{-in\theta})$$

$$= \frac{1}{2i}[(\cos\theta + i\sin\theta)^n - (\cos\theta - i\sin\theta)^n]$$

$$= \frac{1}{2i}\left[\{x + i\sqrt{(1-x^2)}\}^n + \{x - i\sqrt{(1-x^2)}\}^n\right]$$

$$= \frac{1}{2i}\left\{\sum_{r=0}^{n} n_{c_r} x^{n-r}\{i\sqrt{(1-x^2)}\}^2 - \sum_{r=0}^{n} n_{c_r} x^{n-r}\{-1\sqrt{(1-x^2}\}^\rho\right\}$$

(By Binomial Theorem)

$$= \frac{1}{2i}\sum_{r=0}^{n} {}^nc_r\, x^{n-r}\{1-(-1)^r\}\, i^r(1-x^2)^{r/2}$$

when r is even $(-1)^r = 1$; $\therefore 1-(-1)^r = 0$

and when r is odd $(-1)^r = -1$ $\therefore 1-(-1)^r = 0$

$\therefore$ $$U_n(x) = \frac{1}{2i}\sum_{r=0}^{n} {}^nc_r\, x^{n-r}{}_2 i^r (1-x^2)^{r/2}$$

(r is odd $\leq n$)

Taking $r = 2s + 1$, where s is an integral, $r \leq n$ means $s \leq \frac{n-1}{2}$, s is integral.

Hence $\frac{n-1}{2}$ is greatest integer less than or equal to $\frac{n-1}{2}$.

We have $$U_n(x) = \frac{1}{i}\sum_{s=o}^{(n-1)/2} {}^nc_{2s+1}\, x^{n-2s-1}\, i^{2s+1}(1-x^2)^{s+1/2}$$

$$= \sum_{s=o}^{(n-1)/2} (-1)^s \frac{(n)!}{(2s+1)!(n-2s-1)!}(1-x^2)^{s+1/2}\, x^{n-2s-1}$$

$$= \sum_{s=o}^{(n-1)/2} (-1)^{sr} \frac{(n)!}{(2r+1)!(n-2r-1)!}(1-x^2)^{r+1/2}\, x^{n-2r-1}$$

7.19 First few chebyshev Polynomials

From § 7.18, we have

$$T_n(x) = \sum_{r=0}^{(n/2)} (-1)^r \frac{n!}{(2r)!(n-2r)!}(1-x^2)^r x^{n-2r}$$

and $$U_n(x) = \sum_{r=0}^{(n-1)/2} (-1)^r \frac{(n)!}{(2r+1)!(n-2r-1)!}(1-x^2)^{r+1/2} x^{n-2r-1}$$

Putting n = 0, 1, 2, 3, ... , we have

$T_0(x) = 1$

$T_1(x) = x$

$$T_2(x) = \sum_{r=0}^{1} (-1)^r \frac{(2)!}{(2r)!(2-2r)!}(1-x^2)^r x^{2-2r}$$

$$x^2 - (1-x^2) = 2x^2 - 1$$

$$T_3(x) = \sum_{r=0}^{1} (-1)^r \frac{(3)!}{(2r)!\,(3-2r)!} (1-x^2)^r\, x^{2-2r}$$

$$= x^3 - 3(1-x^2)\,x = 4x^3 - 3x$$

Similarly, $T_4(x) = 8x^4 + 8x^2 + 1$

and $T_5(x) = 16x^5 - 20x^3 + 5x$ etc.

Similarly,

$$U_0(x) = 0$$

$$U_1(x) = \sqrt{(1-x^2)}$$

$$U_2(x) = \sqrt{(1-x^2)}\,.\,2x$$

$$U_3(x) = \sum_{r=0}^{1} (-1)^r \frac{(3)!}{(2r+1)!\,(2-2r)!} (1-x^2)^{r+1/2}\, x^{2-2r}$$

$$= 3(1-x^2)^{1/2}\,.\,x^2 - (1-x^2)^{3/2}\,.\,x^0$$

$$= (4x^2-1)\sqrt{(1-x^2)}$$

Similarly. $U_4(x) = (8x^3-4x)\sqrt{(1-x^2)}$

and $U_5(x) = (16x^4 - 12x^2 + 1)\sqrt{(1-x^2)}$ etc.

7.20 Generating Function

To Prove that

(i) $$\frac{1-t^2}{1-2tx+t^2} = T_0(x) + 2\sum_{n=1}^{\infty} T_n(x)\,.\,t^n$$

and (ii) $$\frac{\sqrt{(1-x^2)}}{1-2tx+t^2} = \sum_{n=0}^{\infty} U_{n+1}(x)\,.\,t^n$$

(i) Putting $x = \cos\theta = \frac{1}{2}(e^{i\theta} + e^{-i\theta})$, we get

$$\frac{1-t^2}{1-2tx+t^2} = \frac{1-t^2}{1-t(e^{i\theta}+e^{-i\theta})+t^2} = \frac{1-t^2}{(1-te^{i\theta})(1-te^{-i\theta})}$$

$$= (1-t^2)(1-te^{i\theta})^{-1}(1-te^{-i\theta})^{-1}$$

$$= (1-t^2)\sum_{r=0}^{\infty}(te^{i\theta})^r \sum_{s=0}^{\infty}(te^{-i\theta})^s$$

(By Binomial Therem)

$$= (1-t^2)\sum_{r,s=0}^{\infty} t^{r+s}\, e^{i(r-s)\theta}$$

$$= \sum_{r,s=0}^{\infty} t^{r+s}\, e^{i(r-s)\theta} - \sum_{r,s=0}^{\infty} t^{r+s+2}\, e^{i(r-s)\theta} \qquad ...(i)$$

Now, coefficient of t^0 in (i) is

$$e^{1(0-0)\theta} = 1 = T_0(x)$$

[obtained by putting $r = 0$, $s = 0$ in the first summation]

Again coefficient of t in (i) is

$e^{i(0-1)\theta} + e^{i(1-0)\theta}$

[obtained by putting $r = 0$,

$= e^{-i\theta} + e^{i\theta}$ s = 1, and r = 1, s = 0 in the first summation]

$= 2 \cos \theta = 2x = 2T_1(x)$

Hence, the coefficient of t^n in (i)

$$= \sum_{r=0}^{n} e^{i[r-(n-r)]\theta} - \sum_{r=0}^{n-2} e^{i[r-(n-r-2)]\theta}$$

[obtained by putting r + s = n, i.e., s = n – r in the first summation and r + s + 2 = n, i.e., s = n – r – 2 in the second summation, s ≥ 0 gives n – r ≥ 0, i.e., r ≤ n and n – r – 2 ≥ 0, i.e., r ≤ n – 2]

$$= e^{-in\theta} \sum_{r=0}^{n} e^{i.2r\theta} - e^{-i\theta(n-2)} \sum_{r=0}^{n-2} e^{i2r\theta}$$

$$= e^{-in\theta} \left[1 + e^{2i\theta} + e^{4i\theta} + \ldots + t_0 (n+1) \text{ terms}\right]$$

$$- e^{-i(n-2)\theta} \left[1t\, e^{2i\theta} + e^{4i\theta} + \ldots + t_0 (n-1) \text{ terms}\right]$$

$$= e^{in\theta} . \frac{1-(e^{2i\theta})^{n+1}}{1-e^{2i\theta}} - e^{-i(n-2)\theta} . \frac{1-(e^{2i\theta})^{n-1}}{1-e^{2i\theta}}$$

$$= \frac{e^{-in\theta} - e^{i(n+2)\theta} - e^{-i(n-2)\theta} + e^{in\theta}}{(1-e^{2i\theta})}$$

$$= \frac{e^{-in\theta}(1-e^{2i\theta}) + e^{in\theta}(1-e^{2i\theta})}{(1-e^{2i\theta})}$$

$$= e^{ni\theta} + e^{-ni\theta} = 2 \cos n\theta$$

$$= 2 \cos (n \cos^{-1} x) = 2\, T_n(x)$$

∴ From (i) we have

$$\frac{1-t^2}{1-2tx+t^2} = T_0(x) + 2 \sum_{n=1}^{\infty} T_n(x) . t^n$$

(ii) Putting $x = \cos \theta = \frac{1}{2}(e^{i\theta} + e^{-i\theta})$ and simplifying as in case (i), we have

$$\frac{\sqrt{(1-x^2}}{1-2tx+t^2} = \sin \theta \sum_{r,s=0}^{\infty} t^{r+s} e^{i(r-s)\theta} \qquad \text{...(ii)}$$

∴ coefficient of t^n on the R.H.S. will be $\sin \theta . \sum_{r=0}^{n} e^{i[r-(n-r)]\theta}$

[obtained by putting r + s = n, i.e., s = n – r, s ≥ 0 given (n – r) ≥ 0 i.e., r ≤ n]

$$= \sin \theta .\ e^{-in\theta} \sum_{r=0}^{n} e^{2ir\theta}$$

$$= \sin \theta .\ e^{-in\theta} [\ 1 + e^{2i\theta} + e^{4i\theta} + \ldots\ t_0 (n+1) \text{ terms}]$$

$$= \sin\theta \,.\, e^{-in\theta}\, \frac{1 - e^{2(n+)i\theta}}{1 - e^{2i\theta}}$$

$$= \frac{e^{i\theta} - e^{i\theta}}{2i} \cdot \frac{e^{-in\theta}\,(1 - e^{2(n+1)i\theta})}{-e^{i\theta}\,(e^{i\theta} - e^{-i\theta})}$$

$$= \frac{e^{-i(n+1)\theta}\,(-1 + e^{2(n+1)i\theta})}{2i}$$

$$= \frac{e^{(n+1)i\theta} - e^{-(n+1)i\theta}}{2i} = \sin(n+1)\,\theta$$

$$= \sin\{(n+1)\cos^{-1}x\} = U_{n+1}(x)$$

Hence from (ii) we have

$$\frac{\sqrt{(1-x^2)}}{1 - 2tx + t^2)} = \sum_{r=0}^{\infty} U_{n+1}(x)\,.\,t^n.$$

7.21 Orthogonal properties

To prove that

(i) $$\int_{-1}^{1} \frac{T_m(x)\,T_n(x)}{\sqrt{(1-x^2)}}\,dx = \begin{cases} 0 & m \neq n \\ \pi/2 & m = n \neq 0 \\ \pi & m = n = 0 \end{cases}$$

and (ii) $$\int_{-1}^{1} \frac{U_m(x)\,U_n(x)}{\sqrt{(1-x^2)}}\,dx = \begin{cases} 0 & m \neq n \\ \pi/2 & m = n \neq 0 \\ 0 & m = n = 0 \end{cases}$$

(i) we have

$$T_m(x) = \cos(m\cos^{-1}x)$$
$$T_n(x) = \cos(n\cos^{-1}x)$$

$$\therefore \int_{-1}^{1} \frac{T_m(x)\,T_n(x)}{\sqrt{(1-x^2)}}\,dx$$

$$= \int_{-1}^{1} \frac{\cos(m\cos^{-1}x)\cos(n\cos^{-1}x)}{\sqrt{(1-x^2)}}\,dx$$

Putting $x = \cos\theta$, i.e., $dx = -\sin\theta\,d\theta$ we get

$$= \int_{\pi}^{0} \frac{\cos m\theta\,\cos n\theta}{\sin\theta}\,(-\sin\theta)\,d\theta$$

$$= \int_{0}^{\pi} \cos m\theta \cos n\theta\,d\theta \qquad \text{...(i)}$$

$$= \frac{1}{2}\int_{0}^{\pi} [\cos(m+n)\theta + \cos(m-n)\theta]\,d\theta$$

$$= \frac{1}{2}\int_{0}^{\pi} \left[\frac{1}{m+n}\sin(m+n)\theta + \frac{1}{m-n}\sin(m-n)\theta\right]_0^{\pi}$$

$$= 0, \quad \text{if } m \neq n$$

If $m = n \neq 0$, from (i), we have

$$\int_{-1}^{1} \frac{T_m(x)\, T_n(x)}{\sqrt{(1-x^2)}}\, dx = \int_0^{\pi} \cos^2 n\,\theta\, d\theta$$

$$= \frac{1}{2}\int_0^{\pi} (1 + \cos 2n\,\theta)\, d\theta$$

$$= \frac{1}{2}\left[\theta + \frac{1}{2n}\sin 2n\,\theta\right]_0^{\pi} = \pi/2$$

If m = n = 0, from (i), we have

$$\int_{-1}^{1} \frac{T_m(x)\, T_n(x)}{\sqrt{(1-x^2)}}\, dx = \int_0^{\pi} d\theta = \pi,$$

(ii) we have

$$U_m(x) = \sin(m \cos^{-1}x)$$
$$U_n(x) = \sin(n \cos^{-1}x)$$

$$\therefore \quad \int_{-1}^{1} \frac{U_m(x)\, U_n(x)}{\sqrt{(1-x^2)}}\, dx = \int_{-1}^{1} \frac{\sin(m\cos^{-1}x)\sin(n\cos^{-1}x)}{\sqrt{1-x^2}}\, dx$$

Putting $x = \cos\theta$, $dx = -\sin\theta\, d\theta$

$$= \int_0^{\pi} \sin m\,\theta \,.\, \sin n\,\theta\, d\theta \qquad \text{...(ii)}$$

$$= \frac{1}{2}\int_0^{\pi} [\cos(m-n)\,\theta - \cos(m+n)\,\theta]\, d\theta$$

$$= \frac{1}{2}\left[\frac{\sin(m-n)\,\theta}{m-n} - \frac{\sin(m+n)\,\theta}{m+n}\right]_0^{\pi}$$

$= 0,$ if $m \neq n$

If $m = n \neq 0$, from (ii), we have

$$\int_{-1}^{1} \frac{U_m(x)\, U_n(x)}{\sqrt{(1-x^2)}}\, dx = \int_0^{\pi} \sin^2 n\,\theta\, d\theta$$

$$= \frac{1}{2}\int_0^{\pi} (1 - \cos 2n\,\theta)\, d\theta$$

$$= \frac{1}{2}\left[\theta - \frac{1}{2n}\sin 2n\,\theta\right]_0^{\pi}$$

$= \pi/2.$

If $m = n = 0$, from (ii), we have

$$\int_{-1}^{1} \frac{U_m(x)\, U_n(x)}{\sqrt{(1-x^2)}}\, dx = 0$$

7.22 Recurrence Formulae for $T_n(x)$ and $U_n(x)$

(I) $T_{n+1}(x) - 2x\, T_n(x) + T_{n-1}(x) = 0$

We have $T_n(x) = \cos(n \cos^{-1}x)$

$= \cos n\,\theta$, Putting $x = \cos\theta$

$$\therefore \quad T_{n+1}(x) - 2x\, T_n(x) + T_{n-1}(x)$$
$$= \cos(n+1)\theta - 2\cos\theta\cos n\,\theta + \cos(n-1)\,\theta$$
$$= \cos(n+1)\theta - [\cos(n+1)\theta + \cos(n-1)\theta]$$

$$+ \cos (n-1)\theta$$

$$= 0.$$

(II) $(1 - x^2) T_n'(x) = - nx\, T_n(x) + n\, T_{n-1}(x)$

we have $T_n(x) = \cos (n \cos^{-1} x)$

$= \cos n\,\theta$, putting $x = \cos\theta$

Also $T'_n(x) = \dfrac{d}{dx} \cos (n \cos^{-1} x)$

$$= -\sin (n \cos^{-1} x) \cdot \frac{-n}{\sqrt{(1-x^2)}}$$

$$= \frac{n}{\sqrt{(1-x^2)}} \sin (n \cos^{-1} x)$$

$$= \frac{n \sin n\,\theta}{\sin\theta}$$

$\therefore$ $(1 - x^2)\, T_n'(x) = (1 - \cos^2\theta) \cdot \dfrac{n}{\sin\theta} \cdot \sin n\,\theta$

$$= n \sin\theta \sin n\,\theta$$

and $-n\,x\, T_n(x) + n\, T_{n-1}(x)$

$= -n \cos\theta \cos n\,\theta + n \cos (n-1)\,\theta$

$= -n \cos\theta \cos n\,\theta + n\, [\cos n\,\theta \cos\theta + \sin n\,\theta \sin\theta]$

$= n \sin\theta \sin n\,\theta$

$\therefore$ $(1 - x^2)\, T_n'(x) = - nx\, T_n(x) + n\, T_{n-1}(x)$

(III) $U_{n+1}(x) - 2x\, U_n(x) + U_{n-1}(x) = 0$

We have

$U_n(x) = \sin (n \cos^{-1} x)$

$= \sin n\theta$ where $x = \cos\theta$

$\therefore$ $U_{n+1}(x) - 2x\, U_n(x) + U_{n-1}(x)$

$= \sin (n+1)\,\theta - 2 \cos\theta \sin n\,\theta + \sin (n-1)\,\theta$

$= \sin (n+1)\,\theta - \{\sin (n+1)\,\theta + \sin (n-1)\,\theta\} + \sin(n-1)\theta$

$= 0.$

(IV) $(1-x^2)\, U_n'(x) = -nx\, U_n(x) + n\, U_{n-1}(x)$

We have

$U_n(x) = \sin (n \operatorname{Cos}^{-1} x)$

$= \sin n\,\theta$, putting $x = \cos\theta$

Also, $U_n'(x) = \dfrac{d}{dx} \sin (n \cos^{-1} x)$

$$= \cos (n \cos^{-1} x) \cdot \frac{-n}{\sqrt{(1-x^2)}}$$

$$= -\frac{n \cos n\,\theta}{\sin\theta}$$

$\therefore$ $(1-x^2)\, U_n'(x) = (1-\cos^2\theta) \dfrac{-n}{\sin\theta} \cos n\theta$

$$= -n \sin\theta \cos n\theta$$

$= n\ (\cos\theta \sin n\theta - \sin\theta \cos n\theta) - n \cos\theta \sin n\theta$

$= n\ U_{n-1}(x) - nx\ U_n(x)$

$\therefore \quad (1-x^2)\ U_n'(x) = -nx\ U_n(x) + n\ U_{n-1}(x)$

Illustrative Examples

Ex. 5. *Prove that*

(i) $T_n(1) = 1$, (ii) $T_{2n}(0) = (-1)^n$

(iii) $U_n(1) = 0$, (iv) $U_{2n}(0) = 0$.

Solution. We have $T_n(x) = \cos(n \cos^{-1} x)$...(i)

(i) Putting $x = 1$ in (i), we have

$T_n(1) = \cos(n \cos^{-1} 1) = \cos o° = 1$

(ii) Putting $x = 0$, in (i), we get

$$T_n(0) = \cos(n \cos^{-1} 0) = \cos \frac{n\pi}{2}$$

If n is even, say $n = 2m$

$\therefore \quad T_{2m}(0) = \cos m\pi = (-1)^m$

$\therefore \quad T_{2n}(0) = (-1)^n$

(iii) $U_n(x) = \sin(n \cos^{-1} x)$ ...(ii)

Putting $x = 1$ in (ii), we have

$U_n(1) = \sin(n \cos^{-1} 1) = \sin 0° = 0.$

(iv) Putting $x = 0$ in (ii), we get

$$U_n(0) = \sin(n \cos{-1}\ 0) = \sin \frac{n\pi}{2},$$

if n is even, say $n = 2m$, then

$U_{2m}(0) = \sin m\pi = 0.$

$\therefore \quad U_{2n}(0) = 0.$

Ex. 6. *Prove that*

$$[T_n(x)]^2 - T_{n+1}(x)\ T_{n-1}(x) = 1-x^2.$$

Solution. We have $T_n(x) = \cos(n \cos^{-1} x)$

$= \cos n\theta$, when $x = \cos\theta$

$\therefore \quad [T_n(x)]^2 - \cos(n+1)\theta \cos(n-1)\theta$

$= \cos^2 n\theta - \cos(n+1)\theta \cos(n-1)\theta$

$= \cos^2 n\theta - (\cos^2 n\theta - \sin^2\theta) = \sin^2\theta$

$= 1 - \cos^2\theta = 1 - x^2.$

Ex. 7. *Prove that* $T_n'(x) = \dfrac{n}{\sqrt{1-x^2)}} U_n(x)$

Solution. We have $T_n'(x) = \cos(n \cos^{-1} x)$

and $U_n(x) = \sin(n \cos^{-1} x)$

$$\therefore \quad T_n'(x) = \frac{d}{dx} \cos(n \cos^{-1} x)$$

$$= -\sin(n \cos^{-1} x) \cdot \frac{-n}{\sqrt{(1-x^2)}}$$

$$= \frac{n}{\sqrt{1-x^2}} \sin(n \cos^{-1} x)$$

$$= \frac{n}{\sqrt{1-x^2}} \mathrm{U}_n(x).$$

Ex. 8. *Show that*

$$\sqrt{(1-x^{2)}}\, T_n(x) = U_{n+1}(x) - x\, U_n(x)$$

Solution. We have

$$\mathrm{T}_n(x) = \cos(n \cos^{-1} x) = \cos n\,\theta, \text{ where } x = \cos\theta$$

and $\mathrm{U}_n(x) = \sin(n \cos^{-1} x) = \sin n\,\theta$

$\therefore$ $\sqrt{(1-x^{2)}}\, \mathrm{T}_n(x) = \sin\theta \cos n\,\theta$

$$= (\sin\theta\cos n\,\theta + \cos\theta \sin n\,\theta) - \cos\theta \sin n\,\theta$$

$$= \sin(n+1)\,\theta - \cos\theta \sin n\,\theta$$

$$= \mathrm{U}_{n+1}(x) - x\,\mathrm{U}_{n.}(x).$$

Ex. 9. *Show that*

$$\sqrt{(1-x^{2)}}\, U_n(x) = x\, T_n(x) - T_{n+1}(x)$$

Solution. We have

$$\mathrm{T}_n(x) = \cos(n \cos^{-1} x) = \cos n\,\theta, \text{ where } x = \cos\theta$$

and $\mathrm{U}_n(x) = \sin(n \cos^{-1} x) = \sin n\,\theta$

$\therefore$ $= \sqrt{(1-x^2)}\, U_n(x) = \sin\theta \sin\theta\, x$

$$= \cos\theta\cos n\,\theta - (\cos\theta\cos n\,\theta - \sin\theta\sin n\,\theta)$$

$$= \cos\theta\cos n\,\theta - \cos(n+1)\,\theta$$

$$= x\,\mathrm{T}_n(x) - \mathrm{T}_{n+1}(x).$$

Ex. 10. *Show that* $\frac{1}{\sqrt{(1-x^{2)}}} U_n(x)$ *satisfies the differential equation* $(1 - x^2)\frac{d^2y}{dx^2} - 3x\frac{dy}{dx} + (n^2-1)\,y = 0.$

Solution. Let $y = \frac{1}{\sqrt{1-x^{2)}}} \mathrm{U}_n(x)$

$$\therefore \quad \frac{dy}{dx} = \frac{1}{\sqrt{1-x^2)}} \mathrm{U}_n'(x) + \frac{x}{(1-x^2)^{3/2}} \mathrm{U}_n(x)$$

and

$$\frac{d^2y}{dx^2} = \frac{1}{\sqrt{1-x^2)}} \mathrm{U}_n''(x) + \frac{2x}{(1-x^2)^{3/2}} \mathrm{U}_n'(x)$$

$$+ \frac{1}{(1-x^2)^{3/2}} \mathrm{U}_n(x) + \frac{3x^2}{(1-x^2)^{5/2}} \mathrm{U}_n(x)$$

$$\therefore \quad (1-x^2)\frac{d^2y}{dx^2} - 3x\frac{dy}{dx} + (\mathrm{n}^2-1)\,y$$

$$= (1-x^2)\left[\frac{1}{\sqrt{(1-x^2)}} U_n''(x) + \frac{2x}{(1-x^2)^{3/2}} U_n'(x) + \frac{1}{(1-x^2)^{3/2}} U_n(x) + \frac{3x^2}{(1-x^2)^{3/2}} U_n(x)\right]$$

$$- 3x\left[\frac{1}{\sqrt{(1-x^{2)}}} U_n'(x) + \frac{x}{(1-x^2)^{3/2}} U_n(x) + \frac{(n^2-1)}{\sqrt{(1-x^2)}} U_n(x)\right]$$

$$= \frac{1}{\sqrt{(1-x^2)}} [(1 - x^2) U_n'' (x) - x U_n' (x) + n^2 U_n (x)] = 0$$

Since $U_n (x)$ is the solution of

$$(1-x^2) \frac{d^2y}{dx^2} - x \frac{dy}{dx} + n^2y = 0.$$

Exercise – 7

1. Prove that $L_n (0) = n\,!$

2. Show that $\int_x^{\infty} x^5 e^{-x} L_{10} (x) \, dx = 0.$

3. Prove that

$$L_n' (x) - x L'_{n-1} (x) + n L_{n-1} (x) = 0.$$

4. From $L^{\alpha}_n (x) = \frac{e^x x^{-\alpha}}{n\,!} \frac{d^n}{dx^n} (e^{-x} . x^{n+\alpha}).$

prove that $L_1^2 (x) = 3-x.$

5. Prove that

(i) $\int_0^{\infty} e^{-x} L_3 (x) L_5 (x) \, dx = 0.$

and (ii) $\int_0^{\infty} e^{-x} L_4^2 (x) \, dx = 1.$

6. Prove that

$$2 [T_n (x)]^2 = 1 + T_{2n} (x).$$

7. Prove that

$$T_{m+n} (x) + T_{m-n} (x) = 2T_m (x) T_n (x).$$

8. Prove that

$$T_n (x) - 2x T_{n-1} (x) + T_{n-2} (x) = 0.$$

8

Hypergeometric Functions

8.1 Hypergeometric Function

The Peohhammer symbol $(\alpha)_r$ is defined by

$$(\alpha)_r = \alpha\,(\alpha+1)\,(\alpha+2)\,...\,(\alpha+r-1)$$

$$= \frac{\Gamma(\alpha+r)}{\Gamma(\alpha)}, \text{ where } r \text{ is a positive integer}$$

and $\quad (\alpha)_0 = 1.$

The general *hypergeometric function.*

$${}_mF_n\,(\alpha_1, \alpha_2, ... ; \alpha_m ; \beta_1, \beta_2 ... , \beta_n ; x)$$

is defined by

$${}_mF_n\,(\alpha_1, \alpha_2, ... , \alpha_m ; \beta_1, \beta_2 ... \beta_n ; x) = \sum_{r=0}^{\infty} \frac{(\alpha_1)_r\,(\alpha_2)_r \cdots (\alpha_m)_r}{(\beta_1)_r\,(\beta_2)_r \cdots (\beta_n)_r} \cdot \frac{x^r}{r\,!}$$

Another notation often used for general hypergeometric function is

$${}_mF_n = \left[\begin{matrix} \alpha_1, & \alpha_2, & .... & \alpha_m ; \\ \beta_1, & \beta_2, & .... & \beta_n ; \end{matrix} \; x\right]$$

Here we shall consider only two cases.

Case I $\quad m = n = 1.$

In this case the hypergeometric function ${}_1F_1\,(\alpha, \beta, x)$ will be called the' confluent hypergeometric function or kummer function. Thus

$${}_1F_1\,(\alpha, \beta, x) = \sum_{r=0}^{\infty} \frac{(\alpha)_r}{(\beta)_r} \cdot \frac{x^r}{r!}$$

The confluent hypergeometric function ${}_1F_1\,(\alpha, \beta, x)$ is also denoted by M (α, β, x).

Case II $\quad m = 2, n = 1.$

In this case the hypergeometric function ${}_2F_1\,(\alpha_1, \alpha_2, \beta, x)$ will merely be called the *hypergeometric function.* Thus

$${}_2F_1\,(\alpha_1, \alpha_2, \beta, x) = \sum_{r=0}^{\infty} \frac{(\alpha_1)_r\,(\alpha_2)_r}{(\beta)_r} \cdot \frac{x^r}{r\,!}$$

The hypergeometric function ${}_2F_1\,(\alpha_1, \alpha_2, \beta, x)$ is also denoted by $F\,(\alpha_1, \alpha_2, \beta, x)$

8.2 Gauss's Hypergeometric equation

A differential equation of the type

$$x(1-x)\frac{d^2y}{dx^2}+[c-(a+b+1)x]\frac{dy}{dx}-aby=0$$

is called *Gauss's hypergeometric equation* or *hypergeomtric equation* or simply *Gauss's equation.*

8.3 The Hypergeometric Series

The series $1+\frac{ab}{1!c}x+\frac{a(a+1)b(b+1)}{2!c(c+1)}x^2$

$$+\frac{a(a+1)(a+2)b(b+1)(b+2)}{3!c(c+1)(c+2)}x^3+\ldots$$

is called the *hypergeometric series* and is denoted by ${}_2F_1(a, b, c, x)$.

This series converges absolutely if $|x|<1$ and if $|x|= 1$, and series converges absolutely if $c-a-b>0$ or $c>a+b$.

8.4 Particular cases of Hypergeometric Series

1. $$\log(1+x)=x-\frac{x^2}{2}+\frac{x^3}{3}-\frac{x^4}{4}+\ldots$$

$$=x\left[1-\frac{x}{2}+\frac{x^2}{3}-\frac{x^3}{4}+\ldots\right]$$

$$=x\left[1+\frac{1.1}{1!2}(-x)+\frac{1(1+1).1(1+1)}{2!2(2+1)}(-x)^2+\frac{1.(1+1)(1+2).1(1+1)(1+2)}{3!2(2+1)(2+2)}(-x)^3+\ldots\right]$$

$$=x\,.\,{}_2F_1(1,1,2,-x).$$

2. $$(1+x)^n=1+nx+\frac{n(n-1)}{2!}x^2+\frac{n(n-1)(n-2)}{3!}x^3+\ldots$$

$$=1+\frac{(-n).1}{1!1}(-x)+\frac{(-n)(-n+1)(1)(1+1)}{2!1(1+1)}+\frac{(-n)(-n+1)(-n+2).1(1+1)(1+2)}{3!.1(1+1).(1+2)}(-x)^3+\ldots$$

$$={}_2F_1(-n,1,1,-x).$$

3. $$\tan^{-1}x=x-\frac{x^3}{3}+\frac{x^5}{5}-\frac{x^7}{7}+\ldots$$

$$=x\left[1-\frac{x^2}{3}+\frac{x^4}{5}-\frac{x^6}{7}+\ldots\right]$$

$$=x\left[1+\frac{\frac{1}{2}.1}{1!.\frac{3}{2}}(-x^2)+\frac{\frac{1}{2}\left(\frac{1}{2}+1\right).1(1+1)}{2!\frac{3}{2}\left(\frac{3}{2}+1\right)}(-x^2)^2+\ldots\right]$$

$$=x\,.\,{}_2F_1\left(\frac{1}{2},1,\frac{3}{2},-x^2\right)$$

8.5 Different forms of Hypergeometric Function

The hypergeometric function $F\ (a, b, c, x)$ can be put in the following forms as well :

$$F\ (a,\ b,\ c,\ x) = (1-x)^{c-a-b}\ {}_2F_1\ (c-a,\ c-b,\ c-x) \qquad \text{...(i)}$$

$$= (1-x)^{-a}\ {}_2F_1\left(a, c-b, c, \frac{x}{x-1}\right) \qquad \text{...(ii)}$$

$$= (1-x)^{-b}\ {}_2F_1\left(b, c-a, c, \frac{x}{x-1}\right) \qquad \text{...(iii)}$$

8.6 Solution of the Hypergeometric Equation

Deviding the hypergeometric differential equation throughout by (x^2-x), we have

$$\frac{d^2y}{dx^2} + x_1 \frac{dy}{dx} + x_2 y = 0$$

where $\quad x_1 = \dfrac{(1+\alpha+\beta)\,x - \nu}{(x^2-x)}$ and $x_2 = \dfrac{\alpha\beta}{(x^2-x)}$

Hence $\quad x_1 \longrightarrow \infty$ when $x = 0$ or 1, or ∞

and $\quad x_2 \longrightarrow \infty$ when $x = 0$ or 1, or ∞

Hence $\quad x = 0$, $x = 1$ and $x = \infty$ are the singular points.

Since $(x^2 - x)\ x_1$ and $(x^2-x)^2\ x_2$ remain finite for all finite values of x therefore hypergeometric differential equation can be solved by series integration method.

The hypergeometric differential equation is

$$x\ (1-x)\ \frac{d^2y}{dx^2} + [\nu - (\alpha + \beta + 1)\ x]\ \frac{dy}{dx} - \alpha\beta y = 0 \qquad \text{...(i)}$$

(a) When x is small. Let us consider the solution of (i) in ascending *powers of* x as

$$y = \sum_{r=0} a_r x^{k+r}$$

so that
$$\frac{dy}{dx} = \sum_{r=0}^{\infty} a_r\ (k+r)\ x^{k+r-1}$$

and
$$\frac{d^2y}{dx^2} = \sum_{r=0}^{\infty} a_r\ (k+r)\ (k+r-1)\ x^{k+r-2} \qquad \text{...(ii)}$$

Substituting in (i), we have

$$\sum_{r=0}^{\infty} a_r\ [\ (x^2 - x)\ (k+r)\ (k+r-1)\ x^{k+r-2} + \{\ (1+\alpha+\beta)\ x-\nu\ \}\ (k+r)\ x^{k+r-1} + \alpha\beta\ x^{k+r}\ ] = 0$$

or
$$\sum_{r=0}^{\infty} a_r\ [\ \{\ (k+r)^2 + (\alpha + \beta)\ (k+r) + \alpha\beta\ \}\ x^{k+r} - (k+r)\ (k+r+\nu-1)\ x^{k+r-1}\ \} = 0 \qquad \text{...(iii)}$$

Now (iii) being an identity, we can equate to zero the coefficients of various powers of x.

$\therefore$ Equating to zero the coefficient of lowest power of x, i.e., of x^{k-1}, we have

$$a_0\, k\,(k+\nu-1) = 0$$

Now, $a_0 \neq 0$, as it is the coefficient of the first term with which the series is started.

$$\left.\begin{aligned} \therefore \quad & k = 0 \\ \text{or} \quad & k = 1-\nu \end{aligned}\right\} \qquad \text{...(iv)}$$

Equating the coefficient of the next higher power of x, i.e., of x^k, to zero, we get

$$a_0\,\{k^2 + (\alpha+\beta)\,k + \alpha\beta\} - (k+1)\,(k+\nu)\,a_1 = 0$$

$$\therefore \quad a_1 = \frac{k^2 + (\alpha+\beta)\,k + \alpha\beta}{(k+1)\,(k+\nu)}\,a_0$$

or

$$a_1 = \frac{(k+\alpha)\,(k+\beta)}{(k+1)\,(k+\nu)}\,a_0$$

Again equating to zero the coefficient of the general term, i.e., of x^{k+r}, we get

$$a_r\,\{(k+r)^2 + (\alpha+\beta)\,(k+r) + \alpha\beta\} - (k+r+1)\,(k+r+\nu)\,a_{r+1} = 0$$

$$\therefore \quad a_{r+1} = \frac{(k+r+\alpha)\,(k+r+\beta)}{(k+r+1)\,(k+r+\nu)}\,a_r \qquad \text{...(v)}$$

Case I When $k = 0$

From (v), we have

$$a_{r+1} = \frac{(\alpha+r)\,(\beta+r)}{(r+1)\,(\nu+r)}\,a_r$$

Puttin $r = 0, 1, 2, \ldots$

$$a_1 = \frac{\alpha.\beta}{1.\nu}$$

$$a_2 = \frac{(\alpha+1)\,(\beta+1)}{2.(\nu+1)}\,a_1 = \frac{\alpha(\alpha+1)\,\beta\,(\beta+1)}{2\,!\,\nu\,(\nu+1)}\,a_0\,.$$

$$a_3 = \frac{(\alpha+2)\,(\beta+2)}{2\,!\,(\nu+2)}\,a_2 = \frac{\alpha\,(\alpha+1)\,(\alpha+2)\,\beta\,(\beta+1)\,(\beta+2)}{2\,!\,\nu\,(\nu+1)\,(\nu+2)}\,a_0$$

$\therefore$ From (ii) we have

$$y = a_0 x^k + a_1\,x^{k+1} + a^2\,x^{k+2} + \ldots$$

or

$$y = a_0\left[1 + \frac{\alpha\beta}{1.\nu}\,x + \frac{\alpha\,(\alpha+1)\,\beta\,(\beta+1)}{2\,!\,\nu\,(\nu+1)}\,x^2 + \frac{\alpha(\alpha+1)\,(\alpha+2)\,\beta\,(\beta+1)\,(\beta+2)}{3\,!\,\nu\,(\nu+1)\,(\nu+2)}\,x^3 + \ldots + \frac{(\alpha)_n\,(\beta)_n}{n\,!\,(\nu)_n}\,x^n + \ldots\right]$$

Since $k = 0$

$$= a_0 \sum_{n=0}^{\infty} \frac{(\alpha)_n (\beta)_n}{n!(\nu)_n} x^n$$

$$= a_0 \cdot {}_2F_1(\alpha, \beta, \nu, x). \quad \text{where } (\alpha)_n = \alpha(\alpha+1) \ldots (\alpha+n-1)$$

If $a_0 = 1$, this series called the *hypergeometric series* and its sum y denoted by ${}_2f_1(\alpha, \beta, \nu, x)$ is called the *hypergeometric function.*

In case $\alpha = 1$ and $\beta = \nu$ then the hypergeometric series becomes

$$y = 1 + x + x^2 + x^3 + \ldots$$

which is a geometric series. That is why it is called *hypergeometric series.*

Case II. When $k = 1-\nu$, from (v) we have

$$a_{r+1} = \frac{(1-\nu+r+\alpha)(1-\nu+r+\beta)}{(1-\nu+r+1)(1-\nu+r+\nu)} \cdot a_r.$$

or
$$a_{r+1} = \frac{(\alpha'+r)(\beta'+r)}{(\nu'+r)(r+1)} a_r$$

where
$$\alpha' = 1 - \nu + \alpha$$
$$\beta' = 1 - \nu + \beta$$

and
$$\nu' = 2 - \nu$$

Putting $r = 0, 1, 2, \ldots$ we have

$$a_1 = \frac{\alpha' . \beta'}{1.\nu'} a_0$$

$$a_2 = \frac{(\alpha'+1)(\beta'+1)}{2.(\nu'+1)} a_1$$

$$= \alpha' \frac{(\alpha'+1)\beta'(\beta'+1)}{2!\nu'(\nu'+1)} a_0$$

$$a_3 = \frac{(\alpha'+2))(\beta'+2)}{3(\nu'+2)} a_2$$

$$= \frac{\alpha'(\alpha'+1)(\alpha'+2)\beta'(\beta'+1)(\beta'+2)}{3!\nu'(\nu'+1)(\nu'+2)} a_0 \text{ etc.}$$

$\therefore$ from (iii), we have

$$y = a_0 x^k + a_1 x^{k+1} + a_2 x^{k+2} + \ldots$$

$$= a_0 x^k \left[1 + \frac{\alpha' . \beta'}{1.\nu'} x + \frac{\alpha'(\alpha'+1)\beta'(\beta'+1)}{2!\nu'(\nu'+2)} x^2 + \ldots\right]$$

$$= a_0 x^{1-\nu} \left[1 + \frac{\alpha'.\beta'}{1.\nu} x + \frac{\alpha'(\alpha'+1)\beta'(\beta'+1)}{2!\nu'(\nu'+1)} x^2 + \ldots + \frac{(\alpha')_n(\beta')_n}{n!(\nu')_n} x^n + \ldots\right]$$

$$= a_0 x^{1-\nu} \sum_{n=0}^{\infty} \frac{(\alpha')_n (\beta')_n}{(n!(\nu')_n} x^n$$

$$= a_0 x^{1-\nu} {}_2F_1(\alpha', \beta'; \nu'; x)$$

$$= x^{1-\nu} {}_2F_1(\alpha - \nu + 1, \beta - \nu + 1; 2-\nu; x) \quad \ldots\text{(vii)}$$

as $a_0 = 1$.

Thus we get two independent particular solutions (vi) and (vii) of the hypergeometric equation about $x = 0$.

Hence the general solution is given by

$$y = A\,{}_2F_1(\alpha, \beta; \nu; x) + Bx^{1-\nu}\,{}_2F_1(\alpha-\nu+1, \beta-\nu+1; 2-\nu; x) \quad \ldots\text{(viii)}$$

Note ν should not be a negative interger or unity. Since when ν = –ve integer ${}_2F_1$ (α, β; ν ; x) can not be obtained and when ν = 1, the solution (vii) is identical with solution (vi).

(b) **When $x = 1$** If $1-x = z$.

Then
$$\frac{dz}{dx} = -1.$$

$$\frac{dy}{dx} = \frac{dy}{dz} \cdot \frac{dz}{dx} = -\frac{dy}{dz}$$

and
$$\frac{d^2y}{dx^2} = \frac{d}{dx}\left(\frac{dy}{dx}\right) = \frac{d}{dx}\left(-\frac{dy}{dz}\right)$$
$$= -\frac{d^2y}{dz^2} \cdot \frac{dz}{dx} = \frac{d^2y}{dz^2}.$$

Thus equation (i) reduces to

$$z(1-z)\frac{d^2y}{dz^2} + [\nu - (\alpha+\beta+1)(z+1)]\left(-\frac{dy}{dz}\right) - \alpha\beta\nu = 0.$$

or
$$z(1-z)\frac{d^2y}{dz^2} + [(\alpha+\beta-\nu+1) - (\alpha+\beta+1)z]\frac{dy}{dz} - \alpha\beta\nu = 0,$$

which is identical with (i) with ν replaced by α + β – ν + 1 and x by $z = 1-x$.

Hence from (viii), the required solution is

$$y = A\,{}_2F_1(\alpha, \beta; \alpha+\beta-\nu+1; 1-x)$$
$$+ B(1-x)^{\nu-\alpha-\beta}\,{}_2F_1(\nu-\beta, \nu-\alpha; \nu-\alpha+\beta+1; 1-x)$$

or
$$y = A \,.\, {}_2F_1(\alpha, \beta; \alpha+\beta-\nu+1; 1-x)$$
$$+ B.(1-x)^{\nu-\alpha-\beta}\,{}_2F_1(\nu-\beta, \nu-\alpha; \nu-\alpha+\beta+1; 1-x) \quad \text{...(ix)}$$

(c) **When $x = \infty$.** In this case we consider the solution of (i) as

$$y = \sum_{r=0}^{\infty} a_r x^{-k-r}$$

Substituting in (i), we have

$$\sum_{r=0}^{\infty} a_r [(-k-r)(-k-r-1+\nu)x^{-k-r-1}$$
$$- (k-r+\alpha)(-k-r+\beta)x^{-k-r}] = 0 \quad \text{...(x)}$$

Equating to zero coefficient of x^{-k}, we have

$$a_0(-k+\alpha)(-k+\beta) = 0$$

$$\because \quad a_0 \neq 0$$

$$\therefore \quad \left.\begin{aligned} k &= \alpha \\ \text{or} \quad k &= \beta \end{aligned}\right\} \quad \text{...(xi)}$$

Again equating to zero the coefficient of the general term, i.e., of x^{-k-r}, we have

$$a_{r-1}(-k-r+1)(-k-r+\nu) - a_r(-k-r+\alpha)(-k-r+\beta) = 0$$

$$\therefore \quad a_r = \frac{(-k-r+1)(-k-r-\nu)}{(-k-r+\alpha)(-k-r+\beta)} a_{r-1}$$

Case I. When $k = \alpha$,

$$a_r = \frac{(r+\alpha-1)(r+\alpha-\nu)}{r(r+\alpha+\beta)} a_{r-1}.$$

Putting $r = 1, 2, 3, \ldots$

$$a_1 = \frac{\alpha(1+\alpha-\nu)}{1.(1+\alpha+\beta)} a_0$$

$$a_2 = \frac{(\alpha+1)(2+\alpha-\nu)}{2.(2+\alpha-\beta)} a_1$$

$$= \frac{(\alpha+1)(2+\alpha-\nu)}{2.(2+\alpha-\beta)} \cdot \frac{\alpha.(1+\alpha-\nu)}{1.(1+\alpha-\beta)} a_0$$

$$= \frac{\alpha(\alpha+1).(1+\alpha-\nu)(2+\alpha-\nu)}{2!(1+\alpha-\beta)(2+\alpha-\beta)} a_0$$

--- --- ---

--- --- ---

$$a_n = \frac{[\alpha(\alpha+1)\ldots(\alpha+r-1).(1+\alpha-\nu)(1+1+\alpha-\nu)\ldots(1+r-1+\alpha-\nu)\ldots]}{2!(\alpha+\alpha-\beta)(1+1+\alpha-\beta)\ldots(1+r-1+\alpha-\beta)} a_0$$

$$= \frac{(\alpha)_r(1+\alpha-\nu)_r}{r!(\alpha-\beta+1)_r} a_0$$

$$\therefore \qquad y = \sum_{r=0}^{\infty} \frac{(\alpha)_r(1+\alpha-\nu)_r}{r!(\alpha-\beta+1)_r} x^{-\alpha-r} \text{ when } a_0 = 1$$

or

$$y = x^{-\alpha} \sum_{r=0}^{\infty} \frac{(\alpha)_r(\alpha+\beta-1)_r}{r!(\alpha-\beta+1)_r} \left(\frac{1}{x}\right)^r$$

or

$$y = x^{-\alpha}\, {}_2F_1\left(\alpha, \alpha-\nu+1; \alpha-\beta+1; \frac{1}{x}\right)$$

Case II. When $k = \beta$

$$y = x^{-\beta}\, {}_2F_1\left(\beta, \beta-\nu+1; \beta-\alpha+1; \frac{1}{x}\right).$$

Hence the general solution is

$$y = A x^{-\alpha}\, {}_2F_1\left(\alpha, \alpha-\nu+1; \alpha-\beta+1; \frac{1}{x}\right)$$
$$+ B x^{-\beta}\, {}_2F_1\left(\beta, \beta-\nu+1; \beta+\alpha+1; \frac{1}{x}\right) \qquad \ldots(\text{xii})$$

8.7 Linear relation between the solution of the hypergeometric equation

In the solution (vii) of § 8.6 the series will be convergent if $|x| < 1$, i.e., in the interval $(-1, 1)$. Similarly, the series in the solution (ix) are convergent in the interval $(0, 2)$. Thus in the interval $(0, 1)$ all the four series in (viii) and (ix) are convergent. Since only two solutions of the differential equation (i) are linearly independent there must exist a linear relation between the solutions (viii) and (ix) in the interval $(0, 1)$. So let

$${}_2F_1(\alpha, \beta; \nu; x) = A . {}_2F_1(\alpha, \beta; \alpha-\beta-\nu+1; 1-x)$$
$$+ B(1-x)^{\nu-\alpha-\beta}\, {}_2F_1(\nu-\alpha, \nu-\beta; \nu-\alpha-\beta+1; 1-x) \qquad \ldots(\text{i})$$

To determine the constants A and B, suppose that $\alpha + \beta < \nu < 1$, so that three series

$${}_2F_1(\alpha, \beta; \nu; 1),\ {}_2F_1(\alpha, \beta; \alpha+\beta-\nu+1; 1),$$
$${}_2F_1(\nu-\alpha, \nu-\beta; \nu-\alpha-\beta+1; 1) \text{ are convergent.}$$

Putting $x = 0$ and $x = 1$ in (i), we have

$$1 = A\,.\,{}_2F_1(\alpha, \beta; \alpha+\beta-\nu+1; 1) + B\,.\,{}_2F_1(\nu-\alpha, \nu-\beta; \nu-\alpha-\beta+1; 1)$$

and
$${}_2F_1(\alpha, \beta; \nu; 1) = A$$

or
$$A = \frac{\Gamma(\nu)\,\Gamma(\nu-\alpha-\beta)}{\Gamma(\nu-\alpha)\,\Gamma(\nu-\beta)}$$

and
$$1 = A.\frac{\Gamma(\alpha+\beta-\nu+1)\,\Gamma(1-\nu)}{\Gamma(\beta-\nu+1)\,\Gamma(\alpha-\nu+1)} + B\,.\,\frac{\Gamma(\nu-\alpha-\beta+1)\,.\,\Gamma(1-\nu)}{\Gamma(1-\beta)\,\Gamma(1-\alpha)}$$

[from Gauss's Theorem]

or
$$1 = \frac{\Gamma(\nu)\,\Gamma(\nu-\alpha-\beta)}{\Gamma(\nu-\alpha)\,\Gamma(\nu-\beta)}\cdot\frac{\Gamma(\alpha+\beta-\nu+1)\,\Gamma(1-\nu)}{\Gamma(\beta-\nu+1)\,\Gamma(\alpha-\nu+1)} + B\,\frac{\Gamma(\nu-\alpha-\beta+1)\,\Gamma(1-\nu)}{\Gamma(1-\beta)\,\Gamma(1-\alpha)}$$

or
$$1 = \frac{\{\Gamma(\nu)\,\Gamma(1-\nu)\}\,\{\Gamma(\nu-\alpha-\beta)\,\Gamma(\alpha+\beta-\nu+1)\}}{\{\Gamma(\nu-\alpha)\,.\,\Gamma(\alpha-\nu+1)\}\,.\,\{\Gamma(\nu-\beta)\,\Gamma(\beta-\nu+1)\}} + B\,.\,\frac{\Gamma(\nu-\alpha-\beta+1)\,\Gamma(1-\nu)}{\Gamma(1-\beta)\,\Gamma(1-\alpha)}$$

or
$$1 = \frac{(\pi\, coses\, \pi\,\nu)\,.\,\pi\{cosec\,\pi(\nu-\alpha-\beta)\}}{\{\pi\, cosec\,\pi(\nu-\alpha)\}\,.\,\{\pi\, cosec\,\pi(\nu-\beta)\}} + B\,.\,\frac{\Gamma(\nu-\alpha-\beta+1)\,\Gamma(1-\nu)}{\Gamma(1-\beta)\,\Gamma(1-\alpha)}$$

(Since $\Gamma(\alpha)\,\Gamma(1-\alpha) = \pi\,\text{cosec}\,\pi\ \iota$)

or
$$B.\frac{\Gamma(\nu-\alpha+\beta-1)\,\Gamma(1-\nu)}{\Gamma(1-\beta)\,\Gamma(1-\alpha)} = 1 - \frac{\sin\pi(\nu-\alpha)\sin\pi(\nu-\beta)}{\sin\pi\nu\,.\,\sin\pi(\nu-\alpha-\beta)}$$

$$= \frac{\sin\pi\nu\,.\,\sin\pi(\nu-\alpha-\beta) - \sin\pi(\nu-\alpha)\,.\,\sin\pi(\nu-\beta)}{\sin\pi\nu\,.\,\sin\pi(\nu-\alpha-\beta)}$$

$$= \frac{\cos\pi(\alpha-\beta) - \cos\pi(2\nu-\alpha-\beta) - \cos\pi(\alpha-\beta) + \cos\pi(2\nu-\alpha-\beta)}{2\sin\pi y\,.\,\sin\pi(\nu-\alpha-\beta)}$$

$$= \frac{\cos\pi(\alpha+\beta) - \cos\pi(\alpha-\beta)}{2\sin\pi\nu\,.\,\sin\pi(\nu-\alpha-\beta)}$$

$$= \frac{-2\sin\pi\beta\sin\pi\alpha}{2\sin\pi\nu\,.\,\sin\pi(\nu-\alpha-\beta)}$$

or
$$B\,.\,\frac{\Gamma(\alpha)\,\Gamma(\beta)}{\Gamma(\nu)\,\Gamma(\alpha+\beta-\nu)} \times \frac{\{\Gamma(\alpha+\beta-\nu)\,\Gamma(\nu-\alpha-\beta+1)\}\,\{\Gamma(\nu)\,.\,\Gamma 1(-\nu)\}}{\{\Gamma(\beta)\,\Gamma(1-\beta)\}\,\{\Gamma(\alpha)\,.\,\Gamma(1-\alpha)\}} = \frac{\sin\pi\alpha\,.\,\sin\pi\beta}{\sin\pi\nu\,.\,\sin\pi(\alpha+\beta-\nu)}$$

or
$$B\,.\,\frac{\Gamma(\alpha)\,\Gamma(\beta)}{\Gamma(\nu)\,.\,\Gamma(\alpha+\beta-\nu)} \times \frac{\{\pi\, cosec\,\pi(\alpha+\beta-\nu)\}\,\{\pi\, cosec\,\pi\nu\}}{\{\pi\, cosec\,\pi\beta\}\,\{\pi\, cosec\,\pi\alpha\}}$$

$$= \frac{\sin \pi \alpha \,.\, \sin \pi \beta}{\sin \pi \nu \sin \pi (\alpha+\beta-\nu)}$$

$$\therefore \qquad B = \frac{\Gamma(\nu)\,\Gamma(\alpha+\beta-\nu)}{\Gamma(\alpha)\,\Gamma(\beta)}$$

Hence from (i), we have

$$_2F_1(\alpha, \beta; \nu; x) = \frac{\Gamma(\nu)\,\Gamma(\nu-\alpha-\beta)}{\Gamma(\nu-\alpha)\,\Gamma(\nu-\beta)} \,.\, {}_2F_1(\alpha, \beta; \alpha+\beta-\nu+1; 1-x)$$

$$+ \frac{\Gamma(\nu)\,\Gamma(\alpha+\beta-\nu)}{\Gamma(\alpha)\,\Gamma(\beta)} \,.\, (1-x)^{\nu-\alpha-\beta}$$

$$\times\ {}_2F_1(\nu-\alpha, \nu-\beta; \nu-\alpha-\beta+1; 1-x).$$

8.8 Symmetric Property of hypergeometric function

It is obvious that hypergeometric function does not change if the parameters α and β are interchanged, keeping ν fixed,

i.e., $\qquad {}_2F_1(\alpha, \beta, \nu, x) = {}_2F_1(\beta, \alpha, \nu, x)$

This is known as the *symmetric property* of hypergeometric function.

8.9 Integral formaula

If $|x| < 1$ *and if* $\nu > \beta > 0$, *then*

$$_2F_1(\alpha, \beta; \nu; x) = \frac{\Gamma(\nu)}{\Gamma(\beta)\,\Gamma(\nu-\beta)} \int_0^1 t^{\beta-1} (1-t)^{\nu-\beta-1} (1-xt)^{-\alpha}\, dt$$

We have

$$_2F_1(\alpha, \beta; \nu; x) = \sum_{n=0}^{\infty} \frac{(\alpha)_n (\beta)_n}{n!\,(\nu)_n} x^n \qquad \text{...(i)}$$

where $\qquad (\alpha)_n = \alpha(\alpha+1) \ldots (\alpha+n-1)$

$$= \frac{1.2 \ldots (\alpha-1)\,\alpha\,(\alpha+1) \ldots (\alpha+n-1)}{1.2 \ldots (\alpha-1)}$$

$$= \frac{\Gamma(\alpha+n)}{\Gamma(\alpha)}$$

$$\therefore \qquad \frac{(\beta)_n}{(\nu)_n} = \frac{\Gamma(\beta+n)}{\Gamma(\beta)} \cdot \frac{\Gamma(\nu)}{\Gamma(\nu+n)}$$

$$= \frac{\Gamma(\nu)\,\Gamma(\beta+n)\,\Gamma(\nu-\beta)}{\Gamma(\beta)\,\Gamma(\nu+n)\,\Gamma(\nu-\beta)}$$

$$= \frac{\Gamma(\nu)\,\Gamma(\beta+n)\,\Gamma(\nu-\beta)}{\Gamma(\beta)\,\Gamma(b+n+\nu-\beta)} \cdot \frac{1}{\Gamma(\nu-\beta)}$$

$$= \frac{\Gamma(\nu)}{\Gamma(\beta)\Gamma(\nu-\beta)} \cdot \int_0^1 (1-t)^{\nu-\beta-1}\, t^{\beta+n-1}\, dt$$

$$\left[\text{Since } \frac{\Gamma(m)\,\Gamma(n)}{\Gamma(m+n)} = B(m, n) = \int_0^1 (1-t)^{n-1}\, t^{m-1}\, dt\right]$$

$$= \frac{1}{\frac{\Gamma(\beta)\,\Gamma(\nu-\beta)}{\Gamma(\beta+\nu-\beta)}} \cdot \int_0^1 t^{\beta+n-1} (1-t)^{\nu-\beta-1}\, dt$$

$$= \frac{1}{B(\beta, \nu-\beta)} \cdot \int_0^1 t^{\beta+n-1} (1-t)^{\nu-\beta-1}\, dt$$

$\therefore$ From (i), we have

$${}_2F_1(\alpha, \beta, \nu, x) = \sum_{n=0}^{\infty} \frac{1}{B(\beta, \nu-\beta)} \cdot \int_0^1 t^{\beta+n-1} (1-t)^{\nu-\beta-1} \left\{\frac{(\alpha)_n x^n}{n!}\right\} dt$$

$$= \sum_{n=1}^{\infty} \frac{1}{B(\beta, \nu-\beta)} \int_0^1 t^{\beta-1} (1-t)^{\nu-\beta-1} \frac{(\alpha)_n (xt)^n}{n!}\, dt$$

$$= \frac{1}{B(\beta, \nu-\beta)} \cdot \int_0^1 t^{\beta-1} (1-t)^{\nu-\beta-1} \times \left[\sum_{n=0}^{\infty} \frac{(\alpha)_n \cdot (xt)^n}{n!}\right] dt$$

$$= \frac{1}{B(\beta, \nu-\beta)} \cdot \int_0^1 t^{\beta-1} (1-t)^{\nu-\beta-1} \times \left\{1+\alpha \,.\, xt + \frac{\alpha(\alpha+1)}{2!}(xt)^2 + \ldots\right\} dt$$

or

$${}_2F_1(\alpha, \beta, \nu, x) = \frac{\Gamma(\nu)}{\Gamma(\beta)\,\Gamma(\nu-\beta)} \int_0^1 t^{\beta-1} (1-t)^{\nu-\beta-1} (1-xt)^{-\alpha}\, dt.$$

This is known as the *integral formula* for hypergeometric function and is valid if

$$|x| < 1, \nu > \beta > 0.$$

8.10 Kummer's Theorem

Puttin $x = -1$ and $\nu = \beta - \alpha + 1$ in the integral formula for hypergeometric function, we have

$${}_2F_1(\alpha, \beta, \beta-\alpha+1, -1) = \frac{1}{B(\beta, 1-\alpha)} \cdot \int_0^1 t^{\beta-1} (1-t)^{-\alpha} (1+t)^{-\alpha} dt$$

$$= \frac{1}{\frac{\Gamma(\beta)\,\Gamma(1-\alpha)}{\Gamma(\beta-1+\alpha)}} \cdot \int_0^1 t^{\beta-1} (1-t^2)^{-\alpha}\, dt$$

$$= \frac{1}{2} \cdot \frac{\Gamma(\beta-\alpha+1)}{\Gamma(\beta)\,\Gamma(1-\alpha)} \int_0^1 z^{(\beta-2)/2} (1-z)^{-\alpha}\, dz$$

Putting $t^2 = z$

$$= \frac{1}{2} \cdot \frac{\Gamma(\beta-\alpha+1)}{\Gamma(\beta)\,\Gamma(1-\alpha)} \int_0^1 z^{B/2-1} (1-z)^{(1-\alpha)-1}\, dz$$

$$= \frac{1}{2} \frac{\Gamma(\beta-\alpha+1)}{\Gamma(\beta)\,\Gamma(1-\alpha)} \cdot B\left(\frac{\beta}{2}, 1-\alpha\right)$$

$$= \frac{1}{2} \frac{\Gamma(\beta-\alpha+1)}{\Gamma(\beta)\,\Gamma(1-\alpha)} \cdot \frac{\Gamma(\beta/2)\,.\,\Gamma(1-\alpha)}{\Gamma(\beta/2-\alpha+1)}$$

$$= \frac{\Gamma(\beta-\alpha+1)\,.\,\frac{\beta}{2}\,.\,\Gamma\beta/2}{\alpha.\Gamma(\beta)\,\Gamma(\beta/2-\alpha+1)}$$

$$= \frac{\Gamma(\beta-\alpha+1)\,\Gamma(\beta/2+1)}{\Gamma(\beta+1)\,\Gamma(\beta/2+\alpha-1)}$$

Hence

$${}_2F_1(\alpha, \beta, \beta-\alpha+1, -1) = \frac{\Gamma(\beta-\alpha+1)\,\Gamma(\beta/2+1)}{\Gamma(\beta+1)\,\Gamma(\beta/2-\alpha+1)}$$

This is known as *Kumer's theorem.*

8.11 Gauss's Theorem

Putting x = 1 in the integral formula for hypergeometric function, we get

$${}_2F_1(\alpha, \beta, \nu, 1) = \frac{1}{B(\beta, \nu-\beta)} \int_0^1 t^{\beta-1}(1-t)^{\nu-\beta-1}.(1-t)^{-\alpha}\, dt$$

$$= \frac{1}{B(\beta, \nu-\beta)} \int_0^1 t^{\beta-1}(1-t)^{(\nu-\beta-\alpha)-1}\, dt$$

$$= \frac{B(\beta, \nu-\beta-\alpha)}{B(\beta, \nu-\beta)}$$

$$\frac{\Gamma(\beta)\,\Gamma(\nu-\beta-\alpha)}{\Gamma(\nu-\alpha)}$$

$$= \frac{\Gamma(\beta)\,\Gamma(\nu-\beta)}{\Gamma(\nu)}$$

$$= \frac{\Gamma(\nu).(\Gamma(\nu-\beta-\alpha)}{\Gamma(\nu-\alpha).\Gamma(\nu-\beta)}$$

Hence $${}_2F_1(\alpha, \beta, \nu, 1) = \frac{\Gamma(\nu)\,\Gamma(\nu-\beta-\alpha)}{\Gamma(\nu-\alpha).\Gamma(\nu-\beta)}$$

This is known as *Gauss's theorem.*

8.12 Vandermonde's Theorem

Putting $\alpha = -n$ in Gauss's theorem, we get

$${}_2F_1(-n, \beta, \nu, 1) = \frac{\Gamma(\nu)\,\Gamma(\nu-\beta+n)}{\Gamma(\nu+n)\,\Gamma(\nu-\beta)}$$

$$= \frac{\Gamma(\nu)\,(\nu-\beta+n-1)\,(\nu-\beta+n-2)\ldots(\nu-\beta)\,\Gamma(\nu-\beta)}{(\nu+n-1)\,(\nu+n-2)\ldots\nu\,\Gamma(\nu)\,\Gamma(\nu-\beta)}$$

$$= \frac{(\nu-\beta+n-1)\,(\nu-\beta+n-2)\ldots(\nu-\beta)}{(\nu+n-1)\,(\nu+n-2)\ldots\nu}$$

Hence

$${}_2F_1(-n, \beta, \nu, 1) = \frac{(\nu-\beta)\,(\nu-\beta+1)\ldots(\nu-\beta+n-1)}{\nu\,(\nu+1)\ldots(\nu+n-1)}$$

$$= \frac{(\nu-\beta)_n}{(\nu)_n}.$$

This is known as *Vandermonde's theorem.*

8.13 Differentiation of hypermonde's functions

We have

$$_2F_1(\alpha, \beta, v, 1) = \sum_{n=0}^{\infty} \frac{(\alpha)_n (\beta)_n}{n!(v)_n} x_n$$

Differentiating both sides, w.r.t. x, we have

$$\frac{d}{dx}\{_2F_1(\alpha, b, v, x)\} = \sum_{n=1}^{\infty} \frac{(\alpha)_n (\beta)_n}{n!(v)_n} \cdot nx^{n-1}$$

$$= \sum_{n=1}^{\infty} \frac{(\alpha)_n (\beta)_n}{(n-1)!(v)_n} x^{n-1}$$

$$= \sum_{m=0}^{\infty} \frac{(\alpha)_{m+1} (\beta)_{m+1}}{m!(v)_{m+1}} x^m, \text{ putting } n-1 = m.$$

$$= \sum_{m=0}^{\infty} \frac{\alpha(\alpha+1)_m \beta(\beta+1)_m}{m!\, v(v+1)_m} x^m.$$

Since

$$(\alpha)_{m+1} = \alpha(\alpha+1) \ldots (\alpha+m+1-1)$$

$$= \alpha(\alpha+1)(\alpha+2) \ldots (\alpha+1+m-1)$$

$$= \alpha \cdot (\alpha+1)_m$$

$$= \frac{\alpha\beta}{v} \sum_{m=0}^{\infty} \frac{(\alpha+1)_m (\beta+1)_m}{m!(v+1)_m} x^m$$

$$= \frac{\alpha\beta}{v} 2F_1(\alpha+1, \beta+1, v+1, x)$$

$$\therefore \quad \frac{d}{dx}\{_2F_1(\alpha, \beta, v, x) = \frac{\alpha\beta}{v} \cdot {_2F_1}(\alpha+1, \beta+1, v+1, x)$$

Differentiating once again, w.r.t. x, we get

$$\frac{d^2}{dx^2} 2F_1(\alpha, \beta, v, x) = \frac{\alpha\beta}{v} \cdot \frac{d}{dx} 2F_1(\alpha+1, \beta+1, v+1, x)$$

$$= \frac{\alpha\beta}{v} \sum_{m=1}^{\infty} \frac{(\alpha+1)_m (\beta+1)_m}{(m-1)!(v+1)_m} x^{m-1}$$

$$= \frac{\alpha\beta}{v} \sum_{m=1}^{\infty} \frac{(\alpha+1)(\alpha+2)_{m-1}(\beta+1)(\beta+2)_{m-1}}{(m-1)!(v+1)(v+2)_{m-1}} x^{m-1}$$

$$= \frac{\alpha(\alpha+1)\beta(\beta+1)}{v(v+1)} \sum_{n=0}^{\infty} \frac{(\alpha+2)_n (\beta+2)_n}{n!(v+2)_n} \cdot x^n$$

Putting $m-1 = n$

$$= \frac{\alpha(\alpha+1)\beta(\beta+1)}{v(v+1)} \cdot {_2F_1}(\alpha+2, \beta+2, v+2, x).$$

Proceeding in similar way, we will get

$$\frac{d^p}{dx^p}\{_2F_1(\alpha, \beta, v, x) = \frac{\alpha(\alpha+1)\ldots(\alpha+p-1)\beta(\beta+1)\ldots(\beta+p-1)}{v(v+1)\ldots(v+p-1)}$$

$$_2f_1(\alpha+p, \beta+p, v+p, x)$$

$$= \frac{(\alpha)_p (\beta)_p}{(\nu)_p} \cdot {}_2F_1 (\alpha+p, \beta+p, \nu+p, x)$$

Particular Cases — If $x = 0$, we have

(i) $${}_2F_1 (\alpha, \beta, \nu, 0) = \left[1 + \frac{\alpha\beta}{\nu} x + \frac{\alpha(\alpha+1)\beta(\beta+1)}{2!\,\nu(\nu+1)} x^2 + \ldots\right]_{x=0}$$

$$= 1.$$

(ii) $$\frac{d}{dx}\{{}_2F_1 (\alpha, \beta, \nu, x)\}_{x=0} = \frac{\alpha\beta}{\nu} \cdot {}_2f_1 (\alpha+1, \beta+1, \nu+1, 0)$$

$$= \frac{\alpha\beta}{\nu}\left[1 + \frac{(\alpha+1)(\beta+1)}{(\nu+1)} x + \ldots\right]_{x=0}$$

$$= \frac{\alpha\beta}{\nu}$$

(iii) $$\frac{d^2}{dx^2}\, {}_2F_1 (\alpha, \beta, \nu, x)_{x=0} = \frac{\alpha(\alpha+1)\beta(\beta+1)}{\nu(\nu+1)}$$

(iv) $$\frac{d^p}{dx^p}\, {}_2F_1 (\alpha, \beta, \nu, x)_{x=0} = \frac{\alpha(\alpha+1)\ldots(\alpha+p-1)\,\beta(\beta+1)\ldots(\beta+p-1)}{\nu(\nu+1)\ldots(\nu+p-1)}$$

$$= \frac{(\alpha)_p (\beta)_p}{(\nu)_p}.$$

8.14 The Confluent hypergeometric function

The hypergeometric differential equation is

$$x(1-x)\frac{d^2y}{dx^2} + \{\nu - (1+\alpha+\beta)x\}\frac{dy}{dx} - \alpha\beta y = 0 \qquad \text{...(i)}$$

Replacing x by $\frac{x}{\beta}$, we have

$$\frac{x}{\beta}\left(1 - \frac{x}{\beta}\right)\beta^2 \frac{d^2y}{dx^2} + \left\{\nu - \left(1 + \frac{1+\alpha}{\beta}\right)x\right\}\frac{dy}{dx} - \alpha\beta y = 0$$

or $$x\left(1 - \frac{x}{\beta}\right)\frac{d^2y}{dx^2} + \nu - \left(1 + \frac{1+\alpha}{\beta}\right)x\,\}\frac{dy}{dx} - \alpha y = 0 \qquad \text{...(ii)}$$

Since ${}_2F_1 (\alpha, \beta; \nu, x)$ is the solution of (i)

$\therefore\ {}_2F_1\left(\alpha, \beta; \nu; \frac{x}{\beta}\right)$ is the solution of (ii)

Now, if $\beta \to \infty$, we have

$$\lim_{\beta \to \infty} {}_2F_1\left(\alpha, \beta; \nu; \frac{x}{\beta}\right)$$

is the solution of differential equation

$$x\frac{d^2y}{dx_2} + (\nu - x)\frac{dy}{dx} - \alpha y = 0 \qquad \text{...(iii)}$$

Now,

$$\underset{\beta \to \infty}{\text{Lim}}\ {}_2F_1\left(\alpha, \beta; \nu; \frac{x}{\beta}\right) = \underset{\beta \to \infty}{\text{Lim}} \sum_{r=0}^{\infty} \frac{(\alpha)_r (\beta)_r}{(\nu)_r\, r\,!} \left(\frac{x}{\beta}\right)^r$$

$$\sum_{r=0}^{\infty} \frac{(\alpha)_r}{(\nu)_r} \cdot \frac{x^r}{r\,!} \qquad \left(\text{Since } \underset{\beta \to \infty}{\text{Lim}} \frac{(\beta)_r}{\beta^r} = 1\right)$$

This is denoted by ${}_1F_1(\alpha; \nu; x)$ and is called *confluent hypergeometric function* and the equation (ii) is called *confluent hypergeometric function Kummer's equation.*

Note

Equation of type (iii) occur in theorectical and methematical physics in the discussion of boundery value problems in potential theory.

8.15 Whittaker's Confluent Hypergeometric Functions

The confluent hypergeometric equation is

$$x\frac{d^2y}{dx^2} + (\nu - x)\frac{dy}{dx} - \alpha y = 0 \qquad \text{...(i)}$$

whose general solution is

$$y = Ay_1(x) + By_2(x) \qquad \text{...(ii)}$$

where A and B are arbitrary constants and

$$y_1(x) = {}_1F_1(\alpha, \nu, x) \qquad \text{...(iii)}$$

and $$y_2(x) = x^{1-\nu}\ {}_1F_1(\alpha - \nu + 1, 2 - \nu, x) \qquad \text{...(iv)}$$

Putting $$y(x) = x^{-\nu/2} e^{x/2} w(x) \qquad \text{...(v)}$$

in equation (i), we have

$$x\left[x^{-\nu/2} e^{x/2}\frac{d^2w}{dx^2} + 2\left\{-\frac{\nu}{2}x^{-\frac{\nu}{2}-1} e^{x/2} + \frac{1}{2}x^{-\nu/2} e^{x/2}\right\}\frac{dw}{dx}\right.$$

$$\left. + w(x)\left\{\frac{\nu}{2}\left(\frac{\nu}{2}+1\right)x^{-\nu/2-1} e^{x/2} - \frac{\nu}{2}x^{-\nu/2-1}\,.\, e^{x/2} + \frac{1}{4}x^{-\nu/2}\,.\, e^{x/2}\right\}\right]$$

$$+ (\nu - x)\left[x^{-\nu/2} e^{x/2}\frac{dw}{dx} + w(x)\left\{-\frac{\nu}{2}x^{-\nu/2-1} + \frac{1}{4}x^{-\nu/2}\,.\, e^{x/2}\right\}\right]$$

$$- \alpha x^{-\nu/2} e^{x/2} w(x) = 0$$

or $$\frac{d^2w}{dx^2} + \left[-\frac{1}{4} + \frac{\frac{\nu}{2} - \alpha}{x} + \frac{\left(\frac{1}{4} - \frac{\nu}{2} + \frac{\nu^2}{4}\right)}{x^2}\right] w(x) = 0$$

or $$\frac{d^2w}{dx^2} + \left[-\frac{1}{4} + \frac{k}{x} + \frac{\frac{1}{4} - m^2}{x^2}\right] + w(x) = 0 \qquad \text{...(vi)}$$

where $k = \frac{\nu}{2} - x$ and $m = \frac{1}{2} - \frac{\nu}{2}$.

The solutions $w(x)$ of the equation (vi) are known as *Whittaker's Confluent hypergeometric functions.*

If $2m$ is neither 1 nor an integer the solution of the equation (i) corresponding to equation (vi) are given by (ii) with

$$\nu = 1 + 2m \quad \text{and} \quad \alpha = \frac{\nu}{2} - k = \frac{1}{2} + m - k.$$

Thus the solutions of equation (vi) are the *Whittakar functions*

$$M_{k,\,m}(x) = -x^{\nu/2} e^{-x/2} y_1(x)$$

$$= x^{1/2+m} e^{-x/2} {}_2F_1\left(\frac{1}{2} - k + m, 1 + 2m, x\right)$$

and

$$M_{k,\,m}(x) = x^{1/2-m} e^{-x/2} {}_2F_1\left(\frac{1}{2} - k + m, 1 + 2m, x\right)$$

8.16 Integral representation of the confluent hypergeometric function $_1F_1$ (α, ν, x) i.e.

$$_2F_1(\alpha, \nu, x) = \frac{\Gamma(\nu)}{\Gamma(\alpha)\Gamma(\nu-\alpha)} \int_0^1 (1-t)^{\nu-\alpha-1} t^{\alpha-1} e^{xt}\, dt.$$

We have

$$_2F_1(\alpha, \nu, x) = \sum_{n=0}^{\infty} \frac{(\alpha)_n x^n}{(\nu)_n n!} \qquad \text{...(i)}$$

where

$$(\alpha)_n = \frac{\Gamma(\alpha+n)}{\Gamma(\alpha)}.$$

$$\therefore \quad \frac{(\alpha)_n}{(\nu)_n} = \frac{\Gamma(\alpha+n)}{\Gamma(\alpha)} \cdot \frac{\Gamma(\nu)}{\Gamma(\nu+n)}$$

$$= \frac{\Gamma(\nu)}{\Gamma(\alpha)\Gamma(\nu-\alpha)} \frac{\Gamma(\nu-\alpha)\Gamma(\alpha+n)}{\Gamma(\beta+n+\nu-\alpha)}$$

$$= \frac{\Gamma(\nu)}{\Gamma(\alpha)\Gamma(\nu-\alpha)} \cdot B(\alpha+n, \nu+\alpha)$$

$$= \frac{\Gamma(\nu)}{\Gamma(\alpha)\Gamma(\nu-\alpha)} \int_0^1 (1-t)^{\nu-\alpha-1} \cdot t^{\alpha+n-1}\, dt$$

$\therefore$ from (i), we have

$$_1F_1(\alpha, \nu, x) = \sum_{n=0}^{\infty} \frac{\Gamma(\nu)}{\Gamma(\alpha)\Gamma(\nu-\alpha)} (1-t)^{\nu-\alpha-1} \cdot t^{\alpha+n-1} \frac{x_n}{n!}\, dt$$

$$= \frac{\Gamma(\nu)}{\Gamma(\alpha)\Gamma(\nu-\alpha)} \int_0^1 (1-t)^{\nu-\alpha-1} \cdot t^{\alpha-1} \left\{\sum_{n=0}^{\infty} \frac{(xt)^n}{n!}\right\} dt$$

or

$$_1F_1(\alpha, \nu, x) = \frac{\Gamma(\nu)}{\Gamma(\alpha)\Gamma(\nu-\alpha)} \int_0^1 (1-t)^{\nu-\alpha-1} \cdot t^{\alpha-1} e^{xt}\, dt$$

or

$$_1F_1(\alpha, \nu, x) = \frac{1}{B(\alpha, \nu-\alpha)} \int_0^1 (1-t)^{\nu-\alpha-1} \cdot t^{\alpha-1} e^{xt}\, dt$$

8.17 Differentiation of confluent hypergeometric function

We have

$$_1F_1(\alpha, \nu, x) = \sum_{n=0}^{\infty} \frac{(\alpha)_n}{(\nu)_n} \cdot \frac{x^n}{n!}$$

Differentiating both sides with respect to x, we get

$$\frac{d}{dx}\{{}_1F_1(\alpha, \nu, x) = \sum_{n=0}^{\infty} \frac{(\alpha)_n}{(\nu)_n} \cdot \frac{nx^{n-1}}{n!}$$

$$= \sum_{n=1}^{\infty} \frac{(\alpha)_n}{(\nu)_n} \cdot \frac{nx^{n-1}}{(n-1)!}$$

$$= \sum_{m=0}^{\infty} \frac{(\alpha)_{m+1}}{(\nu)_{m+1}} \cdot \frac{x^m}{m!}$$

$$= \frac{\alpha}{\nu} \cdot \sum_{m=0}^{\infty} \frac{(\alpha+1)_m}{\nu+1_m} \cdot \frac{x^m}{m!} \qquad \text{Putting } n-1 = m$$

$$[\because (\alpha)_{m+1} = \alpha.\ (\alpha+1)_m]$$

$$\therefore \qquad \frac{d}{dx}\{{}_1F_1(\alpha, \nu, x)\} = \frac{\alpha}{\nu} \cdot {}_1F_1(\alpha+1, \nu+1, x)$$

Differentiating again, with respect to x, we get

$$\frac{d^2}{dx^2}\{{}_1F_1(\alpha, \nu, x)\} = \frac{\alpha(\alpha+1)}{\nu(\nu+1)}\, {}_1F_1(\alpha+2, \nu+2, x)$$

Proceeding similarly, we have

$$\frac{d^p}{dx^p}\{{}_1F_1(\alpha, \nu, x)\} = \frac{(\alpha)_p}{(\nu)_p}\, {}_1F_1(\alpha+p, \nu+p, x)$$

8.18 Dixon's Theorem

It states that

$${}_3F_2\begin{bmatrix}\alpha & ,\beta, & \nu & 1\\ 1+\alpha-\beta, & & 1+\alpha-\nu & \end{bmatrix}$$

$$= \frac{\Gamma\left(a+\frac{\alpha}{2}\right)\Gamma\left(1+\frac{\alpha}{2}-\beta-\nu\right)\Gamma(1+\nu-\beta)\Gamma(1+\alpha-\nu)}{\Gamma(1+\nu)\Gamma(1+\alpha-\beta-\nu)\Gamma\left(1+\frac{\alpha}{2}-\beta\right)\Gamma\left(1+\frac{\alpha}{2}-\nu\right)}$$

We have

$$\frac{\Gamma(\alpha)\Gamma(\beta)\Gamma(\nu)}{\Gamma(1+\alpha-\beta)\Gamma(1+\alpha-\nu)} \cdot {}_3F_2\begin{bmatrix}\alpha & ,\beta, & \nu & 1\\ 1+\alpha-\beta, & & 1+\alpha-\nu & \end{bmatrix}$$

$$= \sum_{n=0}^{\infty} \frac{\Gamma(\alpha+n)\Gamma(\beta+n)\Gamma(\nu+n)}{\Gamma(1+\alpha-\beta+n)\Gamma(1+\alpha-\nu+n)} \cdot \frac{1}{n!}$$

$$= \sum_{n=0}^{\infty} \frac{\Gamma(\alpha+n)\Gamma(\beta+n)\Gamma(\nu+n)}{n!\,\Gamma(1+\alpha+2n)\Gamma(1+\alpha-\beta-\nu)} \times \left\{\frac{\Gamma(1+\alpha+2n)\Gamma(1+\alpha-\beta-\nu)}{\Gamma(1+\alpha-\beta+n).\Gamma(1+\alpha-\nu+n)}\right\}$$

$$= \sum_{n=0}^{\infty} \frac{\Gamma(\alpha+n)\Gamma(\beta+n)\Gamma(\nu+n)}{n!\,\Gamma(1+\alpha+2n)\Gamma(1+\alpha-\beta-\nu)} \times {}_2F_1(\beta+n, \nu+n; 1+\alpha+2n; 1)$$

$$\left\{\text{Since Gauss's theorem } {}_2F_1(\alpha, \beta; \nu; 1) = \frac{\Gamma(\nu)\Gamma(\nu-\alpha-\beta)}{\Gamma(\nu-\alpha)\Gamma(\nu-\beta)}\right\}$$

$$= \sum_{n=0}^{\infty} \frac{\Gamma(\alpha+n)\,\Gamma(\beta+n)\,\Gamma(\nu+n)}{n\,!\,\Gamma(1+\alpha+2n)\,\Gamma(1+\alpha-\beta-\nu)}$$

$$\left\{ \sum_{m=0}^{\infty} \frac{(\beta+n)_m\,(\nu+n)_m}{(1+\alpha+2n)_m} \cdot \frac{1}{m\,!} \right\}$$

$$= \sum_{n=0}^{\infty} \sum_{m=0}^{\infty} \frac{\Gamma(\alpha+n)\,\{\Gamma(\beta+n)\,(\beta+n)_m\}\,\{\Gamma(\nu+n)\,(\nu+n)_m\}}{\{\Gamma(1+\alpha+2n)\,(1+\alpha+2n)_m\}\,\Gamma(1+\alpha-\beta-\nu)\,n\,!\,m\,!}$$

$$= \sum_{n=0}^{\infty} \sum_{m=0}^{\infty} \frac{\Gamma(\alpha+n)\,\Gamma(\beta+n+m)\,\Gamma(\nu+n+m)}{\Gamma(1+\alpha+2n+m)\,\Gamma(1+\alpha-\beta-\nu)\,n\,!\,m\,!}$$

$$= \sum_{m=0}^{\infty} \sum_{n=0}^{\infty} \frac{\Gamma(\beta+n+m)\,\Gamma(\nu+n+m)\,\Gamma(\alpha+n)}{\Gamma(1+\alpha-\beta-\nu)\,\Gamma(1+\alpha+2n+m)\,m\,!\,n\,!}$$

[Changing the order of summation] and putting $p = n + m$

$$= \sum_{p=0}^{\infty} \frac{\Gamma(\beta+p)\,\Gamma(\nu+p)}{1+\alpha-\beta-\nu} \sum_{n=0}^{\infty} \frac{(\alpha+n)}{n\,!\,(p-n)\,!\,\Gamma(1+\alpha+n+p)}$$

$$= \sum_{p=0}^{\infty} \frac{\Gamma(\beta+p)\,\Gamma(\nu+p)}{\Gamma(1+\alpha-\beta-\nu)} \sum_{n=0}^{\infty} \frac{\Gamma(\alpha+n)}{n\,!\,\Gamma(1+\alpha+n+p)} \times (-1)^n \frac{(-p)^n}{p\,!}$$

$$\left(\text{since } \frac{1}{(p+n)\,!}\,(-1)^n \Big/ \frac{(-p)^n}{p\,!} \right)$$

$$= \sum_{p=0}^{\infty} \frac{\Gamma(\beta+p)\,\Gamma(\nu+p)\,\Gamma(\alpha)}{p\,!\,\Gamma(1+\alpha-\beta-\nu)\,.\,\Gamma(1+\alpha+p)} \times \sum_{r=0}^{\infty} \frac{(\alpha)_n\,(-p)_n}{(1+\alpha+p)_n} \cdot \frac{(-1)^n}{n\,!}$$

$$= \sum_{p=0}^{\infty} \frac{\Gamma(\alpha)\,\Gamma(\beta+p)\,\Gamma(\nu+p)}{p\,!\,\Gamma(1+\alpha-\beta-\nu)\,\Gamma(1+\alpha+p)} \times {}_2F_1(\alpha, -p; 1+\alpha+p; -1)$$

$$= \sum_{p=0}^{\infty} \frac{\Gamma(\alpha)\,\Gamma(\beta+p)\,\Gamma(\nu+p)}{p\,!\,\Gamma(1+\alpha-\beta-\nu)\,\Gamma(1+\alpha+p)} \times \frac{\Gamma(1+\alpha+p)\,.\,\Gamma\left(\frac{\alpha}{2}+1\right)}{\Gamma(\alpha+1)\,\Gamma\left(\frac{\alpha}{2}+p+1\right)}$$

(from Kummer's theorem)

$$= \sum_{p=0}^{\infty} \frac{\Gamma(\alpha)\,\Gamma(\beta+p)\,\Gamma(\nu+1)\,\Gamma\left(\frac{\alpha}{2}+1\right)}{p\,!\,\Gamma(1+\alpha-\beta-\nu)\,\Gamma(\alpha+1)\,\Gamma\left(\frac{\alpha}{2}+p+1\right)}$$

$$= \frac{\Gamma(\alpha)\,\Gamma(\beta)\,\Gamma(\nu)}{\Gamma(1+\alpha)\,\Gamma(1+\alpha-\beta-\nu)} \sum_{p=0}^{\infty} \frac{(\beta)_p\,(\nu)_p}{\left(\frac{\alpha}{2}+1\right)_p} \cdot \frac{1}{p\,!}$$

$$= \frac{\Gamma(\alpha)\,\Gamma(\beta)\,\Gamma(\nu)}{\Gamma(1+\alpha)\,\Gamma(1+\alpha-\beta-\nu)}\,{}_2F_1\left(\beta; \nu; \frac{\alpha}{2}+1; 1\right)$$

$$= \frac{\Gamma(\alpha)\Gamma(\beta)\Gamma(\nu)}{\Gamma(1+\alpha)\Gamma(1+\alpha-\beta-\nu)} \cdot \frac{\Gamma\left(\frac{\alpha}{2}+1\right)\Gamma\left(\frac{\alpha}{2}+1-\beta-\nu\right)}{\Gamma\left(\frac{\alpha}{2}+1-\beta\right)\Gamma\left(\frac{\alpha}{2}+1-\nu\right)}$$

[From Gauss's theorem]

Hence

$${}_3F_2\left[\begin{matrix}\alpha\ , & \beta, & \nu & 1\\ 1+\alpha-\beta\ , & & 1+\alpha-\nu & \end{matrix}\right]$$

$$= \frac{\Gamma\left(1+\frac{\alpha}{2}\right)\Gamma\left(1+\frac{\alpha}{2}-\beta-\nu\right)\Gamma(1+\alpha-\beta)\Gamma(1+\alpha-\nu)}{\Gamma(1+\alpha)\Gamma(1+\alpha-\beta-\nu)\Gamma\left(1+\frac{\alpha}{2}-\beta\right)\Gamma\left(1+\frac{\alpha}{2}-\nu\right)}$$

Illustrative Examples

Ex. 1. *Prove that*

(i) $e^x = {}_1F_1(\alpha; \alpha; x)$

(ii) $Sin^{-1}\, x = x\, F\left(\frac{1}{2}, \frac{1}{2}; \frac{3}{2}; x^2\right)$

Solution

(i) We have

$${}_1F_1(\alpha; \beta; x) = \sum_{r=0}^{\infty} \frac{(\alpha)_r}{(\beta)_r} \cdot \frac{x^2}{r\,!} + \ldots$$

$$= 1 + \frac{\alpha}{\beta} \cdot \frac{x}{1\,!} + \frac{\alpha(\alpha+1)}{\beta(\beta+1)} \frac{x^2}{2\,!} + \ldots \qquad \ldots(i)$$

Replacing β by α in (i), we have

$${}_1F_1(\alpha; \alpha; x) = 1 + \frac{x}{1\,!} + \frac{x^2}{2\,!} + \ldots = e^x.$$

(ii) We have, by definition

$$F(\alpha, \beta; \nu; x) = 1 + \frac{\alpha.\beta}{\nu} \cdot \frac{x}{1\,!} + \frac{\alpha(\alpha+1)\beta(\beta+1)}{\nu(\nu+1)} \frac{x^2}{2\,!} + \ldots \qquad \ldots(i)$$

Replacing α, β, ν, x by $\frac{1}{2}, \frac{1}{2}, \frac{3}{2}$ and x^2 respectively in (i), we get

$$F\left(\frac{1}{2}, \frac{1}{2}; \frac{3}{2}; x^2\right) = 1 + \frac{\frac{1}{2}\cdot\frac{1}{2}}{\frac{3}{2}} \cdot \frac{x^2}{1\,!} + \frac{\frac{1}{2}\left(\frac{3}{2}\right)\cdot\frac{1}{2}\left(\frac{3}{2}\right)}{\frac{3}{2}\cdot\frac{5}{2}} \cdot \frac{x^4}{2\,!}$$

$$\therefore \qquad x\,F\left(\frac{1}{2}, \frac{1}{2}; \frac{3}{2}\right) = x + 1^2 \cdot \frac{x^3}{3\,!} + 1^2.3^2 \cdot \frac{x^5}{5\,!} + \ldots = \sin^{-1} x.$$

Ex. 2. *If* $|z| < 1$ *and* $\left|\frac{z}{1-z}\right| < 1$, *prove that*

Ex. 2. *If* $|z| < 1$ *and* $\left|\frac{z}{1-z}\right| < 1$*, prove that*

$$_2F_1\,(a, b, c, z) = (1-z)^{-a}\ _2f_1\left(a, c-b, c, -\frac{z}{1-z}\right)$$

Solution. From integral formula for the hypergeometric function, we have

$$_2F_1\,(a, b, c, z) = \frac{1}{B\,(b, c-b)}\int_0^1 t^{b-1}\,(1-t)^{c-b-1}\,(1-zt)^{-a}\,dt$$

$$= \frac{1}{B\,(b, c-b)}\int_0^1 (1-\mu)^{b-1}\,\mu^{c-b-1}\,(1-z+\mu z)^{-a}\,d\mu$$

Putting $t = 1-\mu$
i.e. $dt = -d\mu$

$$= \frac{1}{B\,(b, c-b)}\int_0^1 \mu^{(c-b)-1}\,(1-\mu)^{c-(c-b)-1} \times (1-z)^{-a}\left(a-\frac{z}{-1+z}\right)^{-a} d\mu$$

$$= (1-z)^{-a}\cdot\frac{1}{B\,(b, c-b)}\int_0^1 \mu^{(c-b)-1}\,(1-\mu)^{c-(c-b)-1} \times \left(1-\frac{z}{-1+z}\right) d\mu$$

$$= (1-z)^{-a}\ _2F_1\left(1, c-b, c, -\frac{z}{1-z}\right).$$

Ex. 3. *Prove that*

$$P_n\,(x) = {}_2F_1\left(-n, n+1, 1, \frac{1-x}{2}\right)$$

Solution. From Rodrigue's formula, we have

$$P_n\,(x) = \frac{1}{2^n\,.\,n\,!}\,\frac{d^n}{dx^n}\,(x^2-1)^n$$

$$= \frac{1}{n\,!}\,\frac{d^n}{dx^n}\left[(x-1)^n\left\{\frac{1}{2}\,(x+1)\right\}^n\right]$$

$$= \frac{1}{n\,!}\,\frac{d^n}{dx^n}\left[(x-1)^n\left\{1-\frac{1}{2}\,(1-x)\right\}^n\right]$$

$$= \frac{(-1)^n}{n\,!}\,\frac{d^n}{dx^n}\left[(1-x)^n\,.\left\{1-n\,.\,\frac{1}{2}\,(1-x)+\frac{n\,(n-1)}{2\,!}\,.\,\frac{(1-x)^2}{4} - \frac{n\,(n-1)\,(n-2)}{3\,!}\,.\,\frac{(1-x)^3}{8}\ldots\right\}\right]$$

$$= \frac{(-1)^n}{n\,!}\,\frac{d^n}{dx^n}\left[(1-x)^n - \frac{n}{2}\,(1-x)^{n+1} + \frac{n\,(n-1)}{2\,!\,.\,2^2}\,(1-x)^{n+2} - \frac{n\,(n-1)\,(n-2)}{3\,!\,2^3}\,(1-x)^{n+3}\ldots\right]$$

$$= \frac{(-1)^n}{n\,!}\left[(-1)^n\, n\,! - \frac{n}{2}(-1)^n \frac{(n+1)\,!}{1\,!}(1-x)\right.$$

$$\left. + \frac{n\,(n-1)}{2\,!} \cdot \frac{(-1)^n}{2^2} \cdot \frac{(n+2)\,!}{2\,!}(1-x)^2 \ldots\right]$$

$$= 1 + \frac{(-n)}{1} \cdot \frac{(n+1)}{1\,!}\left(\frac{1-x}{2}\right)$$

$$+ \frac{(-n)\,(-n+1)\,.\,(n+1)\,(n+2)}{2.1\,.\,2\,!}\left(\frac{1-x}{2}\right)^2 + \ldots$$

$$= {}_2F_1\left(-n, n+1; 1, \frac{1-x}{2}\right).$$

Ex. 4. *Show that*

$$P_n\,(\cos\,\theta) = \cos^n\theta\,.\,{}_2F_1\left(-\frac{n}{2}, -\frac{n-1}{2}, 1, -\tan^2\theta\right)$$

Solution. From Laplace's first integral, we have

$$P_n\,(x) = \frac{1}{\pi}\int_0^{\pi}\left[x + \sqrt{(x^2-1)}\,\cos\phi\right]^n d\phi$$

Putting $x = \cos\theta$, we have

$$P_n\,(\cos\theta) = \frac{1}{\pi}\int_0^{\pi}\left[\cos\theta + \sqrt{(\cos^2\theta-1)}\,\cos\phi\right]^n d\phi$$

$$= \frac{1}{\pi}\int_0^{\pi}(\cos\theta + i\,\sin\theta\,\cos\phi)^n\, d\phi$$

$$= \frac{1}{\pi}\cos^n\theta\int_0^{\pi}(1 + i\,\tan\theta\,\cos\phi)^n\, d\phi$$

$$= \frac{1}{\pi}\cos^n\theta\int_0^{\pi} 1 + n\,i\,\tan\theta\,\cos\phi$$

$$+ \frac{n\,(n-1)\,(n-2)}{3\,!}\,i^3\,\tan^3\theta\,\cos^3\theta + \ldots\,]\,d\phi$$

$$= \frac{1}{\pi}\cos^n\theta\left[\int_0^{\pi} d\Phi + 0 + 2\,.\,\frac{n\,(n-1)}{2\,!}\right.$$

$$\left.\times\, i^2\,\tan^2\,\theta\int_0^{\pi/2}\cos^2\Phi\, d\,\Phi + 0 \ldots\right]$$

By the property of definite integrals.

$$= \frac{1}{\pi}\cos^n\theta\left[\pi + i^2\,\frac{n\,(n-1)}{1\,!}\tan^2\theta\,.\,\frac{\pi}{4}\right.$$

$$\left. + i^4\,\frac{n\,(n-1)\,(n-2)\,(n-3)}{4\,!}\,.\,2\,.\,\frac{1.3}{2.4}\frac{\pi}{4}\ldots\right]$$

$$= \cos^n\theta\left[\frac{1 + \left(-\frac{n}{2}\right)\left(-\frac{n-1}{2}\right)}{1!}(-\tan^2\theta) + \right.$$

$$+ \frac{\left(-\frac{n}{2}\right)\left(-\frac{n}{2}+1\right)\left(-\frac{n-1}{2}\right)\left(\frac{-n-1}{2}+1\right)}{2.1.2\,!}(-\tan^2\theta)^2 + \ldots\Bigg]$$

$$= \cos^n\theta \cdot {}_2F_1\left(-\frac{n}{2}, -\frac{n-1}{2}, 1, -\tan^2\theta\right).$$

Ex. 5. *Prove that*

(i) $P_n(\cos\theta) = {}_2F_1\left(-n, n+1; 1; \sin^2\frac{\theta}{2}\right).$

and (ii) $P_n(\cos\theta) = (-1)^n\, {}_2F_1\left(n+1, -n; 1; \cos^2\frac{\theta}{2}\right)$

Solution. From Example 3 above, we have

$$P_n(x) = {}_2F_1\left(-n, n+1; 1, \frac{1-x}{2}\right) \quad \ldots\text{(i)}$$

Putting $x = \cos\theta$ in (i), we have

$$P_n(\cos\theta) = {}_2F_1\left(-n, n+1; 1; \sin^2\frac{\theta}{2}\right)$$

(ii) Putting $x = -\cos\theta$ in (i), we have

$$P_n(-\cos\theta) = {}_2F_1\left(-n, n+1; 1; \cos^2\frac{\theta}{2}\right)$$

or $$(-1)^n P_n(\cos\theta) = {}_2F_1\left(-n, n+1; 1; \cos^2\frac{\theta}{2}\right)$$

or $$P_n(\cos\theta) = (-1)^n\, {}_2F_1\left(-n, n+1; 1; \cos^2\frac{\theta}{2}\right)$$

$$\because \quad P_n(-x) = (-1)^n P_n(x)$$

or $$P_n(\cos\theta) = (-1)^n\, {}_2F_1\left(n+1, -n; 1; \cos^2\frac{\theta}{2}\right)$$

Since in hypergeometric series α and β can be interchanged.

Ex. 6. *Prove that*

$${}_1F_1(\alpha, \nu, x) = e^x\, {}_1F_1(\nu-\alpha, \nu, -x).$$

Solution. We have

$${}_1F_1(\alpha, \nu, x) = \frac{1}{B(\alpha, \nu-\alpha)}\int_0^1 (1-t)^{\nu-\alpha-1}\, t^{\alpha-1}\, e^{xt}\, dt \quad \ldots\text{(i)}$$

Replacing x by $-x$ and α by $\nu-\alpha$, we have

$${}_1F_1(\nu-\alpha, \nu, -x) = \frac{1}{B(\nu-\alpha, \alpha)}\int_0^1 (1-t)^{\alpha-1}\, t^{\nu-\alpha-1}\, e^{-xt}\, dt$$

$$\frac{e^{-x}}{\beta(\alpha, \nu-\alpha)}\int_0^1 (1-t)^{\alpha-1}\, t^{\nu-\alpha-1} e^{x(1-t)}\, dt$$

Putting $1-t = \mu$ so that $dt - du$

$$= \frac{e^{-x}}{B(\alpha, \nu-\alpha)} \int_0^1 \mu^{\alpha-1} (1-\mu)^{\nu-\alpha-1} e^{\mu x} \, d\mu$$

or $$e^x \,.\, {}_1F_1 (\nu-\alpha, \nu, -x) = \frac{1}{B(\alpha, \nu-\alpha)} \int_0^1 t^{\alpha-1} (1-t)^{\nu-\alpha-1} e^{tx} \, dt$$

or $$e^x \,.\, {}_1F_1 (\nu-\alpha, \nu, -x) = {}_1F_1 (\alpha, \nu, x).$$

Ex. 7. *Prove that*

$$F\left(\alpha, \beta; \nu; \frac{1}{x}\right) = \frac{\Gamma(\nu)\,\Gamma(\nu-\alpha-\beta)}{\Gamma(\nu-\alpha)\,\Gamma(\nu-\beta)} x^{\alpha}.$$

$${}_2F_1 (\alpha, \alpha-\nu+1; \alpha+\beta-\nu+1; 1-x)$$

$$+ \frac{\Gamma(\nu)\,\Gamma(\alpha+\beta-\nu)}{\Gamma(\alpha)\,\Gamma(\beta)} \times x^{\beta} (x-1)^{\nu-\alpha-\beta}$$

$${}_2F_1 (\nu-\alpha, 1-\alpha; \nu-\alpha-\beta+1; 1-x)$$

where $1 < x < 2$ *and* $a > \nu > \alpha + \beta$.

Solution From linear relations of hypergeometric functions, we have

$${}_2F_1 (\alpha, \beta; \nu; x) = \frac{\Gamma(\nu)\,\Gamma(\nu-\alpha-\beta)}{\Gamma(\nu-\alpha)\,\Gamma(\nu-\beta)} \, {}_2F_1 (\alpha, \beta; \alpha + \beta - \nu + 1, 1-x$$

$$+ \frac{\Gamma(\nu)\,\Gamma(\alpha+\beta-\nu)}{\Gamma(\alpha)\,\Gamma(\beta)} (1-x)^{\nu-\alpha+\beta}$$

$${}_2F_1 (\nu-\alpha, \nu-\beta; \nu-\alpha-\beta+a; 1-\alpha)$$

Replacing x by $\frac{1}{x}$, we have

$${}_2F_1 \left(\alpha, \beta; \nu; \frac{1}{x}\right) = \frac{\Gamma(\nu)\,\Gamma(\nu-\alpha-\beta)}{\Gamma(\nu-\alpha)\,\Gamma(\nu-\beta)}$$

$${}_2F_1 \left(\alpha, \beta; \alpha+\beta-\nu+1, 1-\frac{1}{x}\right) + \frac{\Gamma(\nu)\,\Gamma(\alpha+\beta-\nu)}{\Gamma(\alpha)\,\Gamma(\beta)} \left(1-\frac{1}{x}\right)^{\nu-\alpha-\beta}$$

$${}_2F_1 \left(\nu-\alpha, \nu-\beta; \nu-\alpha-\beta+1; 1-\frac{1}{x}\right) \quad \text{...(i)}$$

Now, from example 2, we have

$${}_2F_1 (\alpha, \beta, \nu; x) = (1-x)^{-\alpha} \, {}_2F_1 \left(\alpha, \nu-\beta; \nu; \frac{1}{x}\right) \quad \text{...(ii)}$$

Replacing ν by $\alpha + \beta - \nu + 1$, and x by $1-\frac{1}{x}$, we have

$${}_2F_1 \left(\alpha, \beta; \alpha+\beta-\nu+1, 1-\frac{1}{x}\right)$$
$$= x^{\alpha} \, {}_2F_1 (\alpha, \alpha-\nu+1; \alpha+\beta-\nu+1; 1-x) \quad \text{...(iii)}$$

Again replacing α by $\nu-\alpha$, β by $\nu-\beta$, ν by $\nu-\alpha-\beta+1$ and x by $1-\frac{1}{x}$ in (ii), we have

$$ {}_2F_1\left(\nu-\alpha, \nu-\beta; \nu-\alpha-\beta+1, 1-\frac{1}{x}\right) $$

$$ = x^{\nu-\alpha}\ {}_2F_1\ (\nu-\alpha; 1-\alpha; \nu-\alpha-\beta+1; 1-x) \qquad \text{...(iv)} $$

Hence from (i), (iii) and (iv), we have

$$ {}_2F_1\left(\alpha, \beta; \nu; \frac{1}{x}\right) $$

$$ = \frac{\Gamma(\nu)\,\Gamma(\nu-\alpha-\beta)}{\Gamma(\nu-\alpha)\,\Gamma(\nu-\beta)} x^{\alpha}\ .\ {}_2F_1\ (\alpha, \alpha-\nu+1; \alpha+\beta-\nu+1; 1-x) $$

$$ + \frac{\Gamma(\nu)\,\Gamma(\alpha+\beta-\nu)}{\Gamma(\alpha)\,\Gamma(\beta)} \left(1-\frac{1}{x}\right)^{\nu-\alpha-\beta} x^{\nu-\alpha} $$

$$ \times\ {}_2F_1\ (\alpha, \alpha-\nu+1; \alpha+\beta-\nu+1; 1-x) $$

$$ = \frac{\Gamma(\nu)\,\Gamma(\nu-\alpha-\beta)}{\Gamma(\nu-\alpha)\,\Gamma(\nu-\beta)}\ .\ x^{\alpha}\ {}_2F_1\ (\alpha, \alpha-\nu+1; \alpha+\beta-\nu+1; 1-x) $$

$$ + \frac{\Gamma(\nu)\,\Gamma(\alpha+\beta-\nu)}{\Gamma(\alpha)\,\Gamma(\beta)} x^{\beta}\ (x-1)^{\nu-\alpha-\beta} $$

$$ {}_2F_1\ (\alpha, \alpha-\nu+1; \alpha+\beta-\nu+1; 1-x) $$

Exercise – 8

1. Show that

 (i) $(1-x)-1 = F(1, 1; 1; x), |x| < 1$

 (ii) $\log \frac{1+x}{1-x} = 2x\, F\left(\frac{1}{2}, 1; \frac{3}{2}, x^2\right)$

2. If $P_n(x)$ be Legendre's polynomial of degree n, prove that

 $$ P_n(x) = \left(\frac{x-1}{2}\right)^n {}_2F_1\left(-n, -n; 1, \frac{x+1}{x-1}\right) $$

3. Show that

 $$ (1-x)^{-2} = {}_2F_1\ (\alpha, \beta; \beta; x) $$

4. Show that

 $$ \int_0^{\pi/2} (1-k^2 \sin^2\phi)^{-1/2}\, d\phi = \frac{\pi}{2} F\left(\frac{1}{2}, \frac{1}{2}; 1; k^2\right) \text{ where } |k| < 1. $$

5. Show that

 $$ {}_2F_1\left(\alpha, \beta; \frac{1}{2}\alpha+\frac{1}{2}\beta+\frac{1}{2}; \frac{1}{2}\right) = \frac{\Gamma\left(\frac{1}{2}\right)\Gamma\left(\frac{1}{2}+\frac{1}{2}\alpha+\frac{1}{2}\beta\right)}{\Gamma\left(\frac{1}{2}+\frac{1}{2}\alpha\right)\Gamma\left(\frac{1}{2}+\frac{1}{2}\beta\right)} $$

6. Show that

$$F\left(\alpha, 1-\alpha; \nu; \frac{1}{2}\right) = \frac{\Gamma\left(\frac{1}{2}\nu\right)\Gamma\left(\frac{1}{2}\nu+\frac{1}{2}\right)}{\Gamma\left(\frac{1}{2}\alpha+\frac{1}{2}\nu\right)\Gamma\left(\frac{1}{2}-\frac{1}{2}\alpha+\frac{1}{2}\nu\right)}$$

7. Prove that

$$F(\alpha, \beta+1; \nu+1; x) - F(\alpha, \beta; \nu; x)$$
$$= \frac{\alpha(\nu-\beta)}{\nu(\nu+1)} x F(\alpha+1; \beta+1; \nu+2; x)$$

9

Riccati's Equation

9·1. Riccati's Equation

The differential equation

$$y_1 = P + Qy + Ry^2 \qquad \text{...(1)}$$

where P, Q, R are functions of x and y_1 stands for derivative of y w. r. t. x, i.e. $\frac{dy}{dx}$, is called as *Generalised Riccati's equation.* Due to its importance in practice, we will study here in detail.

9·2. General Solution of Riccati's Equation

To solve equation (i), we change the dependent variable y to u by the subtitution

$$y = -u_1/Ru = -u_1\,(Ru)^{-1} \qquad \text{...(ii)}$$

Differentiating it, $y_1 = -u_2 \,.\, (Ru)^{-1} + (Ru)^{-2}\,[R_1 u + Ru_1]\,u_1$

Putting these values in (i), we get

$$-\frac{u_2}{R\,u} + \frac{R_1 u_1}{R^2\,u} + \frac{u_1{}^2}{R\,u^2} = P + Q\left(\frac{-u_1}{R\,u}\right) + R\left(\frac{u_1{}^2}{R^2\,a^2}\right)$$

or

$$Ru_2 - (QR + R_1)\,u_1 + PR^2\,u = 0 \qquad \text{...(iii)}$$

This is an ordinary linear differential equation of second order in u. Its general solution will be of the form

$$u = Af\,(x) + B\phi\,(x) = Af + B\phi, \text{ (say)} \qquad \text{...(iv)}$$

A and B being arbitrary constants.

Hence the value of y from (ii) is given by

$$y = -\frac{(Af_1 + B\phi_1)}{R\,(Af + B\phi)} = \frac{(A/B)\,(-f_1/R) + (-\phi_2/R)}{(A/B)\,R + \phi}$$

or

$$y = \frac{cg(x) + \varphi(x)}{cf(x) + \phi(x)} = \frac{cg + \psi}{cf + \phi} \qquad \text{.... (v)}$$

where c ($= A/B$) is an arbitrary constant.

Thus (v) gives general solution of the Riccati's equation (i).

Note that by the substitution (ii), the equation (i) is reduced to a linear form. So it is also named as this method of *reduction to linear form.*

9·3. Cross-ratio

The cross-ratio of any four particular integrals of a Riccati's equation is always constant, i.e., independent of x.

The solution of the Riccati's equation (i) is given by (v). Let its four particular solutions be $p(x)$, $q(x)$, $r(x)$ and $s(x)$ obtained by putting α, β, υ, δ respectively in place of c in (v), we have

$$p(x) = \frac{\alpha g + \psi}{\alpha f + \phi},\ q(x) = \frac{\beta g + \psi}{\beta f + \phi}$$

$$r(x) = \frac{\nu g + \psi}{\nu f + \phi},\ s(x) = \frac{\delta g + \psi}{\delta f + \phi}$$

$$\therefore \qquad p(x) - q(x) = \frac{(\alpha - \beta)\ (g\phi - f\psi)}{(\alpha f + \phi)\ (\beta f + \phi)}$$

Similarly determining $p(x) - s(x)$, $r(x) - s(x)$, $r(x) - q(x)$, we can obtain the cross-ratio as

$$\frac{\{p(x) - q(x)\}\ \{r(x) - s(x)\}}{\{p(x) - s(x)\}\ \{r(x) - q(x)\}} = \frac{(\alpha - \beta)\ (\nu - \delta)}{(\alpha - \delta)\ (\nu - \beta)}$$

$$= \text{constant} \quad = k \text{ (say)}$$

9·4. Methods of solving the Riccati's Equation

(a) **When three particular integrals are known –**

Let the general solution of (i) be given by (v). Let its three particular integrals be $q(x)$, $r(x)$, $s(x)$ are given in § 9.3. Then by the above theorem

$$\frac{\{y - q(x)\}\ \{r(x) - s(x)\}}{\{y - s(x)\}\ \{r(x) - q(x)\}} = \frac{(c - \beta)\ (\nu - \delta)}{(c - \delta)\ (\nu - \beta)}$$

$$= k \text{ (constant)}$$

Hence by solving

$$\frac{\{y - q(x)\}\ \{r(x) - s(x)\}}{\{y - s(x)\}\ \{r(x) - q(x)\}} = k,$$

for y, one can obtain the general solution of the Riccati's equation. Note that this general solution is obtained without integration.

(b) **When two particular integrals are known—**

Suppose two particular integrals say $y = q(x)$ and $y = r(x)$ are known. Then by Riccati's equation.

$$y_1 = p + Qy + Ry^2$$

we have

$$q_1 = P + Qq + Rq^2$$

and

$$r_1 = P + Qr + Rr^2$$

Subtracting,

$$y_1 - q_1 = (y - q)\ Q + (y^2 - q^2)\ R^2$$

or

$$\frac{y_1 - q_1}{y - q} = Q + (y + q)\ R$$

and simailarly

$$\frac{y_1 - r_1}{y - r} = Q + (y + r)\ R$$

Again subtracting, we get

$$\frac{y_1 - q_1}{y - q} - \frac{y_1 - r_1}{y - r} = (q - r)\ R$$

Integrating,

$$\log (y - q) - \log (y - r) = \int (q - r) R\, dx + d$$

or

$$\log \{(y - q) / (y - r)\} = \int (q - r) R\, dx + d,$$

where d is an arbitrary constant. This gives the required general solution of the given Riccati's equation.

(c) **When one particular integral is known**

Let the Riccati's equation be $y_1 = P + Qy + Ry^2$ and its one particular integral by $y = q(x)$, so that $q_1 = P + Qq + Rq^2$.

Change the dependent variable y to u by the substitution

$$y = q(x) + 1/v$$

so that

$$y_1 = q_1 - v_1/v^2 = P + Qq + Rq^2 - v_1/v^2$$

Putting these values in the given Riccati's equation, we obtain

$$P + Qq + Rq^2 - \frac{v_1}{v^2} = P + Q\left(q + \frac{1}{v}\right) + R\left(q^2 + \frac{2q}{v} + \frac{1}{v^2}\right)$$

or

$$-\frac{v_1}{v^2} = \frac{Q}{v} + \left(\frac{2q}{v} + \frac{1}{v^2}\right)$$

or

$$\frac{dv}{dx} + (Q + 2Rq)\, v = -R.$$

This is an ordinary linear differential equation of order one in v. Its integrating factor will be

$$\text{I.F.} = e^{\int (Q+2Rq)\, dx}$$

Hence its solution is given by

$$v \,.\, e^{\int (Q + 2Rq)\, x} = -\int \{ R e^{\int (Q + 2Rq)\, x}\}\, dx + d.$$

Replacing υ by $1/(y - q)$, we obtain the desired general solution of the Riccati's equation.

ILLUSTRATIVE EXAMPLES

Ex. 1. *Solve the equation*

$$x^2 y_1 + 2 - 2xy + x^2 y^2 = 0.$$

Solution. The given equation is

$$y_1 = -(2/x^{2)} + (2/x)\, y - y^2 \qquad \text{...(i)}$$

comparing it with Riccati's standard equation, we get $P = -(2/x^2)$, $Q = (2/x)$, $R = -1$.

So we transform the dependent variable y to v by the substitution.

$$y = -u_1/Ru = -u_1/(-u) = \frac{u_1}{u}$$

$$\therefore \quad y_1 = \frac{u_2}{u} - \frac{u_1{}^2}{u^2}$$

Putting these values in (i), we obtain

$$\frac{u_2}{u} - \frac{u_1^{\,2}}{u^2} = -\frac{2}{x^2} + \frac{2}{x} \cdot \frac{u_1}{u} - \frac{u_1^{\,2}}{u^2}$$

or $$x^2 u_2 - 2x\, u_1 + 2u = 0 \qquad \text{...(ii)}$$

It is a homogeneous linear differential equation of second order. Now putting x = e^z in this and denoting d/dx by Δ, the above equation (ii) reduces to

$$\Delta\,(\Delta - 1)\, u - 2\Delta u + 2u = 0$$

or $$(\Delta^2 - 3\Delta + 2)\, u = 0$$

or $$(\Delta - 1)\,(\Delta - 2)\, u = 0$$

its general solution is

$$u = Ae^z + Be^{2z} = Ax + Bx^2$$

Differentiating it, $u_1 = A + 2Bx$.

∴ General solution of (i) is given by

$$y = \frac{u_1}{u} = \frac{A + 2Bx}{Ax + Bx^2} = \frac{c + 2x}{cx + x^2}$$

or $$y\,(cx + x^2) = c + 2x, \text{ where } c = A/B.$$

Ex. 2. *Solve*

$$y_1 = 2 + \frac{1}{2}\left(x - \frac{1}{x}\right) y - \frac{1}{2}\, y^2 \qquad \text{...(i)}$$

Solution. Putting $y = x + \frac{1}{2}$, So that $y_1 = 1 - \frac{1}{x^2}$, in eqn. (i), we get

$$1 - \frac{1}{x^2} = 2 + \frac{1}{2}\left(x - \frac{1}{x}\right)\left(x + \frac{1}{x}\right) - \frac{1}{2}\left(x + \frac{1}{x}\right)^2$$

or $$1 - \frac{1}{x^2} = 1 - \frac{1}{x^2}$$

Hence $y = x + \frac{1}{x}$ is one integral of the given equation (i).

Let us change y to v by the substitution

$$y = x + \frac{1}{x} + \frac{1}{v}, \text{ so that } y_1 = 1 - \frac{1}{x^2} - \frac{1}{v^2} \cdot \frac{dv}{dx}$$

Putting these in (i), it reduces to

$$1 - \frac{1}{x^2} - \frac{1}{v^2} \cdot \frac{dv}{dx} = 2 + \frac{1}{2}\left(x - \frac{1}{x}\right)\left(x + \frac{1}{x} + \frac{1}{v}\right) - \frac{1}{2}\left(x + \frac{1}{x} + \frac{1}{v}\right)^2$$

$$= 2 + \frac{1}{2}\left(x^2 - \frac{1}{x^2}\right) + \frac{1}{2v}\left(x - \frac{1}{x}\right) - \frac{1}{2}\left[\left(x + \frac{1}{x}\right)^2 + \frac{2}{v}\left(x + \frac{1}{x}\right) + \frac{1}{v^2}\right]$$

on simplification, we obtain

$$\frac{dv}{dx} - \left(\frac{x}{2} + \frac{3}{2x}\right) v = \frac{1}{2} \qquad \text{...(ii)}$$

This is a linear differential eqn. of order one.

Its I.F. $= e^{-\int\left(\frac{x}{2} + \frac{3}{2x}\right) dx}$

$$= e^{-\int\left(\frac{x}{2}+\frac{3}{2x}\right)dx} = x^{-3/2}\, e^{-x^2/4}$$

Hence the general solution of (ii) is given by

$$v \,.\, x^{-3/2} \,.\, e^{-x^2/4} = \frac{1}{2}\int x^{-3/2} \,.\, e^{-x^2/4}\, dx + d$$

Putting $1/v = y - x - 1/x$ or $v = \dfrac{1}{(xy - x^2 - 1)}$ in this, we get the general solution of (i) as $\dfrac{(x^{-3/2} \,.\, e^{-x^2/4})}{(xy - x^2 - 1)} = \dfrac{1}{2}\int x^{-3/2} \,.\, e^{x^2/4}\, dx + d.$

Ex. 3. *Show that 1, x, x^2 are three integrals of the equation $x(x^2 - 1)\, y_1 + x^2 - (x^2 - 1)\, y - y^2 = 0$, and hence obtain the general solution as $y\,(x + k) = x + kx^2$.*

Solution. The given equation can be written as

$$y_1 = -\frac{x}{x^2 - 1} + \frac{1}{x} \,.\, y + \frac{x}{x\,(x^2 - 1)}\, y^2 \qquad \text{...(i)}$$

Putting $y = 1$ and hence $y_1 = 0$, the above equation is satisfied. Therefore $y = 1$ is a solution of this equation. Similarly $y = x$. $y = x^2$ can be shown to be the two integrals of (i).

Since three particular integrals of (i) are known so the method explained in § 9.4 (a) will be used.

If $q(x) = 1$, $r(x) = x$, $s(x) = x^2$, then the general solution of (i) is given by

$$\frac{\{y - q(x)\}\,\{r(x) - s(x)\}}{\{y - s(x)\}\,\{r(x) - q(x)\}} = k$$

or $$\frac{(y - 1)\,(x - x^2)}{(y - x^2)\,(x - 1)} = k$$

or $$k\,(y - x^2) + x\,(y - 1) = 0$$

or $$y\,(k + x) = x + kx^2 \,.$$

Ex. 4. *Show that tan x is one integral of $y_1 = 1 + y^2$, and hence obtain the general solution in the form*

$$y\,(c - \tan x) = c \tan x + 1.$$

Solution. If $y = \tan x$, then $y_1 = \sec^2 x$.

also $\quad 1 + y^2 = 1 + \tan^2 x = \sec^2 x = y_1$.

Hence $\quad y = \tan x$ is one integral of the equation $y_1 = 1 + y^2$.

Now change the dependent variable y to v by substitution $y = \tan x + \dfrac{1}{v}$, so that $y_1 = \sec^2 x - v_1/v^2$

Putting these values in the given equation we get

$$\sec^2 x - \frac{v_1}{v^2} = 1 + \left(\tan x + \frac{1}{v}\right)^2$$

or $$\frac{v^1}{v^2} = \frac{1}{v^2} + \frac{2\tan x}{v}$$

or $$v_1 + 2 \tan x \, . \, v = -1 \qquad \text{...(i)}$$

This is linear equation in v of first order.

Its $$\text{I.F.} = e^{\int 2 \tan x \, dx} = e^{2 \log \sec x}$$
$$= \sec^2 x$$

$\therefore$ The general solution of (i) is given by

$$v \, . \sec^2 x = -\int \sec^2 x \, dx + c = -\tan x + c$$

or $$v = (c - \tan x) / \sec^2 x$$

Now, putting $v = 1/(y - \tan x)$, we get

$$\frac{1}{(y - \tan x)} = \frac{c - \tan x}{\sec^2 x}$$

or $$y\,(c - \tan x) = c \tan x + 1.$$

Ex. 5. *Show that there are two values of the constant for which k/x is an integral of $x^2 (y_1 + y^2) = 2$, and hence obtain the general solution.*

Solution. The given equation can be rewritten as

$$y_1 = (2/x^2) - y^2 \qquad \text{...(i)}$$

putting $y = k/x$, so that $y_1 = -k/x^2$ in this, we get

$$-k/x^2 = 2/x^2 - k^2/x^2$$

or $$k^2 - k - 2 = 0, \text{ i.e., } k = -1, 2.$$

Hence for the two values of k, viz. -1 and 2, $y = k/x$ is an integral of the equation (i).

Hence $y = -1/x$ and $y = 2/x$ are two P.I.S. of (i).

Let $q(x) = 2/x$ are two P.I.S. of (i).

Since two particular integrals are known, the method of § 9.4 (*b*) will be used.

By the formula obtained in § 9.4 (*b*), the general equation of Riccati's equation $y_1 = P + Qy + Ry^2$ is given by

$$\log [(y - q) / (y - r)] = \int (q - r) R \, dx + d$$

Comparing the equation (i) with the Riccati's equation, we get $R = -1$

Hence the general solution of the equation (i) is given by

$$\log [\,(y - 2/x) / (y + 1/x)\,] = \int \left(\frac{2}{x} + \frac{1}{x}\right) (-1) \, dx + d$$

or $$\log [\,(xy - 2) / (xy + 1)\,] = -3 \log x + \log \lambda$$

or $$\frac{(xy - 2)}{(xy + 1)} = \lambda / x^3$$

or $$x^3 (xy - 2) = \lambda (xy + 1),$$

where λ is an arbitrary constant.

EXERCISE – 9

Solve the following equations

1. $y_1 = -2 - 5y - 2y^2$.
2. $x(1 - x^3)\, y_1 = x^2 + y - 2xy^2$, x^2 is an integral.
3. $x(x - 1)\, y_1 - (2x + 1)\, y + y^2 + 2x = 0$, x is an integral.
4. $y_1 = e^{2x} - ye^x + e^{-x} y^2$, e^x is an integral.

5. $y_1 = \cos x - y \sin x + y^2$, $\sin x$ is an integral.

ANSWERS

1. $2y(1 + c\,e^{3x}) + (4 + c\,e^{3x}) = 0.$
2. $(x^4 - x)/(y - x^2) = c - 2x^3/3$.
3. $y = (x^2 + c)/(x + c)$
4. $y = e^x - (e^{2x - ex}) / \left\{d + \int e^{x - e^x}\, dx\right\}$
5. $\dfrac{e^{-\cos x}}{(2 - \sin x)} - d - \int e^{-\cos x}\, dx$.

10

Orthogonal Set of Functions

10.1 Introduction

The concept of an orthogonal set of functions arises in a natural way from an analogy with vectors in a vector space. This is a natural generalization of the concept of an orthogonal set of vectors, i.e., a set of mutually perpendicular vectors. In fact, a function can be considered as a generalized vector so that fundamental properties of the set of functions are suggested by an analogous Properties of the set of vectors.

10.2 Some Basic Definitions

Inner Product. The inner product of two functions $f(x)$ and $g(x)$ is the number defined by the equation

$$(f, g) = \int_a^b f(x)\, g(x)\, dx \text{ [on internal } a \le x \le b]$$

Orthogonal function The condition that the two functions be orthogonal is written as

$$(f, g) = 0$$

i.e.,
$$\int_a^b f(x)\, g(x)\, dx = 0$$

Norm of the function—The norm of the function $f(x)$ is defined as the non-negative number

$$\| f \| = \left\{ \int_a^b [f(x)]^2\, dx \right\}^{1/2}.$$

Orthogonality with respect to a weight (or density) function. The concept of orthogonality can be extended as follows. Let $p(x) \ge 0$. Then the condition that the two functions $f(x)$ and $g(x)$ be orthogonal with respect to the weight function $p(x)$ is written as

$$\int_a^b p(x)\, f(x)\, g(x)\, dx = 0.$$

Further the norm of the function $f(x)$ is defined as

$$\| f \|_p = \sqrt{\left\{ \int_a^b p(x) f^2(x)\, dx \right\}}$$

Again $f(x)$ is said to be normalized when

$$\int_a^b p(x) f^2(x)\, dx = 1$$

Note that the orthogonality with respect to a weight function $p(x)$ can be reduced to the ordinary type by using the product $\sqrt{\{p(x)\}}\, f(x)$ and $\sqrt{\{p(x)\}}\, g(x)$ as two functions.

Orthogonal set of functions — If we have a set $\{f_n(x)\}$ $(n = 1, 2, 3, ...)$ of real functions defined on an internal $a \le x \le b$ then the set $\{f_n(x)\}$ is said to be an orthogonal set of functions on the internal $a \le x \le b$ if

$$\int_a^b f_m(x) f_n(x)\, dx = 0, \text{ whenever } m \ne n.$$

Orthogonal set of functions with respect to a weight function

Let there is a set $\{f_n(x)\}$ $(n = 1, 2, 3, ...)$ of real functions defined on an internal $a \le x \le b$. Let $p(x) \ge 0$. Then the set $\{f_n(x)\}$ is said to be an orthogonal set of functions on the internal $a \le x \le b$ if

$$\int_a^b p(x) f_m(x) f_n(x)\, dx = 0, \text{ whenever } m \ne n.$$

Orthonormal set of functions — If we have a set $\{f_n(x)\}$ $(n = 1, 2, 3, ...)$ of real functions, defined on an interval $a \le x \le b$ is said to be an orthonormal set of functions on the interval, if

$$\int_a^b f_n(x) f_m(x)\, dx = \{0 \text{ when } m \ne n, 1 \text{ when } m = n\}$$

i.e.,

$$\int_\alpha^\beta f_m(x) f_n(x)\, dx = \delta_{mn},$$

where the Kronecker delta $\delta\, mn = \{0 \text{ when } m \ne n, 1 \text{ when } m = n\}$

Orthonormal set of functions with respect to a weight function

Let $\{\phi_n(x)\}$ $(n = 1, 2, 3, ...)$ be a set of real functions defined on an internal $a \le x \le b$ and $p(x) \ge 0$. Then the set $\{\phi_n(x)\}$ is said to be orthonormal set of functions on the internal $a \le x \le b$ if

$$\int_a^b p(x)\, \phi_m(x)\, \phi_n(x)\, dx = \begin{cases} 0 \text{ when } m \ne n, \\ \text{when m = n} \end{cases}$$

i.e.,

$$\int_a^b p(x)\ \theta\mu(x)\ \phi_m(x)\ \phi_n(x)\, dx = \delta\, mn.$$

10.3 Cram-Schmidt Orthonormalization method

From an orthogonal set we may obtain an orthonormal set by dividing each function by its norm on the internal under consideration. This method of orthonormalization is called Gram-Schmidt orthonormalisation method.

Illustrative Examples

Ex. 1. *Show that the functions* g_m = *cos mx ; m* = 0, 1, 2, ------- *form orthogonal set of functions on the interval* $-\pi \le x \le \pi$, and determine the corresponding orthenormal set of functions.

Solution. We have, when $m \neq n$

$$\int_{-\pi}^{\pi} \cos mx \cos nx \, dx$$

$$= 2\int_{o}^{\pi} \cos mx \cos nx \, dx$$

$$= \int_{0}^{\pi} [\cos (m+n)x - \cos (m-n)\, x] \, dx$$

$$= \left[\frac{\text{Sin}\,(m+n)\,x}{m+n} - \frac{\sin (m-n)\,x}{m-n}\right]_0^{\pi} = 0$$

Hence the given functions form an orthogonal set.

Now, norm of g_m is

$$\| g_m \| = \| \cos mx \| = \left[\int_{-\pi}^{\pi} \cos^2 mx \, dx\right]^{1/2}$$

$$= \left[2\int_{o}^{\pi} \cos^2 mx \, dx\right]^{1/2}$$

$$= \sqrt{(2\pi)}, \text{ when } m = 0$$

and $$\| \cos mx \| = \sqrt{\pi} \text{ when } m = 1, 2 \text{------}$$

Hence the orthonormal set is

$$\frac{1}{\sqrt{(2\pi)}}, \frac{\cos x}{\sqrt{\pi}}, \frac{\cos 2x}{\sqrt{\pi}}, \frac{\cos 3x}{\sqrt{\pi}}, \ldots$$

Ex.2 *Show that the function 1, cosx, sinx, cos 2x, sin 2x, — form an orthogonal set on an interval* $-\pi \le x \le \pi$ *and obtain the orthonormal set.*

Solution. Here $\int_{-\pi}^{\pi} \cos mx \sin nx \, dx,$

for all $m = 0, 1, 2, \ldots$

$n = 1, 2, 3, \ldots$ and $m \neq n$

$$= \frac{1}{2}\int_{-\pi}^{\pi} \{\sin (m+n)\, x \pm \sin (n-m)\, x\} \, dx$$

according as $n >$ or $< m$

$$= \frac{1}{2}\left[\frac{\cos (m+n)x}{m+n} \mp \frac{\cos (n-m)\,x}{n-m}\right]_{-\pi}^{\pi} = 0$$

Also $\int_{-\pi}^{\pi} 1. \cos mx\, dx = 0 , \int_{-\pi}^{\pi} \text{Sin}^2 mx\, dx = 0$

and $\int_{-\pi}^{\pi} \text{Cos}^2 mx\, dx = 0$

Hence the functions form orthogonal set.

Now $$\| 1 \| = \left\{\int_{-\pi}^{\pi} 1^2\, dx\right\}^{1/2} = \sqrt{(2\pi)}$$

$$\| \cos mx \| = \left[\int_{-\pi}^{\pi} \cos^2 mx\, dx\right]^{1/2}$$

$$= \left[\int_{0}^{\pi} (1-\cos 2mx)\, dx\right]^{1/2} = \sqrt{\pi}$$

and $$\| \sin mx \| = \left[\int_{-\pi}^{\pi} \sin^2 mx\, dx\right]^{1/2} = \sqrt{\pi}$$

Hence the orthonormal set of functions is

$$\frac{1}{\sqrt{(2\pi)}}, \frac{\cos x}{\sqrt{\pi}}, \frac{\sin x}{\sqrt{\pi}}, \frac{\cos 2x}{\sqrt{\pi}}, \frac{\sin 2x}{\sqrt{\pi}} \ldots$$

Ex. 3. *Show that the functions $f_1(x) = 1$, $f_2(x) = x$ are orthogonal on the internal (-1, 1) and determine the constants A and B so that function $f_3(x) = 1 + A x + Bx^2$ is orthogonal to both f_1 and f_2 on the interval.*

Solution. Here

$$\int_{-1}^{1} f_1(x) f_2(x)\, dx = \int_{-1}^{1} 1.\, x\, dx = \left[\frac{x^2}{2}\right]_{-1}^{1} = 0$$

Hence $f_1(x)$ and $f_2(x)$ are orthogonal on the interval (–1, 1).

If $f_3 = 1 + Ax + Bx^2$ is orthogonal to both $f_1(x) = 1$ and $f_2(x) = x$ on the interval (–1, 1), then

$$\int_{-1}^{1} f_1(x) f_3(x)\, dx = 0$$

or $$\int_{-1}^{1} 1. (1 + Ax + Bx^2)\, dx = 0$$

or $$\left[x + \frac{Ax^2}{2} + \frac{Bx^3}{3}\right]_{-1}^{1} = 0$$

or $$2 + \left(\frac{2}{3}\right) B = 0 \qquad \therefore \quad B = -3,$$

and $$\int_{-1}^{1} f_2(x) f_3(x)\, dx = 0$$

or $$\int_{-1}^{1} (x + Ax^2 + Bx^3)\, dx = 0$$

or
$$\left[\frac{x^2}{2}+\frac{A}{3}x^3+\frac{B}{4}x^4\right]_{-1}^{1} = 0$$

or
$$\frac{2}{3}A = 0 \qquad \therefore A = 0$$

Hence the function f_3 (x) is orthogonal to both f_1 (x) and f_2 (x) if A = 0 and B = –3.

10.4 Generalized Fourier series

$\{\phi_n(x)\}$ $\{n = 1, 2, 3, ...\}$ be an orthogonal set of functions on an interval (a,b). It may be possible to represent an arbitrary function f on the some interval by a linear combination of these functions, in the form

$$f(x) = \sum_{n=1}^{\infty} c_n \phi_n(x) = c_1 \phi_1(x) + c_2 \phi_2(x) + ... + c_n \phi_n(x) + \quad ...(i)$$
$$(a \le x \le b)$$

If the series (i) converges and represents $f(x)$, it is called a *generalized fourier series* of $f(x)$, and its coefficients are called the *fourier constants* of $f(x)$ with repect to the orthogonal set $\{\phi_n\}$

Multiplying both sides of (i) by $\phi_n(x)$ and then integrating over the interval $a \le x \le b$ on which the funtions are orthonormal, we have

$$c_n = \int_a^b f(x)\, \phi_n(x)\, dx.$$

10.5 Strum - Liouville Equation

Various important orthogonal sets of function arise in solution of second - order differential equations of the form

$$[R(x)\, y']' + [Q(x) + \lambda P(x)]\, y = 0 \qquad ...(i)$$

on some internal $a \le x \le b$ satisfying conditions of the form

$$\left.\begin{aligned} &(a) \quad a_1 y + a_2 y' = 0 \text{ at } x = a \\ \text{and} \quad &(b) \quad b_1 y + b_2 y' = 0 \text{ at } x = b \end{aligned}\right\} \qquad ...(ii)$$

here λ is a real parameter and a_1, a_2, b_1, b_2, are given real constants atleast one in each condition (ii) being different from zero.

The equation (i) is known as the *Strum Liouville equation.*

We may see that legendre's equation, Bessel's equation and other important equations can be written in the form (i) Conditions (ii) are called the *boundary conditions.*

Strum–Liouville Problem (Eigen functions and Eigen values)

The boundry value problem given by (i), (ii) is called a *Strum–Liouville problem.*

The solutions $y \ne 0$ are called the *characteristic functions or eigen functions* and λ *Characteristic values or eigen values* of the problem.

10.6 Theorem 1

Let the function P, Q, R in the Strum-Liouville equation be real and continuous on the internal $a \le x \le b$. *Let* $y_m(x)$ *and* $y_n(x)$ *be given functions of Strum-Liouville problem corresponding to distinct eigen values* λ_m and λ_n *respectively, and let the derivatives* $y'_m(x)$, $y'_n(x)$ *be continuous on the inetrval. Then* y_m *and* y_n *are orthogonal on that interval with respect to the weight function P.*

Since $y_m(x)$ and $y_n(x)$ be the solutions of the Strum-Liouville problem

$$[R(x)y']' + [Q(x) + \lambda P(x)]y = 0 \qquad ...(i)$$

on some internal $a \le x \le b$, satisfying conditions

(a) $a_1 y + a_2 y^1 = 0$ at $x = a$

and (b) $b_1 y + b_2 y^1 = 0$ at $x = b$

$\therefore$ we have

$$(R y'_m)' + (Q + \lambda_m P) y_m = 0 \qquad ...(ii)$$

and

$$(Ry'_n)' + (Q + \lambda_n P) y_n = 0 \qquad ...(iii)$$

Multiply (ii) by y_n and (iii) by y_m and subtracting we have

$$(\lambda_m - \lambda_n) P\ y_m y_n = y_m (R y'_n)' - y_n (R y'_m)'$$

or

$$(\lambda_m - \lambda_n P y_m y_n = (R y'_n y_m - R y'_m y_n)'$$

Integrating both sides from a to b, we have

$$(\lambda_m - \lambda_n \int_a^b P y_m y_n\, dx = [R y' y_m - R y'_m y_n]_a^b$$

$$= R(b)[y'_n(b) y_m(b) - y'm(b) y_n(b)]$$
$$-R(a)[y'_n(a) y_m(a) - y_m'(y_m'(a) y_n(a)] \qquad ...(iv)$$

Now following different cases arise :

Case I If R (a) = R (b) = 0 (each)

$\therefore$ From (iv) we have

$$(\lambda_m - \lambda_n) \int_a^b P y_m y_n\, dx = 0$$

or

$$\int_a^b P y_m y_n\, dx = 0 \qquad \text{since } \lambda_m \ne \lambda_n.$$

from which it follows that y_m and y_n are orthogonal with respect to the weight funcion P.

Case II If R (a) = 0 but R $(b) \ne 0$.

$\therefore$ from (iv), we have

$$(\lambda_m - \lambda_n) \int_a^b P y_m y_n\, dx = R(b)[y'_n(b) y_m(b) - y'_m(b) y_n(b)] \qquad ...(v)$$

Also from (b), we have

$$b_1 y_m(b) + b_2 y_m'(b) = = 0 \qquad ...(vi)$$

and

$$b_1 y_n(b) + b_2 y_n'(b) = 0 \qquad ...(vii)$$

If $b_2 \ne 0$, then multiplying (vi) by y_n (b) and (vii) by y_m (b) and subtracting, we have

$$b_2 [y_m' (b) - y_n (b) - y_n (b) y_m (b)] = 0$$

and $$y'_m (b) y_n (b) - y_n' (b) y_m (b) = 0$$

∴ from (v) we have

$$\int_a^b P y_m y_n dx = 0,$$

i.e., y_m and y_n are orthogonal with respect to the weight function P.

If $b_2 = 0$ then assuming $b_1 \neq 0$, -then multiplying (vi), by y'_n (b) and (vii) by y_m' (b) and subtracting, we have

$$b_1 [y_m (b) y_n' (b) - Y_m' (b) y_n (b)] = 0$$

or $$y_m (b) y_n' (b) - y_m' (b) y_n (b) = 0$$

∴ from (v), we have

$$\int_a^b P y_m y_n dx = 0$$

∴ y_m and y_n are orthoonarmal with respect to the weight function P.

Case III. If R (b) = 0, but R (a) ≠ 0

∴ from (iv), we have

$$(\lambda_m - \lambda_n) \int_a^b P y_m y_n dx = - R (a) [y_n (a) y_m (a) - y_m (a) y_n (a)] \quad ...(viii)$$

Also, formula, we have

$$a_1 y_m (a) + a_2 y'm (a) = 0 \quad ...(ix)$$

and $$a_1 y_n (a) + a_2 y_n (a) = 0 \quad ...(x)$$

If $a_2 \neq 0$, then multiplying (ix) by y_n (a) and (x) by y_m (a) and subtracting, we have

$$a_1 [y_m' (a) y_n (a) - y_n' (a) y_m (a)] = 0$$

or $$y_m' (a) y_n (a) - y_n' (a) y_m (a) = 0$$

∴ from (viii) , we have $\int_a^b P y_m y_n dx = 0$

∴ y_m and y_n are orthogonal with respect to the weight function P.

If $a_2 = 0$, then we assume $a_1 \neq 0$

Then multiplying (ix) by y_n' (a) and (x) by ym' (a) and subtracting, we have

$$a_1 [y_n' (a) y_m (a) - y_m' (a) y_n (a)] = 0$$

or $$y_n' (a) y_m (a) - y_m' (a) y_n (a) = 0$$

∴ from (viii), we have $\int_a^b P y_m y_n dx = 0$

∴ y_m and y_n are orthogonal with respect to the weight function P.

Case IV. If R (a) ≠ 0 , R (b) ≠ 0.

Thus using (a) and (b) and proceeding an in case II and III, we have from (iv)

$$\int_a^b P y_m y_n dx = 0$$

Case V . If R (a) = R (b)

∴ from (iv), we have

$$(\lambda_m - \lambda_n) \int_a^b P\, y_m\, y_n\, dx$$

$$= R(b)[y_n'(b)\, y_m(b) - y_m'(b)\, y_n(b)$$

$$- y_m(a)\, y_m(a) + y_m'(a)\, y_n(a)] \quad ...(xi)$$

nd

$$a_1 y_m(a) + a_2 y_n(a) = 0 \quad ...(xii)$$

$$a_1 y_n(a) + a_2 y_n(a) = 0 \quad ...(xiii)$$

$$b_1 y_m(b) + b_2 y_m(b) = 0 \quad ...(xiv)$$

$$b_1 y_n(b) + b2\, y_n(b) = 0 \quad ...(xv)$$

If $a_1 \neq 0$, $b_1 \neq 0$, multiplying (xii) by $y_n(a)$ and (xiii) by y_m (a) and subtracting ve have

$$y_m(a)\, y_n(a) - y_m(a)\, y_n(a) = 0$$

Also multiplying (xiv) by y_n (b) and (xv) by y_m (b) and subtracting, we have

$$Y'_{m(b)}\, Y_n(b) - Y'_{n(b)}\, Y_{m(b)} = 0$$

∴ from (xi), we have

$$\int_a^b P\, y_m\, y_n\, dx = 0$$

Hence Y_m and Y_n are orthogonal with respect to the weight function P.

0.7. Theorem 2

Eigen values of the Strum-Liouville problem are all real.

Strum-Liouville problem is

$$(r x')' + (q + \lambda p) x = 0 \quad ...(i)$$

on the internal a, satisfying the conditions

$$a_1\, x(a) + a_2\, x'(a) = 0 \quad ...(ii)$$

and

$$b_1\, x(b) + b_2\, x'(b) = 0 \quad ...(iii)$$

Let x be an eigen function corresponding to an eigen value

$$\lambda = \alpha + i\beta$$

where α, β are real numbers. This eigen function on X (x) will satisfy equations (i), (ii) and (iii) and it may be complex valued function.

Taking the complex conjugete of all the terms in equations (i), (ii) and (iii), we get

$$(r\, \bar{x}')' + (q + \lambda p)\, \bar{x} = 0 \quad ...(iv)$$

$$a_1\, \bar{x}(a) + a_2\, \bar{x}'(a) = 0 \quad ...(v)$$

and

$$b_1\, \bar{x}(b) + b_2\, \bar{x}'(b) = 0 \quad ...(vi)$$

which shows that $\bar{x}$ (x) is the eigen function corresponding to the eigen values $\bar{\lambda} = \alpha - i\beta$.

Multiplying (i) by $\bar{x}$ and (iv) by x and subtracting, we get

$$(r\bar{x}')\, \bar{x} - (r\, x)'\, x + (\lambda - \bar{\lambda})\, p\, x\, \bar{x} = 0$$

or

$$(\lambda - \bar{\lambda}).\, p(x)\, x(x)\, \bar{x}(x) = (r\bar{x}')\, x - (r\bar{x}')'\, \bar{x}$$

$$= (r\, \bar{x}'\, x - r\, x'\, \bar{x})'$$

Integrating both sides from a to b, we have

$$(\lambda - \bar{\lambda}) \int_a^b p(x)\, x(x)\, \bar{x}(x)\, dx = [r\, \bar{x}'\, x - r\bar{x}\, x']_a^b$$

or $$(\lambda-\bar{\lambda})\int_a^b p(x)\,x(x)\,\bar{x}(x)\,dx$$
$$= r(b)\,[\bar{x}'(b) - x'(b)\,\bar{x}(b)]$$
$$- r(a)\,[\bar{x}(a)\,x'(a) - x'(a)\,\bar{x}(a)]$$

or $$(\lambda-\bar{\lambda})\int_a^b p(x)\,x(x)\,\bar{x}(x)\,dx = 0$$

with the help of equations (ii), (iii), (v) and (vi).

But $p(x) > 0$ when $a < b$ and $x(x)\,\bar{x}(x) = |x(x)|^2$

$\therefore$ $\int_a^b p(x)\,x(x)\,\bar{x}(x)\,dx$ has a positive value in the given internal.

$\therefore$ $\lambda - \bar{\lambda} = 0$ or $2\iota\beta = 0$

or $\beta = 0$, i.e., λ is real.

Hence eigen-values of Sturn - Liouville problem are all real.

10.8. Theorem 3

If $r(a) > 0$ or $r(b) > 0$, the Strum Liouville problem can not have two linearly independent eigen functions corresponding to the same eigen value. Also each eigen function can be made real valued by multiplying it by an appropriate non - zero constant.

The Strum - Liouville problem is
$$(r\,x')' + (q + \lambda p)\,x = 0 \qquad \text{...(i)}$$
on the intervel $a \le x \le b$

satisfying the condition
$$a_1\,x(a) + a_2\,x^1(a) = 0 \qquad \text{...(ii)}$$
and
$$b_1\,x(b) + b_2\,x^1(b) = 0 \qquad \text{...(iii)}$$

Let x and y be two eigen functions of the Strum–Liouville problem corresponding to the same eigen value λ.

Now if $r(a) > 0$.

Let us consider the function $w(x)$ such that
$$w(x) = x(x)\,y(a) - y'(x)\,x'(a) \qquad \text{...(iv)}$$

It may be easily seen - that w(x) satisfies the equation
$$(r\,w')' + (q + \lambda p)\,w = 0$$

Also $w'(a) = [w'(x)]_{x=0} = [x'(x)\,y'(a) - y(x)\,x'(a)]_{x=0} = 0$

Now if $a_1 \neq 0$, then from (ii), we have
$$\left.\begin{aligned} a_1\,x(a) + a_2\,x'(a) &= 0 \\ \text{and} \quad a_1\,y(a) + a_2\,y'(a) &= 0 \end{aligned}\right\} \qquad \text{...(vi)}$$

which gives
$$a_1\,[x(a)\,y'(a) - y(a)\,x'(a)] = 0$$
or
$$x(a)\,y'(a) - y(a)\,x'(a) = 0 \qquad \text{or} \qquad w(a) = 0.$$

But according to the uniqueness theorem for the solution of linear differential equations, we see that $w(x) = 0$ is the only solution of equation (v), such that

$$W(a) = W'(a) = 0 \quad \text{...(viii)}$$

Thus $\qquad x(x)\, y'(a) - y(x)\, x'(a) = 0$

If either $x' \neq 0$ or $y'(a) \neq 0$ then (vi) implies that the functions $x(x)$ and $y(x)$ are linearly dependent, i.e., one function is a constant multiple of the other function.

If $x'(a) = 0$ and $y'(a) = 0$ then from (vi), we have $a_1 = 0$. In this case we can take the function v(x) such that

$$V(x) = y(a)\, x(x) - x(a)\, y(x)$$

and proceeding similarly we shall get $V(x) = 0$.

Hence $x(x)$ and $y(x)$ are linearly dependent.

Now let $x = a + i\beta$ be a complex valued eigen function corresponding to a real eigen-value λ. Substituting $x = a + i\beta$ in (i), (ii), and (iii) and seperating the real and imaginary party we see that α and β are also eigen functions of the Strum- Liouville problem corresponding to the same eigen value λ. Hence according to the first part one must be equal to constant time the other. Say $\beta = k\alpha$ where k is a constant.

$$\therefore \qquad x = \alpha(1 + ik)$$

$\therefore$ x is real, if k is imaginary constant factor.

If k is real constant then x may be made real by multiplying it by an appropriate non-zero constant.

Hence each eigen function can be made real valued by multiplying it by an appropriate non-zero constant.

Illustrative Examples

Ex. 4. *For the eigen value problem*

$$x'' + \lambda x = 0, \quad x(0) = 0, \quad x(\pi) = 0$$

Obtain the set of eigen function and the eigen values

Solution

Case I If $\lambda = 0$, we have

$$x'' = 0 \quad \therefore x(x) = Ax + B, \quad \therefore x(0) = 0 = B$$

and $x(\pi) = 0 = A\pi + B$. Hence $A = 0$ and $B = 0$.

$\therefore$ $x(x) = 0$ which is not an eigen function.

Case II If $\lambda = n^2$, we have $x'' + n^2 x = 0$

$$\therefore \qquad x(x) = A\cos nx + B\sin nx, \ \therefore x(0) = 0 = A$$

and $x(\pi) = 0 = B \operatorname{Sin} n\pi$

giving $A = 0$ and either $B = 0$ or $\operatorname{Sin} n\pi = 0$.

If $B = 0$, $x(x) = 0$ and which is not eigen value.

$$\therefore \qquad \text{taking } \sin n\pi = 0$$

which gives $n = \pm 1, \pm 2, \ldots$

$\therefore$ Eigen functions are $x(x) = \operatorname{Sin} nx$, taking $B = 1$ and eigen value are $\lambda = n^2$, $n = 1, 2, 3, \ldots$

Case III. If $\lambda = -n^2$, we have $x'' - n^2 x = 0$

$$\therefore \qquad x(x) = Ae^{nx} + be^{-nx} \ \therefore x(0) = 0 = A + B$$

and $x(\pi) = 0\ Ae^{n\pi} + Be^{-n\pi}$ giving $A = 0$ and $B = 0$

$\therefore$ $x(x) = 0$ which is also not an eigen function.

Ex. 5. *Find all eigen values and eigen functions of the Strum- Liouville problem* $x'' + \lambda x = 0$, $x(0) = x'\left(\frac{\pi}{2}\right) = 0$.

Solution.

Case I. If $\lambda = 0$, we have x'' *(0)*

$$\therefore \quad X(x) = Ax + B, \quad \therefore x(0) = 0 = B$$

and $x'(\pi/2) = 0 = A$.

$\therefore$ $X(x) = 0$, which is not an eigen function.

Case II, If $\lambda = n^2$, we have $x'' + n^2 x = 0$

$$\therefore \quad X(x) = A \cos nx + B \operatorname{Sin} nx \quad \therefore \quad x(0) = 0 = A$$

and $$X'(\pi/2) = 0 = Bn \cos \frac{n\pi}{2} \quad \therefore \quad A = 0$$

if $B = 0$, then $X(x) = 0$, which is not an eigen function.

$\operatorname{Cos} \frac{n\pi}{2} = 0$ giving $n = (2m - 1)$, $m = 1, 2, 3, \ldots$

$$\therefore \quad X(x) = B \operatorname{Sin} \{(2m-1)x\}$$

$\therefore$ eigen functions are $X(x) = \operatorname{Sin} \{(2m-1)x\}$ and eigen values are $\lambda = (2m-1)^2$, $m = 1, 2, 3, \ldots$

Case III If $\lambda = -n^2$, we have $x'' - n^2 x = 0$

$$\therefore \quad X(x) = Ae^{nx} + Be^{-nx} \quad \therefore \quad X(0) = 0 = A + B$$

$$X'(\pi/2) = 0 = Ane^{n\pi/2} - Bne^{-n\pi/2}$$

giving $A = 0 = B$. $\therefore$ $X(x) = 0$ which is not an eigen function.

Ex. 6. *Find all the eigen values and eigen function of the Strum Liouville problem*

$$x'' + \lambda x = 0, \; x'(0) = 3, \; x'(c) = 0$$

Solution

Case I If $\lambda = 0$, we have $x'' = 0$

$$\therefore \quad x(x) = Bx + A, \; X'(x) = B, \quad \therefore X'(0) = 0 = B$$

and $$X'(c) = 0 = B \; \therefore \; X(x) = A,$$

which is the eigen function and the corresponding eigen value is $\lambda = 0$

Case II. If $X = n^2$, we have

$$X'' + n^2 x = (0) \quad \therefore X(x) = A \cos nx + B \operatorname{Sin} nx$$

$$\therefore \quad X'(0) = 0 = Bn \quad \therefore B = 0$$

and $X'(e) = -An \operatorname{Sin} nc + B\,n \operatorname{Cos} nc = 0$

or $$A \operatorname{Sin} nc = 0.$$

If $A = 0$ then $x(x) = 0$, which is not an eigen function.

$\therefore$ taking $\operatorname{Sin} nc = 0$

$$\therefore \quad nc = m\pi \text{ or } n = \frac{m\pi}{c}, \; m = 1, 2, \ldots$$

$$\therefore \quad x(x) = A \cos \frac{m\pi x}{c}$$

$$\therefore \quad \text{eigen function } X(x) = \cos \frac{m\pi x}{c}. \text{ by taking } A = 1.$$

and eigen values are $\lambda = \frac{m^2 \pi^2}{c^2}$, $m = 1, 2, 3 ...$

Case III. If $\lambda = -n^2$, we have

$$X'' - n^2 x = 0 \qquad \therefore \qquad X(x) = Ae^{nx} + Be^{-nx}$$

$$\therefore \qquad x'(0) = 0 \qquad \therefore \qquad X'(x) = Ane^{nx} + Be^{-nx}$$

and $x'(c) = 0 = Ane^{nc} - Bne^{-nc}$, giving $A = 0 = B$

$X(x) = 0$, which is not an eigen function.

Ex. 7. *Find the eigen values and eigen functions for the problem* $\{xy'(x)\}$ $+ \frac{\lambda}{x} y(x) = 0$, $y(1) = y(e^{2\pi}) = 0$.

Solution. The given equation can be written as

$$xy''(x) + y'(x) + \frac{\lambda}{x} y(x) = 0$$

or

$$x^2 y''(x) + x\, y'(x) + \lambda\, y(x) = 0.$$

Changing the independent variable from x to z, by the substitution $x = e^z$ so that $x \frac{dy}{dx} = \frac{dy}{dz} = \Delta y$

and $x^2 \frac{d^2y}{dx^2} = D(D-1)y$ where $D = \frac{d}{dz}$

The equation reduces to

$$\{D(D-1)y + Dy + \lambda y\} = 0$$

or

$$D^2 y + \lambda y = 0 \qquad \text{or} \qquad \frac{d^2 y}{dz^2} + \lambda y = 0.$$

Case I When $\lambda = 0$, we have $\frac{d^2 y}{dz^2} = 0$

$$\therefore \qquad y = Az + B \qquad \text{or } y(x) = A \log x + B$$

so that $\quad y'(x) \frac{A}{x}$

$$\therefore \qquad y'(1) = A = 0$$

$\therefore$ Corresponding to the eigen value $\lambda = 0$ $y(x) = B$ is the eigen function.

Case II When $\lambda = k^2$

The equation is $\frac{d^2y}{dz^2} + k^2 y = 0$

$$\therefore \qquad y = A \cos kz + B \text{ Sin } kz$$

or

$$y(x) = A \cos(k \log x) + B \text{ Sin }(k \log x)$$

so that $\quad y'(x) = \frac{Ak}{x} \text{ Sin }(K \log x) + \frac{Bk}{x} \cos(K \log x)$

$$\therefore \qquad y'(1) = BK = 0 \qquad \therefore \quad B = 0$$

$\therefore$ either $A = 0$ or $\text{Sin } 2\pi K = 0$.

But $A \neq 0$, otherwise $y(x) = 0$, which is not an eigen function

$$\therefore \qquad \text{Sin } 2\pi K = 0 \qquad \therefore \quad 2\pi K = n\pi$$

or

$$K = \frac{n}{2}, \quad n = 1, 2, ...$$

$\therefore \qquad \lambda = k^2 = \frac{n^2}{4}, \quad n = 1, 2, 3, ...$

$\therefore \qquad y(x) = A \cos (\frac{n}{2} \log x)$

$\therefore$ eigen functions are

$y_n (x) = An \cos (\frac{n}{2} \log x)$

and eigen values are $\lambda = \frac{n^2}{4}, n = 1, 2, ...$

Case III. when $\lambda = - k^2$

The equation is $\frac{d^2y}{dz^2} - k^2 y = 0$

$\therefore \qquad y = Ae^{kz} + Be^{-kz}$

or $\qquad y(x) = Ax^k + bx^{-k}$

so that $\qquad y'(x) = AK x^{k-1} - BK x^{-k-1}$

$\therefore \qquad y'(1) = AK - Bk = 0 \qquad$ or B = A

and $\qquad y'(e^{2\pi}) = AK (e^{2\pi})^{k-1} - BK (e^{2\pi})^{-k-1} = 0$

or $\qquad Ae^{2\pi K} \; Ae^{-2\pi K} = 0, \qquad \therefore B = - A$

or $\qquad A (e^{2\pi K} - e^{-2\pi k}) = 0 \qquad \therefore A = D, B = 0$

so that $y(x) = 0$, which is not an eigen function.

10.9 Orthogonality of Legendre Polynomials

The Legendre's differential equation

$$(1-x^2) y'' - 2xy' + n (n + 1) y = 0$$

may be written as

$$[(1-x^2) y'] + \lambda y = 0 \qquad ...(i)$$

where $\lambda = n (n+1)$,

and is therefore a Strum-Liouville equation with

$$R(x) = 1-x^2, P(x) = 1 \text{ and } Q(x) = 0$$

Here no boundary conditions are needed to form a Strum-Liouville problem on the internal (–1, 1) since R = 0 when x = ± 1.

Further we know that Legendre Polynomials

$$P_n (x), (n = 0, 1, 2 ...)$$

are the solutions of the problem, hence they are the eigen functions and since they have continuous derivatives, therefore it follows that $\{P_n (x)\}$, $n = 0, 1, 2, ...$ are orthogonal on the interval $-1, \leq n \leq 1$ with respect to the wight function P = 1, i.e, $\int_{-1}^{1} P_m (x) P_n (x) dx = 0 \; (m \neq n)$

and $\qquad \| P_m \|^2 = \int_{-1}^{1} P_m^2 (x) \, dx = \frac{1}{2m + 1}, \; m = 0, 1, 2, ...$

If $g_0 (x)$, $g_1 (x)$, are eigen functions which are orthogonal on an interval $a \leq x \leq c$ with respect to the weight function $p(x)$, and if a given function $f(x)$ can be represented by a generalised Fourier series

$$f(x) = \sum_{n=1}^{\infty} c_m \, g_n(x),$$

then,
$$C_m = \frac{1}{\| gm \|2} \int_a^b p(x) f(x) g_m(x) \, dx$$

(m = 0, 1, 2, ...)

where
$$\| gm \|^2 = \int_a^b p(x) g_m^2(x) \, dx.$$

10.10 Orthogonality of Bessel's Function

We know that $J_n(\vartheta)$ is the solution of Bessel's equation.

$$v^2 \frac{d^2 y}{dv^2} + v \frac{dy}{dv} + (v^2 - n^2) y = 0,$$

where n is a positive integer.

$$\therefore \quad v^2 \frac{d2\, J_n(v)}{dv^2} + \frac{dJ_n(v)}{dv} + (v^2 - n^2) J_n(v) = 0.$$

Putting $v = \lambda x$, we have

$$\frac{dJ_n}{dv} = \frac{dJ_n}{dx} \cdot \frac{dx}{dv} = \frac{1}{\lambda} J'_n$$

and
$$\frac{d^2 Jn}{dv^2} = \frac{1}{\lambda} J_n'' \frac{dx}{dv} = \frac{1}{\lambda^2} J_n'',$$

where λ is a constant.

$$x^2 J_n''(\lambda x) + x J'_n(\lambda x) + (\lambda^2 x^2 - n^2) J_n(\lambda x) = 0$$

which may be written as

$$[x J_n'(\lambda x)]' + \left(-\frac{n^2}{x} + \lambda^2 x \right) J_n(x) = 0 \qquad \text{...(i)}$$

which is Strum-Liouville equation for each fixed n with

$$R(x) = x, \; Q(x) = -\frac{n^2}{x} \text{ and } P(x) = x$$

here parameter being λ^2 instead of λ.

Since $R(x) = 0$ for $x = 0$, it follows that solution of (i) on an interval $0 \le x \le a$ satisfying the boundary conditions

$$J_n(\lambda a) = a, \qquad \text{....(ii)}$$

form an orthogonal set with respect to the weight function $P(x) = x$.

Let $\alpha_n < \alpha_{2n} < \alpha_{3n}$ ... denote the positive zeros of $J_n(v)$, therefore (ii) holds for

$$\lambda a = \alpha_{mn} \text{ or } \lambda = \lambda_{mn} = \frac{\alpha_{mn}}{a}$$

(m = 1, 2, ... n fixed)

and since J_n' is continuous, also at $x = 0$, therefore for each fixed n = 0, 1, 2,

... the Bessel function $J_n(\lambda_{mn} x)$ $(m = 1, 2, \ldots$ with $\lambda_{mn} = \frac{\alpha_{mn}}{a}$, form an orthogonal set on an interval $0 \le x \le a$ with respect to weight function $p(x) = x$.

$$\therefore \qquad \int_o^a x\, J_n(\lambda_{mn} x)\, J_n(\lambda(\lambda_{pn} x) = 0 \; (p \neq m)$$

Thus we obtained infinitely many orthogonal sets corresponding to each fixed value of n.

If a function is represented by generalised fourier Bessel series

$$f(x) = \sum_{m=1}^{\infty} C_m\, J_r(\lambda_{mn} x), \text{ for } n \text{ fixed} \qquad \text{....(iii)}$$

then $$C_m = \frac{1}{\| J_n(\lambda mn\, x) \|^2} \int_o^a x\, f(c)\, J_n(\lambda_{mn} x)\, dx,\; m = 1, 2, \ldots$$

Since $$p(x) = x. \qquad \lambda_{mn} = \frac{\lambda\, mn}{a}$$

where $$\| J_n(\lambda_{mn} x) \|^2 = \int_o^a x\, J_n^2(\lambda_{mn} x)\, dx \qquad \text{...(iv)}$$

To find $\| J_n(\lambda_{mn}^2)^2 \|$ let us proceed as follows :

Multiplying (i) by $2x\, J_n'(\lambda x)$, we have

$$2x\, J_n'(\lambda x)\, [\, x\, J_n'(\lambda x)]' + (\lambda_{mn} \frac{n^2}{x} + \lambda^2 x)$$

$$2x\, J_n(\lambda x)\, J_n' \lambda x) = 0$$

or $$[\{x\, J_n'(\lambda x)\}^2] + (\lambda^2 x^2 - n^2)\, [\, J_o^2(\lambda x)' = 0$$

Integrating over the limits o to a, we have

$$[\{x\, J_n'(\lambda x)\}^2]_o^a = -\int_o^a (\lambda^2 x^2 - n^2)\, (J_n^2(\lambda x)]'\, dx$$

Integrating R.H.S. by parts, we have

$$[\{x\, J_n'(\lambda x)\}^2]_o^a = -[(\lambda^2 x^2 - n^2)\, J_n^2(\lambda x)]_o^a$$

$$+ 2x^2 \int_o^a x\, J_n^2(\lambda x)\, dx \qquad \text{...(v)}$$

From Recurrence formula for $J_n(\mu)$, we have

$$\frac{d}{dv}\{v^{-n} J_n(v)\} = -v^{-n} J_{n+1}(v)$$

or $$\mu^{-n} \frac{d}{dv} J_n(v) - v^{-n-1} J_n(v) = -v^{-n} J_{n+1}(v),$$

Multiplying both sides by v^{n+1}

$$v \frac{d}{dv} J_n(v) - n\, J_n(v) = -v\, J_{n+1}(v)$$

Putting $v = \lambda x$,

$$\lambda x \frac{d J_n(\lambda x)}{d(\lambda x)} - n\, J_n(\lambda x) = -\lambda x\, J_{n+1}(\lambda x)$$

or $$\lambda x \frac{d J_n (\lambda x)}{d (\lambda x)} = n\ J_n (\lambda x) - \lambda x\ J_{n+1} (\lambda x)$$

or $$\lambda x \frac{d J_n (\lambda x)}{dx} \cdot \frac{1}{\lambda} = n\ J_n (\lambda x) - \lambda x\ J_{n+1} (\lambda x)$$

or $$x\ J_n' (\lambda x) = n\ J_n (\lambda x) - \lambda x\ J_{n+1} (\lambda x)$$

Substituting in (v), we have

$$[\{n\ J_n (\lambda x) - \lambda x\ J_{n+1} (\lambda x)\}^2]_o^a$$

$$= - [\lambda^2 x^2 - n^2) J_n^2 (\lambda x)]_o^a + 2\lambda^2 \int_o^a x\ J_n^2 (\lambda x)\ dx$$

If $\lambda = \lambda_{mn}$, then $J_n (\lambda a) = J_n (\lambda_{mn} a) = 0$

and since $J_n (0) = 0$, $(n = 1, 2, ...)$

$\therefore$ We have

$$\lambda^2_{mn}\ a^2\ J^2_{n+1} (\lambda_{mn}\ a) = 2\lambda^2_{mn} \int_o^a x\ J_n^2 (\lambda_{mn}^2)\ dx$$

$$= 2\ \lambda^2_{mn} \| J_n (\lambda_{mn}\ x)\|^2$$

[Since weight function $p(x) = x$]

$$\| J_n (\lambda_{mn}\ x)\|^2 = \frac{a^2}{2} J^2_{n+1} (\lambda_{mn}\ a)$$

$$= \frac{a^2}{2} J^2_{n+1} (\alpha_{mn})$$

Where $\alpha_{mn} = \lambda_{mn}\ a$

$\therefore$ $$C_m = \frac{2}{a^2 J^2_{n+1}(\alpha_{mn})} \int_o^a x\ f(x)\ J_n (\lambda_{mn}{}^x)\ dx \quad ...(vi)$$

n fixed.

$$\lambda_{mn} = \frac{\alpha_{mn}}{a}, \qquad m = 1, 2, ...$$

Thus generalised Fourier Bessel series is given by (iii) with the coefficients given by (vi),

10.11 Orthogonality of Hermite Polynomials

The Hermite polynomials $H_n (x)$, given by

$$H_n (x) = (-1)^n\ e^{x^2} \frac{d^n e^{-x^2}}{dx^n}$$

are orthogonal with respect to the weight function $p(x) = e^{-x^2}$ on the interval $-\infty \le x \le \infty$.

$$\int_{-\infty}^{\infty} H_m(x) Hn(x) e^{-x^2} dx = (-1)^n \int_{-\infty}^{\infty} H_m (x) \frac{d^n e^{-x^2}}{dx^n} dx$$

$$= (-1)^n \left[H_m (x) \frac{d^{n-1} (e^{-x^2})}{dx^{n-1}} \right]_{-\infty}^{\infty}$$

$$-(-1)^n \int_{-\infty}^{\infty} H'_m(x) \{\frac{d^{n-1}}{dx^{n-1}} e^{-x^2} dx$$

$$= -(-1)^n \int_{-\infty}^{\infty} 2m\, H_{m-1}(x) \frac{d^{n-1}}{dx^{n-1}} e^{-x^2} dx$$

[Since e^{-x2} and all its derivatives vanish for infinite x and $H' = 2n\, H_{n-1}$]

$$= (-1)^{n-1}\, 2m \int_{-\infty}^{\infty} H_{m-1}(x) \frac{d^{n-1}}{dx^{n-1}} e^{-x^2} dx \quad n > m$$

proceeding similarly again and again

$$= (-1)^{n-m}\, 2^m\, m! \int_{-\infty}^{\infty} H_0(x) \frac{d^{n-m}}{dx^{n-m}} e^{-x^2} dx \quad n > m$$

$$= (-1)^{n-m}\, 2^m\, m! \int_{-\infty}^{\infty} \frac{d^{n-m}}{dx^{n-m}} e^{-x^2} dx$$

$[\because H_0(x) = 1]$

$$= (-1)^{n-m}\, 2^m\, m! \left[\frac{d^{n-m-1}}{dx^{n-m-1}} e^{-x^2} \right]_{-\infty}^{\infty}$$

$$= 0.$$

$$\int_{-\infty}^{\infty} H_n^2(x)\, e^{-x^2} dx$$

$$= \int_{-\infty}^{\infty} H_n(x) \frac{d^n}{dx^n} e^{-x^2} dx$$

integerating as above n lines

$$= 2^n\, n \int_{-\infty}^{\infty} H_o(x)\, e^{-x^2} dx$$

$$= 2^n\, n! \int_{-\infty}^{\infty} e^{-x^2} dx$$

$$= 2^n\, n!.\, 2 \int_0^{\infty} e^{-x^2} dx$$

$$= 2^n\, n!\, \sqrt{\pi}.$$

The functions of the orthogonal system are

$$\Psi_n(x) = \frac{H_n(x)\, e^{-x^2/2}}{\sqrt{\{2^n\, n!\, \sqrt{n}\}}}, \quad (n = 0, 1, 2, ...)$$

10.12 Orthogonality of Laguerre polynomials

The Laguerre polynomials $L_n(x)$ given by

$$L_n(x) = e^x \frac{d^n}{dx^n}(x^n e^{-x})$$

are orthogonal w.r.t the weight function $p(x) = e^{-x}$ on the interval $0 \leq x \leq \infty$

$$\int_0^\infty L_m(x) \cdot L_n(x)\, e^{-x}\, dx$$

$$= \int_0^\infty L_m(x) \frac{d^n}{dx^n}(x^n e^{-x})\, dx$$

$$= \left[L_m(x) \frac{d^{n-1}}{dx^{n-1}}(x^n e^{-x}) \right]_0^\infty - \int_0^\infty$$

$$L'_m(x) \frac{d^{n-1}}{dx^{n-1}}(x^n e^{-x})\, dx$$

$$= -\int_0^\infty L_m'(x) \frac{d^{n-1}}{dx^{n-1}}(x^n e^{-x})\, dx$$

proceeding similarly

$$= (-1)^m \int_0^\infty L_m^{m'}(x) \frac{d^{n-m}}{dx^{n-m}}(x^n e^{-x})\, dx \quad n \le m$$

$$= (-1)^m \int_0^\infty (-1)^m\, m!\, \frac{d^{n-m}}{dx^{n-m}}(x^n e^{-x})\, dx \quad n \le m$$

$$= m! \left[\frac{d^{n-m-1}}{dx^{n-m-1}}(x^n e^{-x}) \right]_0^\infty = 0$$

Now,

$$\int_0^\infty L_n^2(x).\, e^{-x}\, dx$$

$$= \int_0^\infty L_n(x) \frac{d^n}{dx^n}(x^n e^{-x})\, dx$$

$$= (-1)^n \int_0^\infty L_n^{n!}(x)\,(x^n e^{-x})\, dx$$

$$= (-1)^n (-1)^n\, n! \int_0^\infty x^n e^{-x}\, dx = (n!)^2$$

Thus the functions of the orthogonal system are

$$\Psi_n(x) = \frac{e^{-x/2} L_n(x)}{n!} \qquad (n = 0, 1, 2, \ldots)$$

10.13 Orthogonelity of chebyshev Polynomials

Chebyshev polynomials $T_n(x)$ given by

$$T_n(x) = \cos(n \cos^{-1} x)$$

are orthogonal with respect to the weight function $p(x) = \dfrac{1}{\sqrt{(1-x^{2})}}$ on the interval $-1 < x < 1$

$$\int_{-1}^{1} \frac{T_m(x)\, T_n(x)}{\sqrt{(1-x^2)}}\, dx$$

$$= \int_{-1}^{1} \frac{\cos(m \cos^{-1} x) \cos(n \cos^{-1} x)}{\sqrt{(1-x^{2})}}\, dx \qquad \ldots(i)$$

Putting $x = \cos\theta$

$$\int_o^\pi \cos m\theta \cos n\theta \, d\theta$$

$$= \frac{1}{2}\int_0^\pi [\cos (m+n)\,\theta + \cos (m-n)\,\theta]\, d\theta$$

$$= \frac{1}{2}\left[\frac{1}{m+n}\sin (m+n)\,\theta + \frac{1}{m-n}\sin (m-n)\,\theta\right]_0^\pi$$

$= 0$, if $m \neq n$, i.e., $m-n \neq 0$

10.14 Orthogonality of Jacabi Polynomials.

The Jacobi polynomials $G_n(x)$ are orthogonal with respect to weight function

$$p(x) = (1-x)^{q-1} \quad (q > 0,\ p-q > -1)$$

on tthe interval $0 \leq x \leq 1$.

$$G_n(x) = \frac{x^{1-q}(1-x)^{q-p}}{q(1+1)\ldots(q+n-1)}\frac{d^n}{dx^n}[x^{q+n-1}(1-x)^{p+n-q}]$$

Since $\int_0^1 p(x).\, G_m(x)\, G_n(x)\, dx = 0$ for $m \neq n$

(it may be proved easily).

10.15 Bessel's Ineguality and completeness Relation

Let $x_1, x_2, \ldots$ be an orthonormal system and let f be any function. Then the numbers c_v, $v = 1, 2, \ldots$ such that

$$C_v = (f, \Psi_v) = \int f\,\Psi_v\, dx \qquad \text{...(i)}$$

are called the *expansion coefficients of components of f* with respect to the given orthonormal system.

Obviously $$\int\left(f - \sum_{v=1}^{n} C_v \Psi_v\right)^2 dx \geq 0 \qquad \text{...(ii)}$$

By writing out the square and inegrating term by term, we get

$$0 \leq \int f^2\, dx - 2\sum_{v=1}^{n} C_v \int f.\,\Psi_v\, dx + \sum_{v=1}^{n} C_v^2$$

or $$0 \leq (nf)^2 - 2\sum_{v=1}^{n} C_v^2 + \sum_{v=1}^{n} C_v^2$$

[Nf means norm of f]

or $$0 \leq (Nf)^2 - \sum_{v=1}^{n} C_v^2$$

or $$\sum_{v=1}^{n} C_v^2 \leq (Nf)^2 \qquad \text{...(iii)}$$

Since the number on the right is Independent of *n*, it follows that

$$\sum_{\nu=1}^{n} C_\nu^2 < (Nf)^2$$

This fundamental inequality is known as *Bessel's inequality* and is true for every orthenormal system. It proves that the *sum of the squares of the expansion coefficients always converges.*

For systems of functions with complex values the corresponding relation is

$$\sum_{\nu=1}^{n} |C_\nu|^2 \leq (Nf)^2 = (f\bar{f}) \quad \text{...(iv)}$$

holds, where Cv is the expansion coefficient Cv = (f. Ψ v).

This relation may be obtained from the inquality

$$\int \left| f(x) - \sum_{\nu=1}^{n} C_\nu \psi_\nu \right|^2 dx = (Nf)^2 - \sum_{\nu=1}^{n} |C_\nu|^2 \geq 0$$

The significance of the intergal in (ii) is that it occurs in the problem of approximating the given function $f(x)$ by a linear combination $\sum_{\nu=1}^{n} \lambda_\nu \psi_\nu$ with λ_ν as constant coefficient and fixed n, in such a way that the mean square error

$$M = \int (f - \sum_{\nu=1}^{n} \lambda_\nu \psi_\nu)^2 \, dx$$

is as small as possible.

An approximation of this type is known as an approximation by the method of least squares, or an *approximation in the mean.*

If, for a given otheonormal system Ψ_1, Ψ_2 ...., any piecewise cotinuous function *f*, can be approximated in the mean to any desired degree of accuracy by choosing *n* large enough, c.e., if *n* may be so chosen that the mean square error

$$\int (f - \sum_{\nu=1}^{n} C_\nu \Psi_\nu)^2 \, dx$$

is less than a given arbitrary small positive number, then the system of functions Ψ_1, Ψ_2 ... is said to be *complete.*

For a complete or orthonormal system of functions Bessel's inequality becomes an equality for every function *f*

i.e., $$\sum_{\nu=1}^{n} C_\nu^2 = (Nf)^2$$

or $$\sum_{\nu=1}^{n} (f, \Psi_\nu)^2 = \| f \|^2$$

The relation is known as the *completeness relation* or *Perseval's equation.*

10.16 Definitions

Closed Set. The set $\{\phi_n\}$ is closed in the sense of mean convergence if for each function f of the function space

$$\sum_{n=1}^{\infty} (f,\phi_n)^2 = \| f \|^2$$

Complete Set. An orthonormal set $\{\phi_n\}$ is complete in the function space if there is no function in that space, with positive norm which to orthogonal is each of the function

10.17 Theorem. If an orthonormal set $\{\phi_n (x)\}$ is closed it is complete

If an orthonormal set is closed then for each function f of the function space

$$\sum_{\nu=1}^{\infty} (f, \phi_n)^2 = \| f \|^2 \qquad \text{... (i)}$$

Now, let us suppose a function Ψ in the space which is orthogonal to each function $\{\phi_n (x)\}$ of the closed orthonormal set such that

$$\| \phi \| \neq 0$$

$\therefore$ $\qquad (f, \phi_n) \neq 0$

$\therefore$ from (i), we have $\| f \| = 0$,

which is a contradiction.

Therefore there is no function is space, with positive norm which is orthogonal to each of the function $\phi_n (x)$

Hence the closed orthonormal set $\{\phi_n (x)\}$ is complete also.

EXERCISE 10.

1 Show that the function sin x, sin $2x$, sin $3x$, are orthogonal on the interval $(0, \pi)$.

2 In the following cases, show that the given set is orthogonal on the given interval, and determine the corresponding, orthonormal set.

(a) 1, cos $2x$, cos $4x$, cos $6x$, ... $0 \leq x \leq \pi$

(b) sin πx, sin $2\pi x$, sin $3\pi x$, ... $-1 \leq x \leq 1$

(c) $\{\cos nx\}$, $n = 0, 1, 2, ...$. $0 \leq x \leq \pi$

3. Show that the function $f_1(x) = 4$ and $f_2(x) = x^3$ are orthogonnal on the interval $(-2, 2)$ and determine the constants a and B so that the function $f_3 (x) = 1 + Ax + Bx^2$ is orthogonal to both f_1 and f_2.

4 Show that the set of functions $\left\{\sin \frac{n\pi x}{c}\right\}$ $(n = 1, 2,...)$ is ortogonel on the interval $(0,c)$ and find the orthonormal set.

5 Find all eigen values and eigen functions of the strum– Lioville problem

$x'' + \lambda x' = 0$, $x' (-\pi) = 0$,

$x' (\pi) = 0$,

6. Find the characterstic functions of the following case of the strum-liouville's problem
$x''+\lambda x=0$, $x(0)=0$, $x'(L)=0$

Answers

2 (a) $\frac{1}{\sqrt{\pi}}, \sqrt{\left(\frac{2}{\pi}\right)} \cos 2x, \sqrt{\left(\frac{2}{\pi}\right)} \text{Cos } 4x \ldots$

(b) Sin πx, Sin $2\pi x$, ...

(c) $\frac{1}{\sqrt{\pi}} \sqrt{\left(\frac{2}{\pi}\right)} \cos nx$, $n = 1, 2 \ldots$

4. $\left\{\frac{\sqrt{2}}{C} \sin \frac{n\pi x}{C}\right\}. (0 \le x \le c, n = 1, 2 \ldots)$

5. $X(x) = \cos \frac{n(\pi + x)}{2}, n = 0, 1, 2 \ldots$

6. $X(x) = \frac{\sin(2n-1)\pi x}{2L}, n = 1, 2, \ldots$

11

Elliptic Functions

11.1 Introduction

It is not possible to express the length of the are of on ellipse in terms of algebraic, trigonometric or exponential functions. In order to evaluate the integal which results from the attempt to rectify the ellipse, a new function-elliptic function was introduced. Elliptic functions have many applications in the fields of mechanics and mathematics. In this chapter, knowledge of complex variables has been assumed.

11.2 Singly-periodic and Doubly-periodic Functions

A function which satisfies the relation

$$f(z + w) = f(z), \; w \neq 0 \qquad \text{...(i)}$$

for values of z for which $f(z)$ exists, is known as a *singly-periodic function* or simply *periodic function*. w is called the *period* of function $f(z)$. From (i), we have

$$f(z + nw) = f(z), \text{ for each integer } n, \; n \neq, 0 \qquad \text{...(ii)}$$

This shows that if w is a period of $f(z)$. then nw is also a period of $f(z)$.

This period w is said to be *fundamental period* of $f(z)$ if no submultiples of w satisfies (i).

Again suppose that w_1, w_2 are any two constants whose ratio is not real. Then a function which satisfies the relations

$$f(z + 2\,w_1) = f(z), \; f(z + 2\,w_2) = f(z) \qquad \text{...(iii)}$$

for all values of z for which $f(z)$ exists, is known as a doubly periodic function of z, with two distinct periods $2\,w_1$ and $2\,w_2$.

The relations in (iii) are equivalent to single relation

$$f(z + 2\,mw_1 + 2nw_2) = f(z), \; m \text{ and } n \text{ being integers} \qquad \text{...(iv)}$$

Define

$$\Omega_{m,n} = 2mw_1 + 2nw_2 \qquad \text{...(v)}$$

Then (iv) may be written as

$$f(z + \Omega_{m,n}) = f(z) \qquad \text{...(vi)}$$

11.3 Elliptic function

A doubly-periodic analytic function $f(z)$ which has no singular points other than poles in the finite part of the plane, is called an elliptic function.

11.4 Period-parallelograms (or meshes) and cells

It is known from the theory of complex variables that if 0 is the origin in the complex z- plane and the complex points z_1 and z_2 are the points P and Q, then the complex number $z_1 + z_2$ is the points R, such that O P R Q is a parallelogram. If z_1/z_2 is real, the points z_1, z_2 and $z_1 + z_2$ are on the same line.

Suppose that w_1/w_2 is not real. Then if we plot all the periods $\Omega_{m,n} = 2mw_1 + 2nw_2$ (m, n are integers), of a doubly periodic function $f(z)$, we get a net work of parallelograms shown in fig. 11.1.

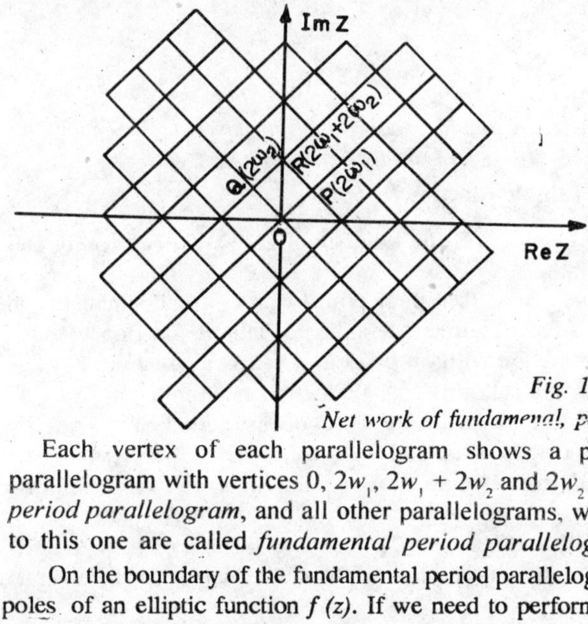

Fig. 11.1
Net work of fundamenal, promitive parallelograms.

Each vertex of each parallelogram shows a period of $f(z)$. The parallelogram with vertices 0, $2w_1$, $2w_1 + 2w_2$ and $2w_2$ is called the *primitive period parallelogram*, and all other parallelograms, which are equal in area to this one are called *fundamental period parallelograms*.

On the boundary of the fundamental period parallelograms there may lie the poles of an elliptic function $f(z)$. If we need to perform integration along the boundaries of these parallelograms, we have to replace the network of these parallelograms with network, called the *cells*.

Consider the primitive period parallelogram, of an elliptic function $f(z)$ whose vertices are 0, $2w_1$, $2w_1 + 2w_2$ and $2w_2$. By hypothesis there are only a finite number of poles and zeros of $f(z)$ in the closed region of this parallelogram.

We may find a point t in the region of this parallelogram, such that the parallelogram with vertices t, $t + 2w_1$, $t + 2w_1 + 2w_2$ and $t + 2w_2$ has, on its boundary, no poles and no zeros of $f(z)$. This new parallelogram is known as **cell.** Constructing such cells we get a network of these (Fig. 11.2).

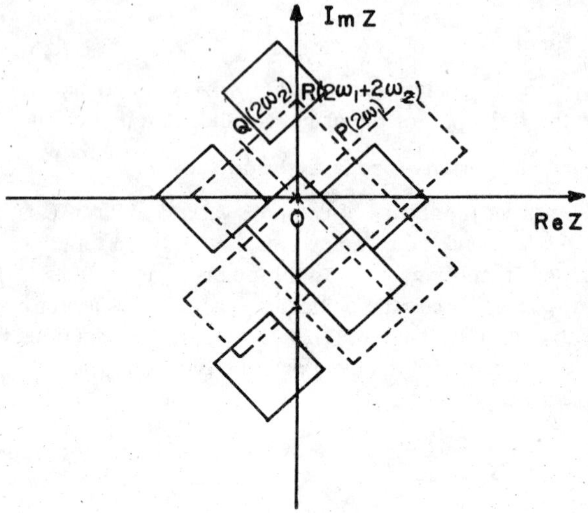

Fig. 11.2

Shows a net work of cells (solid) and a net work of fundamental Parallelogram (dashed).

11.5 Properties of an Elliptic function

(I) The number of poles and the number of zeros of f (z) in any cell are finite.

If their number is not finite, then these will be an essential singularity in the finite plane, which is contrary to the definition of elliptic function.

(II) **An elliptic Function with no poles in a cell is a constant.**

If $f(z)$ has no poles is a cell, it is analytic and bounded in the closed cell, and also throughout the finite plane, because of its periodicity. Then by Liouville's theorem of complex variable $f(z)$ is constant.

(III) **The sum of the residues at the poles in a cell of an elliptic function is zero.**

Consider the cell with vertices t, $t + 2w_1$, $t + 2w_1 + 2w_2$ an $t + 2w_2$ and let S_R be the sum of the residues at the poles in the cell. Then by the theorem of residues.

$$2\pi i S_R = \int_t^{t+2w_1} f(z)\,dz + \int_{t+2w_1}^{t+2w_1+2w_2} f(z)\,dz$$

$$+ \int_{t+2w_1+2w_2}^{t+2w_2} f(z)\,dz + \int_{t+2w_2}^{t} f(z)\,dz$$

$$= I_1 + I_2 + I_3 + I_4 \text{ (say)} \qquad \ldots(i)$$

But $$I_2 = \int_{t+2w_1}^{t+2w_1+2w_2} f(z)\,dz$$

$$= \int_t^{t+2w_2} f(z+2w_1)\,dz = \int_t^{t+2w_2} f(z)\,dz$$

$$= -I_4$$

and Similarly

$$I_3 = \int_{t+2w_1+2w_2}^{t+2w_2} f(z)\, dx$$

$$= \int_{t+2w_1}^{t} f(z + 2\, w_2)\, dz = \int_{t+2w_1}^{t} f(z)\, dz = -\, I_1$$

Hence $2\pi i\, S_P = 0$, i.e., $S_P = 0$.

(IV) For an elliptic function, the number of zeros in a cell equals the number of poles in the cell.

Let the number of of poles in a cell be N_1 and the number of zeros be N_2. Then from complex variable, we have

$$2\pi i\,(N_2 - N_1) = \int_B \frac{f'(z)}{f(z)}\, dz \qquad \text{...(i)}$$

where B is the boundary of the cell.

Now since $\quad f(z + 2w_1) = f(z)$ and $f(z + 2w_2) = f(z)$

we have $\quad f'(z + 2w_1) = f''(z)$ and $f'(z + 2w_2) = f'(z)$

i.e. $\dfrac{f'(z)}{f(z)}$ is also an elliptic function, with the periods $2w_1$ and $2w_2$

Therefore by property III above we get that the integral on the right of (i) is zero.

Hence $\qquad N_1 = N_2$.

(V) For an elliptic function $f(z)$ and for any finite number *c*, the number of zeros of $f(z) - c$ is independent of *c*.

Let $2w_1$ and $2w_2$ be the periods of $f(z)$

Then we have,

$$f(z + 2w_1) - c = f(z) - c \text{ and } f(z + 2w_2) - c = f(z) - c.$$

Therefore, $f(z) - c$ and $f(z)$ have the same periods, and we have already seen that $f'(z)$ also has the same period.

Since c is finite, the poles of $f(z) - c$ are the poles of $f(z)$. Hence by complex analysis we observe that the difference between the number of poles and the number of zeros and $f(z) - c$, is

$$\frac{1}{2\pi i}\int_B \frac{f'(z)\, dz}{f(z) - c}$$

But this integral is zero, as in property III above. Hence the theorem.

11.6. Order of an Elliptic Function

The order of an elliptic function is defined as the number of its poles in a cell.

(VI) **An Elliptic Function of order less than two is a constant.**

We know that an elliptic function of order zero is constant.

If the function is of order one, it has a single pole in a cell, and must be zero, so that

$$\int_B f(z)\, dx = 0$$

Hence, by Cauchy's integral theorem of complex analysis, we can say that $f(z)$ is analytic within and on the boundary B of the cell i.e., $f(z)$ has no pole in the cell.

Hence $f(z)$ must be constant.

11.7 The Weierstrass Elliptic function P (z)

Let m and n be integers and let

$$\Omega_{m,n} = 2mw_1 + 2nw_2 \qquad \text{...(i)}$$

Where $2w_1$ and $2w_2$ are two distinct funda-mental periods of the proposed elliptic function and $\frac{w_1}{w_2}$ is not real. Then the Weierstrass's elliptic function or simply Weierstrass function is denoted by P (z) and is defined by

$$P(z) = \frac{1}{z^2} + \sum_{m,n=-\infty}^{\infty}{}' \left\{ \frac{1}{(z-\Omega_{m,n})^2} - \frac{1}{\Omega_{m,n}^2} \right\} \qquad \text{...(ii)}$$

Where the prime attached to the summation signifies that the term for which $m = n = o$ must be omitted.

11.8 Properties of Weierstrass Function P (z)

(I) **P(z) is an even function of z,**

By definition of p (z), we have

$$p(z) = \frac{1}{z^2} + \sum_{m,n=-\infty}^{\infty}{}' \left\{ \frac{1}{(z-\Omega_{m,n})^2} - \frac{1}{\Omega_{m,n}^2} \right\} \qquad \text{...(i)}$$

Where the prime attached to the summation signifies that the term for which $m = n = 0$ must be omitted.

From (i), we also have

$$p(-z) = \frac{1}{z^2} + \sum_{m,n=-\infty}^{\infty} \left\{ \frac{1}{(z+\Omega_{m,n})^2} - \frac{1}{\Omega_{m,n}^2} \right\}$$

If we reverse the order of summation on replacing m by - m and n by –n, we get

$$p(-z) = \frac{1}{z^2} + \sum_{m,n=-\infty}^{\infty} \left\{ \frac{1}{(z-\Omega_{m,n})^2} - \frac{1}{\Omega_{m,n}^2} \right\}$$

i.e. $$p(-z) = p(z) \qquad \text{...(ii)}$$

which shows that p (z) is an even function.

(II) **P′ (z) is an odd function of z.**

By differentiating, we get

$$P'(z) = \sum_{m,n=-\infty}^{\infty} \frac{-2}{(z-\Omega_{m,n})^3} \qquad \text{...(iii)}$$

Where the derivative, - $2/z^3$ of $1/z^2$, has been included in the summation, and hence the prime over Σ is deleted.

From (iii), we get

$$P'(-z) = \sum_{m,n=-\infty}^{\infty} \frac{2}{(z+\Omega_{m,n})^3} = \sum_{m,n=-\infty}^{\infty} \frac{2}{(z-\Omega_{m,n})^3}$$

the last term being obtained by replacing m by $-m$ and n by $-n$. Hence we obtain

$$P'(-z) = -p'(z)$$

i.e. $P'(z)$ is an odd function of z.

(III) **$p'(z)$ is an elliptic function**

As shown in property (II), we have

$$P'(z) = \sum_{m,n=-\infty}^{\infty} \frac{-2}{(z-\Omega_{m,n})^3} \qquad ...(i)$$

From (i), we have

$$P'(z+2w_1) = \sum_{m,n=-\infty}^{\infty} \frac{-2}{(z+2w_1-\Omega_{m,n})^3} \qquad ...(ii)$$

But

$$\begin{aligned} z+2w_1-\Omega_{m,n} &= z+2w_1-(2mw_1+2nw_2) \\ &= z-[2(m-1)w_1-2nw_2] \\ &= z-\Omega_{m-1,n} \text{ by definition} \end{aligned}$$

Hence (ii) reduces to

$$\begin{aligned} P'(z+2w_1) &= \sum_{m,n=-\infty}^{\infty} \frac{-2}{(z-\Omega_{m-1,n})^3} \\ &= \sum_{m,n=-\infty}^{\infty} \frac{-2}{(z-\Omega_{m,n})^3} \qquad ...(iii) \end{aligned}$$

where the second series is obtained from the first series by replacing m by $m+1$

From (i) and (iii), we have

$$P'(z+2w_1) = P'(z) \qquad ...(iv)$$

Proceeding similarly, we may show that

$$P'(z+2w_2) = P'(z) \qquad ...(v)$$

From (iv) and (v) we conclude that $P'(z)$ is an elliptic function with fundamental periods, $2w_1$ and $2w_2$.

(IV) **$P(z)$ is an elliptic function**

As shown in property (III),

$$P'(z+2w_1) = P'(z) \qquad ...(i)$$

and

$$P'(z+2w_2) = P'(z) \qquad ...(ii)$$

Integrating both sides of (i), we have

$$P(z+2w_1) = P(z) + c \qquad ...(iii)$$

where c is a constant of integration. Putting $z = -w_1$ is (iii), we have

$$P(w_1) = P(-w_1) + c \qquad ...(iv)$$

Since $P(z)$ is an even function of z, $P(w_1) = P(-w_1)$ and hence $c = 0$ from (iv). Thus, we have

$$P(z + 2w_1) = P(z) \quad \text{...(v)}$$

Similarly by (ii), we will get

$$P(z + 2w_2) = P(z) \quad \text{...(vi)}$$

Thus P (z) is an elliptic function with fundamental periods $2w_1$ and $2w_2$.

11.9 The differential equation satisfied by P (z)

By the definition of P (z), we have

$$P(z) - \frac{1}{z^2} = \sum_{m,n=-\infty}^{\infty}{}' \left\{\frac{1}{(z-\Omega_{m,n})^2} - \frac{1}{\Omega^2_{m,n}}\right\} \quad \text{...(i)}$$

This shows that P (z) - z^{-2} is analytic at the origin and zero there. Since P (z) is an even function of z, it follows that P (z) -z^2 is also an even function. Hence a Taylar expansion must exist, i.e.

$$P(z) - z^{-2} = \sum_{n=1}^{\infty} C_n z^{2n} \quad \text{...(ii)}$$

Which is valid for sufficiently small values of (z). Using (1) for P (z) - z^{-2} and comparing the coefficients of z^2 and z^4, (ii) gives

$$C_1 = 4 \sum_{m.n=-\infty}^{\infty}{}' \Omega^{-4}_{mn} \text{ and } C_2 = 5 \sum_{m,n=-\infty}^{\infty} \Omega^{-6}_{m,n} \quad \text{...(iii)}$$

Let O (z^n) denote a function which is analytic in a neighbourhood of the origin and possesses a zero of order n there.

Then (ii) may be expressed as

$$P(z) - z^{-2} = c_1 z^2 = c_2 z^4 = O(z^6)$$

or

$$P(z) = z^{-2} + c_1 z^2 + c_2 z^4 + O(z^6) \quad \text{...(iv)}$$

Differentiating both sides of (iv), we get

$$P'(z) = -2 z^{-3} + 2c_1 z + 4c_2 z^3 + O(z^5) \quad \text{...(v)}$$

From (iv) and (v) we have

$$P^3(z) = z^{-6} + 3c_1 z^{-2} + 3c_2 + O(z^2) \quad \text{...(vi)}$$

$$P'^2(z) = 4 z^{-6} - 8c_1 z^{-2} - 16 c_2 + O(z^2) \quad \text{...(vii)}$$

Multiplying both sides of (vi) by 4 and then subtracting the resulting equation from (vii),

we get

$$P'^2(z) - 4 P^3(z) = -20c_1 z^{-2} - 28c_2 + O(z^2) \quad \text{...(viii)}$$

From (iv), we have

$$P(z) = z^{-2} + o(z^2)$$

$$\therefore \quad 20c_1 P(z) = 20c_1 z^{-2} + O(z^2) \quad \text{...(ix)}$$

Adding (viii) and (ix), we get

$$\therefore \quad P'^2(z) - 4p^3(z) + 20c_1 p(z) = -28 c_2 = 0(z^2)$$

i.e.,

$$P'^2(z) - 4 P^3(z) = 20c_1 P(z) + 28c_2 = 0(z^2) \quad \text{...(x)}$$

Since P (z) and P$'$ (z) both are elliptic functions with periods $2w_1$ and $2w_2$, it follows that the function on L.H.S of (x), $f(z)$ say, is also an elliptic function with periods $2w_1$ and $2w_2$. Clearly $f(z)$ is analytic at the origin, and hence it is also at all congruent points $z = \Omega_{m,n}$ w here m and n are integers. But they are the only possible singular points of $f(z)$. Thus elliptic function $f(z)$ has no poles in a cell and hence $f(z)$ must be a constant, say A. Then (x) reduces to

$$f(z) = A + 0\,(z^2) \qquad \text{...(xi)}$$

where $$f(z) = P'^2(z) - 4P^3(z) + 20c_1 P(z) + 28c_2 \qquad \text{...(xii)}$$

Taking limit as $z \to 0$, (xi) gives A = 0

Hence (xi) and (xii) give

$$P'^2(z) - 4P^3(z) + 20c_1 P(z) + 28c_2 = 0$$

or $$P'^2(z) = 4P^3(z) - 20c_1 P(z) - 28c_2 \qquad \text{...(xiii)}$$

where c_1 and c_2 are given by (iii) . (xiii) shows that $w = p(z)$ is a solution of the differential equation

$$\left(\frac{dw}{dz}\right)^2 = 4w^3 - 20\,c_1\,w - 28\,c_2 \qquad \text{...(xiv)}$$

This is the desired differential equation satisfied by the Weirestrass's elliptic function.

In practice, we take $20c_1 = g_2$ and $28\,c_2 = g_3$. Then (xiv) reduces to

$$\left(\frac{dw}{dz}\right)^2 = 4\,w^2 - g_2\,y - g_3 \qquad \text{...(xv)}$$

where g_2 and g_3 are called the **invariants** of P (z).

11.10 Weierstrass's Zeta function ζ (z)

Weierstrass's zeta function is denoted by ζ (z) and is defined by

$$\zeta(z) = \frac{1}{z} + \sum_{m,n=-\infty}^{\infty}{}' \left\{\frac{1}{z - \Omega_{m,n}} + \frac{1}{\Omega_{m,n}} + \frac{z}{\Omega^2_{m,n}}\right\} \qquad \text{...(i)}$$

where the prime attached to the summation signifies that the term for which $m = n = 0$ must be omitted.

11.11 Properties of Weierstrass's Zeta Function

(I) ζ (z) is not an elliptic function

The general term of the series in equation (i) of § 11.10 is

$$0(|\Omega m, n|^{-3}) \text{ as } |\Omega_{m,n}| \to \infty \qquad \text{...(i)}$$

Accordingly, ζ (z) is an analytic function of z over the entire z – plane except at poles of residue 1 at each of the points $\Omega_{m,n}$, where m and n are integers.

Thus the sum of residues at all poles of ζ (z) is non-zero. Hence ζ (z) is not an elliptic function because the sum of the residues of an elliptic function at its poles in any cell is zero.

(II) ζ (z) is an odd function

For this we re-write ζ (z) as

$$\zeta(z) = \frac{1}{z} + \sum_{m,n=-\infty}^{\infty} \left[\left\{\frac{1}{z-\Omega_{m,n}} + \frac{1}{\Omega_{m,n}} + \frac{z}{\Omega^2_{m,n}}\right\} + \left\{\frac{1}{z+\Omega_{m,n}} - \frac{1}{\Omega_{m,n}} + \frac{z}{\Omega^2_{m,n}}\right\}\right]$$

where the second term in the summation (ii) is obtained by replacing m by ($-m$) and n by ($-n$) in the first term and using the following fact

$$\Omega_{-m,-n} = 2(-m)\,w_1 + 2(-n)\,w_2$$
$$= -\Omega_{-m,n} \qquad \text{...(ii)}$$

Replacing z by $-z$ in (i) and simplifying, we get

$$\zeta(-z) = -\frac{1}{z} + \sum_{m,n=-\infty}^{\infty}{}' \left[\left\{\frac{-1}{z+\Omega_{m,n}} + \frac{1}{\Omega_{m,n}} - \frac{z}{\Omega^2_{m,n}}\right\} + \left\{\frac{-1}{z-\Omega_{m,n}} - \frac{1}{\Omega_{m,n}} - \frac{z}{\Omega^2_{m,n}}\right\}\right] \quad ...(iii)$$

From (i) and (iii),

$$\zeta(-z) = -\zeta(z).$$

Hence $\zeta(-z)$ is an odd function of z.

11.12. The pseudo (or quasi) - periodicity of the function $\zeta(z)$

From the definitions of P (z) and $\zeta(z)$, we can easily show that

$$\frac{d\zeta(z)}{dz} = -P(z) \quad ...(i)$$

Since P (z) is an elliptic function with periods $2w_1$ and $2w_2$, we have

$$P(z + 2w_1) = P(z) \quad ...(ii)$$

$$P(z + 2w_2) = P(z) \quad ...(iii)$$

Using the result (i), (ii) may be rewritten

as
$$\frac{d\zeta(z' + 2\omega_1)}{dz} = \frac{d\zeta(z)}{dz} \quad ...(iv)$$

integrating (iv), we get

$$\zeta(z + 2w_1) = \zeta(z) + 2n_1 \quad ...(v)$$

where $2n_1$ is a constant of integration.

Putting $z = -w_1$ in (v) and using the fact that $\zeta(z)$ is an odd function so that

$$z(-w_1) = -\zeta(w_1),$$

we have

$$\zeta(w_1) = -\zeta(w_1) + 2n_1, \text{ so that}$$

$$\zeta(w_1) = n_1, \quad ...(vi)$$

Similarly, from , (i) and (iii), we have

$$\zeta(z + 2w_2) = \zeta(z) + 2n_2 \quad ...(vii)$$

where n_2 is another constant of integration, Putting $z = -w_2$ we obtain

$$\zeta(w_2) = n_2 \quad ...(viii)$$

From (v) and (vii), it follows that n_1 and n_2 cannot be both zero because $n_1 = n_2 = 0$ would imply that $\zeta(z)$ is an elliptic function. This contradicts the known fact that $\zeta(z)$ is not an elliptic function. The nature of (v) and (vii) with the condition that at least one of n_1 and n_2 is non-zero shows that $\zeta(z)$ has a pseude-periodicity.

11.13 Weierstrass's sigma function $\sigma(z)$

Weierstrass's sigma function is denoted and defined by

$$\sigma(z) = z \prod_{m,n\to\infty}^{\infty}{}' \left\{\left(1 - \frac{z}{\Omega_{m,n}}\right) exp. \left(\frac{z}{\Omega_{m,n}} + \frac{z^2}{2\Omega^2_{m,n}}\right)\right\} \quad ...(i)$$

where the prime attached to the product signifies that the term for which $m = n = 0$ must be omitted.

The following facts may be easily verified

(i) $\sigma(z)$ is not an elliptic function.

(ii) $\sigma(z)$ is an odd function of z

(iii) $\sigma(z)$ may be defined by the relation

$$\frac{d}{dz} \log \sigma(z) = \zeta(z)$$

together with condition $\lim_{z \geq 0} \left\{ \frac{\sigma(z)}{z} \right\} = 1$

11.14 The Jacobion Elliptic Function

An elliptic function with two simple zeros in a cell is said to be a Jacobion elliptic function.

Let σ devote Weierstrass's sigma function and $\sigma_r(z)$ is defined as

$$\sigma_r(z) = e^{-n_r z} \frac{\sigma(z+w_r)}{\sigma(w_r)} \quad (r = 1, 2, 3)$$

Then we define elliptic functions as

$$S(z) = (e - e_2)^{1/2}.\ \sigma(z)/\ \sigma_2(z) \qquad \text{...(i)}$$

$$c(z) = \sigma_1(z)/\sigma_2(z) \qquad \text{...(ii)}$$

$$D(z) = \frac{\sigma_3(z)}{\sigma_2(z)} \qquad \text{...(iii)}$$

It can be shown very easily that

$$\sigma_r(z) = \sigma(z) \{ P(z) - e_r \}^{1/2} \ (r = 1, 2, 3) \qquad \text{...(iv)}$$

Using (iv), (i), (ii), and (iii) may be written as

$$S(z) = \left\{ \frac{e_1 - e_2}{P(z) - e_2} \right\}^{½} \qquad \text{...(v)}$$

$$C(z) = \left\{ \frac{P(z) - e_1}{P(z) - e_2} \right\}^{½} \qquad \text{...(vi)}$$

$$D(z) = \left\{ \frac{P(z) - e_3}{P(z) - e_2} \right\}^{½} \qquad \text{(vii)}$$

It may be shown that S(z), C(z) and D(z) are elliptic functions. The *modulus* *k* of these functions is given by

$$k = -\left(\frac{e_3 - e_2}{e_1 - e_2} \right)^{½} \qquad \text{...(viii)}$$

The *complementary modules k' of the above functions is defined by*

$$k' = \left(\frac{e_1 - e_3}{e_1 - e_2} \right)^{½} \qquad \text{...(ix)}$$

Obviously

$$k^2 + k'^2 = 1 \qquad \text{...(x)}$$

11.15 The Jacobion elliptic functions $S_n(u)$, $C_n(u)$, $d_n(u)$

The Jacabion elliptic functions $s_n(u)$, $c_n(u)$ and $d_n(u)$ are defined by the equations

$$s_n(u) = S\{(e_1 - e_2)^{-1/2} u\} \quad ...(i)$$
$$C_n(u) = C\{(e_1 - e_2)^{-1/2} u\} \quad ...(ii)$$
$$d_n(u) = D\{(e_1 - e_2)^{-1/2} u\} \quad ...(iii)$$

Since $4w_1$ and $4w_2$ are periods of functions S, C an D, it fallows that $s_n(u)$, $c_n(u)$ and $d_n(u)$ also do not change on adding $4w_1 (e_1 - e_2)^{1/2}$ or $4w_2 (e_1 - e_2)^{1/2}$ to u.

Let. $k = w_1 (e_1 - e_2)^{1/2}$, $ik' = w_2 (e_1 - e_2)^{1/2}$ — (iv)

Then k and ik' are known as the *quarte periods* of the Jacobion elliptic functions. These are also given by (taking $t = \text{Sin}\ \theta$)

$$K = \int_0^1 \frac{dt}{\sqrt{\{(1-t^2)(1-k^2t^2)\}}} = \int_0^{\pi/2} \frac{d\theta}{\sqrt{1-k^2 \sin^2\theta}} \quad ...(v)$$

and $$K' = \int_0^1 \frac{dt}{\sqrt{\{(1-t^2)(1-k'^2t^2)\}}} = \int_0^{\pi/2} \frac{d\theta}{\sqrt{(1-k'^2 \sin^2\theta}} \quad ...(vi)$$

It can be verified that periods of

s_n are $4k$ and $2ik$ ...(vii)

c_n are $4k$ and $2k + 2ik'$ ...(viii)

d_n are $2k$ and $4\ ik'$ ...(ix)

Let $z = (e_1 - e_2)^{-1/2} u$, so that $u = (e_1 - e_2)^{1/2} z$ ...(x)

$$\text{Then } u = \frac{w_1 (e_1 - e_2)^{1/2} z}{w_1} = \frac{kz}{w_1}, \text{ by (iv)} \quad ...(xi)$$

using (x) and (xi), (i) to (iii) reduce to

$$s_n (kz/w_1) = s(z) \quad ...(xii)$$
$$c_n (kz/w_1) = c(z) \quad ...(xiii)$$
$$d_n (kz/w_1) = d(z) \quad ...(xiv)$$

Now $$(e_1 - e_2)^{1/2} = \frac{w_1 (e_1 - e_2)^{1/2}}{w_1} = \frac{K}{w_1}, \text{ by (iv)} \quad (xv)$$

Using (xv) and definitions (i), (ii), (iii), of § 11.14, equations (xii) to (xiv) may be re-written as

$$s_n \left(\frac{kz}{w_1}\right) = S(z) = \frac{K\sigma(z)}{w_1 \sigma 2(z)} \quad ...(xvi)$$

$$c_n \left(\frac{kz}{w_1}\right) = c(z) = \frac{\sigma_1(z)}{\sigma_2(z)} \quad ...(xvii)$$

$$d_n \left(\frac{kz}{w_1}\right) = D(z) = \frac{\sigma_3(z)}{\sigma_2(z)} \quad ....(xviii)$$

11.16 Values of $s_n(0)$, $c_n(0)$ and $d_n(0)$

We know that

$$\sigma_r(z) = e^{-\eta_r z} \frac{\sigma(z+w)}{\sigma(w_r)} \ (r = 1, 2, 3) \quad ...(i)$$

and $$\sigma(z) = z \prod_{m,n=-\infty}^{\infty} \left\{1 - \frac{z}{\Omega_{m,n}}\right\} \exp. \left\{\frac{z}{\Omega_{m,n}} + \frac{z^2}{2\Omega^2_{m,n}}\right\} \quad \text{...(ii)}$$

Putting $z = (0)$ in (i), we have

$$\sigma_r(0) = 1 \text{ for } r = 1, 2, 3$$

$$\sigma_1(0) = \sigma_2(0) = \sigma_3(0) = 1$$

Again, putting $z = 0$ in (ii), we have

$$\sigma(0) = 0$$

Now putting $z = 0$ in (xvi), (xvii), (xviii) of § 11.15, we get

$$s_n(0) = 0\ c_n(0) = 1 \text{ and } d_n(0) = 1.$$

12

Beta and Gamma Functions

12.1 Euler's Integral

First and second Eulerian integrals are known as *Beta and Gamma Functions*. These integrals occupy a very important place in definite integrals and have got wide applications in Mechanics, Physics, Statistics and many other applied sciences.

12.2 Beta Functions.

The *beta functions,* denoted by B(m, n) is defined by the integral

$$B\,(m,\,n) = \int_o^1 x^{m-1}\,(1-x)^{n-1}\,dx \qquad \text{...(i)}$$

for positive values of m and n. The integral is convergent for $m > 0$, $n > 0$.

Putting $x = 1-y$, we have

$$B\,(m,n) = \int_1^0 (1-y)^{m-1}\,.\,y^{n-1}\,(-dy)$$

$$= \int_0^1 y^{n-1}\,(1-y)^{m-1}\,dy = B\,(n,m)$$

Hence $\qquad$ **B (*m,n*) = B (*n, m*)** $\qquad$ ...(ii)

12.3 Other forms of Beta function

(i) $\qquad$ Putting $x = \dfrac{y}{1+y}$ in (i), we obtain

$$B\,(m,n) = \int_0^1 x^{m-1}\,(1-x)^{n-1}\,dx$$

$$= \int_0^\infty \frac{y^{m-1}\,dy}{(1+y)^{m+n}}$$

Replacing y by x, *we obtain*

$$\mathbf{B\,(m,n)} = \int_0^\infty \frac{x^{m-1}\,dx}{(1+x)^{m+n}}\,dx \qquad \text{...(iii)}$$

(ii) Putting $x = sin^2\,\theta$ in (i), we get

$$B\,(m,n) = \int_0^{\pi/2} (\sin^2\theta)^{m-1}\,(\cos^2\theta)^{n-1}\,.\,2\sin\theta\cos\theta\,d\theta$$

$$\therefore \quad B(m,n) = 2\int_0^{\pi/2} \sin^{2m-1}\theta \cos^{2n-1}\theta \, d\theta \qquad \text{...(iv)}$$

12.4 Gamma Function

The *gamma function* denoted by $\Gamma(n)$ is defined by the improper integral

$$\Gamma n = \int_0^{\infty} x^{n-1} e^{-x} \, dx \qquad \text{...(i)}$$

which is convergent for $n > 0$

12.5 Recurrence relation for gamma function

By definition

$$\Gamma(n+1) = \int_0^{\infty} x^n e^{-x} \, dx$$

$$= \lim_{b \to \infty} \int_0^b x^n e^{-x} \, dx$$

$$= \lim_{b \to \infty} \left[\left| x^n (-e^{-x}) \right|_0^b - \int_0^b n x^{n-1} (-e^{-x}) \, dx \right]$$

$$= \lim_{b \to \infty} \left[-b^n e^{-b} + n \int_0^b x^{n-1} e^{-x} \, dx \right]$$

$$= \lim_{b \to \infty} \left[-b^n e^{-b} \right] + \lim_{b \to \infty} n \int_0^b x^{n-1} e^{-x} \, dx \qquad \text{...(i)}$$

$$\therefore \quad \Gamma(n+1) = n\,\Gamma(n), \text{ if } n > 0 \qquad \text{...(i)}$$

Again, by definition, we have

$$\Gamma(1) = \int_0^{\infty} \varepsilon^{-x} \, dx = \lim_{b \to \infty} \int_0^b e^{-x} \, dx$$

$$= \lim_{b \to \infty} \left[-e^{-x} \right]_0^b = \lim_{b \to \infty} \left[1 - e^{-b} \right] = 1$$

$$\therefore \quad \Gamma(1) = 1 \qquad \text{...(ii)}$$

Putting $n = 1, 2, 3, ...$ in (i), we get

$$\Gamma 2 = 1.\,\Gamma(1) = 1!, \quad \Gamma(3) = 2\,\Gamma(2) = 2.1 = 21$$

$$\Gamma 4 = 3\,\Gamma[3) = 3.2! = 3\,!, \quad \text{and so on.}$$

In general, $\Gamma(n+1) = n\,!$, when $n = 1, 2, 3, \ ...$

Thus, this fundamental property of the gamma function helps us in its evaluation. This is also called a *recurrence relation* for the gamma function.

We can generalize the gamma function for $n < 0$ by the use of the recurrence relation in the form

$$\Gamma(n) = \frac{\Gamma(n+1)}{n}$$

This process is called *analytic continuation.* It may further be remarked that $\Gamma(0) = \infty$, $\Gamma(1-n) = \infty$, n being a positive integer.

12.6 Value of $\Gamma\left(\frac{1}{2}\right)$

By definition, we have

$$\Gamma\left(\frac{1}{2}\right) = \int_0^\infty x^{-1/2}\, e^{-x}\, dx = 2\int_0^\infty e^{y^2}\, dy \qquad \text{...(i)}$$

on putting $x = y^2$ and $dx = 2y\, dy$.

Rewriting this result, with x instead of y, we get

$$\Gamma\left(\frac{1}{2}\right) = 2\int_0^\infty e^{-x^2}\, dx \qquad \text{...(ii)}$$

Multiplying (i) and (ii), we get

$$\left[\Gamma\left(\frac{1}{2}\right)\right]^2 = 4\int_0^\infty e^{-x^2}\, dx \times \int_0^\infty e^{-y^2}\, dy$$

$$= 4\int_0^\infty \int_0^\infty e^{-(x^2+y^2)}\, dx\, dy$$

$$= 4\int_0^{\pi/2} \int_0^\infty e^{-r^2} . r\, d\theta\, dr,$$

(on putting $x = r\cos\theta$, $y = r\sin\theta$)

$$= 2\int_0^{\pi/2} \left[-e^{-r^2}\right]_0^\infty d\theta$$

$$= 2\int_0^{\pi/2} d\theta = \pi$$

Hence $\qquad \Gamma\left(\frac{1}{2}\right) = \sqrt{\pi}$

12.7 Transformation of Gamma Function

We have

$$\Gamma(n) = \int_0^\infty e^{-x} . x^{n-1}\, dx$$

Let us put $x = \lambda\, t$, so that $dx = \lambda\; dt$

$$\therefore \qquad \Gamma(n) = \int_0^\infty e^{-\lambda t}\, (\lambda t)^{n-1} . \lambda\, dt$$

$$= \lambda^n \int_0^\infty e^{-\lambda t} x^{n-1}\, dx$$

Hence $\qquad \dfrac{\Gamma(n)}{\lambda^n} = \int_0^\infty e^{-\lambda x}\, x^{n-1}\, dx$

12.8 Relation between Beta and Gamma Functions

To show that $B\,(m, n) = \dfrac{\Gamma(m)\,\Gamma(n)}{\Gamma(m+n)}$

From relation of § 12.7, by replacing λ by z, we get

$$\Gamma(n) = \int_0^\infty e^{-zx} x^{n-1} z^n \, dx$$

$$\therefore \quad \Gamma(n). e^{-z} z^{m-1} = \int_0^\infty e^{-z(1+x)} z^{m+n-1} x^{n-1} \, dx$$

Integrating both sides with respect to z between the limits 0 to ∞, we have

$$\Gamma(n) \int_0^\infty e^{-z} z^{m-1} \, dz = \int_0^\infty x^{n-1} \left[\int_0^\infty e^{-z(1+x)} . z^{m+n-1} \, dz \right] dx.$$

or
$$\Gamma(n) \Gamma(m) = \int_0^\infty x^{n-1} \left[\int_0^\infty \frac{e^{-y} . y^{m+n-1} dy}{(1+x)^{m+n}} \right] dx$$

where $z(1+x) = y$

$$= \int_0^\infty \frac{x^{n-1}}{(1+x)^{m+n}} \left[\int_0^\infty e^{-y} y^{m+n-1} \, dy \right] dx$$

$$= \int_0^\infty \frac{x^{n-1}}{(1+x)^{m+n}} [\Gamma(m+n)] \, dx.$$

$$\therefore \quad \Gamma(n) \; \Gamma(m) = \Gamma(m+n) . \int_0^\infty \frac{x^{n-1}}{(1+x)^{m+n}} dx$$

or
$$\Gamma(n) . \Gamma(m) = \Gamma(m+n) . B(m,n)$$

Hence
$$B(m,n) = \frac{\Gamma(m) . \Gamma(n)}{\Gamma(m+n)} \qquad \text{...(ii)}$$

Deductions.

(i) From the above result and the can. (iv) of § 12.3, we get

$$\frac{\Gamma(m) . \Gamma(n)}{\Gamma(m+n)} = 2\int_0^{\pi/2} \sin^{2m-1} \theta . \cos^{2n-1}\theta \, d\theta$$

or
$$\int_0^{\pi/2} \sin^{2m-1} \theta. \cos^{2n-1} d\theta = \frac{\Gamma(m) . \Gamma(n)}{2\Gamma(m+n)} \qquad \text{...(iii)}$$

or
$$\int_0^{\pi/2} \sin^p\theta. \cos^q \theta \, d\theta = \frac{\Gamma\left(\frac{p+1}{2}\right) . \Gamma\left(\frac{q+1}{2}\right)}{2\Gamma\left(p+q+\frac{2}{2}\right)} \qquad \text{...(A)}$$

(ii) $$B(m,n) = \frac{\Gamma(m) . \Gamma(n)}{\Gamma(m+n)} = \int_0^\infty \frac{x^{n-1}}{(1+x)^{m+n}} dx$$

on putting $m+n = 1$, it gives

$$\frac{\Gamma(1-n) \Gamma(n)}{\Gamma(1)} = \int_0^\infty \frac{x^{n-1}}{1+x} dx$$

But
$$\int_0^\infty \frac{x^{n-1}}{1+x} dx = \frac{\pi}{\sin n\pi}, \text{ where } 0 < n < 1$$

$$\therefore \quad \Gamma(n) \Gamma(1-n) = \frac{\pi}{\sin n\pi} \qquad \text{...(B)}$$

(iii) Putting $n = \frac{1}{2}$ in (B), we get

$$\Gamma\left(\frac{1}{2}\right)\Gamma\left(\frac{1}{2}\right) = \frac{\pi}{\sin \pi/2} = \pi$$

$$\therefore \quad \Gamma\left(\frac{1}{2}\right) = \sqrt{\pi} \qquad ...(C)$$

(iv) Again putting $n = \frac{1}{4}$ in (B), we obtain

$$\Gamma\left(\frac{1}{4}\right)\Gamma\left(\frac{3}{4}\right) = \frac{\pi}{\sin \pi/4} = \pi\sqrt{2}$$

or
$$\Gamma\left(\frac{3}{4}\right) = \frac{\pi\sqrt{2}}{\Gamma\left(\frac{1}{4}\right)} \qquad ....(D)$$

12.9 Duplication Formula

To show that

$$\Gamma(m)\,\Gamma\left(m+\frac{1}{2}\right) = \frac{\sqrt{\pi}}{2^{2m-1}}\,\Gamma(2m)$$

where m is an integer.

From earn. (iii) of § 12.8, we have

$$\int_0^{\pi/2} \sin^{2m-1}\theta \cos^{2n-1}\theta \, d\theta = \frac{\Gamma(m)\,.\,\Gamma(n)}{2\Gamma(m+n)} \qquad ...(i)$$

Putting $2n-1 = 0$ or $n = \frac{1}{2}$ in (i), we get

$$\int_0^{\pi/2} \sin^{2m-1}\theta \, d\theta = \frac{\Gamma(m)\,\Gamma\left(\frac{1}{2}\right)}{2\,\Gamma\left(m+\frac{1}{2}\right)}$$

$$= \frac{\Gamma(m)\sqrt{\pi}}{2\,\Gamma\left(m+\frac{1}{2}\right)} \qquad ...(ii)$$

Again putting $n = m$ in (i), we get

$$\int_0^{\pi/2} \sin^{2m-1}\theta \cos^{2m-1}\theta d\theta = \frac{\Gamma(m)\,\Gamma(m)}{2\,\Gamma(2m)}$$

or
$$\frac{1}{2^{2m-1}}\int_0^{\pi/2} (2\sin\theta\cos\theta)^{2m-1} \, d\theta = \frac{[\Gamma(m)]^2}{2\,\Gamma(2m)}$$

or
$$\frac{1}{2^{2m-1}}\int_0^{\pi/2} \sin 2\theta^{2m-1} \, d\theta = \frac{[\Gamma(m)]^2}{2\,\Gamma(2m)}$$

Now, putting $2\theta = \phi$ and $d\theta = \frac{1}{2} d\phi$, we get

$$\frac{1}{2^{2m}} \int_0^{\pi/2} \sin^{2m-1}\phi \, d\phi = \frac{[\Gamma(m)]^2}{2\Gamma(2m)}$$

or
$$\frac{2}{2^{2m}} \int_0^{\pi/2} \sin^{2m-1}\phi \, d\phi = \frac{[\Gamma(m)]^2}{2\Gamma(2m)}$$

or
$$\int_0^{\pi/2} \sin^{2m-1}\theta \, d\theta = 2^{2m-1} \frac{[\Gamma(m)]^2}{2\Gamma(2m)} \qquad \text{...(iii)}$$

From equations (ii_ and (iii), we get

$$\frac{2^{2m-1}[\Gamma(m)]^2}{2\Gamma(2m)} = \frac{\Gamma(m)\sqrt{(\pi)}}{2\Gamma\left(m+\frac{1}{2}\right)}$$

$$\therefore \quad \Gamma(m) \, . \, \Gamma\left(m+\frac{1}{2}\right) = \frac{\sqrt{\pi}}{2^{2m-1}} \Gamma(2m)$$

12.10 Evaluation of the Integrals

$$\int_0^{\infty} e^{-ax} \cos bx . x^{m-1} \, dx \text{ and } \int_0^{\infty} e^{-ax} \sin bx . x^{m-1} dx$$

We have from § 12.7,

$$\int_0^{\infty} e^{-\lambda x} . x^{m-1} \, dx = \frac{\Gamma(m)}{\lambda^m}$$

Putting λ = a-ib, we get

$$\int_0^{\infty} e^{-(a-ib)x} . x^{m-1} \, dx = \frac{\Gamma(m)}{(a-ib)^m}$$

$$= \frac{\Gamma(m)}{(a^2+b^2)^m} (a+ib)^m \qquad \text{...(i)}$$

Now let $a + ib = r(\cos\theta + i \sin\theta)$, so that

$$r = \sqrt{(a^2+b^2)}, \quad \text{and } \theta = \tan^{-1}\left(\frac{b}{a}\right).$$

Hence from, (i), we get

$$\int_0^{\infty} e^{-ax} e^{ibx} x^{m-1} \, dx = \frac{\Gamma(m)(a^2+b^2)^{m/2}(\cos\theta + i\sin\theta)^m}{(a^2+b^2)^m}$$

or
$$\int_0^{\infty} e^{-ax} x^{m-1} (\cos bx + i \sin bx) \, dx$$

$$= \frac{\Gamma(m)(\cos m\theta + i \sin m\theta)}{(a^2+b^2)^{m/2}}$$

Separating real and imaginary parts, we get

$$\int_0^{\infty} e^{-ax} \cos bx \, x^{m-1} \, dx = \frac{\Gamma(m)}{(a^2+b^2)^{m/2}} \cos m\theta \qquad \text{...(ii)}$$

and
$$\int_0^{\infty} e^{-ax} \sin bx \, x^{m-1} \, dx = \frac{\Gamma(m)}{(a^2+b^2)^{m/2}} \sin m\theta \qquad \text{...(iii)}$$

where $\theta = \tan^{-1}\left(\frac{b}{a}\right)$.

Deductions.

Putting $a = 0$ in (ii) and (iii), we get

$$\int_0^\infty x^{m-1} \cos bx\, dx = \frac{\Gamma(m)}{b^m} \cos \frac{m\pi}{2} \quad \text{...(iv)}$$

and

$$\int_0^\infty x^{m-1} \sin bx\, dx = \frac{\Gamma(m)}{b^m} \sin \frac{m\pi}{2} \quad \text{...(v)}$$

12.11 Evaluation of Integral $\int_0^\infty \cos (bx^{1/n})\, dx$

Putting $x = z^n$ and $dx = nz^{n-1}\, dz$, we get

$$\int_0^\infty \cos (bx^{1/n})\, dx = \int_0^\infty \cos (bz).\, n\, z^{n-1}\, dz$$

$$= n \,.\, \frac{\Gamma(n)}{b^n} \,.\, \cos \frac{n\pi}{2}$$

[By (iv) of § 12.10]

$$\therefore \quad \int_0^\infty \cos (bx^{1/n})\, dx = \frac{\Gamma(n+1)}{b^n} \cos \frac{n\pi}{2}.$$

12.12 To prove that

$$\Gamma\left(\frac{1}{n}\right) \Gamma\left(\frac{2}{n}\right) \Gamma\left(\frac{3}{n}\right) \cdots \Gamma\left(\frac{n-1}{n}\right) = \frac{(2\pi)^{(n-1)/2}}{n^{1/2}}$$

where n is a positive integer greater than unity.

let

$$P = \Gamma\left(\frac{1}{n}\right) . \Gamma\left(\frac{2}{n}\right) . \Gamma\left(\frac{3}{n}\right) \cdots \Gamma\left(\frac{n-2}{n}\right) \Gamma\left(\frac{n-1}{n}\right)$$

$$= \Gamma\left(\frac{1}{n}\right) . \Gamma\left(\frac{2}{n}\right) . \Gamma\left(\frac{3}{n}\right) \cdots \Gamma\left(1-\frac{2}{n}\right) \Gamma\left(1-\frac{1}{n}\right).$$

Now writing the value of P in the reverse order, we get

$$P = \Gamma\left(1-\frac{1}{n}\right) \Gamma\left(1-\frac{2}{n}\right) \cdots \Gamma\left(\frac{3}{n}\right) . \Gamma\left(\frac{2}{n}\right) . \Gamma\left(\frac{1}{n}\right)$$

Multiplying the two values, we get.

$$P^2 = \left[\Gamma\left(\frac{1}{n}\right) . \Gamma\left(1-\frac{1}{n}\right)\right] . \left[\Gamma\left(\frac{2}{n}\right) . \Gamma\left(1-\frac{2}{n}\right)\right]$$

$$\cdots \left[\Gamma\left(1-\frac{2}{n}\right) . \Gamma\left(\frac{2}{n}\right)\right] \left[\Gamma\left(1-\frac{1}{n}\right) . \Gamma\left(\frac{1}{n}\right)\right]$$

But

$$\Gamma\left(\frac{r}{n}\right) \Gamma\left(1-\frac{r}{n}\right) = \frac{\pi}{\sin\left(\frac{r\pi}{n}\right)}$$

[§ 12.8 (B)]

$$\therefore \quad P^2 = \frac{\pi}{\sin\left(\frac{\pi}{n}\right)} \cdot \frac{\pi}{\sin\left(\frac{2\pi}{n}\right)} \cdot \frac{\pi}{\sin\left(\frac{3\pi}{n}\right)} \sin\ (\theta + 2\pi/n) \ \dots \ \frac{\pi}{\sin\frac{(n-1)\pi}{n}}$$

$$= \frac{\pi^{n-1}}{\sin\left(\frac{\pi}{n}\right) . \sin\left(\frac{2\pi}{n}\right) . \sin\left(\frac{3\pi}{n}\right) \dots \sin\frac{(n-1)\pi}{n}} \quad \dots(i)$$

But from trigonometry

$$\frac{\sin n\theta}{\sin\theta} = 2^{n-1} \sin\ (\theta + 2\pi/n) \ \dots \ \sin\left(\theta + \frac{n-1}{n}\pi\right) \quad \dots(ii)$$

Taking the limit as $\theta \to 0$, we get

$$\lim_{\theta \to 0} \frac{\sin n\theta}{\sin\theta} = \lim_{\theta \to 0} \left[n . \frac{\sin n\theta}{n\theta} \cdot \frac{\theta}{\sin\theta}\right] = n$$

Hence by (ii), we have

$$n = 2^{n-1} \sin\frac{\pi}{n} \sin\frac{2\pi}{n} \ \dots \ \sin\frac{(n-1)\pi}{n}$$

Substituting this value in the denominator of (i), we get

$$P^2 = \frac{\pi^{n-1}}{n/2^{n-1}} = \frac{(2\pi)^{n-1}}{n}$$

Hence

$$P = \Gamma\left(\frac{1}{n}\right) \cdot \Gamma\left(\frac{2}{n}\right) \cdot \Gamma\left(\frac{3}{n}\right) \dots \Gamma\left(\frac{n-1}{n}\right)$$

$$= \frac{(2\pi)^{(n-1)/2}}{n^{1/2}}$$

Illustrative Examples

Ex. 1. *Find the values of* $\Gamma\left(-\frac{3}{2}\right), \Gamma\left(-\frac{5}{2}\right)$

Solution We have

$$\Gamma(n)\,\Gamma(1-n) = \frac{\pi}{\sin n\pi} \quad \dots(i)$$

(i) Putting $n = -\frac{3}{2}$ in (i), we get

$$\Gamma\left(-\frac{3}{2}\right), \Gamma\left(\frac{5}{2}\right) = \frac{\pi}{\sin\left(-\frac{3}{2}\pi\right)} = \pi$$

or

$$\Gamma\left(-\frac{3}{2}\right) = \frac{\pi}{\Gamma\left(\frac{5}{2}\right)} = \frac{\pi}{\frac{3}{2} \cdot \frac{1}{2}\sqrt{\pi}} = \frac{4\sqrt{\pi}}{3} \quad \dots(ii)$$

(ii) Putting $n = -\frac{5}{2}$ in (i), we get

$$\Gamma\left(-\frac{5}{2}\right)\cdot\Gamma\left(\frac{7}{2}\right) = \frac{\pi}{\sin\left(\frac{-5\pi}{2}\right)} = -\frac{\pi}{\sin\left(\frac{5\pi}{2}\right)}$$

or
$$\Gamma\left(-\frac{5}{2}\right) = -\frac{\pi}{\Gamma(7/2)} = -\frac{\pi}{\frac{5}{2}\cdot\frac{3}{2}\cdot\frac{1}{2}\sqrt{\pi}}$$

$$= -\frac{8\sqrt{\pi}}{15}.$$

Ex. 2 *Evaluate* : $\int_0^a \frac{x^2}{\sqrt{(a-x)}}\, dx$

Solution. Let $x = a\sin^2\theta$, hence $dx = 2a\ \sin\theta\cos\theta\, d\,\theta$

$$\therefore \quad \int_0^a \frac{x^2}{\sqrt{(a-x)}}\, dx = \int_0^{\pi/2} \frac{a^2\sin^4\theta \,.\, 2a\sin\theta\cos\theta\, d\theta}{\sqrt{a}\cos\theta}$$

$$= 2\, a^{5/2}\int_0^{\pi/2} \sin^5\theta\, d\,\theta$$

$$= 2a^{5/2}\,\frac{\Gamma\left(\frac{6}{2}\right)\Gamma\left(\frac{1}{2}\right)}{2\,\Gamma\left(\frac{7}{2}\right)} = \frac{a^{5/2}\,\Gamma(3)\,.\sqrt{\pi}}{\frac{5}{2}\cdot\frac{3}{2}\cdot\frac{1}{2}\sqrt{\pi}}$$

$$= \frac{16}{15}\, a^{5/2}$$

Ex 3. *Prove that*

(i) $\int_0^\infty \frac{xdx}{1+x^6} = \frac{\pi}{3\sqrt{3}}$,

(ii) $\int_{-\infty}^\infty \cos\frac{\pi x^2}{2}\, dx = 1.$

Solution (i) Let $I = \int_0^\infty \frac{xdx}{1+x^6}$.

Put $\quad x^6 = y$ or $x = y^{1/6}$, hence $dx = \frac{1}{6}\, y^{-5/6}\, dy = \frac{1}{6}\int_0^\infty \frac{y^{-2/3}}{1+y}\, dy$

$$\therefore \quad I = \frac{1}{6}\int_0^\infty \frac{y^{1/6}\,.\,y^{-5/6}}{1+y}\, dy = \frac{1}{6}\int_0^\infty \frac{y^{-2/3}}{1+y}\, dy$$

$$= \frac{1}{6}\int_0^\infty \frac{y^{1/3-1}}{(1+y)}\, dy$$

$$= \frac{1}{6}\cdot\frac{\pi}{\sin\frac{\pi}{3}} \qquad \left[\because \int_0^\infty \frac{x^{n-1}}{1+x}\, dx = \frac{\pi}{\sin n\pi}\right]$$

i.e., $\quad I = \frac{\pi}{3\sqrt{3}}.$

(ii) Let $I = \int_{-\infty}^{\infty} \cos \frac{\pi x^2}{2} \, dx = 2 \int_0^{\infty} \cos \frac{\pi x^2}{2} \, dx$

Put $x^2 = t$ or $x = t^{1/2}$, so that $dx = \frac{1}{2} t^{-1/2} \, dt$.

$\therefore$ $I = 2 \cdot \frac{1}{2} \int_0^{\infty} t^{-1/2} \cos \frac{\pi}{2} t \, dt = \int_0^{\infty} t^{1/2-1} \cos \frac{\pi}{2} t \, dt$

$$= \frac{\Gamma\left(\frac{1}{2}\right)}{\left(\frac{\pi}{2}\right)^{1/2}} \cos\left(\frac{1}{2} \cdot \frac{\pi}{2}\right) \left[\because \int_0^{\infty} x^{m-1} \cos bx \, dx = \frac{\Gamma(m)}{b^m} \cos \frac{m\pi}{2}\right]$$

$$= \frac{\sqrt{\pi}}{\left(\frac{\pi}{2}\right)^{1/2}} \cdot \frac{1}{\sqrt{2}} = 1.$$

Ex. 4. *Show that* $\int_0^1 \left(\log \frac{1}{x}\right)^{n-1} dx = \Gamma(n) \quad n > 0$

Solution. Let $I = \int_0^1 \left(\log \frac{1}{x}\right)^{n-1} dx$

Put $\log \frac{1}{x} = t$ or $x = e^{-t}$, so that $dx = -e^{-t} \, dt$

$\therefore$ $I = \int_0^{\infty} t^{n-1} (-e^{-t}) \, dt = \int_0^{\infty} t^{n-1} e^{-t} \, dt$

$= \Gamma(n)$, $n > 0$, by definition of gamma function.

Ex. 5. *Evaluate* : $\int_0^{\infty} \frac{x^8 (1-x^6)}{(1+x)^{24}} \, dx$

Solution Let $I = \int_0^{\infty} \frac{x^8 (1-x^6)}{(1+x)^{24}} \, dx$

$$= \int_0^{\infty} \frac{x^8 \, (dx)}{(1+x)^{24}} - \int_0^{\infty} \frac{x^{14} \, (dx)}{(1+x)^{24}} \, dx$$

$$= \int_0^{\infty} \frac{x^{9-1}}{(1+x)^{9+15}} \, dx - \int_0^{\infty} \frac{x^{15-1}}{(1+x)^{15+9}} \, dx$$

$= B(9, 15) - B(15, 9) = 0$

$[\because B(m,n) = B(n,m)]$

Ex. 6. *Show that, if* $m > -1$

$$\int_0^{\infty} x^m e^{-n^2 x^2} \, dx = \frac{1}{2n^{m+1}} \Gamma\left(\frac{m+1}{2}\right).$$

Solution. Let $I = \int_0^{\infty} x^m e^{-n^2 x^2} \, dx$

Now, put $n^2x^2 = t$, or $x = \frac{1}{n}, \sqrt{t}$ so that $dx = \frac{1}{2n} t^{-1/2}\, dt.$

$$\therefore \quad I = \int_0^\infty \frac{1}{n^m}.\, t^{m/2} e^{-t} \frac{1}{2n} t^{-1/2}\, dt$$

$$= \frac{1}{2n^{m+1}} \int_0^\infty t^{(m-1)/2} e^{-t}\, dt$$

$$= \frac{1}{2n^{m+1}} \int_0^\infty t^{\left[\left(\frac{m+1}{2}\right)-1\right]} e^{-t}\, dt$$

$$= \frac{1}{2n^{m+1}} \Gamma\left(\frac{m+1}{2}\right), \quad \text{if } \frac{m+1}{2} > 0 \text{ or } m > -1.$$

Ex. 7. *Show that* $\int_0^{\pi/2} \tan^n x\, dx = \frac{\pi}{2} \sec \frac{n\pi}{2}$.

Solution. Here $\int_0^{\pi/2} \tan^n_x\, dx = \int_0^{\pi/2} \sin^n x.\, \cos^{-nx}\, dx$

$$= \frac{\Gamma\left(n+\frac{1}{2}\right)\Gamma\left(\frac{1-n}{2}\right)}{2\Gamma\left[\frac{n+(-n)+2}{2}\right]}$$

$$= \frac{\Gamma\left(\frac{n+1}{2}\right)\Gamma\left(\frac{1-n}{2}\right)}{2\Gamma(1)}$$

$$= \frac{1}{2}.\, \Gamma\left(\frac{n+1}{2}\right).\, \Gamma\left(1-\frac{n+1}{2}\right)$$

$$= \frac{1}{2}.\, \frac{\pi}{\sin\frac{(n+1)\pi}{2}} = \frac{\pi}{2} \sec. \frac{n\pi}{2}.$$

Ex. 8. *Prove that*

$$\int_a^b (x-a)^{m-1} (b-x)^{n-1}\, dx = (b-a)^{m+n-1} B(m,n)$$

where m and n are positive.

Solution. Put $x-a = (b-a)\, y$, so that $dx = (b-a)\, dy$

$$\therefore \quad \int_a^b (x-a)^{x-1} (b-x)^{n-1}\, dx$$

$$= \int_0^1 [\,(b-a)y\,]^{m-1} [(b-a)\,(1-y\,]^{n-1} (b-a)\, dy$$

$$=(b-a)^{m+m-1} \int_0^\infty y^{m-1} (1-y)^{n-1}\, dy$$

$$= (b-a)^{m+n-1}\ B(m,n).$$

Ex. 9. *show that* $B(m,n) = \int_0^1 \frac{x^{m-1}+x^{n-1}}{(1+x)^{m+n}}\, dx.$

Solution By definition, we have

$$B(m,n) = \int_0^\infty \frac{x^{m-1}\,dx}{(1+x)^{m+n}}$$

$$= \int_0^1 \frac{x^{m-1}\,dx}{(1+x)^{m+n}} + \int_1^\infty \frac{x^{m-1}\,dx}{(1+x)^{m+n}}$$

Now put $x = 1/t$ in the second integral on R.H.S.

Then

$$B(m,n) = \int_0^1 \frac{x^{m-1}\,dx}{(1+x)^{m+n}} + \int_1^0 \frac{(1/t)^{m-1}\left(-1/t^2\right)dt}{(1+1/t)^{m+n}}$$

$$\int_0^1 \frac{n^{m-1}\,dx}{(1+x)^{m+n}} + \int_0^1 \frac{t^{n-1}\,dt}{(1+t)^{m+n}}$$

$$= \int_0^1 \frac{x^{m-1}\,dx}{(1+x)^{m+n}} + \int_0^1 \frac{x^{n-1}\,dx}{(1+x)^{m+n}}$$

$$= \int_0^1 \frac{x^{m-1} + x^{n-1}}{(1+x)^{m+n}}\,dx.$$

Ex. 10. *Show that*

$$\int_0^1 \frac{x^2\,dx}{(1-x^4)^{1/2}} \times \int_0^1 \frac{dx}{(1+x^4)^{1/2}} = \frac{\pi}{4\sqrt{2}}.$$

Solution. Let $I_1 = \int_0^1 \frac{x^2\,dx}{(1-x^4)^{1/2}}$

Put $x^4 = t$ or $x = t^{1/4}$, so that $dx = \frac{1}{4}t^{-3/4}\,dt$

$$\therefore \quad I_1 = \frac{1}{4}\int_0^1 \frac{t^{1/2}\,.\,t^{-3/4}\,dt}{(1-t)^{1/2}} = \frac{1}{4}\int_0^1 t^{-1/4}(1-t)^{-1/2}\,dt$$

$$= \frac{1}{4}\int_0^1 t^{(3/4-1)}(1-t)^{1/2-1}\,dt = \frac{1}{4}.\,B\left(\frac{3}{4},\frac{1}{2}\right)$$

$$= \frac{1}{4}\cdot\frac{\Gamma\left(\frac{3}{4}\right)\cdot\Gamma\left(\frac{1}{2}\right)}{\Gamma(5/4)} = \frac{1}{4}\cdot\frac{\Gamma(3/4)\,.\,\sqrt{\pi}}{\frac{1}{4}\Gamma(1/4)}$$

i.e. $$I_1 = \sqrt{\pi}\,\frac{\Gamma(3/4)}{\Gamma(1/4)} \qquad \text{...(i)}$$

Again let $I_2 = \int_0^1 \frac{dx}{(1+x^4)^{1/2}}$

Put $x^2 = \tan\theta$ or $x = \sqrt{\tan\theta}$, so that

$$dx = \frac{sec^2\,d\theta}{2\sqrt{\tan\theta}}$$

$$\therefore \quad I_2 = \int_0^{\pi/4} \frac{sec^2\,\theta\,d\theta}{2\sqrt{(tan\theta)}\,.\,sec\theta} = \int_0^{\pi/4} \frac{d\theta}{2\sqrt{(sin\theta\cos\theta)}}$$

$$= \frac{1}{\sqrt{2}}\int_0^{\pi/4} \frac{d\theta}{\sqrt{(sin\,2\theta)}}$$

Again put $2\theta = \phi$

$$\therefore \quad I_2 = \frac{1}{2\sqrt{2}}\int_0^{\pi/2} \frac{d\theta}{\sqrt{(sin\theta)}} = \frac{1}{2\sqrt{2}}\int_0^{\pi/2} \sin^{-1/2}\theta \, d\theta.$$

$$= \frac{1}{2\sqrt{2}} \cdot \frac{\Gamma\left(\frac{\frac{-1}{2}+1}{2}\right) \cdot \Gamma\left(\frac{1}{2}\right)}{2\Gamma\left(\frac{\frac{-1}{2}+2}{2}\right)}$$

$$= \frac{1}{4\sqrt{2}} \cdot \frac{\Gamma\left(\frac{1}{4}\right) \cdot \sqrt{\pi}}{\Gamma(3/4)} \qquad ...(ii)$$

From (i) and (ii) an multiplication, we get

$$I_1 \times I_2 = \sqrt{\pi} \cdot \frac{\Gamma(3/4)}{\Gamma(1/4)} \times \frac{1}{4\sqrt{2}} \sqrt{\pi} \cdot \frac{\Gamma(1/4)}{\Gamma(3/4)}$$

$$= \frac{\pi}{4\sqrt{2}}.$$

Ex. 11. *Show that* $\int_0^1 \log \Gamma(x)\, dx = \frac{1}{2} \log 2\pi.$

Solution Let $I = \int_0^1 \log \Gamma(x)\, dx$

$$= \int_0^1 \log \Gamma(1-x)\, dx$$

$$\left[\text{By } \int_0^a f(x)\, dx = \int_0^a f(a-x)\, dx\right]$$

$$\therefore \quad 2I = \int_0^1 [\log \Gamma(x) + \log \Gamma(1-x)]\, dx$$

or

$$2I = \int_0^1 \log [\Gamma(x)\, \Gamma(1-x)]\, dx$$

But

$$\Gamma(n)\,\Gamma(1-n) = \frac{\pi}{\sin n\pi}$$

$$\therefore \quad 2I = \int_0^1 \log \left[\frac{\pi}{\sin x\pi}\right] dx$$

$$= \int_0^1 \log \pi \, dx - \int_0^1 \log \sin\pi \, dx$$

$$= \log \pi - \frac{1}{\pi}\int_0^{\pi} \log \sin t\, dt, \text{ on putting } \pi x = t$$

$$= \log \pi - \frac{2}{\pi}\int_0^{\pi/2} \log \sin t\, dt$$

$$= \log \pi - \frac{2}{\pi}\left(-\frac{\pi}{2} \log 2\right)$$

$$= \frac{1}{2}[\log \pi + \log 2] = \frac{1}{2} \log 2\pi.$$

Exercise 12

Show that

1. $\dfrac{\Gamma(1/3)\,\Gamma(5/6)}{\Gamma(2/3)} = 2^{1/3}\sqrt{\pi}$

2.(i) $B(m,n) = B(m+1,n) + B(m,n+1)$ $m,n > 0$.

(ii) $\dfrac{B(m+1,n)}{m} = \dfrac{(B(m,n+1)}{n} = \dfrac{B(m,n)}{m+n}$

3.(i) $\displaystyle\int_0^2 \frac{x^2\,dx}{\sqrt{(2-x)}}\,dx = \frac{64\sqrt{2}}{15}$,

(ii) $\displaystyle\int_0^1 \frac{x^2\,dx}{\sqrt{1-x^3}} = \frac{2}{3}$,

(iii) $\displaystyle\int_0^1 \frac{dx}{\sqrt{1-x^3}} = \frac{\sqrt{\pi}\,\Gamma\left(\frac{1}{3}\right)}{3\,\Gamma(5/6)}$;

(iv) $\displaystyle\int_0^3 \frac{dx}{\sqrt{(3x-x^2)}} = \pi$

4.(i) $\displaystyle\int_0^1 \frac{dx}{\sqrt{(1-x^n)}} = \frac{\sqrt{\pi}\,\Gamma(1/n)}{n\,\Gamma\left(\frac{1}{2}+\frac{1}{n}\right)}$.

(ii) $\displaystyle\int_0^1 (1-x^n)^{1/n}\,dx = \frac{1}{n}\,\frac{[\Gamma(1/n)]^2}{2\,\Gamma(2/n)}$

(iii) $\displaystyle\int_0^1 x^{n-1}\left(\log\frac{1}{x}\right)^{m-1} dx = \frac{\Gamma(m)}{n^m}$, $(m,\ n > 0)$.

(iv) $\displaystyle\int_0^\infty x^4 e^{-x^4}\,dx = \frac{1}{4}\,\Gamma(5/4)$.

5. If $c > 1$, $\displaystyle\int_0^\infty \frac{x^c}{c^x}\,dx = \frac{\Gamma(c+1)}{(\log c)^{c+1}}$

6. $\displaystyle\int_0^{\pi/2} \sqrt{(\tan\theta)}\,d\theta = \int_0^{\pi/2} \sqrt{(\cot\theta)}\,d\theta = \frac{\pi\sqrt{2}}{2}$.

7. $\displaystyle\int_0^{\pi/2} \frac{d\theta}{\sqrt{(\sin\theta)}} \times \int_0^{\pi/2} \sqrt{(\sin\theta)}\,d\theta = \pi$.

8. Show that

$$B(m,n) = a^m b^n \int_0^\infty \frac{x^{m-1}\,dx}{(ax+b)^{m+n}}$$

and deduce that

$$\int_0^{\pi/2} \frac{\sin^{2m-1}\theta\,\cos^{2n-1}\theta}{(a\sin^2\theta + b\cos^2\theta)^{m+n}}\,d\theta = \frac{B(m,n)}{2a^m b^n}$$

9. show that

$$\int_0^1 \frac{x^{m-1}(1-x)^{n-1}}{(x+a)^{m+n}}\,dx = \frac{B(m,n)}{a^n(1+a)^m}\ ; \ a,\ m,\ n > 0.$$

[Hint. Put $\dfrac{x}{x+a} = \dfrac{t}{1+a}$ etc.]

10. Show that

$$\int_0^{\pi/2} \frac{d\theta}{\sqrt{\left(1-\frac{1}{2}\sin^2\theta\right)}} = \frac{\left[\Gamma\left(\frac{1}{4}\right)\right]^2}{4\sqrt{2}}\ .$$

13

Dirac Delta Functions

13.1 Introduction

The concepts of an impulsive force, i.e., a very large force acting for a short interval of time, and that of a load acting at a point of a beam which generates a very large pressure over a very small area of the beam play a very important role in mechanics. In order to deal with these basic ideas mathematically Dirac introduced a new function which is known as Dirac delta function. This functions is utilized to express physical quantities that are defined as a distinct point in time or in space as quantities which are distributed throughout time or space. An extensive use is now made in quantum mechanics and boundary value problems in mathematical physics.

13.2 The Dirac delta Function

The Dirac delta function or simply delta function is denoted by $\delta(x)$ and is defined by

$$\delta(x) = \begin{cases} 0 \text{ if } x \neq 0 \\ \infty \text{ if } x = 0 \end{cases} \quad \text{...(i)}$$

together with condition that

$$\int_{-\infty}^{\infty} \delta(x)\, dx = 1 \quad \text{...(ii)}$$

The above definition does not provide a clear picture of $\delta(x)$. However it is clear that $\delta(x)$ is a function which is very large in the neighbourhood of the point $x = 0$ but is zero outside a very small interval surrounding the origin. $\delta(x)$ may vary in this interval in an arbitrary manner without making its oscillations indefinitely large.

Consider a function $\delta_{\in}(x)$ defined by

$$\delta_{\in}(x) \begin{cases} 0, & x < 0 \\ 1/\in, & 0 < x < \in \\ 0, & x > \in \end{cases} \quad \text{...(iii)}$$

Then
$$\int_{-\infty}^{\infty} \delta_{\in}(x)\, dx = \int_{-\infty}^{0} \delta_{\in}(x)\, dx + \int_{0}^{\in} \delta_{\in}(x)\, dx$$
$$+ \int_{-\in}^{\infty} \delta_{\in}(x)\, dx$$

$$= 0 + \int_0^{\varepsilon} \frac{1}{\varepsilon} dx + 0$$

$$= \frac{1}{\varepsilon} . \in = 1$$

Thus $$\int_{-\infty}^{\infty} \delta_{\in}(x)\, dx = 1 \qquad ...(iv)$$

From (iii) and (iv), it follows that we may treat $\delta(x)$ as the limiting form of $\delta_{\in}(x)$ as $\in \longrightarrow 0$, i.e.

$$\lim_{\in \to 0} \delta_{\in}(x) = \delta(x) \qquad ...(v)$$

13.3 Delta Function δ (x-a)

Generalising the definition of § 13.2, we define

$$\delta(x-a) = \begin{cases} 0 \text{ if } x \neq a \\ \infty \text{ if } x = a \end{cases} \qquad ...(i)$$

together with the condition

$$\int_{-\infty}^{\infty} \delta(x-a)\, dx = 1 \qquad ...(ii)$$

13.4 Properties of delta Functions

(I) *If f(x) is continuous in a certain interval which includes the origin, then*

(i) $$\int_{-\infty}^{\infty} f(x)\, \delta(x)\, dx = f(0)$$

(ii) $$\int_{-\infty}^{\infty} f(x)\, \delta(x-a)\, dx = f(a)$$

(iii) $$\int_{-\infty}^{\infty} f(x)\, \delta(a-x)\, dx = f(a)$$

Proof

(i) $$\int_{-\infty}^{\infty} f(x)\, \delta_{\in}(x)\, dx = \int_{-\infty}^{0} f(x)\, \delta_{\in}(x)\, dx$$

$$+ \int_0^{\varepsilon} f(x)\, \delta_{\in}(x)\, dx + \int_{\varepsilon}^{\infty} f(x)\, \delta_{\in}(x)\, dx$$

$$= 0 + \int_0^{\in} f(x) \frac{1}{\in} dx + 0$$

$$\therefore \quad \int_{-\infty}^{\infty} f(x)\, \delta_{\in}(x)\, dx = \frac{1}{\in} \int_0^{\in} f(x)\, d(x) \qquad ...(i)$$

since $f(x)$ is continuous, by using the mean value theorem of the integral calculus we can find a number θ, where $0 \leq \theta \leq 1$, such that

$$\int_0^{\varepsilon} f(x)\, dx = f(\theta_{\in}) \int_0^{\varepsilon} dx = \in f(\theta_{\in}) \qquad ...(ii)$$

using (ii), (i) may be re-written as

$$\int_{-\infty}^{\infty} f(x)\,\delta_{\epsilon}(x)\,dx = f(\theta_{\epsilon}), 0 \le \theta_{\epsilon} \le 1$$

Now, let $\epsilon \to 0$, then (iii) reduce to

$$\int_{-\infty}^{\infty} f(x)\,\delta(x)\,dx = f(0)$$

(ii) Putting $t = x + a$, i.e., $x = t - a$ and $dx = dt$ in (iv), we have

$$\int_{-\infty}^{\infty} f(t-a)\,\delta(t-a)\,dx = f(0)$$

(iii) Putting $t = a{-}x$, i.e., $x = a{-}t$ and $dx = -dt$ in (iv), we get

$$\int_{-\infty}^{\infty} f(a-t)\,\delta(a-t(-dt)\,dx = f(a)$$

i.e. $$\int_{-\infty}^{\infty} f(a-x)\,\delta(a-t)\,dt = f(a)$$

which may be re-written as

$$\int_{-\infty}^{\infty} f(a-x)\,\delta(a-x)\,dx = f(a)$$

(II) $\delta(-x) = \delta(x)$

Proof

$\delta(-x)$ satisfies the relations

$$\delta(-x) = \begin{cases} 0, & \text{if } x \ne 0 \\ \infty, & \text{if } x = 0 \end{cases}$$

and $$\int_{-\infty}^{\infty} \delta(-x)\,dx = -\int_{+\infty}^{\infty} \delta(t)\,dt$$

Putting $x = -t$ so that $dx = -dt$

$$= \int_{-\infty}^{\infty} \delta(x)\,dx = 1$$

Hence $\delta(-x) = \delta x$.

(III) $\delta(ax) = \dfrac{1}{a}\,\delta(x),\ a > 0$

Proof Since $x \ne 0$ hence $ax \ne 0$ $\therefore$ $a > 0$

$\delta(ax)$ satisfies the relation

$$\delta(ax) = \begin{cases} 0, & \text{if } ax \ne 0 \\ \infty, & \text{if } ax = 0 \end{cases}$$

and $$\int_{-\infty}^{\infty} a\delta(ax)\,dx = \int_{-\infty}^{\infty} \delta(t)\,dt$$

Putting $ax = t$ so that $dx = \dfrac{1}{a}\,dt$

$$= \int_{-\infty}^{\infty} \delta(x)\, dx = 1$$

which implies that

$$a\delta(ax) = \delta(x)$$

or
$$\delta(ax) = \frac{1}{a}\delta(x).$$

13.5 Derivatives of δ (x)

If δ (x) is a continuous differentiable Dirac delta function, vanishing for large x, then

$$\int_{-\infty}^{\infty} f(x)\, \delta'(x)\, dx = -f'(0)$$

Proof Assuming that $f(x)$, $\delta(x)$ and $\delta'(x)$ can be regarded as ordinary functions than by the rule of integeration by parts, we have

$$\int_{-\infty}^{\infty} f(x)\, \delta'\, dx = [f(x)\, \delta(x)]_{-\infty}^{\infty}$$

$$- \int_{-\infty}^{\infty} f'(x)\, \delta(x)\, dx$$

$$= -f'(0).$$

Repeating this process again and again, we get

$$\int_{-\infty}^{\infty} f(x)\, \delta^{n}(x)\, dx = (-1)^{n} f^{n}(0).$$

13.6 The Heaviside Unit Function or the Unit Step Function

The heaviside unit-step function denoted by H (x) is defined as

$$H(x) = \begin{cases} 1, & \text{if } x \geq 0 \\ 0, & \text{if } x < 0 \end{cases}$$

If $a > 0$, then

$$H(x-a) = \begin{cases} 1, & \text{if } x \geq a \\ 0, & \text{if } x < a \end{cases}$$

13.7 The Dirac delta Function is the derivative of the Heaviside unit function H (x) defined by the equation

$$\mathbf{H}(x) = \begin{cases} \mathbf{1}, & \textbf{if } x > \mathbf{0} \\ \mathbf{0}, & \textbf{if } x < \mathbf{0} \end{cases}$$

Proof we have

$$\int_{-\infty}^{\infty} f(x)\, H'(x)\, dx = \lim_{a \to \infty} \int_{-a}^{a} f(x)\, H'(x)\, dx$$

Integrating by parts taking H′ (x) as second function.

$$= \lim_{a\to\infty} \left[\{f(x)\, H(x)\}_{-a}^{a} - \int_{-a}^{a} f'(x)\, H(x)\, dx \right]$$

$$= \lim_{a\to\infty} [\, f(a)\, \mathrm{H}(a) - f(-a)\, \mathrm{H}(-a)\,]$$

$$- \int_{-a}^{0} f'(x)\, \mathrm{H}(x)\, dx - \int_{0}^{a} f'(x)\, \mathrm{H}(x)\, dx$$

$$= \lim_{a\to\infty} \left[f(a) - 0 \int_{0}^{a} f'(x) dx \right]$$

$$= \lim_{a\to\infty} \left[f(a) - \{f(x)\}_{0}^{a} \right]$$

$$= \lim_{a\to\infty} [\, f(a) - f(a) + f(0)]$$

$$= f(0)$$

$$\int_{-\infty}^{\infty} f(x)\, \delta(x)\, dx$$

which implies that

$$\mathrm{H}'(x) = \delta(x).$$

14

Jacobi Polynomials

14.1 Jacobi Polynomials

Jacobi polynomial is denoted and defined as

$$P_n^{(\alpha,\beta)}(x) = \frac{(1+\alpha)_n}{n!}\, {}_2F_1\left[-n, 1+\alpha+\beta+n\,;\, \frac{1-x}{2} \atop 1+\alpha\,;\right] \quad ...(i)$$

or

$$P_n^{(\alpha,\beta)}(x) = \sum_{m=0}^{n} \frac{(1+\alpha)_n\,(1+\alpha+\beta)_{n+m}}{m!\,(n-m)!\,(\alpha+1)_m\,(1+\alpha+n)_m} \left(\frac{x-1}{2}\right)^m \quad ...(ii)$$

showing that $P_n^{(\alpha,\beta)}(x)$ is a polynomial of degree n.

If in summation (ii) we replace m by $n-m$, then

$$P_n^{(\alpha,\beta)}(x) = \sum_{m=0}^{n} \frac{(1+\alpha)_n\,(1+\alpha+\beta)_{2n-m}}{(n-m)!\,m!\,(1+\alpha)_{n-m}\,(1+\alpha+\beta)_n} \left(\frac{x-1}{2}\right)^m$$

$$= \frac{(1+\alpha+\beta)_{2n}}{n!\,(1+\alpha+\beta)_n} \left(\frac{x-1}{2}\right)^n \sum_{m=0}^{n} \frac{(-n)_m\,(-\alpha-n)_m}{(-\alpha-\beta-2n)_m\, m!}$$

$$= \frac{(1+\alpha+\beta)_{2n}}{n!\,(1+\alpha+\beta)_n} \left(\frac{x-1}{2}\right)^n {}_2F_1\left[-n, -\alpha-n; \frac{2}{1-x} \atop -\alpha-\beta-2n;\right] \quad ...(iii)$$

(i) can be re-written as

$$P_n^{(\alpha,\beta)}(x) = \frac{(1+\alpha)_n}{n!} \left(\frac{x+1}{2}\right)^n {}_2F_1\left[-n, -\beta-n; \frac{x-1}{x+1} \atop 1+\alpha;\right] \quad ...(iv)$$

or

$$P_n^{(\alpha,\beta)}(x) = \sum_{m=0}^{n} \frac{(1+\alpha)_n\,(1+\beta)_n}{m!\,(n-m)!\,(1+\alpha)_m\,(1+\beta)_m} \left(\frac{x-1}{2}\right)^m \times \left(\frac{x+1}{2}\right)^{n-m} \quad ...(v)$$

By reversing the order of terms in (v), we get

$$P_n^{(\alpha,\beta)}(x) = \sum_{m=0}^{n} \frac{(1+\alpha)_n\,(1+\beta)_n}{(n-m)!\,m!\,(1+\alpha)_{n-m}\,(1-\beta)_m}$$

$$\left(\frac{x-1}{2}\right)^{n-m}\left(\frac{x+1}{2}\right)^{m}$$

$$= \frac{(1+\beta)_n}{n\,!}\left(\frac{x-1}{2}\right)^{n} {}_2F_1\left[\begin{matrix}-n, -\alpha-n; & \dfrac{x+1}{x-1}\\ 1+\beta\,; & \end{matrix}\right] \quad ...(vi)$$

As a particular case, $P_n^{(\alpha,\,\alpha)}(x)$ is called *ultraspherical polynomial* or *Gegenbaver polynomial.* From (i) it is clear that Legendre polynomial $P_n(x)$ is equal to $P_n^{(\alpha,\,\beta)}(x)$.

14.2 Generating Relations

To prove that

(a) $$\sum_{n=0}^{\infty} \frac{(1+\alpha+\beta)_n P^{(\alpha,\beta)}(x)\,.\,t^n}{(1+\alpha)_n}$$

$$= (1-t)^{-1-\alpha-\beta}\,{}_2F_1\left[\begin{matrix}\frac{1}{2}(1+\alpha+\beta), \frac{1}{2}(2+\alpha+\beta); & \dfrac{2t(x-1)}{(1-t)^2}\\ 1+\alpha; & \end{matrix}\right] \quad ...(i)$$

(b) $$\sum_{n=0}^{\infty} \frac{P_n^{(\alpha,\beta)}(x)\,t^n}{(1+\alpha)_n\,(1+\beta)_n}$$

$$= {}_0F_1\left[\begin{matrix}- & ; & \dfrac{t(x-1)}{2}\\ 1+\alpha & & \end{matrix}\right] {}_0F_1\left[\begin{matrix}- & ; & t\,\dfrac{(x+1)}{2}\\ 1+\beta & ; & \end{matrix}\right] \quad ...(ii)$$

This relation is also known as *Beteman's generating relation.*

(a) By the definition of Jacobi polynomial

$$P_n^{(\alpha,\,\beta)}(x) = \sum_{m=0}^{n} \frac{(1+\alpha)_n\,(1+\alpha+\beta)_{m+n}}{m\,!\,(n-m)\,!\,(1+\alpha)_m\,(1+\alpha+n)_m}\left(\frac{x-1}{2}\right)^m$$

We have

$$\sum_{n=0}^{\infty} \frac{(1+\alpha+\beta)_n P^{(\alpha,\beta)}(x)\,t^n}{(1+\alpha)_n}$$

$$= \sum_{n=0}^{\infty}\sum_{m=0}^{n} \frac{(1+\alpha+\beta)_{m+n}\,(x-1)^m\,t^n\,(1+\alpha+\beta)_m t^m}{m\,!\,(n-m)\,!\,(1+\alpha)_m 2^m}$$

$$= \sum_{n=0}^{\infty}\sum_{m=0}^{n} \frac{(1+\alpha+\beta)_{n+2m}\,(x-1)^m\,t^{m+n}}{n\,!\,m\,!\,(1+\alpha)_m\,2^m}$$

$$= \sum_{m=0}^{\infty}\sum_{n=m}^{\infty} \frac{(1+\alpha+\beta)_n\,t^n}{n\,!}\,\frac{(1+\alpha+\beta)_{2m}\,(x-1)^m\,t^m}{m\,!\,(1+\alpha)_m\,2^m}$$

$$= \sum_{m=0}^{\infty} \frac{(1-t)^{-1-\alpha-\beta-2m}\, 2^{2m} \left(\frac{1+\alpha+\beta}{2}\right)_m \left(\frac{2+\alpha+\beta}{2}\right)_m . (x-1)^m t^m}{m\,!\,(1+\alpha)_m\, 2^m}$$

$$= (1-t)^{-1-\alpha-\beta} \sum_{m=0}^{\infty} \frac{\left(\frac{1+\alpha+\beta}{2}\right)_m \left(\frac{2+\alpha+\beta}{2}\right)_m}{(1+\alpha)_m\, ,m\,!} \left\{\frac{2t\,(x-1)}{(1-t)^2}\right\}^m$$

= R.H.S. of (i)

(b) Using defintion (v) of § 14.1, L.H.S. of (ii)

$$= \sum_{n=0}^{\infty} \sum_{m=0}^{n} \frac{\left(\frac{x-1}{2}\right)^m \left(\frac{x+1}{2}\right)^{n-m} t^n}{m\,!\,(n-m)\,!\,(1+\alpha)_m\,(1+\beta)_{n-m}}$$

$$= \sum_{n=0}^{\infty} \sum_{m=0}^{n} \frac{\left(\frac{x-1}{2}\right)^n \left(\frac{x+1}{2}\right)^n t^{n+m}}{m\,!\,n\,!\,(1+\alpha)_m\,(1+\beta)_n}$$

$$= \left(\sum_{m=0}^{\infty} \frac{\left\{\left(\frac{x-1}{2}\right)t\right\}^m}{m\,!} \times \sum_{n=0}^{\infty} \frac{\left\{\left(\frac{x+1}{2}\right)\right\} t^n}{n\,!}\right)$$

= R.H.S. of (ii)

14.3 Important Results

(i) $\mathbf{P}_n^{(\alpha+\beta)}(-x) = (-1)^n\, \mathbf{P}_n^{(\beta,\,\alpha)}(x)$

Replacing x by $(-x)$ and t by $(-t)$ in (ii) of § 14.2, we get

$$\sum_{n=0}^{\infty} \frac{(-1)^n P_n^{(\alpha,\,\beta)}(-x)\, t^n}{(1+\alpha)_n\,(1+\beta)_n}$$

$$= {}_0F_1\left[\begin{matrix} - & ; & \frac{t\,(x+1)}{2} \\ 1+\alpha & ; & \end{matrix}\right] {}_0F_1\left[\begin{matrix} - & ; & \frac{t\,(x+1)}{2} \\ 1+\beta & ; & \end{matrix}\right]$$

$$= \sum_{n=0}^{\infty} \frac{P_n^{(\alpha,\,\beta)}(x)\, t^n}{(1-\alpha)_n\,(1+\beta)_n}$$

Equating the coefficients of t^n on both sides, we obtained the required results.

(ii) $$\mathbf{P}_n^{(\alpha,\,\beta)}(x) = \frac{(-1)^n\,(1+\beta)_n}{n\,!}\, {}_2F_1\left[-n,\, 1+\alpha+\beta+n,\, \frac{1+x}{2} 1+\beta\right]$$

or $$\mathbf{P}_n^{(\alpha,\,\beta)}(x) = \sum_{m=0}^{n} \frac{(-1)^{n-m}\,(1+\beta)_n\,(1+\alpha+\beta)_{n+m}}{m\,!\,(n-m)\,!\,(1+\beta)_m\,(1+\alpha+\beta)_n} \left(\frac{x+1}{2}\right)^m$$

Hint : Use the above result and definition (i) of § 14.1.

14.4 Rodrigue's Formula

To prove that

$$\mathbf{P}_n^{(\alpha,\beta)}(x) = \frac{(x-1)^{-\alpha}(x+1)^{-\beta}}{2^n \cdot n!}[\mathbf{D}^n (x-1)^{n+\alpha}(1+x)^{n+\beta}]$$

or

$$\mathbf{P}_n^{(\alpha,\beta)}(x) = \frac{(-1)^n (1-x)^{-\alpha}(1+x)^{-\beta}}{2^n\, n!} \mathbf{D}^n [(1-x)^{n+\alpha}(1+x)^{n+\beta}] \quad \text{...(ii)}$$

From definition (v) of § 14.1, we get $P_n^{(\alpha,\beta)}(x)$

$$= \sum_{m=0}^{n} \frac{(1+\alpha)_n (1+\beta)_n (x-1)^m (x+1)^{n-m}}{2^n\, m!\,(n-m)!\,(1+\alpha)_m (1+\beta)_{n-m}}$$

$$= \frac{(x-1)^{-\alpha}(x+1)^{-\beta}}{2^n} \sum_{m=0}^{n} \frac{(1+\alpha)_n (1+\beta)_n (x-1)^{m+\alpha}(x+1)^{n-m+\beta}}{m!\,(n-m)!\,(1+\alpha)_m (1+\beta)_{n-m}} \quad \text{...(iii)}$$

If n and m are non–negative integers, we get

$$D^n (x^{m+\alpha}) = \frac{d^n}{dx^n}(x^{m+\alpha}) = (m+\alpha)(m+\alpha-1) \ldots (m+\alpha-n+1)\,.\, x^{m-n+\alpha}.$$

or

$$D^n (x^{m+\alpha}) = \frac{(1+\alpha)_m}{(1+\alpha)_{m-n}} x^{m-n+\alpha}$$

$$\therefore \quad \left.\begin{aligned} D^m \{(x+1)^{n+\beta}\} &= \frac{(1+\beta)_n (x+1)^{n-m+\beta}}{(1+\beta)_{n-m}} \\ \text{and} \quad D^{n-m}\{(x-1)^{n+\alpha}\} &= \frac{(1+\alpha)_n (x-1)^{m+\alpha}}{(1+\alpha)_m} \end{aligned}\right\} \quad \text{...(iv)}$$

Using (iv), (iii) reduces to

$$P_n^{(\alpha,\beta)}(x) = \frac{(x-1)^{\alpha}(x+1)^{-\beta}}{n!\,2^n} \times \sum_{m=0}^{n} \frac{n!}{m!\,(n-m)!} D^m\{(x+1)^{n+\beta}\} D^{n-m}\{(x-1)^{n+\alpha}\}$$

or

$$P_n^{(\alpha,\beta)}(x) = \frac{(x-1)^{\alpha}(x+1)^{-\beta}}{2^n \cdot n!} D^n [(x-1)^{n+\alpha}(x+1)^{n+\beta}] \quad \text{...(v)}$$

[using Leibnitz' theorem]

(v) can also be re–written as (ii).

14.5 Orthogonal Properties

To prove that

(i) $$\int_{-1}^{1} (1-x)^{\alpha}(1+x)^{\beta}\, \mathbf{P}_n^{(\alpha,\beta)}(x)\, \mathbf{P}_m^{(\alpha,\beta)}(x)\, dx = 0 \quad (m \neq n) \quad \text{...(i)}$$

(ii) $$\int_{-1}^{1} (1-x)^{\alpha}(1+x)^{\beta} \{\mathbf{P}_n^{(\alpha,\beta)}(x)\}^2\, dx$$

$$= \frac{2^{\alpha+\beta+1}\,\Gamma(1+\alpha+n)\,\Gamma(1+\beta+n)}{n\,!\,(1+\alpha+\alpha+2n)\,\Gamma(1+\alpha+\beta+n)} \qquad \text{...(ii)}$$

(i) Let I denote the L.H.S. of (i). Then using Rodrigues formula, we have

$$I = \frac{(-1)^n}{2^n\,.\,n\,!}\int_{-1}^{1} D^n\,[(x-1)^{n+\alpha}\,(x-1)^{n+\beta}]\,P_m^{(\alpha,\,\beta)}(x)\,dx$$

$$= \frac{(-1)^n}{2^n\,.\,n\,!}\left[P_m^{(\alpha+\beta)}(x)\,D^{n-1}\left\{(1-x)^{n+\alpha}\,(1+x)^{n+\beta}\right\}\right]_{-1}^{1}$$

$$-\int_{-1}^{1} D\,[P_m^{(\alpha,\,\beta)}(x)]\,D^{n-1}\,[(1-x)^{n+\alpha}\,(1+x)^{n+\beta}$$

[Integrating by parts]

$$= \frac{(-1)^{n+1}}{2^n\,.\,n\,!}\int_{-1}^{1} D\,[P_m^{(\alpha,\,\beta)}(x)]\,D^{n-1}\,[(1-x)^{n+\alpha}\,(1+x)^{n+\beta}\,dx$$

[$\because$ first term reduces to zero under the conditions Re (α) > –1 and Re (β) > –1]

$$= \frac{(-1)^{2n}}{2^n\,.\,n\,!}\int_{-1}^{1} D^n\,[P_m^{(\alpha,\,\beta)}(x)]\,[(1-x)^{n+\alpha}\,(1+x)^{n+\beta}\,dx \qquad \text{...(iii)}$$

[Repeating the same process (n–1) times more]

$= 0$

[$\because$ if $n > m$, $P_m^{(\alpha,\,\beta)}(x)$ being a polynomial of degree m. $D^n\,[P_m^{(\alpha,\,\beta)}(x)] = 0$]

(ii) As before, from (iii), we have

$$\int_{-1}^{1} (1-x)\,(1+x)^{\beta}\,P_n^{(\alpha,\,\beta)}(x)\,P_m^{(\alpha,\,\beta)}(x)\,dx$$

$$= \frac{1}{2^n n\,!}\int_{-1}^{1} (1-x)^{n+\alpha}\,(1+x)^{n+\beta}\,D^n\,[P_m^{(\alpha,\,\beta)}(x)]\,dx$$

writing $m = n$ and denoting the resulting L.H.S. by I, we have

$$I = \frac{1}{2^n n\,!}\int_{-1}^{1} (1-x)^{n+\alpha}\,(1+x)^{n+\beta}\,D^n\,[P_n^{(\alpha,\,\beta)}(x)]\,dx \qquad \text{...(iv)}$$

Now, we have

$$D^n\,[P_n^{(\alpha,\,\beta)}(x)]$$

$$= \frac{(1+\alpha)_n}{n\,!}\,\frac{d^n}{dx^n}\left\{{}_2F_1\left[\begin{matrix}-n, & 1+\alpha+\beta+n; & \dfrac{1-x}{2}\\ & 1+\alpha & ;\end{matrix}\right]\right\}$$

$$= \frac{(1+\alpha)_n}{n\,!} \times \frac{\left(-\dfrac{1}{2}\right)^n (-n)_n\,(1+\alpha+\beta+n)_n}{(1+\alpha)_n} \times {}_2F_1\left[\begin{matrix}0, & 1+\alpha+\beta+2n; & \dfrac{1-x}{2}\\ & 1+\alpha+n & ;\end{matrix}\right]$$

$$= \frac{(1+\alpha+\beta)_{2n}}{2^n\,(1+\alpha+\beta)_n}$$

$\therefore$ (iv) reduces to

$$I = \frac{(1+\alpha+\beta)_{2n}}{2^{2n}\, n\,!\,(1+\alpha+\beta)_n}\int_{-1}^{1} (1-x)^{\alpha+n}\,(1+x)^{\beta+n}\,dx$$

$$= \frac{(1+\alpha+\beta)_{2n}\,.\,2^{\alpha+\beta+1+2n}}{2^{2n}\,.\,n\,!\,(1+\alpha+\beta)_n}\int_{0}^{1} (1-t)^{\alpha+n}\,t^{\beta+n}\,dt$$

[Putting $(1+x) = 2t$]

$$= \frac{2^{\alpha+\beta+1}\,(1+\alpha+\beta)_{2n}\,\Gamma(1+\alpha+n)\,\Gamma(1+\beta+n)}{n\,!\,(1+\alpha+\beta)_n\,\Gamma(2+\alpha+\beta+2n)}$$

$$\therefore \quad = \int_{-1}^{1} (1-x)^{\alpha}\,(1+x)^{\beta}\,\{P_n^{(\alpha,\,\beta)}(x)\}^2\,dx$$

$$= \frac{2^{\alpha+\beta+1}\,\Gamma(1+\alpha+n)\,\Gamma(1+\beta+n)}{n\,!\,(1+\alpha+\beta+2n)\,\Gamma(1+\alpha+\beta+n)}$$

Combining (i) and (ii), we have

$$\int_{-1}^{1} (1-x)^{\alpha}\,(1+x)^{\beta}\,P_n^{(\alpha,\,\beta)}(x)\,P_m^{(\alpha,\,\beta)}(x)\,dx$$

$$= \frac{2^{\alpha+\beta+1}\,\Gamma(1+\alpha+n)\,\Gamma(1+\beta+n)}{n\,!\,(1+\alpha+\beta+2n)\,\Gamma(1+\alpha+\beta+n)}\,\delta_{nm}.$$

14.6 Recurrence Formulae

(a) **Recurrence formulae in which shift in index *n* only takes place –** In generating relation (i), suppose that

$$\Phi(x,\,t) = \sum_{n=0}^{\infty} \frac{(1+\alpha+\beta)_n\,P_n^{(\alpha,\,\beta)}(x)\,t^n}{(1+\alpha)_n}$$

$$= (1-t)^{-1-\alpha-\beta}\;{}_2F_1\left[\begin{matrix}\frac{1}{2}(1+\alpha+\beta),\ \frac{1}{2}(2+\alpha+\beta); & \frac{2t\,(x-1)}{(1-t)^2}\\ 1+\alpha\ ; & \end{matrix}\right] \quad \text{...(i)}$$

Let $$k = 1+\alpha+\beta,\ y = \frac{1}{2}(1-x) \text{ and } \Psi = {}_2F_1 \quad \text{...(ii)}$$

Then (i) gives

$$\phi(y,\,t) = (1-t)^{-k}\,\phi\left\{\frac{-4ty}{(1-t)^2}\right\} \quad \text{...(iii)}$$

$$\frac{\partial\phi}{\partial y} = -4t\,(1-t)^{-k-2}\,\Psi\,'$$

and $$\left(\frac{\partial\phi}{\partial t}\right) = -\,k\,(1-t)^{-k-2}\,\Psi\,-4y\,(1+t)\,(1-t)^{-n-3}\,\Psi'$$

Eliminating Ψ and Ψ' from above relations, we get

$$y\,(1+t)\,\frac{\partial\phi}{\partial y} - t\,(1-t)\,\frac{\partial\phi}{\partial y} = -kt\,\phi,$$

which can be re–written as :

$$y \frac{\partial \phi}{\partial y} - t \frac{\partial \phi}{\partial t} = -kt\,\phi - t^2 \frac{\partial \phi}{\partial y} - xt \frac{\partial \phi}{\partial y} \quad \text{...(iv)}$$

or
$$y \frac{\partial \phi}{\partial y} - t \frac{\partial \phi}{\partial t} = \frac{-kt}{1-t}\,\phi - \frac{2yt}{1-t} \frac{\partial \phi}{\partial y} \quad \text{...(v)}$$

or
$$y \frac{\partial \phi}{\partial y} - t \frac{\partial \phi}{\partial t} = \frac{-kt}{1-t}\,\phi - \frac{2t^2}{1+t} \frac{\partial \phi}{\partial y} \quad \text{...(vi)}$$

Now, we will prove the following recurrence formulae :

(I)
$$\boldsymbol{(x-1)\left[(\alpha+\beta+n)\frac{d}{dx}P_n^{(\alpha,\beta)}(x) + (\alpha+n)\frac{d}{dx}P_{n-1}^{(\alpha,\beta)}(x)\right] =}$$
$$\boldsymbol{= (\alpha+\beta+n)\,[n\,P_n^{(\alpha,\beta)}(x) - (\alpha+n)\,P_{n-1}^{(\alpha,\beta)}(x)]}$$

From (i) and (ii), we have

$$\phi = \sum_{n=0}^{\infty} \frac{(k)_n P_n^{(\alpha,\beta)}(1-2y)\,t^n}{(1+\alpha)_n}$$

Substituting this into (iv), we have

$$\sum_{n=0}^{\infty} \frac{y\,(k)_n}{(1+\alpha)_n} \frac{d}{dy}\{P_n^{(\alpha,\beta)}(1-2y)\} - \frac{n\,(k)_n}{(1+\alpha)_n} P_n^{(\alpha,\beta)}(1-2y)]\,t^n$$
$$= -\sum_{n=0}^{\infty} \frac{(k)_n\,k}{(1+\alpha)_n} P_n^{(\alpha,\beta)}(1-2y)\,t^{n+1}$$
$$= \sum_{n=0}^{\infty} \frac{n\,(k)_n}{(1+\alpha)_n} P_n^{(\alpha,\beta)}(1-2y)\,t^{n+1} - \sum_{n=0}^{\infty} \frac{y\,(k)_n}{(1+\alpha)_n} \frac{d}{dy}\{P_n^{(\alpha,\beta)}(1-2y)\}t^{n+1}$$
$$= -\sum_{n=1}^{\infty} \frac{(k+n-1)\,(k)_{n-1}}{(1+\alpha)_{n-1}} P_{n-1}^{(\alpha,\beta)}(1-2y)\,t^n - \sum_{n=1}^{\infty} \frac{y\,(1+\alpha+\beta)_{n-1}}{(1+\alpha)_{n-1}} \frac{d}{dy}\{P_n^{(\alpha,\beta)}(1-2y)\}t^n$$

Comparing the coefficients of t^n from both sides, we get

$$y \frac{(k)_n}{(1+\alpha)_n} \frac{d}{dy} P_n^{(\alpha,\beta)}(1-2y) - n \frac{(k)_n}{(1+\alpha)_n} P_n^{(\alpha,\beta)}(1-2y)$$
$$= -\frac{(\alpha+\beta+n)\,(k)_{n-1}}{(1+\alpha)_{n-1}} P_n^{(\alpha,\beta)}(1-2y) - y \frac{(k)_{n-1}}{(1+\alpha)_n} \frac{d}{dy} P_{n-1}^{(\alpha,\beta)}(1-2y)$$

or
$$y = (\alpha+\beta+n)\frac{d}{dy}P_n^{(\alpha,\beta)}(1-2y) + y\,(\alpha+n)\frac{d}{dy}P_{n-1}^{(\alpha,\beta)}(1-2y)$$
$$= n\,(\alpha+\beta+n)\,P_n^{(\alpha,\beta)}(1-2y) - (\alpha+\beta+n)\,(\alpha+n)\frac{d}{dy}P_{n-1}^{(\alpha,\beta)}(1-2y)$$

which reduces to relation (I) since $y = \frac{1}{2}(1-x)$

(I) $$(x-1)\frac{d}{dx}P_n^{(\alpha,\beta)}(x)-nP_n^{(\alpha,\beta)}(x)$$

$$=-\frac{(1+\alpha)_n}{(1+\alpha+\beta)_n}\sum_{m=0}^{n}\frac{(1+\alpha+\beta)_m}{(1+\alpha)_m}\left[(1+\alpha+\beta)P_m^{(\alpha,\beta)}(x)+2(x-1)\frac{d}{dx}P_m^{(\alpha,\beta)}(x)\right]$$

From (i) and (ii), we have

$$\Phi=\sum_{n=0}^{\infty}\frac{(k)_n P_n^{(\alpha,\beta)}(1-2y)\,t^n}{1+\alpha)_n}$$

Substituting this into (v), we have

$$\sum_{n=1}^{\infty}\left[\frac{(k)_n\frac{d}{dy}P_n^{(\alpha,\beta)}(1-2y)}{(1+\alpha)_n}-\frac{n\,(k)_n}{(1+\alpha)_n}P_n^{(\alpha,\beta)}(1-2y)\right]t^n$$

$$=-\frac{kt}{1-t}\sum_{n=0}^{\infty}\frac{(k)_n P_n^{(\alpha,\beta)}(1-2y)\,t^n}{1+\alpha)_n}-\frac{2yt}{1-t}\sum_{n=0}^{\infty}\frac{(k)_n\left\{\frac{d}{dy}P_n^{(\alpha,\beta)}(1-2y)\right\}t^n}{(1+\alpha)_n}$$

$$=-k\sum_{n=0}^{\infty}\sum_{m=0}^{\infty}\frac{(k)_n P_n^{(\alpha,\beta)}(1-2y)\,t^{n+m-1}}{1+\alpha)_n}$$

$$-2y\sum_{n=0}^{\infty}\sum_{m=0}^{\infty}\frac{(k)_n\left\{\frac{d}{dy}P_n^{(\alpha,\beta)}(1-2y)\right\}t^{n+m-1}}{(1+\alpha)_n}$$

$$=-k\sum_{n=0}^{\infty}\sum_{m=0}^{n}\frac{(k)_{n-m}P_{n-m}^{(\alpha,\beta)}(1-2y)\,t^{n+1}}{(1+\alpha)_{n-m}}$$

$$-2y\sum_{n=0}^{\infty}\sum_{m=1}^{n}\frac{(k)_{n-m}\left\{\frac{d}{dy}P_{n-m}^{(\alpha,\beta)}(1-2y)\right\}t^{n+1}}{(1+\alpha)_{n-m}}$$

$$=-k\sum_{n=0}^{\infty}\sum_{m=0}^{n}\frac{(k)_m P_m^{(\alpha,\beta)}(1-2y)\,t^{n+1}}{(1+\alpha)_m}$$

$$-2y\sum_{n=0}^{\infty}\sum_{m=0}^{n}\frac{(k)_n\left\{\frac{d}{dy}P_n^{(\alpha,\beta)}(1-2y)\right\}t^{n+1}}{(1+\alpha)_m}$$

Comparing the coefficients of t^n from both sides and using $y=\frac{1}{2}(1-x)$, we get the required formula II.

(III) from (i) and (ii), we have

$$\Phi=\sum_{n=0}^{\infty}\frac{(k)_n P_n^{(\alpha,\beta)}(1-2y)\,t^n}{(1+\alpha)_n}$$

Substituting this into (vi), we have

$$\sum_{n=0}^{\infty}\left[\frac{y\,(k)_n \dfrac{d}{dy}\{P_n^{(\alpha,\beta)}(1-2y)\}}{(1+\alpha)_n} - \frac{n\,(k)_n}{(1+\alpha)_n} P_n^{(\alpha,\beta)}(1-2y)\right] t^n$$

$$= -\frac{kt}{1+t}\sum_{n=0}^{\infty}\frac{(k)_n P_n^{(\alpha,\beta)}(1-2y)\,t^n}{(1+\alpha)_n} - \frac{2t^2}{1+t}\sum_{n=0}^{\infty}\frac{n\,(k)_n P_n^{(\alpha,\beta)}(1-2y)\,t^{n-1}}{(1+\alpha)_n}$$

$$= -k\sum_{n=0}^{\infty}\sum_{m=0}^{n}\frac{(-1)^m (k)_n P_n^{(\alpha,\beta)}(1-2y)\,t^{n+m+1}}{(1+\alpha)_n}$$

$$= -k\sum_{n=0}^{\infty}\sum_{m=0}^{\infty}\frac{(-1)^m (n-m)\,(k)_{n-m} P_{n-m}^{(\alpha,\beta)}(1-2y)\,t^{n+1}}{(1+\alpha)_{n-m}}$$

$$= -k\sum_{n=0}^{\infty}\sum_{m=0}^{n}\frac{(-1)^{n-m} (k)_m P_n^{(\alpha,\beta)}(1-2y)\,t^{n+1}}{(1+\alpha)_m}$$

$$-2\sum_{n=0}^{\infty}\sum_{m=0}^{n}\frac{(-1)^{n-m}\,m\,(k)_m P_m^{(\alpha,\beta)}(1-2y)\,t^{n+1}}{(1+\alpha)_m}$$

Comparing the coefficients of t^n from both sides and using $y = \frac{1}{2}(1-x)$, we get

$$(x-1)\frac{d}{dx}P_n^{(\alpha,\beta)}(x) - n\,P_n^{(\alpha,\beta)}(x)$$

$$= \frac{(1+\alpha)_n}{(1+\alpha+\beta)_n}\sum_{m=0}^{n-1}(-1)^{n-m}(1-\alpha+\beta+2m)$$

$$(1+\alpha+\beta)_m P_m^{(\alpha,\beta)}(x)\,(1+\alpha)_m$$

(IV) $$(x+1)\left[(\alpha+\beta+n)\frac{d}{dx}P_n^{(\alpha,\beta)}(x) - (\beta+n)\frac{d}{dx}P_{n-1}^{(\alpha,\beta)}(x)\right]$$

$$= (\alpha+\beta+n)\left[n\,P_n^{(\alpha,\beta)}(x) + (\beta+n)\,.\,P_{n-1}^{(\alpha,\beta)}(x)\right].$$

[Replace x by $-x$ in relation I and use the relation $P_n^{(\alpha,\beta)}(-x) = (-1)^n P_n^{(\alpha,\beta)}(x)$].

(V) $$(\alpha+\beta+2n)(x^2-1)\frac{d}{dx}P_n^{(\alpha,\beta)}(x)$$

$$= n\,[\beta-\alpha+x\,(\alpha+\beta+2n)]\,P_n^{(\alpha,\beta)}(x)$$

$$-2\,(\alpha+n)(\beta+n)\,P_{n-1}^{(\alpha,\beta)}(x)]$$

Eliminate $\frac{d}{dx}P_{n-1}^{(\alpha,\beta)}(x)$ from relations I and IV.

(VI) $$2n\,(\alpha+\beta+n)(\alpha+\beta+2n-2)\,P_n^{(\alpha,\beta)}(x)$$

$$= (\alpha+\beta+2n-1)\,[\alpha^2-\beta^2+x\,(\alpha+\beta+2n)\,(\beta+\alpha+2n-2)]$$

$$P_{n-1}^{(\alpha,\beta)}(x) - 2\,(\alpha+n-1)(\beta+n-1)(\alpha+\beta+2n)\,P_{n-1}^{(\alpha,\beta)}(x)$$

Compute the value of $\frac{d}{dx}\{P_n^{(\alpha,\beta)}(x)\}$ from relation (v) and the value of

$\frac{d}{dx}\{P_{n-1}^{(\alpha,\beta)}(x)\}$ from relation (v) by replacing n by $n-1$. Put these values in relation (IV).

(b) Recurrence formulae in which a shift in α and β also takes place.

(I) $$\frac{d}{dx}\mathbf{P}_n^{(\alpha,\beta)}(x) = \frac{1}{2}(1+\alpha+\beta+n)\,P_{n-1}^{(\alpha+1,\beta+1)}(x).$$

L.H.S. $$= \frac{d}{dx}P_n^{(\alpha,\beta)}(x)$$

$$= \frac{(1+\alpha)_n}{n\,!}\frac{d}{dx}\,{}_2F_1\left[\begin{matrix}-n,\ 1+\alpha+\beta+n; & \frac{1-x}{2}\\ 1+\alpha\ ; & \end{matrix}\right]$$

[Using definition (i), § 14.1]

$$= \frac{n\,(1+\alpha)_n\,(1+\alpha+\beta+n)}{2\,(1+\alpha)\,n\,!}\,{}_2F_1\left[\begin{matrix}-n+1,\ 2+\alpha+\beta+n; & \frac{1-x}{2}\\ 2+\alpha\ ; & \end{matrix}\right]$$

$$= \frac{(2+\alpha)_{n-1}\,(1+\alpha+\beta+n)}{2\,(n-1)\,!}\times\,{}_2F_1\left[\begin{matrix}-(n-1),\ 1+(\alpha+1)+(\beta+1)+n-1; & \frac{1-x}{2}\\ 1+\alpha+1\ ; & \end{matrix}\right]$$

$$= \frac{1}{2}(1+\alpha+\beta+n)\,P_{n-1}^{(\alpha+1,\,\beta+1)}(x) = \text{R.H.S.}$$

(II) $$\frac{d^m}{dx^m}\mathbf{P}_n^{(\alpha,\beta)}(x) = \frac{1}{2^m}(1+\alpha+\beta+n)_m\,P_{n-m}^{(\alpha+m,\,\beta+m)}(x),$$

where $0 < m \le n$.

From recurrence formula (I), we have

$$\frac{d^2}{dx^2}P_n(\alpha,\beta)(x) = \frac{1}{2}(1+\alpha+\beta+n)\frac{d}{dx}P_{n-1}^{(\alpha+1,\,\beta+1)}(x)$$

$$= \frac{1}{2^2}(1+\alpha+\beta+n)(2+\alpha+\beta+n)\,P_{n-2}^{(\alpha+2,\,\beta+2)}(x)$$

$$= \frac{1}{2^2}(1+\alpha+\beta+n)_2\,P_{n-2}^{(\alpha+2,\,\beta+2)}(x)$$

Proceeding similarly, we get

$$\frac{d^m}{dx^m}P_n^{(\alpha,\beta)}(x) = \frac{1}{2^m}(1+\alpha+\beta+n)_m\,P_{n-m}^{(\alpha+m,\,\beta+m)}(x).$$

(III) $$(x+1)\frac{d}{dx}\mathbf{P}_n^{(\alpha,\beta)}(x) = n\,\mathbf{P}_n^{(\alpha,\beta)}(x) + (\beta+n)\,P_{n-1}^{(\alpha+1,\beta)}(x)$$

From definition (iv), § 14.1, we get

$$P_n^{(\alpha,\beta)}(x) = \frac{(1+\alpha)_n}{n\,!}\left(\frac{x+1}{2}\right)^n {}_2F_1\left[\begin{matrix}-n,\ -\beta-n; & \frac{x-1}{x+1}\\ 1+\alpha; & \end{matrix}\right]$$

$$\therefore \quad \frac{d}{dx}P_n^{(\alpha,\beta)}(x) = \frac{(1+\alpha)_n}{n\,!}\cdot\frac{n}{2}\left(\frac{x+1}{2}\right)^{n-1} {}_2F_1\left[\begin{matrix}-n,\ -\beta-n; & \frac{x-1}{x+1}\\ 1+\alpha; & \end{matrix}\right]$$

$$+\frac{(1+\alpha)_n}{n!}\left(\frac{x+1}{2}\right)^n \frac{d}{dx}\, {}_2F_1\left[\begin{matrix}-n, -\beta-n; & \frac{x-1}{x+1}\\ 1+\alpha; & \end{matrix}\right]$$

$$=\frac{(1+\alpha)_n}{2\,(n-1)!}\left(\frac{x+1}{2}\right)^{n-1} {}_2F_1\left[\begin{matrix}-n, -\beta-n; & \frac{x-1}{x+1}\\ 1+\alpha; & \end{matrix}\right]$$

$$+\frac{(2+\alpha)_n\,(\beta+n)}{(n-1)!\,(x+1)}\left(\frac{x+1}{2}\right)^{n-1} {}_2F_1\left[\begin{matrix}-(n-1), -\beta-n+1; & \frac{x-1}{x+1}\\ 1+(\alpha+1)\;\;; & \end{matrix}\right]$$

$$=\frac{n}{x+1}\,P_n^{(\alpha,\,\beta)}(x)+\frac{\beta+n}{x+1}\,P_{n-1}^{(\alpha+1,\,\beta)}(x)$$

$$\therefore \qquad (x+1)\frac{d}{dx}P_n^{(\alpha,\,\beta)}(x)=n\,P_n^{(\alpha,\,\beta)}(x)+(\beta+n)\,P_{n-1}^{(\alpha+1,\,\beta)}(x)$$

(IV) $$\boldsymbol{(x-1)\frac{d}{dx}P_n^{(\alpha,\,\beta)}(x)=n\,P_n^{(\alpha,\,\beta)}(x)-(\alpha+n)\,P_{n-1}^{(\alpha,\,\beta+1)}(x)}$$

From definition (vi), of § 14.1, we have

$$P_n^{(\alpha,\,\beta)}(x)=\frac{(1+\beta)_n}{n!}\left(\frac{x-1}{2}\right)^n {}_2F_1\left[\begin{matrix}-n, -\alpha-n; & \frac{x+1}{x-1}\\ 1+\beta; & \end{matrix}\right]$$

$$\therefore \qquad \frac{d}{dx}P_n^{(\alpha,\,\beta)}(x)=\frac{n}{(x-1)}\,P_n^{(\alpha,\,\beta)}(x)-\frac{\alpha+n}{n-1}\,\frac{(1+\beta)_{n-1}}{(n-1)!}\left(\frac{x-1}{2}\right)^{n-1}$$

$$\times\, {}_2F_1\left[\begin{matrix}-(n-1), -\alpha-n+1, & \frac{x+1}{x-1}\\ 1+(1+\beta); & \end{matrix}\right]$$

$$=\frac{n}{x-1}\,P_n^{(\alpha,\,\beta)}(x)-\frac{\alpha+n}{x-1}\,P_{n-1}^{(\alpha,\,\beta+1)}(x)$$

$$\therefore \qquad (x-1)\frac{d}{dx}P_n^{(\alpha,\beta)}(x)=n\,P_n^{(\alpha,\beta)}(x)-(\alpha+n)\,P_{n-1}^{(\alpha,\beta+1)}(x)$$

(V) $$\boldsymbol{2\frac{d}{dx}P_n^{(\alpha,\,\beta)}(x)=(\beta+n)\,P_{n-1}^{(\alpha+1\,\beta)}(x)+(\alpha+n)\,P_{n-1}^{(\alpha,\,\beta+1)}(x)}$$

Subtract recurrence formula (IV) from (III) to get the required formula.

(VI) $$\boldsymbol{(\alpha+\beta+n)\,P_n^{(\alpha,\,\beta)}(x)=(\beta+n)\,P_n^{(\alpha,\,\beta-1)}+(\alpha+n)\,P_n^{(\alpha-1,\,\beta)}(x).}$$

Substituting the value of $\frac{d}{dx}P_n^{(\alpha,\,\beta)}(x)$ from recurrence relation (I) in (v), we get

$$(1+\alpha+\beta+n)\,P_{n-1}^{(\alpha+1,\,\beta+1)}(x)=(\beta+n)\,P_{n-1}^{(\alpha+1,\,\beta)}(x)+(\alpha+n)\,P_{n-1}^{(\alpha,\,\beta+1)}(x)$$

This on shifting n to $n+1$, α to $\alpha-1$ and β to $\beta-1$, gives

$$(\alpha+\beta+n)\,P_n^{(\alpha,\,\beta)}(x)=(\beta+n)\,P_n^{(\alpha,\,\beta-1)}(x)+(\alpha+n)\,P_n^{(\alpha-1,\,\beta)}(x).$$

(vii) $$\boldsymbol{\frac{1}{2}(2+\alpha+\beta+2n)(x-1)\,P_n^{(\alpha+1,\,\beta)}(x)}$$

$$= (n+1)\, P_{n+1}^{(\alpha,\beta)}(x) - (1-\alpha+n)\, P_n^{(\alpha,\beta)}(x)$$

We know that

$$\text{F}(a, b; c; z) = \text{F}(a-1, b+1; c, z) + c^{-1}(b+1-a)\, z\, \text{F}(a, b+1; c+1; z)$$

Let $a = -n,\ b = 1+\alpha+\beta+n,\ c = 1+\alpha$ and $z = \frac{1}{2}(1-x)$. Then

$$\text{F}\left[\begin{matrix}-n, & 1+\alpha+\beta; & \frac{1-x}{2}\\ & 1+\alpha; & \end{matrix}\right] = \text{F}\left[\begin{matrix}-n-1, 2+\alpha+\beta+n; & \frac{1-x}{2}\\ 1+\alpha; & \end{matrix}\right] + \frac{2+\alpha+\beta+2n}{1+\alpha}\left(\frac{1-x}{2}\right) \text{F}\left[\begin{matrix}-n, 2+\alpha+\beta+n; & \frac{1-x}{2}\\ 2+\alpha; & \end{matrix}\right]$$

Multiplying both sides by $\frac{(1+\alpha)_n}{n!}$ and making use of definition (i), § 14.1, we get

$$\text{P}_n^{(\alpha,\beta)}(x) = \frac{n+1}{1+\alpha+n}\, \text{P}_{n+1}^{(\alpha,\beta)}(x) + \frac{(2+\alpha+\beta+2n)(1-x)}{2(1+\alpha+n)}\, \text{P}_n^{(\alpha+1,\beta)}(x)$$

$$\therefore \quad \frac{1}{2}(2+\alpha+\beta+2n)(x-1)\ \text{P}_n^{(\alpha+1,\beta)}(x) = (n+1)\, P_{n+1}^{(\alpha,\beta)}(x) - (1+\alpha+n)\ \text{P}_n^{(\alpha,\beta)}(x)$$

(viii)
$$\frac{1}{2}(2+\alpha+\beta+2n)(x+1)\ \mathbf{P}_n^{(\alpha,\beta)}(x) = (n+1)\, P_{n+1}^{(\alpha,\beta)}(x)\ (1+\beta+n)\ P_n^{(\alpha,\beta)}(x)$$

We have that

$$(c-1-b)\,\text{F}(a, b; c; z) = (c-a)\,\text{F}(a-1, b+1; c; z) + (a-b-1)(1-z)\, F(a, b+1; c; z)$$

Now proceed as in formula (VII).

(ix)
$$(\alpha+\beta+2n)\,\mathbf{P}_n^{(\alpha,\beta-1)}(x) = (\alpha+n)\, P_{n+1}^{(\alpha,\beta)}(x) + (\alpha+\beta+n)\,\mathbf{P}_n^{(\alpha,\beta)}(x)$$

We know that

$$(a-1)\, f(a, b; c; z) = aF(a+1; b; c, z) - bF(a, b+1; c; z)$$

Now proceed as in proof for formula VII.

(x)
$$\text{P}_n^{(\alpha,\beta-1)}(x) - \mathbf{P}_{n-1}^{(\alpha-1,\beta)}(x) = \mathbf{P}_{(n-1)}^{(\alpha,\beta)}(x)$$

Substituing the value of $(\alpha+\beta+n)\,\text{P}_n^{(\alpha,\beta)}(x)$ from recurrence formula (vi) in (ix), we get

$$(\alpha+\beta+2n)\,\text{P}_n^{(\alpha,\beta-1)} = (\alpha+n)\ P_{n-1}^{(\alpha,\beta)}(x) + (\beta+n)\,\text{P}_n^{(\alpha,\beta-1)}(x) + (\alpha+n)\,\text{P}_n^{(\alpha-1,\beta)}(x).$$

(xi)
$$(\alpha+\beta+2n)\,\mathbf{P}_n^{(\alpha-1,\beta)}(x) = (\alpha+\beta+n)\ \text{P}_n^{(\alpha,\beta)}(x) - (\beta+n)\,\mathbf{P}_{n-1}^{(\alpha,\beta)}(x)$$

Eliminating $(\beta+n)\,\text{P}_n^{(\alpha,\beta-1)}(x)$ from recurrence formula vi and ix, we have

$$(\alpha+\beta+2n)\left[\frac{\alpha+\beta+n}{\beta+n}\, P_n^{(\alpha,\beta)}(x) + \frac{\alpha+n}{\beta+n}\, P_n^{(\alpha-1,\beta)}(x)\right]$$

$$= (\alpha+\beta+n)\, P_n^{(\alpha,\beta)}(x) + (\alpha+n)\, P_{n-1}^{(\alpha,\beta)}(x).$$

or $$\left(\frac{\alpha+n}{\beta+n}\right)(\alpha+\beta+2n)\, P_n^{(\alpha-1,\beta)}(x) = (\alpha+\beta+n)\left[\frac{\alpha+\beta+2n}{\beta+n} - 1\right] P_n^{(\alpha,\beta)}(x) - (\alpha+n)\, P_{n-1}^{(\alpha,\beta)}(x).$$

or $$(\alpha+\beta+2n)\, P_n^{(\alpha-1,\beta)}(x) = (\alpha+\beta+n)\, P_n^{(\alpha,\beta)}(x) - (\beta+n)\, P_{n-1}^{(\alpha,\beta)}(x).$$

(xii) $$\mathbf{2 . P_n^{(\alpha,\beta)}(x) = (1+x)\, P_n^{(\alpha,\beta+1)}(x) + (1-x)\, P_n^{(\alpha+1,\beta)}(x).}$$

{Subtract recurrence formula (vii) from (viii).}

15 Miscellaneous Special Functions

15.1 Introduction

In present chapter we will introduce briefly some, other advanced special functions. These functions are very much useful in physical and social sciences. Due to lack of space we will not discuss these in details for which the student may concert some standard book on these functions.

15.2 The sive and cosive Integrals. .

The sive and cosive integrals are defined, respectively, by

$$S_i (x) = \int_0^x \frac{\sin t}{t} dt$$

$$C_i (x) = \int_\infty^x \frac{\cos t}{t} dt$$

$$s_i (x) = \int_\infty^x \frac{\sin t}{t} dt$$

15.3 The Exponential Integral

The exponential integrals are defined by

$$E_1 (x) = \int_x^\infty \frac{e^{-t}}{t} dt$$

$$E_i (x) = \int_{-\infty}^x \frac{e^t}{t} dt$$

15.4 The logarithmic Integral

The logarithmic integral is defined by

$$l_i (x) = \int_0^x \frac{dt}{\ln t}$$

15.5 Incomplete Gamma Functions

Incomplete gamma functions are defined by

$$\Gamma (x, \alpha) = \int_\alpha^\infty e^{-t} t^{x-1} dt$$

$$\nu (x, \alpha) = \int_0^\alpha e^{-t} t^{x-1} dt.$$

Using the definition of the gamma function we see that

$$\Gamma(x, \alpha) + \nu(x, \alpha) = \Gamma(x)$$

15.6 Riemann's Zeta Function

Riemann's zeta function is defined by

$$\zeta(x) = \sum_{n=1}^{\infty} \frac{1}{n^x},$$

in which the series is divergent for $x \le 1$ convergent for $x > 1$. It may be proved that

$$\zeta(2) = \frac{\pi^2}{6};\ \zeta(4) = \pi^4/90.$$

15.7 Debye Functions

These functions are defined by

$$D_n(x) = \int_0^x \frac{t^n}{e^t - 1}\,dt$$

The debye functions and the Riemann zeta functions are connected by the relation

$$D_n(\infty) = n!\,\zeta(n+1)$$

15.8 Elliptic Integral

The elliptic integrals of the first, second and third kinds are defined, respectively, by

$$F(k, \phi) = \int_0^{\Phi} \frac{d\theta}{\sqrt{(1 - k^2 \sin^2\theta)}}\ (0 < k < 1) \quad \text{...(i)}$$

$$E(k, \phi) = \int_0^{\Phi} \sqrt{(1 - k^2 \sin^2\theta)}\,d\theta\ (0 < k < 1) \quad \text{...(ii)}$$

and

$$\pi(k, \phi, a) = \int_0^{\Phi} \frac{d\theta}{\sqrt{\{(1 - k^2 \sin^2\theta)(1 + a^2 \sin^2\theta)\}}} \quad \text{...(iii)}$$

$$(0 < k < 1,\ a \ne k)$$

15.9 Complete Elliptic Integrals

When $\phi = \pi/2$ in (i), (ii), and (iii), the resulting integrals are known as complete elliptic integrals. Thus the complete integrals of the first, second kinds are defined respectively by

$$K(k) = \int_0^{\pi/2} \frac{d\theta}{\sqrt{(1 - k^2 \sin^2\theta)}}$$

$$E(k) = \int_0^{\pi/2} \sqrt{(1 - k^2 \sin^2\theta)}\,d\theta$$

and

$$\pi(k, a) = \int_0^{\pi/2} \frac{d\theta}{\sqrt{(1 - k^2 \sin^2\theta)(1 + a^2 \sin^2\theta)}}$$

15.10 The Error Functions

The error function is used extensively is statistics and probability theory and is defined by

$$\text{erf}\,(x) = \frac{2}{\sqrt{\pi}}\int_0^x e^{-t^2}\,dt \qquad \text{...(i)}$$

and the complementary error functions is defined by

$$\text{erfe}\,(x) = \frac{2}{\sqrt{\pi}}\int_x^\infty e^{-t^2}\,dt \qquad \text{...(ii)}$$

Adding (i), and (ii), we get

$$\text{erf}\,(x) + \text{erfe}\,(x) = \frac{2}{\sqrt{\pi}}\left[\int_0^x e^{-t^2}\,dt + \int_x^\infty e^{-t^2}\,dt\right]$$

$$= \frac{2}{\sqrt{\pi}}\int_0^\infty e^{-t^2}\,dt$$

But $\displaystyle\int_0^\infty e^{-t^2}\,dt \; \frac{\sqrt{\pi}}{2}$

$$\therefore \quad \text{erf}\,(x) + \text{erfe}\,(x) = \frac{2}{\sqrt{\pi}} \times \frac{\sqrt{\pi}}{2} = 1 \qquad \text{...(iii)}$$

Hence erfe (x) is also defined by

$$\text{erfe}\,(x) = 1 - \text{erf}\,(x) \qquad \text{...(iv)}$$

Expansion of erf (x) for small values of x

$$\text{erf}\,(x) = \frac{2}{\sqrt{\pi}}\int_0^x e^{-t^2}\,dt$$

$$= \frac{2}{\sqrt{\pi}}\int_0^x \left[1 - t^2 + \frac{t^4}{2\,!} + \ldots + \frac{(-1)^n\, t^{2n}}{n\,!} + \ldots\right] dt$$

$$= \frac{2}{\sqrt{\pi}}\left[x - \frac{x^3}{1\,!\,3} + \frac{x^5}{2\,!\,5} + \ldots + (-1)^n \frac{x^{2n+1}}{n\,!\,(2n+1)} + \ldots\right]$$

To show that erf $(-x)$ = – erf (x)

From (i),

$$\text{erf}\,(-x) = \frac{2}{\sqrt{\pi}}\int_0^{-x} e^{-t^2}\,dt$$

Putting $t = -r$, so that $dt = -dr$, and we have

$$\text{erf}\,(-x) = \frac{2}{\sqrt{\pi}}\int_0^x e^{-r^2}\,(-dr)$$

$$= -\frac{2}{\sqrt{\pi}}\int_0^x e^{-r^2}\,dt$$

$$= -\,\text{erf}\,(x).$$

To show that | erf (x) | ≤ 1

Suppose $x \geq 0$. Then since $e^{-r^2} > 0$, we have erf $(x) \geq 0$

Again $\displaystyle |\,\text{erf}\,(x)| = \frac{2}{\sqrt{\pi}}\int_0^x \left|e^{-t^2}\right| dt$

$$\leq \frac{2}{\sqrt{\pi}}\int_0^{\infty} e^{-t^2}\, dt$$

$$\leq \frac{2}{\sqrt{\pi}} \times \frac{\sqrt{\pi}}{2}$$

$$\leq 1$$

$$\therefore \quad |\operatorname{erf}(x)| \leq 1.$$

15.11 The Fresnel Integrals

These are defined by

$$S(x) = \int_0^x \sin\left(\frac{\pi}{2}t^2\right) dt$$

$$C(x) = \int_0^x \cos\left(\frac{\pi}{2}t^2\right) dt$$

we can easily verify that

$$S(\propto) = C(\propto)\ 1/2$$

and

$$C(x) + iS(x) = \frac{1+i}{2}\operatorname{erf}\left\{\frac{\sqrt{\pi}}{2}(1-i)\,x\right\}$$

15.12 Mathieu Functions

The Mathieu functions $Ce_p\,(z, q)$ and $Se_p\,(z, q)$ of integral order p are the solutions of the Mathieu's equation

$$\frac{d^2v}{dz^2} + (\alpha - 2q\cos 2z)\,v = 0, \qquad \text{...(i)}$$

where the seperation constants α are the functions of q. The solutions are periodic in z with period π or 2π.

The preferred form of the series is given below for q positive :

$$Ce_p\,(z, q) = \sum_{r=0,1}^{\infty}{}^{*} A_r^{(p)} \cos(rz) \qquad \text{...(i)}$$

$$Se_p\,(z.q) = \sum_{r=0,1}^{\infty}{}^{*} B_r^{(p)} \sin(rz), \qquad \text{...(ii)}$$

where the asterisk (*) over the summation sign indicates that the summation is taken over only even or odd values of r as p is even or odd. Here c_e and s_e are the abbreviations for cosine-elliptic and sine-elliptic respectively.

In these series $Ar^{(p)}$ and $Br^{(p)}$ are the function of p, where p and r are either even or odd.

Special Cases

If $q \to 0$, the cosive-elliptic and sive-elliptic Mathieu functions reduce to cosive and sive functions, respectively, i.e.,

$$\lim_{q\to 0} Ce_p(z, q) = \cos pz,\ \lim_{q\to 0} se_p\,(z, q) = \sin pz.$$

15.13 Spheroidal Wave Functions

The spheroidal wave functions denoted by $S_{mn}\,(c,\eta)$ $R_{mn}\,(c, \zeta,$ $S_{mn}\,(-i$

$e,\eta)$and R_{mn} $(-ie,\ i\ \zeta)$, satisfy the ordinary differential equations :

$$\frac{d}{d\eta}\left[(1-\eta^2)\frac{d}{d\eta}S_{mn}(c,\eta)\right]+\left[\lambda_{mn}-c^2\eta^2-\frac{m^2}{1-\eta^2}\right]S_{mn}(c,\eta)=0 \qquad ...(i)$$

$$\frac{d}{d\xi}\left[(\xi^2-1)\frac{d}{d\xi}R_{mn}(c,\xi)\right]+\left[\lambda_{mn}-c^2\xi^2+\frac{m^2}{\xi^2-1}\right]R_{mn}(c,\xi)=0 \qquad ...(ii)$$

$$\frac{d}{d\eta}\left[(1-\eta^2)\frac{d}{d\eta}S_{mn}(-ie,\eta)\right]+\left[\lambda_{mn}+c^2\eta^2-\frac{m^2}{1-\eta^2}\right]S_{mn}(-i\,c,\eta)=0 \qquad ...(iii)$$

and

$$\frac{d}{d\xi}\left[(\xi^2+1)\frac{d}{d\xi}R_{mn}(-ic,i\xi)\right]-\left[\lambda_{mn}-c^2\xi^2-\frac{m^2}{\xi^2+1}\right]R_{mn}(-ic,i\xi)=0 \qquad ...(iv)$$

respectively.

The seperation constants λ_{mn} are the same in the first pair of these equations, and likewise in the second pair. The functions $S_{mn}(c,\eta)$, $S_{mn}(-ie,\eta)$ are called the *angle wave functions*, whereas $R_{mn}(c,\xi)$ R_{mn} (- ie.,)$i\xi$) are called the *radial wave functions* of order m and degree n.

15.14 Generalized prolate Spheroidal Functions

While treating the case of functions of two variables whose Fourier Transforms vanish outside a circle in the two-dimension frequency plane, slepian was led to consider the integral equation

$$\phi(x)=\int_0^1 J_N(c\,xy)\sqrt{(c\,xy)}\,\phi(y)\,dy \qquad ...(i)$$

The solutions of (i) are the bounded eigen functions of the differential equation

$$(1-x^2)\frac{d^2\phi}{dx^2}-2x\frac{d\phi}{dx}+\left(\frac{\frac{1}{4}-N^2}{x^2}-c^2x^2+\Psi\right)\phi=0 \qquad ...(ii)$$

When $N=\frac{1}{2}$, equation (ii) reduces to the equation for prolate spheroidal functions of order zero. The bounded solutions of (ii), for arbitrary values of N are generally referred to as *Generalized Prolate Spheroidal Functions*. These functions are, in many respects, similar to the prolate spheroidal functions. Bounded solution of (ii) exist only for discrete values of ψ, say $\psi_{n,n}$ $n = 0, 1, 2,$ ... which are labelled so that

$$\psi_{N,0}\le\psi_{N,1}\le\psi_{N,2}\le\ ....$$

The corresponding eigen-functions are denoted by $\phi_{n,n}(x)$.

15.15 Generalized prolate spheroidal wave functions

The generalized prolate spheroidal wave function has been defined by R.K. Gupta as the solution of the differential equation

$$(1 - x^2) \frac{d^2y}{dx^2} + [\,(\beta - \alpha) - (\alpha - \beta + 2)\, x]\, \frac{dy}{dx}$$
$$+ [x\,(c) - c^2x^2]\, y = 0 \qquad \text{...(i)}$$

in the form of an infinite sum

$$y\,(x) = \phi_n^{(\alpha,\,\beta)}\,(c, x) = \sum_{j=0}^{\infty} d_{j,\,n}\,(\alpha, \beta)\,(c).\ P_{n+5}(\alpha, \beta)\,(x) \qquad \text{...(ii)}$$

The eigen values for the equation (i) are given by

$$X_n^{(\alpha,\,\beta)}\,(c) = n\,(n + \alpha + \beta + 1) +$$
$$\left[v_{n,-1}^{\alpha,\,\beta}\, v_{n-1}^{\alpha,\,\beta}, 1\, v_{n+1}^{\alpha,\,\beta}, 1\, v_{n,\,n}^{\alpha,\,\beta} - \left(v_{n,\,0}^{\alpha,\,\beta}\right)\right]^2 c^2 + O\,(c^4), \qquad \text{...(iii)}$$

where

$$v_{n,\,1}^{\alpha,\,\beta} = \frac{2\,(n+1)\,(\alpha+\beta+n+1)}{(\alpha+\beta+2n+2)\,(\alpha+\beta+2n+1)},$$

$$v_{n,\,0}^{\alpha,\,\beta} = \frac{\alpha^2 - \beta^2}{(\alpha+\beta+2n+2)\,(\alpha+\beta+2n)},$$

and

$$v_{n-1,\,1}^{\alpha,\,\beta} = \frac{2\,(n+\alpha)\,(n+\beta)}{(\alpha+\beta+2n)\,(\alpha+\beta+2n+1)}$$

Special Cases :

The results available as the particular cases of $\Phi_n^{(\alpha,\,\beta)}$ are :

(i) Legendre Functions, if $\beta = \alpha = 0$, $c = 0$,

(ii) Associated Legendre functions, if $\beta = \alpha = m$, $c = 0$,

(iii) Ultraspherical polynomials, if $\alpha = \beta \neq 0$, $c = 0$

(iv) Jacobi polynomial, if $c = 0$,

(v) Spheroidal wave functions, if, $\beta = \alpha$, $c = 0$,

(vi) Chebyshev polynomials, if $\beta = \alpha = -\frac{1}{2}$, $c = 0$

(vii) Spheroidal wave functions of zero order if $\beta = 0$, $\alpha = 0$, $c \neq 0$.

(viii) Mathieu functions, if $\beta = \alpha = -\frac{1}{2}$, $c \neq 0$.